T0257997

Handbook of Computational Visual Media

Handbook of Computational Visual Media

Edited by Riley Lewis

CLANRYE
INTERNATIONAL
www.clanryeinternational.com

Clanrye International,
750 Third Avenue, 9ᵗʰ Floor,
New York, NY 10017, USA

ISBN: 978-1-63240-917-1

Cataloging-in-Publication Data

Handbook of computational visual media / edited by Riley Lewis.
p. cm.
Includes bibliographical references and index.
ISBN 978-1-63240-917-1
1. Computer graphics. 2. Computer science. 3. Artificial intelligence. 4. Computer vision.
5. Image processing. I. Lewis, Riley.
T385 .H36 2020
006.6--dc23

For information on all Clanrye International publications
visit our website at www.clanryeinternational.com

Contents

Preface

This book has been an outcome of determined endeavour from a group of educationists in the field. The primary objective was to involve a broad spectrum of professionals from diverse cultural background involved in the field for developing new researches. The book not only targets students but also scholars pursuing higher research for further enhancement of the theoretical and practical applications of the subject.

In the digital age, there is a variety of large-scale visual data available on the Internet. This presents opportunities for the novel processing of visual information that can have commercial advantages. It can be accomplished if this data can be understood, systematically managed, processed and utilized. An interdisciplinary field of science called computer vision deals with enabling computers to gain an understanding of digital images and videos. Its objective is to automate tasks that only the human visual system can achieve. Some of the core tasks of computer vision are acquiring, processing, understanding and analyzing digital images, and extracting high-dimensional data for producing numerical or symbolic information. Image understanding can be thought of as the disentangling of symbolic information from image data with the aid of geometry, learning theory, physics and statistics. The applications of computer vision are varied. It is used for automatic inspection such as in manufacturing applications, computer-human interaction, navigation, assisting humans in identification tasks, etc. Computer vision is an upcoming field of science that has undergone rapid development over the past few decades. Most of the topics introduced in this book cover new techniques and the applications of visual information in computer vision. It is a vital tool for all researching or studying computational visual media as it gives incredible insights into emerging trends and concepts.

It was an honour to edit such a profound book and also a challenging task to compile and examine all the relevant data for accuracy and originality. I wish to acknowledge the efforts of the contributors for submitting such brilliant and diverse chapters in the field and for endlessly working for the completion of the book. Last, but not the least; I thank my family for being a constant source of support in all my research endeavours.

Editor

An interactive approach for functional prototype recovery from a single RGBD image

Yuliang Rong[1], Youyi Zheng[2], Tianjia Shao[1](✉), Yin Yang[3], and Kun Zhou[1]

Abstract Inferring the functionality of an object from a single RGBD image is difficult for two reasons: lack of semantic information about the object, and missing data due to occlusion. In this paper, we present an interactive framework to recover a 3D functional prototype from a single RGBD image. Instead of precisely reconstructing the object geometry for the prototype, we mainly focus on recovering the object's functionality along with its geometry. Our system allows users to scribble on the image to create initial rough proxies for the parts. After user annotation of high-level relations between parts, our system automatically jointly optimizes detailed joint parameters (axis and position) and part geometry parameters (size, orientation, and position). Such prototype recovery enables a better understanding of the underlying image geometry and allows for further physically plausible manipulation. We demonstrate our framework on various indoor objects with simple or hybrid functions.

Keywords functionality; cuboid proxy; prototype; part relations; shape analysis

1 Introduction

That form ever follows function. This is the law.

Louis Sullivan

With the popularization of commercial RGBD cameras such as Microsoft's Kinect, people can easily acquire 3D geometry information with an RGB image. However, due to occlusion and noise, recovering meaningful 3D contents from single RGBD images remains one of the most challenging problems in computer vision and computer graphics. Over the past years, much research effort has been devoted to recovering high-quality 3D information from RGBD images [1, 2]. Most of these approaches, starting either from a single image or multiple images, are dedicated to faithfully recovering the 3D geometry of image objects, while their semantic relations, underlying physical settings, or even functionality are overlooked. More recently, research has explored use of high-level structural information to facilitate 3D reconstruction [3–5]. For example, Shao et al. [3] leverage physical stability to suggest possible interactions between image objects and obtain a physically plausible reconstruction of objects in RGBD images. Such high-level semantic information plays an important role in constraining the underlying geometric structure.

Functionality is the center of object design and understanding. Objects in man-made environments are often designed for single or multiple intended functionalities (see Fig. 1). *That form ever follows*

1 State Key Lab of CAD&CG, Zhejiang University, Hangzhou 310058, China. E-mail: Y. Rong, rongyl@zju.edu.cn; T. Shao, tianjiashao@cad.zju.edu.cn (✉); K. Zhou, kunzhou@cad.zju.edu.cn.

2 ShanghaiTech University, Shanghai 200031, China. E-mail: zhengyy@shanghaitech.edu.cn.

3 The University of New Mexico, Albuquerque, NM 87131, USA. E-mail: yangy@unm.edu.

Fig. 1 Objects in man-made environments are often designed for single or multiple intended functionalities.

function is the law of physical manufacturing [6]. In this paper, we develop an interactive system to recover functional prototypes from a single RGBD image. Our goal is to allow a novice user to be able to quickly lift image objects into 3D using 3D prototypes, using just a few high-level annotations of joint types and geometric/functional relations; the user can meanwhile explicitly explore and manipulate an object's function. We focus on prototypes with simple proxies (e.g., cuboids) representing their parts as a means to alleviate the difficulties of precise 3D reconstruction which is a harder problem. By taking physical functionality into consideration, we may gain a much more faithful interpretation of the underlying objects. The functional properties can then be used for applications like in-context design and manipulation.

It is a challenging problem to infer object function just from user annotated joint types and geometric/functional relations. Our system should automatically optimize the detailed joint parameters (axis and position) in order to make the parts move correctly, whereas this task is typically done in CAD software by the user repeatedly adjusting parameters. Furthermore, initial proxies from user-segmented depths are often rough with incorrect orientation and position, and may be incomplete because of occlusion. Hence initial proxies often fail to satisfy the functional relations such as *A covers B*. Therefore our system should also optimize the proxy parameters (size, orientation, and position), in order to make parts satisfy functional relations.

Our method starts with a single RGBD image. The user segments the image object into parts by scribbling on the image using simple strokes or polygons. Then each segmented part is assembled using a 3D proxy. We use simple cuboids in this paper [7]. Given the initial proxies, our system then allows the user to annotate the joint types and functional/geometric relations between parts. In a key stage, our algorithm simultaneously optimizes the detailed joint parameters (axis and position) and the proxy parameters (size, orientation, and position). Finally, a functional prototype is produced with moving parts satisfying the user annotated relations.

We have tested our system on a variety of man-made hybrid functional objects taken from various sources. Our results show that even using only a few user annotations, the proposed algorithm is capable of faithfully inferring geometry along with appropriate functional relations for the object parts. In summary, this paper makes the following contributions:

- Identifying and characterizing the problem of integrating functionality into image-based reconstruction;
- Simultaneous optimization of detailed joint and geometry parameters from user's high-level annotations of joint types and functional/geometric relations;
- An interactive tool for functional annotation which has been tested on a variety of indoor scene images and physical designs.

2 Related work

Proxy-based analysis. A significant amount of work has leveraged proxies to understand objects or scenes. Li et al. [8] and Lafarge et al. [9] consider global relationships as constraints to optimize initial RANSAC-based proxies to produce structured outputs; similarly, Arikan et al. [10] use prior relations plus user annotations to create abstracted geometry. For scene analysis, many approaches encode input scenes as collections of planes, boxes, cylinders, etc., and study their spatial layout [11–16]. Recently, proxies have frequently been used in functionality analysis of a design. Umetani et al. [17] use physical stability and torque limits for guided furniture design in a modeling and synthesis setting. Shao et al. [18] create 3D proxy models from a set of concept sketches that depict a product from different viewpoints, with different configurations of moving parts. Our work is inspired by Koo et al. [7], who annotate cuboids with high-level functional relationships to fabricate physical work-alike prototypes. Unlike their algorithm, our framework does not require explicitly creating joint positions, as we consider a larger search space to automatically infer the joint and part parameters. To our knowledge, we are the first to focus on proxy-based functionality recovery from a single RGBD image, in particular recovering how the object works by jointly optimizing both part geometry and functional relationships based on user annotations.

Constraint-based modeling. Our work is related to constraint-based modeling research in the graphics and CAD communities. Similar work to ours involves the automatic determination of relevant geometric relationships between parts for high-level editing and synthesis of 3D models [5, 19–21]. Previous mechanical engineering research has used declarative methods for specifying relevant geometric constraints for a mechanical design [22, 23]. Some professional CAD software like AutoCAD and SolidWorks contains constraint-based modeling modules, but users are required to manually adjust the low-level part/joint parameters to specify relationships. In contrast, our system can automatically interpret user annotated high-level functionality to give specific geometric constraints.

3D modeling from a single RGBD image. Much effort has been devoted to obtaining high-quality geometry information from a single RGBD image [1, 24]. To recover structural information, Shen et al. [4] extract suitable model parts from a database, and compose them to form high-quality models from a single RGBD image. Shao et al. [3] use physical stability to recover unseen structures from a single RGBD image using cuboids. However, their techniques focus on creating static 3D geometry and structure, whereas our goal is to produce models with correctly moving parts.

3 Overview

As illustrated in Fig. 2, given a single RGBD image, we first let the user scribble strokes over an image object to separate out its functional parts. These parts, being either a semantic component or an added object, are used during function recovery.

To segment the parts, we use a depth-augmented version of the GrabCut segmentation method [25], as Ref. [3] does. Optionally, if the color and depth are too similar, making it difficult to separate the parts with GrabCut, the user may use a polygon tool as in PhotoShop to perform segmentation (see the accompanying video in the Electronic Supplementary Material (ESM)). We assemble a set of cuboid proxies, one fitted to each individual part. The user then annotates high-level relations between these cuboids. The relations are of three kinds: joint type relations (e.g., hinge, sliding), functional relations (e.g., covers, fits inside, supports, flush, connects with) [7], and geometric relations (e.g., equal size, symmetry).

Given the user annotated relations, in a key step, our method recovers each cuboid's orientation, position, and size along with the joint parameters using a combined optimization approach. We use a combined optimization strategy because the cuboid parameters are always coupled with the joint parameters: given a set of joints, the cuboid geometry must be adjusted to satisfy the functional constraints.

Optimization is done using a two-stage sampling strategy. In the first stage, our algorithm samples possible cuboid edges as joint candidates [18] for the specified joint type. Given one set of possible joint candidates, the cuboid orientation is aligned and the cuboid position is refined, by adjusting the corresponding joint edges. We assume that the joint must be snapped to the nearest cuboid face and be parallel to the nearest cuboid edge (as in Ref. [7]).

Having found one set of adjusted joints with cuboid orientations and positions, our method further samples a set of possible candidate rest

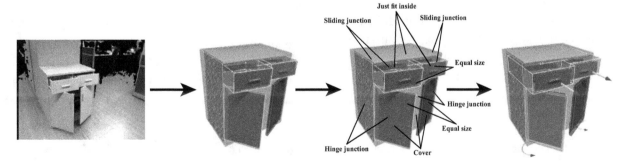

Fig. 2 Algorithmic pipeline. Given the input RGBD image (left), our system generates initial proxy cuboids (mid-left) from parts segmented by the user with strokes or polygon tools. The user then annotates a set of high-level relations between the proxies including joint types and geometric/functional relations (mid-right). Finally our system simultaneously optimizes joint parameters (axis and position) and part parameters (orientation, position, and size) to obtain a functional prototype with parts moving as the user expects (right).

configurations for the cuboids. A rest configuration is a state where the object is in a *closed* state [7]. Because the cuboid size has not yet been definitively determined, the system does not know which state is the *closed* state. Thus we sample possible candidates for the rest configurations, as shown in Fig. 6. For each possible rest configuration, we optimize the cuboid size parameters according to the user annotated functional/geometric relations as in Ref. [7]. Finally, the optimized cuboids which best match the initial point cloud are selected, and the best prototype with best joint and cuboid parameters is produced. We next describe the algorithm in detail.

4 Algorithm

Our method takes as input an RGBD image of a functional object. By *functional* we mean objects having particular moving parts, such as a door which opens by rotating, a sliding drawer, etc. Such objects are very commonly seen in our daily life, for instance, rolling chairs, folding tables, printers, seesaws, etc.

Initial cuboid generation. Given the input RGBD image, our first task is to anchor the object's functional parts. Automatically identifying image objects and object parts in RGBD images has been explored in recent works, but without prior knowledge, such methods do not yet work well enough for our purposes. We resort to an interactive solution. As in Ref. [3], we let the user scribble on the image object to specify object parts. In particular, we allow the user to draw free strokes over parts to indicate a segment (part). We apply a depth-augmented GrabCut algorithm [3] to the underlying point cloud along with its pixel and adjacency information. Optionally, if the color and depth are too similar, making it difficult to separate the parts with GrabCut, the user may use a polygon tool as in PhotoShop to perform segmentation. We then run the *efficient RANSAC* algorithm [26] on the seegmented points to generate candidate planes. The largest plane is selected as the primary plane, and the second largest plane is made orthogonal to the primary one. We extract initial cuboids determined by these orthogonal directions (the third direction is the cross product of the two plane normals). Figure 3 illustrates the process

Fig. 3 Initial proxy generation. The user is allowed to scribble strokes on the image (left); based on the scribbles, depth-augmented GrabCut is applied to segment the input object into different parts (middle). Initial cuboids are then fitted to the corresponding points (right).

of generating the initial cuboids. Note that the generated cuboid may have erroneous orientation, position, and size. In subsequent steps, our goal is to simultaneously optimize these parameters along with the joint parameters so that the extracted cuboids form a prototype whose functionality closely follows the image object.

Relation annotation. Let the set of initial cuboids be $(B_1, \ldots, B_N)$. An important first step is for the user to annotate the high-level relations between the cuboids. To this end, we define three categories of relations. Category I comprises joint relations (e.g., A has a hinge relation w.r.t. B). Category II comprises functional relations (e.g., A covers B), while Category III comprises geometric relations (e.g., symmetry, equal size). In each case, the user selects a pair of cuboids and then indicates the relationship.

To further classify the relations, we define two main types of joint relations: *hinges* and *sliding joints*. For functional relations, following Ref. [7], we define the following function types: *A covers B, A fits inside B, A supports B, A is flush with B*, and *A is connected to B*. The main geometric relations are *symmetry* and *equal size*. These relations impose different geometric constraints during the following optimization stage. Some relations might be dependent on each other; for example, if both A and C cover B, A is geometrically constrained w.r.t. B and C. Figure 4 shows the joint types and some

Fig. 4 User annotated joint types and some typical functional relations. From left to right: hinge joint, sliding joint, exactly covers, just fits, and supports.

typical types of functional relations. Note that unlike Ref. [7], we do not need to explicitly specify joint positions and axes as well as cuboid orientations and positions. Instead, we optimize these parameters in a combined manner.

Combined optimization of cuboids and joints. We now detail our cuboid optimization algorithm. Our goal is to simultaneously optimize the cuboids' orientations and shape parameters (i.e., positions and sizes), as well as the detailed joint parameters, in accordance with the user annotated relations. The optimized cuboid configuration should deviate little from the input point cloud and move as the user expects. Given the input point cloud I and initial cuboids $\mathcal{B} = (B_1, \ldots, B_N)$, along with the user annotated joint types $\mathcal{J} = (J_1, \ldots, J_M)$, functional relations $\mathcal{F} = (F_1, \ldots, F_P)$, and geometric relations $\mathcal{G} = (G_1, \ldots, G_Q)$, we want to obtain the best joint parameters $\boldsymbol{\Theta}^* = (\Theta_1^*, \ldots, \Theta_M^*)$ for the joint types $\mathcal{J}$ along with the best cuboids $\mathcal{B}^* = (B_1^*, \ldots, B_N^*)$, satisfying the functional relations $\mathcal{F}$ and geometric relations $\mathcal{G}$. We do so using the formulation:

$$\underset{\mathcal{B},\boldsymbol{\Theta}}{\arg\min} E(\mathcal{B}, \boldsymbol{\Theta}, I) \quad \text{s.t.} \quad \mathcal{B}, \boldsymbol{\Theta} \text{ satisfy } \mathcal{J}, \mathcal{F}, \mathcal{G} \quad (1)$$

Here $E(\mathcal{B}, \boldsymbol{\Theta}, I)$ measures the deviation of the optimized cuboid configuration from the input point cloud, defined as

$$E(\mathcal{B}, \boldsymbol{\Theta}, I) = \sum_j \sum_k \text{dist}(B_j - p_j^k) \quad (2)$$

where $\sum_k \text{dist}(B_j - p_j^k)$ measures the deviation of cuboid B_j from its associated points p_j^k.

The challenge is how to enforce the annotated relations as geometric constraints while ensuring the cuboids respect the input point cloud. Since the annotated relations are high-level specifications, this leads to a large optimization search space due to the potential ambiguities arising from the rather general annotations. Another challenge is that the cuboid parameters are highly coupled with the joint parameters. That is, given a set of joints, the cuboid geometry should change accordingly to satisfy the functional constraints. Thus we cannot optimize the parameters locally and separately, but must instead do so in a global manner. To solve the above challenges, we use a multi-stage optimization paradigm which first populates the solution space with a two-step sampling algorithm, and then jointly optimize the cuboid parameters and joint parameters.

In the first stage, we sample possible joint parameters, i.e., axial position and orientation. Let us denote the set of joint types as $(J_1, \ldots, J_M)$, and the parameters we wish to estimate as $(\Theta_1, \ldots, \Theta_M)$. We start by building a joint configuration graph. For each cuboid we create a graph node and for each joint type J_i, we create multiple graph connections, with each connection associated with a candidate parameter Θ_i^l for J_i. If A forms a hinge relation with B, each cuboid edge of A can be a candidate hinge axis. We choose only those cuboid edges which are close to B. More specially, we only choose the edges parallel to the face if there is also a *cover* relation, and only choose the edges perpendicular to the face if there is a *fit inside* or *support* relation. This leads to a configuration graph where any traversal path of the graph represents a possible configuration of joints. Figure 5 shows such a graph. Algorithm 1 gives the pseudo-code for building the graph.

Given the joint configuration graph, for each joint configuration we optimize each cuboid's orientation, position, and size based on annotated functional/geometric relations. The cuboid's orientation and position are firstly adjusted based on the current candidate joint configuration, by adjusting the corresponding joint edges. We assume that the joint must be snapped to the nearest cuboid face and be parallel to the nearest cuboid edge (following Ref. [7]). Then we optimize the cuboid's size to satisfy the functional/geometric relations given by the current joint configuration. Note that the functional relations typically indicate the geometry of the cuboids in a *closed* configuration (i.e., a rest configuration [7]). For instance, if A covers B, this typically means that one face of A is rotated about the hinge joint to be in close

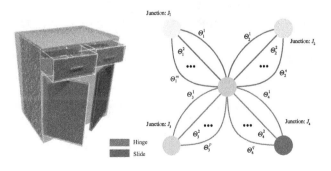

Fig. 5 Junction configuration graph. Each cuboid shown corresponds to a node with the same color. Each annotated joint type corresponds to multiple connections between nodes. One connection is associated with one candidate joint parameter.

Algorithm 1:   Build the junction configuration graph

Input: N initial cuboids $(B_1, \ldots, B_N)$; M junctions $(J_1, \ldots, J_M)$ with unknown parameters $(\Theta_1, \ldots, \Theta_M)$.

Output: Multi-connection junction graph $G := (V, E)$ in which each edge e_i^j corresponds to a parameter Θ_i^j for J_i.

```
G ← ∅
for i = 1 to N do
    V_i ← B_i
end for
/* Build multi-connections between nodes */
for i = 1 to M do
    B_c ← child cuboid of J_i
    B_p ← parent cuboid of J_i
    l ← 1
    /* Test each edge of the child cuboid */
    for j = 1 to 12 do
        E_j ← j-th edge of B_c
        D_j ← direction of E_j
        C_j ← center of E_j
        for k = 1 to 6 do
            F_k ← k-th face of B_p
            N_k ← normal of F_k
            if dist(E_j, F_k) < ε_d and (abs(D_j · N_k) < ε_a or
            abs((D_j · N_k) − 1) < ε_a) then
                Θ_i^l ← (C_j, D_j) // set candidate parameter for J_i
                e_i^l ← Θ_i^l // add a connection e_i^l
                l ← l + 1
            end if
        end for
    end for
end for
```

Fig. 6 Possible rest poses for the hinge joints. As we do not know which face of the cabinet door covers the cabinet, we rotate the hinge joints to sample a set of rest configurations to suggest possible covering faces.

agreement with a face of B (Fig. 6). Since we do not know which face covers B, we enumerate the possible cuboid faces to sample a set of rest configurations (see Fig. 6) and for each rest configuration we optimize the cuboid parameters. Specifically, given a rest configuration of cuboids, we employ the optimization strategy in Ref. [7] to optimize the cuboid parameters $(B_1^*, \ldots, B_N^*)$. We then compute the optimization cost from Eq. (2). Finally, the configuration which best matches the point cloud is selected as the chosen configuration and the optimized cuboids are then computed. The overall algorithm is detailed in Algorithm 2.

5   Results

We show use of our system to recover functionality

Algorithm 2:   Optimize cuboids and junctions

Input: Input point cloud I; N initial cuboids $\mathcal{B} = (B_1, \ldots, B_N)$; junction configuration graph G; functional relations $\mathcal{F}$; geometric relations $\mathcal{G}$.

Output: N optimized cuboids $\mathcal{B}^* = (B_1^*, \ldots, B_N^*)$; M optimized junction parameters $\boldsymbol{\Theta}^* = (\Theta_1^*, \ldots, \Theta_M^*)$.

```
/* Sample candidate junction parameters from G and accordingly
optimize cuboid orientation, position and size */
err ← INF // deviation of cuboids from input point cloud
while true do
    Gather a connection combination (e_1^k, ..., e_M^l) from G
    if no more connection combinations then
        break
    end if
    Create junctions with parameters Θ' = (Θ_1^k, ..., Θ_M^l) from
    (e_i^k, ..., e_i^l)
    adjust the cuboids positions and orientations by snapping the
    junction edges
    /* Calculate possible angles for rest configurations */
    for i = 1 to M do
        calculate candidate angles (α_i^1, ..., α_i^w) to parallelize parent
        and child
    end for
    /* Sample possible rest configurations */
    while true do
        Gather an angle combination (α_1^u, ..., α_M^v)
        if no more angle combinations then
            break
        end if
        Transform to rest configuration with (α_1^u, ..., α_M^v)
        Optimize the cuboids sizes to satisfy F and G, giving a
        solution B' = (B_1', ..., B_N')
        if E(B', Θ', I) < err then
            err ← E(B', Θ', I)
            (B_1^*, ..., B_N^*) ← (B_1', ..., B_N')
            (Θ_1^*, ..., Θ_M^*) ← (Θ_1^k, ..., Θ_M^l)
        end if
    end while
end while
```

prototypes for 6 different objects (see Fig. 7). The first 4 examples (cabinet, drawer, firebox, and chair) are real RGBD images captured with Microsoft Kinect, while the last 2 examples (toolbox and dining table) are synthetic depth data generated from existing 3D designs. See the accompanying video in the ESM for how the various parts move and fit together. Creating a single functional prototype takes 30 to 300 s for these examples. The time for user interaction (segmenting points with strokes and specifying part relationships, plus the waiting time for plane detection for initial cuboid generation) ranges from 27 to 108 s, while the optimization time varies greatly, from 1 to 241 s, depending on the size of the sampling space for joint parameters and rest poses. Experimental statistics (including the numbers of annotated hinge joints, sliding joints, functional relations, and geometric relations) are listed in Table 1.

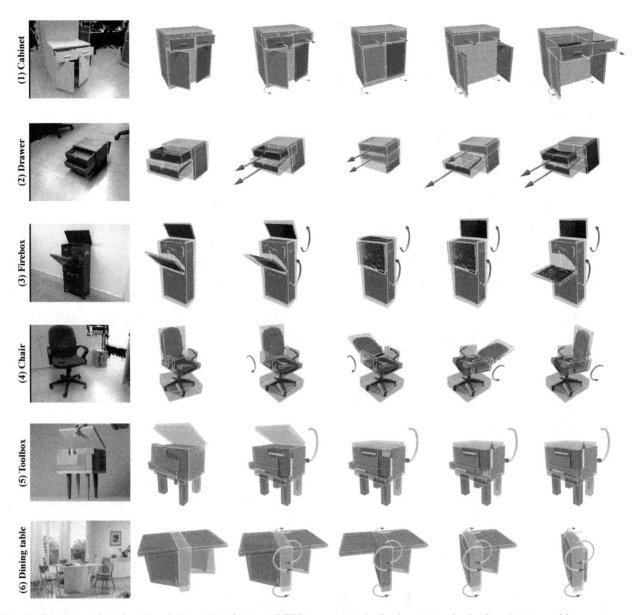

Fig. 7 Experimental results. From left to right: the input RGBD image, initial cuboids, optimized cuboids and joints, and how parts move and fit after the optimization (3 configurations).

Table 1 Statistics for examples: numbers of hinge and sliding joints, numbers of functional and geometric constraints, and time taken for interaction and optimization

Model	Hinge	Slide	Funct.	Geom.	Interact	Optimize
Cabinet	2	2	4	2	62 s	18 s
Drawer	0	2	2	1	29 s	1 s
Firebox	2	0	2	0	27 s	16 s
Chair	2	0	3	0	90 s	2 s
Toolbox	1	3	6	0	108 s	3 s
Dining table	4	0	6	2	55 s	241 s

As shown in Fig. 2, although the geometry of our prototypes may appear simple, the relationships between the moving parts are often complex. Manually adjusting the geometry and relation parameters would be very time and labor consuming. Our system automatically infers the joint parameters (position and axis) and the geometry parameters (size, position, and orientation) by optimizing them simultaneously under the user annotated high-level constraints. Satisfactory part parameters and joint parameters were obtained in all our experiments. For example, in Fig. 7(1), our algorithm automatically places the hinge joints on the correct edges of the cabinet doors, adjusts their orientations appropriately by aligning the hinge joints to the nearest cabinet face, and makes them parallel to the nearest cabinet edges. The sizes of the doors are also optimized to be of equal size and cover the cabinet. The drawers in Figs. 7(1) and 7(2) have the desired orientations with their sliding joints aligned with the cabinet, and have sizes which properly fit inside the cabinet and are equal. In Fig. 7(3), the lid and the front door are both optimized to just cover the firebox. In the chair example (Fig. 7(4)), due to occlusion, the initial cuboids for the leg and the armrest have smaller sizes than they should, but our algorithm successfully extends the leg to support the seat, and extends the armrests to connect with the back. Similarly, the occluded leg in Fig. 7(5) is extended to support the box and has the same size as the other legs. In Fig. 7(6), the orientation and size of the two doors are optimized to support the table top, and the orientation of the top is optimized to be horizontal.

User study. To further evaluate whether our approach can recover correct functional prototypes, we showed our system to 20 students. 5 were computer science undergraduates; 4 students were master candidates in industrial design. The others were 8 master candidates and 3 Ph.D. candidates in computer science. We showed them the captured RGBD images and asked them to imagine how the objects work. These students then used our system to add annotations to the pre-generated initial cuboids based on their imagination. All students reported that our system successfully recovered functional prototypes in which the parts moved as they expected. Furthermore, the optimized part

geometry also met their expectations. One exception was that 6 students said they imagined the hinge joint on the cabinet door in Fig. 7(1) to be exactly at the edge of the cabinet, while our optimization did not consider it to be the best location.

Comparison with real objects and 3D design models. We also checked the recovered prototypes against the captured real objects and 3D design models. As illustrated in the top 2 rows in Fig. 8, the generated prototypes have similar functionality to the real objects, and have parts which after movement give almost the same configurations as the real ones. Furthermore, the optimized simple cuboids approximate the real geometry well, with almost the same size, orientation, and position. We also compared our recovered prototypes with 3D design models whose joints were added and adjusted manually in Autodesk 3DS Max (bottom row in Fig. 8). We can see the prototypes recovered from the user's high-level annotations have very similar functionality to the manually designed models.

6   Conclusions

In this work, we have presented a novel approach to recovering a functional prototype from a user's high-level annotations of relationships. After indicating joint types and other functional/geometric relations, the joint parameters and part geometry parameters are simultaneously optimized. This interface allows

Fig. 8 Top two rows: comparison with input data; bottom row: comparison with the 3D design model. Our system faithfully recovers the functionality the user expects.

users to focus on the functionality of the target object rather than working with low-level geometry and joint parameters. The results demonstrate that our system can generate functional models from a small number of user annotations. In the user study, the recovered prototypes worked correctly, as users expected. The comparison between the real objects and 3D design models further demonstrates the feasibility of our system.

Limitations and future work. The main limitation of our approach is that we use cuboids as proxies to approximate part geometry. While compositions of cuboids are sufficient for representing the functionality of many products, users often prefer higher fidelity geometry to better understand the geometry and relationships. Rough proxies may also cause inaccurate reconstruction. Similarly, the restricted set of joint types is another limitation. In the future, we will add other primitives for part proxies, such as cylinders and spheres. We also plan to integrate more joint types between parts, such as ball joints and simple mechanical links. The current optimization framework may need to be modified to handle more geometry and joint types. Another future direction is to consider other high-level functional constraints between parts. Exploring further high-level relationships could allow more sophisticated functional models.

References

[1] Han, Y.; Lee, J.-Y.; Kweon, I. S. High quality shape from a single RGB-D image under uncalibrated natural illumination. In: Proceedings of IEEE International Conference on Computer Vision, 1617–1624, 2013.

[2] Izadi, S.; Kim, D.; Hilliges, O.; Molyneaux, D.; Newcombe, R.; Kohli, P.; Shotton, J.; Hodges, S.; Freeman, D.; Davison, A.; Fitzgibbon, A. KinectFusion: Real-time 3D reconstruction and interaction using a moving depth camera. In: Proceedings of the 24th Annual ACM Symposium on User Interface Software and Technology, 559–568, 2011.

[3] Shao, T.; Monszpart, A.; Zheng, Y.; Koo, B.; Xu, W.; Zhou, K.; Mitra, N. J. Imagining the unseen: Stability-based cuboid arrangements for scene understanding. *ACM Transactions on Graphics* Vol. 33, No. 6, Article No. 209, 2014.

[4] Shen, C.-H.; Fu, H.; Chen, K.; Hu, S.-M. Structure recovery by part assembly. *ACM Transactions on Graphics* Vol. 31, No. 6, Article No. 180, 2012.

[5] Zheng, Y.; Chen, X.; Cheng, M.-M.; Zhou, K.; Hu, S.-M.; Mitra, N. J. Interactive images: Cuboid proxies for smart image manipulation. *ACM Transactions on Graphics* Vol. 31, No. 4, Article No. 99, 2012.

[6] Sullivan, L. H. The tall office building artistically considered. *Lippincott's Magazine* 57, 1896.

[7] Koo, B.; Li, W.; Yao, J.; Agrawala, M.; Mitra, N. J. Creating works-like prototypes of mechanical objects. *ACM Transactions on Graphics* Vol. 33, No. 6, Article No. 217, 2014.

[8] Li, Y.; Wu, X.; Chrysanthou, Y.; Sharf, A.; Cohen-Or, D.; Mitra, N. J. GlobFit: Consistently fitting primitives by discovering global relations. *ACM Transactions on Graphics* Vol. 30, No. 4, Article No. 52, 2011.

[9] Lafarge, F.; Alliez, P. Surface reconstruction through point set structuring. *Computer Graphics Forum* Vol. 32, No. 2pt2, 225–234, 2013.

[10] Arikan, M.; Schwärzler, M.; Flöry, S.; Wimmer, M.; Maierhofer, S. O-snap: Optimization-based snapping for modeling architecture. *ACM Transactions on Graphics* Vol. 32, No. 1, Article No. 6, 2013.

[11] Gupta, A.; Efros, A. A.; Hebert, M. Blocks world revisited: Image understanding using qualitative geometry and mechanics. In: *Lecture Notes in Computer Science, Vol. 6314.* Daniilidis, K.; Maragos, P.; Paragios, N. Eds. Springer Berlin Heidelberg, 482–496, 2010.

[12] Gupta, A.; Hebert, M.; Kanade, T.; Blei, D. M. Estimating spatial layout of rooms using volumetric reasoning about objects and surfaces. In: *Advances in Neural Information Processing Systems 23.* Lafferty, J.; Williams, C.; Shawe-Taylor, J.; Zemel, R.; Culotta, A. Eds. Curran Associates, Inc., 1288–1296, 2010.

[13] Del Pero, L.; Bowdish, J.; Fried, D.; Kermgard, B.; Hartley, E.; Barnard, K. Bayesian geometric modeling of indoor scenes. In: Proceedings of IEEE Conference on Computer Vision and Pattern Recognition, 2719–2726, 2012.

[14] Jia, Z.; Gallagher, A.; Saxena, A.; Chen, T. 3D-based reasoning with blocks, support, and stability. In: Proceedings of IEEE Conference on Computer Vision and Pattern Recognition, 1–8, 2013.

[15] Jiang, H.; Xiao, J. A linear approach to matching cuboids in RGBD images. In: Proceedings of IEEE Conference on Computer Vision and Pattern Recognition, 2171–2178, 2013.

[16] Zheng, B.; Zhao, Y.; Yu, J. C.; Ikeuchi, K.; Zhu, S.-C. Beyond point clouds: Scene understanding by reasoning geometry and physics. In: Proceedings of IEEE Conference on Computer Vision and Pattern Recognition, 3127–3134, 2013.

[17] Umetani, N.; Igarashi, T.; Mitra, N. J. Guided exploration of physically valid shapes for furniture design. *ACM Transactions on Graphics* Vol. 31, No. 4, Article No. 86, 2012.

[18] Shao, T.; Li, W.; Zhou, K.; Xu, W.; Guo, B.; Mitra, N. J. Interpreting concept sketches. *ACM Transactions*

on Graphics Vol. 32, No. 4, Article No. 56, 2013.

[19] Bokeloh, M.; Wand, M.; Seidel, H.-P.; Koltun, V. An algebraic model for parameterized shape editing. *ACM Transactions on Graphics* Vol. 31, No. 4, Article No. 78, 2012.

[20] Gal, R.; Sorkine, O.; Mitra, N. J.; Cohen-Or, D. iWIRES: An analyze-and-edit approach to shape manipulation. *ACM Transactions on Graphics* Vol. 28, No. 3, Article No. 33, 2009.

[21] Xu, W.; Wang, J.; Yin, K.; Zhou, K.; van de Panne, M.; Chen, F.; Guo, B. Joint-aware manipulation of deformable models. *ACM Transactions on Graphic* Vol. 28, No. 3, Article No. 35, 2009.

[22] Daniel, M.; Lucas, M. Towards declarative geometric modelling in mechanics. In: *Integrated Design and Manufacturing in Mechanical Engineering*. Chedmail, P.; Bocquet, J.-C.; Dornfeld, D. Eds. Springer Netherlands, 427–436, 1997.

[23] Yvars, P.-A. Using constraint satisfaction for designing mechanical systems. *International Journal on Interactive Design and Manufacturing* Vol. 2, No. 3, 161–167, 2008.

[24] Zhang, Q.; Ye, M.; Yang, R.; Matsushita, Y.; Wilburn, B.; Yu, H. Edge-preserving photometric stereo via depth fusion. In: Proceedings of IEEE Conference on Computer Vision and Pattern Recognition, 2472–2479, 2012.

[25] Rother, C.; Kolmogorov, V.; Blake, A. "GrabCut": Interactive foreground extraction using iterated graph cuts. *ACM Transactions on Graphics* Vol. 23, No. 3, 309–314, 2004.

[26] Schnabel, R.; Wahl, R.; Klein, R. Efficient RANSAC for point-cloud shape detection. *Computer Graphics Forum* Vol. 26, No. 2, 214–226, 2007.

degrees from the Department of Mathematics, Zhejiang University. His research interests include geometric modeling, imaging, and human–computer interaction.

2

Practical automatic background substitution for live video

Haozhi Huang[1], Xiaonan Fang[1], Yufei Ye[1], Songhai Zhang[1] (✉), and Paul L. Rosin[2]

Abstract In this paper we present a novel automatic background substitution approach for live video. The objective of background substitution is to extract the foreground from the input video and then combine it with a new background. In this paper, we use a color line model to improve the Gaussian mixture model in the background cut method to obtain a binary foreground segmentation result that is less sensitive to brightness differences. Based on the high quality binary segmentation results, we can automatically create a reliable trimap for alpha matting to refine the segmentation boundary. To make the composition result more realistic, an automatic foreground color adjustment step is added to make the foreground look consistent with the new background. Compared to previous approaches, our method can produce higher quality binary segmentation results, and to the best of our knowledge, this is the first time such an automatic and integrated background substitution system has been proposed which can run in real time, which makes it practical for everyday applications.

Keywords background substitution; background replacement; background subtraction; alpha matting

1 Introduction

Background substitution is a fundamental post-processing technique for image and video editing. It has extensive applications in video composition [1, 2], video conferencing [3, 4], and augmented reality [5]. The process of background substitution can be basically separated into two steps. The first step is to extract the foreground from the input video, and the second step is to combine the original foreground with the new background. Given limited computational resources and time, it is even more challenging to achieve satisfactory background substitution results in real time for live video. In this paper, we focus on background substitution for live video and especially live chat video, in which the camera is monocular and static, and the background is also basically static.

Foreground segmentation, also known as matting, is a fundamental problem. Formally, foreground segmentation takes as input an image I, which is assumed to be a composite of a foreground image F and a background image B. The color of the ith pixel can be represented as a linear combination of the foreground and background colors, where α represents the opacity value:

$$I_i = \alpha_i F_i + (1 - \alpha_i) B_i \tag{1}$$

This is an ill-posed problem which needs assumptions or extra constraints to become solvable.

Generally, existing work on foreground segmentation can be categorized into automatic approaches or interactive approaches. Automatic approaches usually assume that the camera and background are static, and a pre-captured background image is available. They try to model the background using either generative methods [6–9], or non-parametric methods [10, 11]. Those pixels which are consistent with the background model are labeled as background, and the remainder are labeled as foreground. Some recent works incorporate a conditional random field to include color, contrast, and motion cues, and use graph-

---

1 Department of Computer Science, Tsinghua University, Beijing, 100084, China. E-mail: H. Huang, huanghz08@gmail.com; X. Fang, wwjpromise@163.com; Y. Ye, yeyf13.judy@gmail.com; S. Zhang, shz@tsinghua.edu.cn (✉).

2 School of Computer Science and Informatics, Cardiff University, Cardiff, CF24 3AA, UK. E-mail: rosinpl@cardiff.ac.uk.

cut to solve an optimization problem [12–14]. Most online automatic approaches only produce a binary foreground segmentation instead of fractional opacities for the sake of time, and then use feathering [12] or border matting [13] to compute approximate fractional opacities along the boundary. Feathering is a relatively crude, but efficient, technique that fades out the foreground at a fixed rate. Border matting is an alpha matting method that is significantly simplified to only collect the nearby foreground/background samples for each unknown pixel to allow fitting of a Gaussian distribution, which is then used to estimate the alpha value for that pixel. Although border matting also uses dynamic programming to minimize an energy function that encourages alpha values varying smoothly along the boundary, the result of border matting is far from globally optimal. On the other hand, interactive approaches have been proposed to handle more complicated camera motion [1, 15, 16]. Since strictly real-time performance is unnecessary for such applications, they compute more precise fractional opacities along the segmentation boundary from the beginning. Such methods require the user to draw some strokes or a trimap in a few frames to indicate whether a pixel belongs to the foreground/background/unknown region. They then solve for the alpha values in the unknown region and propagate the alpha mask to other frames.

In contrast to the large amount of foreground segmentation publications, there are fewer studies on techniques for compositing the original foreground and a new background for background substitution. Since the light sources of the original video and the new background may be drastically different, directly copying the foreground to the new background will not achieve satisfactory results. Some seamless image composition techniques [17, 18] may seem relevant at first glance, but they require the original and new backgrounds to be similar. Other color correction techniques based on color constancy [19–22] are more suitable in our context. Color constancy methods first estimate the light source color of the image, and then adjust pixel colors according to the specified hypothetical light source color.

In this paper, we present a novel practical automatic background substitution system for live video, especially live chat video. Since real-time performance is necessary and interaction is inappropriate during live chat, our method is designed to be efficient and automatic. We first accomplish binary foreground segmentation by a novel method which is based on *background cut* [12]. To make the segmentation result less sensitive to brightness differences, we introduce a simplified version of the *color line model* [23] during the background modeling stage. Specifically, we build a color line for each background pixel and allow larger variance along the color line than in the perpendicular direction. We also include a more recent promising alpha matting method [24] to refine the segmentation boundary instead of feathering [12] or border matting [13]. To maintain real-time performance when including such a complicated alpha matting process, we perform foreground segmentation at a coarser level and then use simple but effective bilinear upsampling to generate a foreground mask for the finer level. After foreground segmentation, in order to compensate for any lighting difference between the input video and the new background, we estimate the color of the light sources in both the input video and new background, and then adjust the foreground color based on the color ratio of the light sources. This color compensation process follows the same idea as the white-patch algorithm [25], but to our knowledge this is the first time such color compensation has been applied to background substitution. Compared to previous approaches, thanks to its invariance to luminance changes, the binary segmentation result of our method is more accurate, and, thanks to the alpha matting border refinement and foreground color compensation, the appearance of the foreground in our result is more compatible with the new background.

In summary, the main contributions of our paper are:

- A novel practical automatic background substitution system for live video.
- Introduction of a color line model in conjunction with a Gaussian mixture model in the background modeling stage, which makes the foreground segmentation result less sensitive to brightness differences.
- Application of a color compensation step to

background substitution, which makes the inserted foreground look more natural in the new background.

2 Related work

2.1 Automatic video matting

Unlike interactive video matting methods [1, 15, 16, 26], which need user interaction during video playback, automatic video matting is more appropriate for live video. The earliest kind of automatic video matting problem is constant color matting [27], which uses a constant backing color, often blue, so is usually called *blue screen matting*. Although excellent segmentation results can be achieved by blue screen matting, it needs extra equipment including a blue screen and careful setting of light sources. More recent video matting methods loosen the requirement for the background to have constant color, and only assume that the background can be pre-captured and remains static or only contains slight movements. They model the background using either generative methods, such as a Bayesian model [6], a self-organized map [7], a Gaussian mixture model [8], independent component analysis [9], a foreground–background mixture model [28], or non-parametric methods [10, 11]. Such models allow prediction of the probability of a pixel belonging to the background. These methods can create holes in the foreground and noise in the background if the colors of the foreground and background are similar, because they only make local decisions. Some recent techniques utilize the power of graph-cut to solve an optimization problem based on a conditional random field using color, contrast, and motion cues [12–14]; they are able to create more complete foreground masks since they constrain the alpha matte to follow the original image gradient. Other work [29] focuses on foreground segmentation for animation. In our case, in order to acquire real-time online matting for live video, it is inappropriate to include motion cues. Thus our model is only based on color and contrast, like the work of Sun et al. [12]. We also find that stronger shadow resistance can be achieved by employing a *color line model* [23]. Another drawback of existing online methods is that they only acquire a binary foreground segmentation and

then use approximate border refinement techniques such as feathering [12] or border matting [13] to compute fractional opacities along the boundary. In this paper, we will show that a more precise alpha matting technique can be incorporated while real-time performance can still be achieved by performing foreground segmentation at a coarser level and then using simple bilinear upsampling to generate a finer level foreground mask.

2.2 Interactive video matting

Interactive video matting is another popular video matting approach. It no longer requires a known background and static camera, and takes a user drawn trimap or strokes to tell if a pixel belongs to the foreground/background/unknown region. For images, previous methods are often sampling-based [30], affinity-based [24], or a combination of both [31], computing alpha values for the unknown region based on the known region information. For video, Chuang et al. [15] use optical flow to propagate the trimap from one frame to another. *Video SnapCut* [1] maintains a collection of local classifiers around the object boundary. Each classifier subsequently solves a local binary segmentation problem, and classifiers of one frame are propagated to subsequent frames according to motion vectors estimated between frames. However, they need to take all frames all at once to compute reliable motion vectors, which takes a huge amount of time, so are unsuitable for online video matting. Gong et al. [16] use two competing one-class support vector machines (SVMs) to model the background and foreground separately for each frame at every pixel location, use the probability values predicted by the SVMs to estimate the alpha matte; they update the SVMs over time. Near real-time performance is available with the help of a GPU, but they still need an input user trimap and an extra training stage, so are inconvenient for live video applications.

There are three main categories of methods for color adjustment to improve the realism of image composites. The first category focuses on color consistency or color harmony. For example, Wong et al. [32] adjust foreground colors to be consistent with nearby surrounding background pixels, but their method fails when nearby background pixels do not correctly represent the overall lighting conditions.

Cohen-Or et al. [33] and Kuang et al. [34] consider overall color harmony based on either aesthetic rules or models learned from a dataset, but they tend to focus on creating aesthetic images rather than realistic images. The second category of methods focuses on seamless cloning based on solving a Poisson equation or coordinate interpolation [2, 17, 18, 35, 36]. A major assumption in these approaches is that the original background is similar to the new background, which we cannot guarantee in our application. The third category of methods is based on color constancy, estimating the illumination of the image first and then adjusting colors accordingly [19–22]. In this paper, we utilize the most basic and popular color constancy method, the *white-patch algorithm* [25], to estimate the light source color, since we need its efficiency for real-time application.

3 Our approach

3.1 Overview

We now outline our method. The pipeline can be separated into three steps: foreground segmentation, border refinement, and final composition. Firstly, for the foreground segmentation step, we suppose the background can be pre-captured and maintains static. Inspired by *background cut* [12], we build a global Gaussian mixture background model, local single Gaussian background models at all pixel locations, and a global Gaussian mixture foreground model. But unlike background cut, instead of using an isotropic variance for the local single Gaussian background models, we make the variance along the *color line* larger than that in the direction perpendicular to the color line. Here the concept of a color line is borrowed from Ref. [23]. The original color line model built multiple curves to represent all colors of the whole image, and assumed that colors from the same object lie on the same curve. To check which curve a pixel belongs to is a time consuming process. In order to achieve real-time performance, we adapt the color line model to a much simpler and more efficient version. In our basic version of the color line model, for each pixel we build a single curve color line model, which avoids the process of matching a pixel to one of the curves in the multiple curve model. Furthermore, instead of fitting a curve, we fit a straight line

that intersects the origin in RGB space, which means we ignore the non-linear transform of the camera sensor. Our experiments show this simplified model to be sufficient and effective. By utilizing this color line model, we can avoid misclassifying background pixels which undergo color changes due to a shadow passing by, since color changes caused by shadows still remain along the color line. Using this background cut model, we can build an energy function that can be optimized by graph-cut to give a binary foreground segmentation matte. Secondly, we carry out border refinement for this binary foreground matte. Specifically, we use morphological operations to mark the border pixels between foreground and background. Considering these border pixels to be the unknown region results in a trimap. We then carry out closed-form alpha matting [24], which computes fractional alpha values for these border pixels. It is important to emphasize that, only when the binary foreground segmentation result is essentially correct, can a trimap be automatically computed reliably in this way. Lastly, to perform composition, we estimate the light source colors of the original input video and the new background separately, and adjust the foreground colors accordingly to make the foreground look more consistent with the new background.

3.2 Foreground segmentation

3.2.1 Basic background cut model

In this section we briefly describe the background cut model proposed in Ref. [12]. The background cut algorithm takes a video and a pre-captured background as input, and the output is a sequence of binary foreground masks, in which each pixel r is labeled 0 if it belongs to the background or 1 otherwise. Background cut solves the foreground segmentation problem frame by frame. For each frame, the process of labeling can be transformed into solving a global optimization problem. The energy function to be minimized is in the form of a *conditional random field*:

$$E(X) = \sum_r E_d(x_r) + \lambda_1 \sum_{r,s} E_c(x_r, x_s) \quad (2)$$

where $X = \{x_r\}$, x_r denotes the label value, r, s are neighbouring pixels in one frame, E_d (the data term) represents per-pixel energy, and E_c is a contrast term computed from neighbouring pixels. Here λ_1 is a predefined constant balancing E_d and E_c, which is empirically set to 30 in our experiments. This is a classical energy function which can be minimized by graph-cut [37].

Now we explain how to construct E_d and E_c. First we model the foreground and the background using Gaussian models. For the foreground, we build a global Gaussian mixture model (GMM). For the background, we not only build a global GMM, but also a local single Gaussian distribution model at each pixel location (a per-pixel model). The two global GMMs are defined as

$$p(v_r|x_r = i) = \sum_{k=1}^{k_i} w_k^i N(v_r|\mu_k^i, \Sigma_k^i), \ i = 0, 1 \quad (3)$$

where $i = 0$ and $i = 1$ stand for background and foreground respectively, v_r denotes the color of pixel r, k_i denotes the number of mixture components, w_k^i denotes the weight of the kth component, N denotes the Gaussian distribution, μ_k^i denotes the mean, and Σ_k^i denotes the covariance matrix. The single Gaussian distribution at every pixel location is defined as

$$p_s(v_r) = N(v_r|\mu_r^s, \Sigma_r^s) \quad (4)$$

where $\Sigma_r^s = \sigma_r^s I$, so, following Ref. [12], the variance of the per-pixel model is isotropic. The background global GMM and the background per-pixel model are initialized using pre-captured background data. The foreground global GMM is initialized using pixels whose probabilities are lower than a threshold in the background model. After initialization, these Gaussian models are updated frame by frame according to the segmentation results.

Based on the Gaussian models, the data term E_d is defined as

$$E_d(x_r) = \begin{cases} -\log\left(\lambda_2 p(v_r|x_r) + (1 - \lambda_2) p_s(v_r)\right), & x_r = 0 \\ -\log p(v_r|x_r), & x_r = 1 \end{cases} \quad (5)$$

Here λ_2 is a predefined constant balancing the global GMM and the local per-pixel model, which is empirically set to 0.1 in our experiments. The contrast term is

$$E_c(x_r, x_s) = |x_r - x_s| \exp(-\beta \|v_r - v_s\|^2 / d_B(r, s)) \quad (6)$$

$$d_B(r, s) = 1 + (\|v_r^B - v_s^B\| / K)^2 \exp(-z_{rs}^2 / \sigma_z) \quad (7)$$

where $d_B(r, s)$ is a contrast attenuation term proportional to the contrast with respect to the background, $z_{rs} = \max(\|v_r - v_r^B\|, \|v_s - v_s^B\|)$ measures the dissimilarity between the pre-captured

background and the current frame, and β, K, and σ_z are predefined constants. In our experiments, we set $\beta = 0.005$, $K = 1$, $\sigma_z = 10$. The introduction of the contrast attenuation term causes E_c to rely on the contrast from the foreground instead of the background.

The energy function in Eq. (2) can be optimized using the graph-cut algorithm [37]. For more details of the model, please refer to Ref. [12]. One major drawback of this background cut model is that, when the color of a background pixel changes due to changes in illumination, it will have extremely low probability in the per-pixel model, which will cause the pixel to be misclassified as foreground instead of background.

3.2.2 Background cut with color line model

Now we explain how the color line model [23] can improve the effectiveness of the background cut model in the presence of shadows.

Starting from the basic color line model, we make the assumption that colors of a certain material under different intensities of light form a linear color cluster that intersects the origin in RGB space. Suppose the average color at a pixel location is $\mu_r^s = (r, g, b)$. When the illumination of the same pixel location changes, its color will also change from μ_r^s to v_r. According to the color line model, v_r will approximately lie on the line connecting the origin and μ_r^s in the RGB color space. With this insight, we can decompose v_r as

$$v_r = v_\perp + v_\parallel \quad (8)$$

such that $v_\perp \perp \mu_r^s$ and $v_\parallel \parallel \mu_r^s$. Define:

$$f(v_r, \mu_r^s) = N\left(\|v_\perp\| \mid 0, \sigma_{pe}\right) N\left(\|v_\parallel\| \mid \|\mu_r^s\|, \sigma_{pa}\right) \quad (9)$$

where σ_{pe} and σ_{pa} are the respective variances of the Gaussian distributions for the perpendicular direction and parallel direction. Then the per-pixel single Gaussian distribution Eq. (4) is modified to be

$$p_s(v_r) = f(v_r, \mu_r^s) \quad (10)$$

As discussed before, the color of an object is more likely to fluctuate in the parallel direction than in the perpendicular direction. Therefore, we set $\sigma_{pe} = \sigma_r^s$, $\sigma_{pa} = \lambda_3 \sigma_{pe}$, $\lambda_3 > 1$ to constrain variance in the perpendicular direction and tolerate variance in the parallel direction, which gives our model a strong resistance to shadow. Here we do not build a global color line model as in Ref. [23], which uses multiple color lines for the whole image to replace the global

GMM, because it takes a long time to determine which line each pixel belongs to when the number of lines is large (e.g., a model with 40 lines is used in Ref. [23]), precluding real-time performance.

3.3 Border refinement

After graph-cut, we add an extra hole filling step by applying the morphological close operation to fill small holes in the foreground mask. See Fig. 1 for an example. However, we currently still have a binary foreground matte (see Fig. 1(d)). In this subsection, we explain how to automatically compute fractional alpha values for the segmentation border.

First, we automatically generate a mask covering the segmentation border as the unknown region:

$$U_i = 1 - (\mathrm{erode}(F)_i \wedge \mathrm{erode}(B)_i) \qquad (11)$$

Here U_i denotes the value of the ith pixel of the unknown mask, erode() denotes the morphological erosion operation, F is the binary foreground matte, and B is the binary background matte where $B_i = 1 - F_i$. The morphological operation radius is set to 2 for 640×480 input. The eroded foreground mask, eroded background mask, and unknown region mask are separately painted in white, black, and gray in the final trimap. Using this trimap with one of the most popular alpha matting methods [24], we calculate the fractional alpha values for the unknown region. See Fig. 2 for an example of the generated trimap and alpha matting result.

3.4 Composition

For an ideal final composition, the new composite image should be

$$I_{\mathrm{new}} = \alpha F_{\mathrm{old}} + (1 - \alpha)B_{\mathrm{new}} \qquad (12)$$

Here I_{new} denotes the new composite image, F_{old}

Fig. 2 (a) Automatically generated trimap. (b) Alpha matting result.

denotes the original foreground, and B_{new} denotes the new background (Fig. 3(c)). For previous methods whose pre-captured background (Fig. 3(a)) is unavailable, F_{old} is approximated by I_{old}:

$$I_{\mathrm{new}} = \alpha I_{\mathrm{old}} + (1 - \alpha)B_{\mathrm{new}} \qquad (13)$$

However, in our case, since the pre-captured background B_{old} is available, we can calculate the original foreground more accurately:

$$F_{\mathrm{old}} = [I_{\mathrm{old}} - (1 - \alpha)B_{\mathrm{old}}]/\alpha \qquad (14)$$

This gives a final composition formula:

$$I_{\mathrm{new}} = I_{\mathrm{old}} + (1 - \alpha)(B_{\mathrm{new}} - B_{\mathrm{old}}) \qquad (15)$$

Directly applying the above composition will create unrealistic results due to the difference in light source colors between the original input and the new background. Thus, we propose a color compensation process to deal with this problem.

First, we need to estimate the light source colors of the original input video and the new background image. The *white-patch method* [25], a popular color constancy method, assumes that the highest values in each color channel represent the presence of white in the image. In this paper, we use the variant of the white-patch method designed for CIE-Lab space, a color space that is naturally designed to separate lightness and chroma. We first calculate

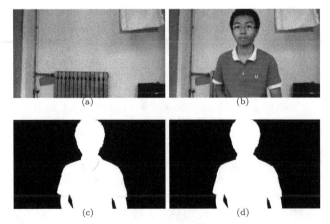

Fig. 1 (a) Pre-captured background. (b) One frame of the input video. (c) Binary foreground matte after graph-cut. (d) Foreground matte after filling holes.

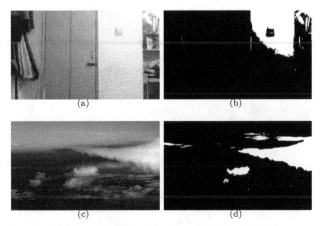

Fig. 3 (a) Pre-captured background. (b) Estimated light source mask of the pre-captured background (a). (c) New background. (d) Estimated light source mask of the new background (c).

the accumulated histogram in the lightness channel L of an image in CIE-Lab space, and consider those 10% pixels with the largest lightness values to be the white pixels. Figure 3 shows an example of the light source masks. The estimated light source color is then computed as the mean color value of all light source pixels. Denote the estimated light source color of the input video as c_{old}, that of the new background image as c_{new}. Then the new composite image after color compensation is

$$I_{\text{new}} = rI_{\text{old}} + (1 - \alpha)(B_{\text{new}} - rB_{\text{old}}) \qquad (16)$$

$$r = c_{\text{new}}/c_{\text{old}} \qquad (17)$$

Figure 4 compares results with and without light source color compensation. We can clearly see that the result with color compensation is more realistic.

4 Results and discussion

In this section, we report results generated under different conditions. All results shown were generated using fixed parameters.

Results for different frames of the same input video. Figure 5 shows that our method can create generally good background substitution results for different frames, no matter what the gesture is. Sometimes there may be residual background between the fingers (e.g., Fig. 5(c)) due

(a)   (b)

Fig. 4 (a) Composite result without color compensation. (b) Composite result with color compensation.

to the hole-filling post-processing, but it does not do much harm to the overall effect.

Results for different input videos. Figure 6 shows that our method can deal with different kinds of foreground and background. Color compensation works fine for various lighting condition. Although the matting border is not 100% perfect for Fig. 6(b) due to confusion of hair and background, the composition result is generally good.

Comparison with previous methods. We compare various methods: *fuzzy Gaussian* [38], *adaptive-SOM* [7], *background cut* [12] using RGB color space and CIE-Lab color space, and our color line model. To implement the fuzzy Gaussian and adaptive-SOM methods, we used the code in the BGSLibrary [39]. There are also other background subtraction methods in the BGSLibrary, we choose these two methods because they show the most promising results under real-time conditions. Figure 7 shows foreground masks created by different methods. After the person walks into the picture, some shadow will be cast onto the wall. The fuzzy Gaussian and adaptive-SOM methods create a lot of noise and holes since they do not utilize gradient information between neighbouring pixels. Background cut used in RGB color space does a better job by using the graph-cut model to introduce gradient information. However, it is sensitive to brightness differences, which causes shadow to be misclassified as foreground. If we set the variance of the Gaussian to be larger to tolerate some shadow, part of the true foreground is then misclassified as background. Background cut in CIE-Lab color space also suffers from the same issue. Although allowing a larger variance in the L channel can give

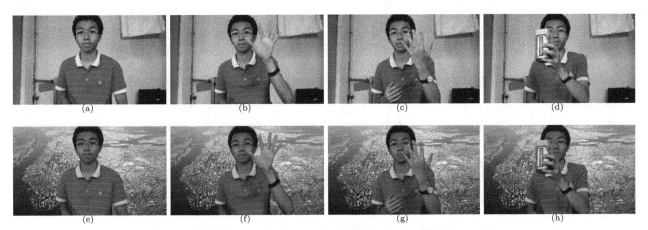

(a)   (b)   (c)   (d)

(e)   (f)   (g)   (h)

Fig. 5 (a)–(d) Input video frames. (e)–(h) Background substitution results.

Fig. 6 (a)–(c) Input frames from different videos. (d)–(f) Background substitution results.

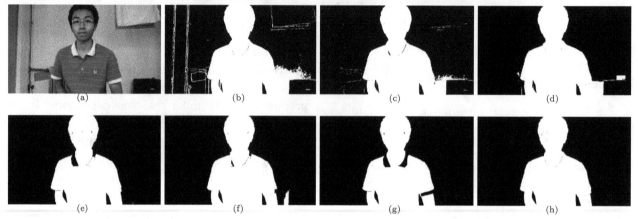

Fig. 7 (a) Input frame. (b) Foreground mask created by fuzzy Gaussian. (c) Adaptive-SOM result. (d) Background cut in RGB space result with a low variance ($\sigma_r^s = (5/255)^2$) Gaussian model. (e) Background cut in RGB space result with a larger variance ($\sigma_r^s = (20/255)^2$). (f) Background cut in CIE-Lab space result with $\sigma_L = \sigma_a = \sigma_b = (5/255)^2$. (g) Background cut in CIE-Lab space result with larger variance in the L channel ($\sigma_L = 5 * (5/255)^2$). (h) Result of our method ($\sigma_{pe} = (10/255)^2, \sigma_{pa} = 10 * (10/255)^2$).

greater tolerance to brightness changes, in actual test cases, even when we only increase the variance in the L channel by a small amount, part of the collar disappears. In contrast, using our color line model with background cut constantly creates a better foreground segmentation result.

To further quantitatively evaluate the comparison, we created a large number of "ground truth" foreground masks following a similar approach to one in Ref. [40]. The key idea is to use some balls as the moving foreground objects, and use a circle detection technique to detect the balls, which will automatically create "ground truth" masks for evaluation of our foreground segmentation methods. Specifically, we first calculate the difference image between the pre-captured background and the current frame (where one or more balls appear). Then we perform circle detection using the Hough transform [41] on the difference image, which generally produces reliable and accurate detection

results. Finally, we manually eliminate the small number of outliers that occur when circle detection fails. In total, 4105 frames and their circle detection results are collected as the ground truth. Figure 8 shows a few examples. We did not use the ground truth from the *VideoMatting* benchmark [42], because their synthetic test images do not have shadows on the background, which is one of the fundamental aspects we wish to test. Using the generated ground truth, we tested different methods including fuzzy Gaussian, adaptive-SOM, background cut using RGB color space and CIE-Lab color space, and our color line model. For fuzzy Gaussian and adaptive-SOM, we used the default parameters provided by the BGSLibrary. For the background cut method, we tested several parameters and gave results with the highest F1 score. Table 1 shows that background cut with our color line model achieves the highest F1 score, the CIE-Lab space method follows closely, and others are

  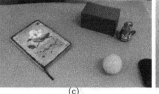 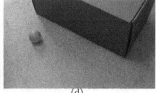

(a)   (b)   (c)   (d)

Fig. 8 Example frames for creating ground truth.

Table 1 Method comparison on ground truth dataset

Method	Precision	Recall	F1
Fuzzy Gaussian	0.252	0.993	0.402
Adaptive-SOM	0.510	0.963	0.667
BC-RGB	0.839	0.962	0.896
BC-Lab	0.900	0.968	0.933
BC-Colorline	0.907	0.964	0.935

substantially worse. However, as we have already shown in Fig. 7, CIE-Lab space has an obvious drawback in actual application scenarios. We also tested an outdoor scene with different methods to show the effectiveness of our model: see Fig. 9. In conclusion, our color line model generally creates a better foreground segmentation boundary, and is effective at coping with differences in brightness.

Results with new background. We also tested our color compensation method using new backgrounds with different light sources. In Fig. 10, the first row shows the new input backgrounds, and the second row shows the light source pixel masks. The third row contains the composition results; we can see that the color of the foreground varies correctly according to different backgrounds.

Acceleration. Although we restrict the alpha matting computation to a very small region, it is still computationally expensive. In order to enable our algorithm to run in real time, we first downsample the input frames by a scale of two, carry out foreground cut and alpha matting on the downsampled images, and then upsample the matting result to the original scale. We finish the final composition step at the original scale. We call this process "sampling acceleration". As we can see in Fig. 11, the matting result using sampling acceleration is very similar to the result produced by processing the full frames. If we do not use alpha matting to refine the border, the border is jagged (see Fig. 11(c)).

Performance. We have implemented our method in C++ on a PC with an Intel 3.4 GHz Core i7-3770 CPU. For a 640×480 input video, our background substitution program can run at 10 frames per second using just the CPU, and it can run at a real-time frame rate with GPU parallelization.

5 Conclusions

In this paper, we have presented a novel background

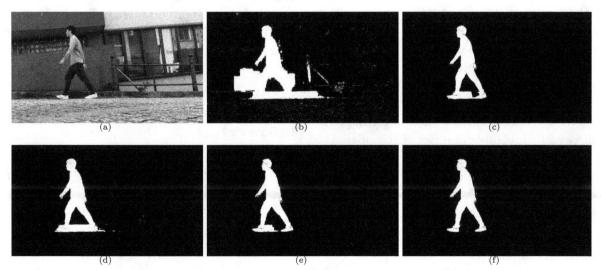

(a)   (b)   (c)

(d)   (e)   (f)

Fig. 9 (a) Input frame. (b) Background cut in RGB space result with a low variance ($\sigma_r^s = (5/255)^2$) Gaussian model. (c) Background cut in RGB space result with a larger variance ($\sigma_r^s = (20/255)^2$). (d) Background cut in CIE-Lab space result with $\sigma_L = \sigma_a = \sigma_b = (5/255)^2$. (e) Background cut in CIE-Lab space result with larger variance in the L channel ($\sigma_L = 5 * (5/255)^2$). (f) Result of our method ($\sigma_{pe} = (10/255)^2, \sigma_{pa} = 10 * (10/255)^2$).

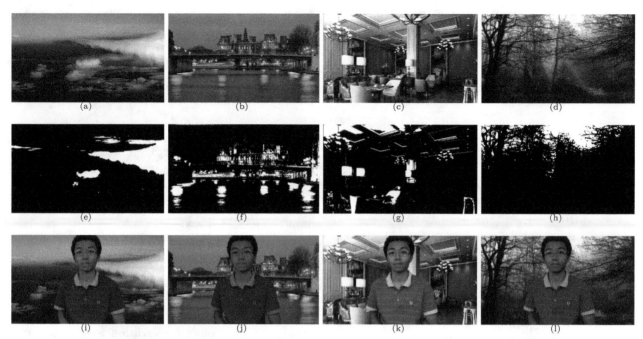

Fig. 10   (a)–(d) Input new backgrounds. (e)–(h) Estimated light source pixel mask. (i)–(l) Background substitution results.

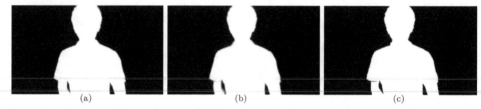

Fig. 11   (a) Matting result without sampling acceleration. (b) Matting result with sampling acceleration. (c) Foreground segmentation result with sampling acceleration but without alpha matting border refinement.

substitution method for live video. It optimizes a cost function based on Gaussian mixture models and a conditional random field, using graph-cut. A color line model is used when computing the Gaussian mixture model to make the model less sensitive to brightness differences. Before final composition, we use alpha matting to refine the segmentation border. Light source colors of the input video and new background are estimated by a simple method, and we adjust the foreground colors accordingly to give more realistic composition results. Compared to previous methods, our approach can automatically produce more accurate foreground segmentation masks and more realistic composition results, while still maintaining real-time performance.

Acknowledgements

We thank the reviewers for their valuable comments. This work was supported by the National High-Tech R&D Program of China (Project No. 2012AA011903), the National Natural Science Foundation of China (Project No. 61373069), the Research Grant of Beijing Higher Institution Engineering Research Center, and Tsinghua–Tencent Joint Laboratory for Internet Innovation Technology.

References

[1] Bai, X.; Wang, J.; Simons, D.; Sapiro, G. Video SnapCut: Robust video object cutout using localized classifiers. *ACM Transactions on Graphics* Vol. 28, No. 3, Article No. 70, 2009.

[2] Chen, T.; Zhu, J.-Y.; Shamir, A.; Hu, S.-M. Motion-aware gradient domain video composition. *IEEE Transactions on Image Processing* Vol. 22, No. 7, 2532–2544, 2013.

[3] Liu, Z.; Cohen, M. Head-size equalization for better visual perception of video conferencing. In:

Proceedings of the IEEE International Conference on Multimedia and Expo, 4, 2005.

[4] Zhu, Z.; Martin, R. R.; Pepperell, R.; Burleigh, A. 3D modeling and motion parallax for improved videoconferencing. *Computational Visual Media* Vol. 2, No. 2, 131–142, 2016.

[5] Van Krevelen, D. W. F.; Poelman, R. A survey of augmented reality technologies, applications and limitations. *International Journal of Virtual Reality* Vol. 9, No. 2, 1–21, 2010.

[6] Apostoloff, N.; Fitzgibbon, A. Bayesian video matting using learnt image priors. In: Proceedings of the IEEE Computer Society Conference on Computer Vision and Pattern Recognition, Vol. 1, I-407–I-414, 2004.

[7] Bouwmans, T.; El Baf, F.; Vachon, B. Background modeling using mixture of Gaussians for foreground detection—A survey. *Recent Patents on Computer Science* Vol. 1, No. 3, 219–237, 2008.

[8] Maddalena, L.; Petrosino, A. A self-organizing approach to background subtraction for visual surveillance applications. *IEEE Transactions on Image Processing* Vol. 17, No. 7, 1168–1177, 2008.

[9] Tsai, D.-M.; Lai, S.-C. Independent component analysis-based background subtraction for indoor surveillance. *IEEE Transactions on Image Processing* Vol. 18, No. 1, 158–167, 2009.

[10] Barnich, O.; Van Droogenbroeck, M. ViBe: A universal background subtraction algorithm for video sequences. *IEEE Transactions on Image Processing* Vol. 20, No. 6, 1709–1724, 2011.

[11] Hofmann, M.; Tiefenbacher, P.; Rigoll, G. Background segmentation with feedback: The pixel-based adaptive segmenter. In: Proceedings of the IEEE Computer Society Conference on Computer Vision and Pattern Recognition Workshops, 38–43, 2012.

[12] Sun, J.; Zhang, W.; Tang, X.; Shum, H.-Y. Background cut. In: *Computer Vision–ECCV 2006*. Leonardis, A.; Bischof, H.; Pinz, A. Eds. Springer Berlin Heidelberg, 628–641, 2006.

[13] Criminisi, A.; Cross, G.; Blake, A.; Kolmogorov, V. Bilayer segmentation of live video. In: Proceedings of the IEEE Computer Society Conference on Computer Vision and Pattern Recognition, 53–60, 2006.

[14] Yin, P.; Criminisi, A.; Winn, J.; Essa, I. Bilayer segmentation of webcam videos using tree-based classifiers. *IEEE Transactions on Pattern Analysis and Machine Intelligence* Vol. 33, No. 1, 30–42, 2011.

[15] Chuang, Y.-Y.; Agarwala, A.; Curless, B.; Salesin, D. H.; Szeliski, R. Video matting of complex scenes. *ACM Transactions on Graphics* Vol. 21, No. 3, 243–248, 2002.

[16] Gong, M.; Qian, Y.; Cheng, L. Integrated foreground segmentation and boundary matting for live videos. *IEEE Transactions on Image Processing* Vol. 24, No. 4, 1356–1370, 2015.

[17] Pérez, P.; Gangnet, M.; Blake, A. Poisson image editing. *ACM Transactions on Graphics* Vol. 22, No. 3, 313–318, 2003.

[18] Jia, J.; Sun, J.; Tang, C.-K.; Shum, H.-Y. Drag-and-drop pasting. *ACM Transactions on Graphics* Vol. 25, No. 3, 631–637, 2006.

[19] Buchsbaum, G. A spatial processor model for object colour perception. *Journal of the Franklin Institute* Vol. 310, No. 1, 1–26, 1980.

[20] Finlayson, G. D.; Hordley, S. D.; Hubel, P. M. Color by correlation: A simple, unifying framework for color constancy. *IEEE Transactions on Pattern Analysis and Machine Intelligence* Vol. 23, No. 11, 1209–1221, 2001.

[21] Cheng, D.; Prasad, D. K.; Brown, M. S. Illuminant estimation for color constancy: Why spatial-domain methods work and the role of the color distribution. *Journal of the Optical Society of America A* Vol. 31, No. 5, 1049–1058, 2014.

[22] Cheng, D.; Price, B.; Cohen, S.; Brown, M. S. Beyond white: Ground truth colors for color constancy correction. In: Proceedings of the IEEE International Conference on Computer Vision, 298–306, 2015.

[23] Omer, I.; Werman, M. Color lines: Image specific color representation. In: Proceedings of the IEEE Computer Society Conference on Computer Vision and Pattern Recognition, Vol. 2, II-946–II-953, 2004.

[24] Levin, A.; Lischinski, D.; Weiss, Y. A closed-form solution to natural image matting. *IEEE Transactions on Pattern Analysis and Machine Intelligence* Vol. 30, No. 2, 228–242, 2008.

[25] Land, E. H.; McCann, J. J. Lightness and retinex theory. *Journal of the Optical Society of America* Vol. 61, No. 1, 1–11, 1971.

[26] Zhang, Y.; Tang, Y.-L.; Cheng, K.-L. Efficient video cutout by paint selection. *Journal of Computer Science and Technology* Vol. 30, No. 3, 467–477, 2015.

[27] Smith, A. R.; Blinn, J. F. Blue screen matting. In: Proceedings of the 23rd Annual Conference on Computer Graphics and Interactive Techniques, 259–268, 1996.

[28] Mumtaz, A.; Zhang, W.; Chan, A. B. Joint motion segmentation and background estimation in dynamic scenes. In: Proceedings of the IEEE Conference on Computer Vision and Pattern Recognition, 368–375, 2014.

[29] Zhang, L.; Huang, H.; Fu, H. EXCOL: An extract-and-complete layering approach to cartoon animation reusing. *IEEE Transactions on Visualization and Computer Graphics* Vol. 18, No. 7, 1156–1169, 2012.

[30] Gastal, E. S. L.; Oliveira, M. M. Shared sampling for real-time alpha matting. *Computer Graphics Forum* Vol. 29, No. 2, 575–584, 2010.

[31] Chen, X.; Zou, D.; Zhou, S.; Zhao, Q.; Tan, P. Image matting with local and nonlocal smooth priors. In: Proceedings of the IEEE Conference on Computer Vision and Pattern Recognition, 1902–1907, 2013.

[32] Wong, B.-Y.; Shih, K.-T.; Liang, C.-K.; Chen, H. H. Single image realism assessment and recoloring by color compatibility. *IEEE Transactions on Multimedia* Vol. 14, No. 3, 760–769, 2012.

[33] Cohen-Or, D.; Sorkine, O.; Gal, R.; Leyvand, T.; Xu, Y.-Q. Color harmonization. *ACM Transactions on Graphics* Vol. 25, No. 3, 624–630, 2006.

[34] Kuang, Z.; Lu, P.; Wang, X.; Lu, X. Learning self-adaptive color harmony model for aesthetic quality classification. In: Proceedings of SPIE 9443, the 6th International Conference on Graphic and Image Processing, 94431O, 2015.

[35] Chen, T.; Cheng, M.-M.; Tan, P.; Shamir, A.; Hu, S.-M. Sketch2Photo: Internet image montage. *ACM Transactions on Graphics* Vol. 28, No. 5, Article No. 124, 2009.

[36] Farbman, Z.; Hoffer, G.; Lipman, Y.; Cohen-Or, D.; Lischinski, D. Coordinates for instant image cloning. *ACM Transactions on Graphics* Vol. 28, No. 3, Article No. 67, 2009.

[37] Boykov, Y.; Kolmogorov, V. An experimental comparison of min-cut/max-flow algorithms for energy minimization in vision. In: *Energy Minimization Methods in Computer Vision and Pattern Recognition.* Figueiredo, M.; Zerubia, J.; Jain, A. K. Eds. Springer Berlin Heidelberg, 359–374, 2001.

[38] Sigari, M. H.; Mozayani, N.; Pourreza, H. R. Fuzzy running average and fuzzy background subtraction: concepts and application. *International Journal of Computer Science and Network Security* Vol. 8, No. 2, 138–143, 2008.

[39] Sobral, A. BGSLibrary. 2016. Available at https://github.com/andrewssobral/bgslibrary.

[40] Rosin, P. L.; Ioannidis, E. Evaluation of global image thresholding for change detection. *Pattern Recognition Letters* Vol. 24, No. 14, 2345–2356, 2003.

[41] Kerbyson, D. J.; Atherton, T. J. Circle detection using Hough transform filters. In: Proceedings of the 5th International Conference on Image Processing and its Applications, 370–374, 1995.

[42] Graphics and Media Lab. Videomatting benchmark. 2016. Available at http://videomatting.com.

3

Feature-based RGB-D camera pose optimization for real-time 3D reconstruction

Chao Wang[1], Xiaohu Guo[1] (✉)

Abstract In this paper we present a novel feature-based RGB-D camera pose optimization algorithm for real-time 3D reconstruction systems. During camera pose estimation, current methods in online systems suffer from fast-scanned RGB-D data, or generate inaccurate relative transformations between consecutive frames. Our approach improves current methods by utilizing matched features across all frames and is robust for RGB-D data with large shifts in consecutive frames. We directly estimate camera pose for each frame by efficiently solving a quadratic minimization problem to maximize the consistency of 3D points in global space across frames corresponding to matched feature points. We have implemented our method within two state-of-the-art online 3D reconstruction platforms. Experimental results testify that our method is efficient and reliable in estimating camera poses for RGB-D data with large shifts.

Keywords camera pose optimization; feature matching; real-time 3D reconstruction; feature correspondence

1 Introduction

Real-time 3D scanning and reconstruction techniques have been applied to many areas in recent years with the prevalence of inexpensive depth cameras for consumers. The sale of millions of such devices makes it desirable for users to scan and reconstruct dense models of the surrounding environment by themselves. Online reconstruction techniques have various popular applications, e.g., in augmented reality (AR) to fuse supplemented elements with the real-world environment, in virtual reality (VR) to provide users with reliable environment perception and feedback, and in simultaneous localization and mapping (SLAM) for robots to automatically navigate in complex environments [1–3].

One of the earliest and most notable methods among RGB-D based online 3D reconstruction techniques is KinectFusion [4], which enables a user holding and moving a standard depth camera such as Microsoft Kinect to rapidly create detailed 3D reconstructions of a static scene. However, a major limitation of KinectFusion is that camera pose estimation is performed by frame-to-model registration using an iterative closest point (ICP) algorithm based on geometric data, which is only reliable for RGB-D data with small shifts between consecutive frames acquired by high-frame-rate depth cameras [4, 5].

To solve the aforementioned limitation, a common strategy adopted by most subsequent online reconstruction methods is to introduce photometric data into the ICP-based framework to estimate camera poses by maximizing the consistency of geometric information as well as color information between two adjacent frames [2, 5–11]. However, even though an ICP-based framework can effectively deal with RGB-D data with small shifts, it solves a non-linear minimization problem and always converges to a local minimum near the initial input because of the small angle assumption [4]. This indicates that pose estimation accuracy relies strongly on a good initial guess, which is unlikely to be satisfied if the camera moves rapidly or is shifted suddenly by the user. For the same reason, ICP-

1 University of Texas at Dallas, Richardson, Texas, USA. E-mail: C. Wang, chao.wang3@utdallas.edu; X. Guo, xguo@utdallas.edu (✉).

based online reconstruction methods always generate results with drifts and distortion for scenes with large planar regions such as walls, ceilings, and floors, even if consecutive frames only contain small shifts. Figure 1 illustrates this shortcoming for several current online methods using an ICP-based framework, and also shows the advantage of our method on RGB-D data with large shifts on a planar region.

Another strategy to improve the robustness of camera tracking is to introduce RGB features into camera pose estimation by maximizing the 3D position consistency of corresponding feature points between frames [12–14]. These feature-based methods are better than ICP-based ones in handling RGB-D data with large shifts, since they simply run a quadratic minimization problem to directly compute the relative transformation between two consecutive frames [13, 14]. However, unlike ICP-based methods using frame-to-model registration, current feature-based methods estimate camera pose only based on pairs of consecutive frames, which usually brings in errors and accumulates drifts in reconstruction on RGB-D data with sudden change. Moreover, current feature-based methods always inaccurately estimate camera pose because of unreliable feature extractors and matching. Practically, the inaccurate camera poses are not utilized directly in reconstruction, but pushed into an offline backend post-process to improve their reliability, such as global pose graph optimization [12, 15] or bundle adjustment [13, 14]. For this reason, most current feature-based reconstruction methods are strictly offline.

In this paper, we combine the advantages of the two above strategies and propose a novel feature-based camera pose optimization algorithm for online 3D reconstruction systems. To solve the limitation that the ICP-based framework always converges to a local minimum near the initial input, our approach estimates the global camera poses directly by efficiently solving a quadratic minimization problem to maximize the consistency of matched feature points across frames, without any initial guess. This makes our method robust in dealing with RGB-D data with large shifts. Meanwhile, unlike current feature-based methods which only consider pairs of consecutive frames, our method utilizes matched features from all previous frames to reduce the impact of bad features and accumulated error in camera pose during scanning. This is achieved by keeping track of RGB features' 3D points information from all frames in a structure called the feature correspondence list.

Our algorithm can be directly integrated into current online reconstruction pipelines. We have implemented our method within two state-of-the-art online 3D reconstruction platforms. Experimental results testify that our approach is efficient and improves current methods in estimating camera pose on RGB-D data with large shifts.

2   Related work

Following KinectFusion, many variants and other brand new methods have been proposed to overcome its limitations and achieve more accurate reconstruction results. Here we mainly consider camera pose estimation methods in online

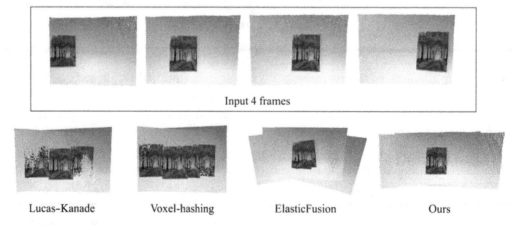

Fig. 1 Camera pose estimation comparison between methods. Top: four real input point clouds scanned using different views of a white wall with a painting. Bottom: results of stitching using camera poses provided by the Lucas–Kanade method [6], voxel-hashing [2], ElasticFusion [9], and our method.

and offline reconstruction techniques, and briefly introduce camera pose optimization in some other relevant areas.

2.1 Online RGB-D reconstruction

A typical online 3D reconstruction process takes RGB-D data as input and fuses the dense overlapping depth frames into one reconstructed model using some specific representation, of which two most important categories are volume-based fusion [2, 4, 5, 10, 16, 17] and point/surfel-based fusion [1, 9]. Volume-based methods are very common since they can directly generate models with connected surfaces, and are also efficient in data retrieval and use of the GPU. While KinectFusion is limited to a small fixed-size scene, several subsequent methods introduce different data processing techniques to extend the original volume structure, such as moving volume [16, 18], octree-based volume [17], patch volume [19], or hierarchical volume [20]. However, these online methods simply inherit the same ICP framework from KinectFusion to estimate camera pose.

In order to handle dense depth data and stitch frames in real time, most online reconstruction methods prefer an ICP-based framework which is efficient and reliable if the depth data has small shifts. While KinectFusion runs a frame-to-model ICP process with vertex correspondence obtained by projective data association, Peasley and Birchfield [6] improved it by providing ICP with a better initial guess and correspondence based on a warp transformation between consecutive RGB images. However, this warp transformation is only reliable for images with very small shifts, just like the ICP-based framework. Nießner et al. [2] introduced voxel-hashing technique into volumetric fusion to reconstruct scenes at large scale efficiently and used color-ICP to maintain geometric as well as color consistency of all corresponding vertices. Steinbrucker et al. [21] proposed an octree-based multi-resolution online reconstruction system which estimates relative camera poses between frames by stitching their photometric and geometric data together as closely as possible. Whelan et al.'s method [10] and a variant [5] both utilize a volume-shifting fusion technique to handle large-scale RGB-D data, while Whelan et

al.'s ElasticFusion approach [9] extends it to a surfel-based fusion framework. They introduce local loop closure detection to adjust camera poses at any time during reconstruction. Nonetheless, these methods still rely on an ICP-based framework to determine a single joint pose constraint and therefore are still only reliable on RGB-D data with small shifts. Figure 1 gives a comparison between our method and these current methods on a rapidly scanned wall. In Section 4 we compare voxel-hashing [2], ElasticFusion [9], and our method on an RGB-D benchmark [22] and a real scene.

Feature-based online reconstruction methods are much rarer than ICP-based ones, since camera poses estimated only using features are usually unreliable due to the noisy RGB-D data, and must be subsequently post-processed. Huang et al. [13] proposed one of the earliest SLAM systems which estimates an initial camera pose in real time for each frame by utilizing FAST feature correspondence between consecutive frames, and sending all poses to a post-process for global bundle adjustment before reconstruction, which makes this method less efficient and not strictly an online reconstruction technique. Endres et al. [12] considered different feature extractors and estimated camera pose by simply computing the transformation between consecutive frames using an RANSAC algorithm based on feature correspondences. Xiao et al. [14] provided an RGB-D database with full 3D space views and used SIFT features to construct the transformation between consecutive frames, followed by bundle adjustment to globally improve pose estimates. In summary, current feature-based methods utilize feature correspondences only between pairs of consecutive frames to estimate the relative transformation between them. Unlike such methods, our method utilizes the feature-matching information from all previous frames by keeping track of the information in a feature correspondence list. Section 4.4 compares our method and current feature-based frameworks utilizing only pairs of consecutive frames.

2.2 Offline RGB-D reconstruction

The typical and most common scheme for offline reconstruction methods is to take advantage of some global optimization technique to determine consistent camera poses for all frames, such as bundle adjustment [13, 14], pose graph optimization [5, 14, 23], and deformation graph optimization with loop closure detection [9]. Some offline works utilize similar strategies to online methods [2, 5, 9] by introducing feature correspondences into an ICP-based framework. They maximize the consistency of both dense geometric data and sparse image features, such as one of the first reconstruction systems proposed by Henry et al. [7] using SIFT features.

Other work introduces various special points of interest into camera pose estimation and RGB-D reconstruction. Zhou and Koltun [24] proposed an impressive offline 3D reconstruction method which focuses on preserving details of points of interest with high density values across RGB-D frames, and runs pose graph optimization to obtain globally consistent pose estimations for these points. Two other works by Zhou et al. [25] and Choi et al. [26] both detect smooth fragments as point of interest zones and attempt to maximize the consistency of corresponding points in fragments across frames using global optimization.

2.3 Camera pose optimization in other areas

Camera pose optimization is also very common in many other areas besides RGB-D reconstruction. Zhou and Koltun [3] presented a color mapping optimization algorithm for 3D reconstruction which optimizes camera poses by maximizing the color agreement of 3D points' 2D projections in all RGB images. Huang et al. [13] proposed an autonomous flight control and navigation method utilizing feature correspondence to estimate relative transformation between consecutive frames in real time. Steinbrücker et al. [27] presented a real-time visual odometry method which estimates camera poses by maximizing photo-consistency between consecutive images.

3 Camera pose estimation

Our camera pose optimization method attempts to maximize the consistency of matched features'

corresponding 3D points in global space across frames. In this section we start with a brief overview of the algorithmic framework, and then describe the details of each step.

3.1 Overall scheme

The pipeline is illustrated in Fig. 2. For each input RGB-D frame, we extract the RGB features in the first step (see Section 3.2), and then generate a good feature match with correspondence-check (see Section 3.3). Next, we maintain and update a data structure called the feature correspondence list to store matched features and corresponding 3D points in the camera's local coordinate space across frames (see Section 3.4). Finally, we estimate camera pose by minimizing the difference between matched features' 3D positions in global space (see Section 3.5).

3.2 Feature extraction

2D feature points can be utilized to reduce the amount of data needed to evaluate the similarity between two RGB images while preserving the accuracy of the result. In order to estimate camera pose efficiently in real time while guaranteeing the reconstruction reliability, we need to select a feature extraction method with a good balance between feature accuracy and speed. We ignore corner-based feature detectors such as BRIEF and FAST, since the depth data from consumer depth cameras always contains much noise around object contours due to the cameras' working principles [28]. Instead, we simply use an SURF detector to extract and describe RGB features, for two main reasons. Firstly, SURF is robust, stable, and scale and rotation invariant [29], which is important for establishing reliable feature correspondences between images. Secondly, existing methods can efficiently compute SURF in parallel on the GPU [30].

3.3 Feature matching

Using the feature descriptors, a feature match can be obtained easily but it usually contains many

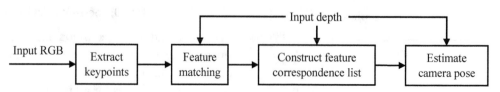

Fig. 2 Algorithm overview.

mismatched pairs. To remove as many outliers as possible, we run an RANSAC-based correspondence-check based on 2D homography and relative transformation between pairs of frames.

For two consecutive frames $i - 1$ and i with RGB images and corresponding 3D points in the camera's local coordinate space, we first obtain an initial feature match between 2D features based on their descriptors. Next, we run a number of iterations, and in each iteration we randomly select 4 feature pairs to estimate the 2D homography $\boldsymbol{H}_z$ using the direct linear transformation algorithm [31] and the 3D relative transformation $\boldsymbol{T}_z$ between the corresponding 3D points. $\boldsymbol{H}_z$ and $\boldsymbol{T}_z$ with lowest re-projection errors amongst all feature pairs are selected as the final ones to determine the outliers. After iterations, feature pairs with a 2D re-projection error larger than a threshold σ_H or a 3D re-projection error larger than a threshold σ_T are treated as outliers, and are removed from the initial feature match.

During the correspondence-check, we only select feature pairs with valid depth values. Meanwhile, in order to reduce noise in the depth data, we pre-smooth the depth image with a bilateral filter before computing 3D points from 2D features. After the correspondence-check, if the number of valid matched features is too small, the estimated camera pose obtained based on them will be unreliable. Therefore, we abandon all subsequent steps after feature matching and use a traditional ICP-based framework if the number of validly matched features is smaller than a threshold σ_F. In our experiment, we empirically choose $\sigma_H = 3$, $\sigma_T = 0.05$, and $\sigma_F = 10$.

Figure 3 shows a feature matching comparison before and after the correspondence-check for two consecutive images captured by a fast-moving camera. The blue circles are feature points, while the green circles and lines are matched feature pairs. Note that almost all poorly matched correspondence pairs are removed.

3.4 Feature correspondence list construction

In order to estimate the camera pose by maximizing the consistency of the global positions of matched features in all frames, we establish and update a feature correspondence list (FCL) to keep track of matched features in both the spatial and temporal

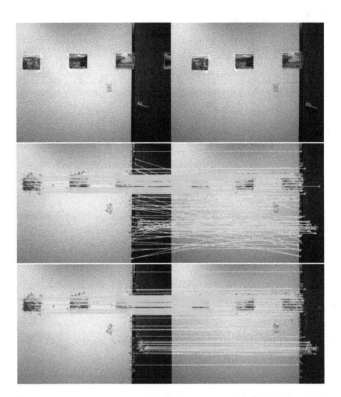

Fig. 3 Two original images (top), feature matching before (middle) and after (bottom) correspondence checking.

domain. The FCL is composed of 3D point sets, each of which denotes a series of 3D points in the camera's local coordinate space, whose corresponding 2D pixels are matched features across frames. Thus, the FCL in frame i is denoted by $\boldsymbol{L} = \{\boldsymbol{S}_j | j = 0, \ldots, m_i - 1\}$, where each $\boldsymbol{S}_j$ contains 3D points whose corresponding 2D points are matched features, j is the point set index, and m_i is the number of point sets in the FCL in frame i. The FCL can be simply constructed: Fig. 4 illustrates the process used to construct FCL for two consecutive frames.

By keeping track of all RGB features' 3D positions in each camera's local space, we can estimate camera poses by maximizing the consistency of all these 3D points' global positions. By utilizing feature information from all frames instead of just two consecutive frames, we aim to reduce the impact of possible bad features, such as incorrectly matched features or features from ill-scanned RGB-D frames. Moreover, this also avoids the accumulation of error in camera pose from previous frames.

3.5 Camera pose optimization

For the 3D points in each point set in FCL, their

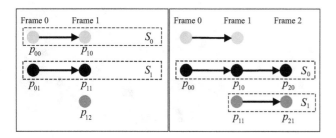

Fig. 4 Feature correspondence lists for frame 1 (left) and frame 2 (right). To construct the FCL for frame 2, we remove point sets with unmatched features (green), add matched points whose corresponding features are in the previous frame's FCL into the corresponding point sets (red), and add new point sets for matched features whose corresponding features are not in the previous frame's FCL (blue). Finally we re-index all points in the FCL. The number of point sets in the two FCLs is the same; here $m_1 = m_2 = 2$.

corresponding RGB features can be regarded as 2D projections from one 3D point in the real world on the RGB images in a continuous series of frames. For these 3D points in the camera coordinate space, we aim to ensure that their corresponding 3D points in the world space are as close as possible.

Given the FCL $L = \{S_j | j = 0, \cdots, m_i - 1\}$ in frame i, for each 3D point $p_{ij} \in S_j$, our objective is to maximize the agreement between p_{ij} and its target position in the world space with respect to a rigid transformation. Specifically, we seek a rotation R_i and translation vector t_i that minimize the following energy function:

$$E_i(R_i, t_i) = \sum_{j=0}^{m_i-1} w_j \| R_i p_{ij} + t_i - q_j \|^2 \quad (1)$$

where w_j is a weight to distinguish the importance of points, and q_j is the target position in the world space of p_{ij} after transformation. In our method we initially set:

$$q_j = \frac{1}{|S_j| - 1} \sum_{k=n_j}^{i-1} (R_k p_{kj} + t_k) \quad (2)$$

which is the average position of the 3D points in the world frame obtained from all points in S_j except for p_{ij} itself, where n_j is the frame index for S_j's first point. Intuitively, the more frequently a 3D global point appears in frames, the more reliable this point's measured data will be for the estimation of camera pose. Therefore, we use $w_j = |S_j|$ to balance the importance of points. q_j in Eq. (2) can be easily computed from the stored information in frame i's FCL.

The energy function $E_i(R_i, t_i)$ in Eq. (1) is

a quadratic least-squares objective and can be minimized by Arun et al.'s method [32]:

$$R_i = V D U^{\mathrm{T}} \quad (3)$$

$$t_i = \overline{q} - R_i \overline{p}_i \quad (4)$$

Here $D = \mathrm{diag}(1, 1, \det(V U^{\mathrm{T}}))$ ensures that R_i is a rotation matrix without reflection. U, V are both $3 \times m_i$ matrices from the singular value decomposition (SVD) of matrix $S = U \Sigma V^{\mathrm{T}}$, which is constructed by $S = X W Y^{\mathrm{T}}$ where:

$$X = [p_{i0} - \overline{p}_i, \ldots, p_{i(m_i-1)} - \overline{p}_i] \quad (5)$$

$$W = \mathrm{diag}(w_0, \ldots, w_{m_i-1}) \quad (6)$$

$$Y = [q_0 - \overline{q}, \ldots, q_{m_i-1} - \overline{q}] \quad (7)$$

$$\overline{p}_i = \frac{\sum_k w_k p_{ik}}{\sum_k w_k}, \quad \overline{q} = \frac{\sum_k w_k q_k}{\sum_k w_k} \quad (8)$$

Here X and Y are both $3 \times m_i$ matrices, W is a diagonal matrix with weight values, and $\overline{p}_i$ and $\overline{q}$ are the mass centers of all p_{ij} and q_j in frame i respectively. In general, by minimizing the energy function in Eq. (1), we seek a rigid transformation which makes each 3D point's global position in the world space as close as possible to the average position of all its corresponding 3D points from all previous frames.

After solving Eq. (1) for the current frame i, each p_{ij}'s target position q_j in Eq. (2) can be updated by

$$q'_j = \frac{1}{|S_j|} \sum_{k=n_j}^{i} (R_k p_{kj} + t_k) \quad (9)$$

This is simply done by putting p_{ij} and the newly obtained transformation R_i and t_i into Eq. (2), and estimating q_j as the average center of all points in S_j. Note that we can utilize the new q'_j in Eq. (9) to further decrease the energy in Eq. (1) and obtain another new transformation, which can be utilized again to update q'_j in turn. Therefore, an iterative optimization process updating q'_j and minimizing the energy E_i can be repeatedly used to optimize the transformation until the energy converges.

Furthermore, the aforementioned iterative process can also be run on previous frames to further maximize the consistency of matched 3D points' global positions between frames. If an online reconstruction system contains techniques to update the previously reconstructed data, then the further optimized poses in previous frames can be used to update the reconstruction quality further. Actually, we only need to optimize poses between frame r to

i, where r is the earliest frame index of all points in frame i's FCL. A common case during online scanning and reconstruction is that, the camera stays steady on a same scene for a long time. Then, the correspondence list will keep too many old redundant matched features from very early previous frames, which will greatly increase the computation cost of optimization. To avoid this, we check the gap between r and i for every frame i. If $i - r$ is larger than a threshold δ, we only run optimization between frame $i - \delta$ and i. In the experiments, we use $\delta = 50$.

In particular, minimizing each energy $E_k (r \leqslant k \leqslant i)$ is equivalent to minimizing the sum of the energy between these frames:

$$E(E_r, \ldots, E_i) = \sum_{k=r}^{i} E_i$$
$$= \sum_{k=r}^{i} \sum_{j=0}^{m_k-1} w_j \| \boldsymbol{R}_k \boldsymbol{p}_{kj} + \boldsymbol{t}_k - \boldsymbol{q}_j \|^2 \quad (10)$$

According to the solutions in Eqs. (5)–(8), the computation of each transformation $\boldsymbol{R}_k$ and $\boldsymbol{t}_k$ in Eq. (10) is independent of that in other frames. The total energy E is estimated each time in the iterative optimization process to determine if the convergence condition is satisfied or not.

Algorithm 1 describes the entire iterative camera pose optimization process in our method. In the experiments we set the energy threshold $\varepsilon = 0.01$. Our optimization method is very efficient in that it only takes $O(m_i)$ multiplications and additions as well as a few SVD processes on 3×3 matrices.

4 Experimental results

To assess the capabilities of our camera pose estimation method, we embedded it within two state-of-the-art platforms: a volume-based method based on voxel-hashing [2] and a surfel-based method, ElasticFusion [9]. In the implementation, we first estimate camera poses using our method, and then regard them as good initial guesses for the original ICP-based framework in each platform. The reason is that the reconstruction quality is possibly low if the online system does not run a frame-to-model framework to stitch dense data from the current frame with the previous model during reconstruction [5]. Note that for each frame, even though our method optimizes camera poses from all relevant frames, we only use the optimized

---

Algorithm 1 Camera pose optimization

Input: Feature correspondence list for frame i, earliest frame index r, and energy threshold ε.
Output: Optimized camera poses between frame r and frame i.
1: Update $\{\boldsymbol{q}_j\}$ via Eq. (2);
2: Compute energy E_i in Eq. (1) with $\{\boldsymbol{q}_j\}$ and obtain $\boldsymbol{R}_i$ and $\boldsymbol{t}_i$;
3: Compute total energy E in Eq. (10);
4: **while** (**true**) **do**
5:     $E' \Leftarrow E$;
6:     Update $\{\boldsymbol{q}'_j\}$ with $\{\boldsymbol{R}_k, \boldsymbol{t}_k | k = r, \ldots, i\}$ via Eq. (9);
7:     **for all** $(r \leqslant k \leqslant i)$ **do**
8:        Compute energy E_k in Eq. (1) with $\{\boldsymbol{q}'_j\}$ and obtain $\boldsymbol{R}'_k$ and $\boldsymbol{t}'_k$;
9:     **end for**
10:    Compute new energy E in Eq. (10) with $\{\boldsymbol{R}'_k, \boldsymbol{t}'_k | k = r, \ldots, i\}$;
11:    **if** $(|E' - E| < \varepsilon)$ **then**
12:      **break**;
13:    **end if**
14:    **for all** $(r \leqslant k \leqslant i)$ **do**
15:      $\boldsymbol{R}_k \Leftarrow \boldsymbol{R}'_k, \boldsymbol{t}_k \Leftarrow \boldsymbol{t}'_k$;
16:    **end for**
17: **end while**
18: **Return** $\{\boldsymbol{R}'_k, \boldsymbol{t}'_k | k = r, \ldots, i\}$

---

pose for the current frame for the frame-to-model framework to update the reconstruction, and the optimized poses in previous frames are only utilized to estimate the camera poses in future frames.

4.1 Trajectory estimation

We first compare our method with both voxel-hashing [2] and ElasticFusion [9], evaluating the trajectory estimation performance using several datasets from the RGB-D benchmark [22]. In order to compare with ElasticFusion [9], we utilize the same error metric as in their work, absolute trajectory root-mean-square error (ATE) which measures the root-mean-square of Euclidean distances between estimated camera poses and ground truth ones associated with timestamps [9, 22].

Table 1 shows the results from each method with and without our improvement. We denote the smallest error for each dataset in bold. Here "dif1" and "dif5" denote the frame difference used for each dataset during reconstruction. In other words, for "dif5", we only use the first frame of every 5 consecutive frames in each original dataset, and omit the other 4 intermediate frames

Table 1 Trajectory estimation comparison of methods using ATE metric

System	fr1/desk		fr1/floor		fr1/room		fr3/ntf	
	dif1	dif5	dif1	dif5	dif1	dif5	dif1	dif5
Voxel-hashing	1.10	0.74	1.01	0.70	0.61	1.08	1.32	1.30
Ours	0.32	0.32	**0.16**	**0.19**	0.34	0.61	0.18	0.08
ElasticFusion	**0.03**	0.30	0.41	0.54	0.38	0.48	**0.08**	0.15
Ours	0.04	**0.21**	0.17	0.22	**0.32**	**0.35**	**0.08**	**0.08**

in order to estimate the trajectories on RGB-D data with large shifts, while for "dif1" we just use the original dataset. Note that our results are different when embedded in the two platforms even for the same dataset. This is because, firstly, the two online platforms utilize different data processing and representation techniques, and different frame-to-model frameworks during reconstruction. Secondly, the voxel-hashing platform does not contain any optimization technique to modify previously constructed models and camera poses, while ElasticFusion utilizes both local and global loop closure detection in conjunction with global optimization techniques to optimize previous data and generate a globally consistent reconstruction [9]. Results in Table 1 show that our method improves upon the other two methods for estimating trajectories, especially on large planar regions such as fr1/floor and fr3/ntf which both contain floor with textures. Furthermore, our method also estimates trajectories better than the other methods when the shifts between the RGB-D frames are large.

4.2 Pose estimation

To estimate the pose estimation performance, we compared our methods with the same two methods on the same benchmark using relative pose error (RPE) [22], which measures the relative pose difference between each estimated camera pose and the corresponding ground truth. Table 2 gives the results, which show that our method can improve camera pose estimation on datasets with large shifts, even though our result is only on a par with the others on the original datasets with small shifts between consecutive frames.

4.3 Surface reconstruction

In order to compare the influence of computed camera poses on the final reconstructed models for our method and the others, we firstly compute camera poses by each method on its corresponding platform, and then use all the poses on the same voxel-hashing platform to generate reconstructed models. Here our method runs on the voxel-hashing platform. Figure 5 gives the reconstruction results for different methods on the fr1/floor dataset from the same benchmark, with frame difference 5. The figure shows that our method improves the reconstructed surface by producing good camera poses for the RGB-D data with large shifts.

To test our method on a fast-moving camera on

Table 2 Pose estimation comparison of methods using RPE metric

System	fr1/desk		fr1/floor		fr1/room		fr3/ntf	
	dif1	dif5	dif1	dif5	dif1	dif5	dif1	dif5
Voxel-hashing	1.57	1.16	1.25	0.98	1.15	1.49	1.60	1.62
Ours	0.91	0.94	0.80	0.80	0.84	1.14	1.36	1.42
ElasticFusion	**0.04**	0.41	**0.42**	0.58	**0.51**	0.63	**0.11**	**0.11**
Ours	0.05	**0.29**	0.43	**0.48**	0.54	**0.61**	0.12	**0.11**

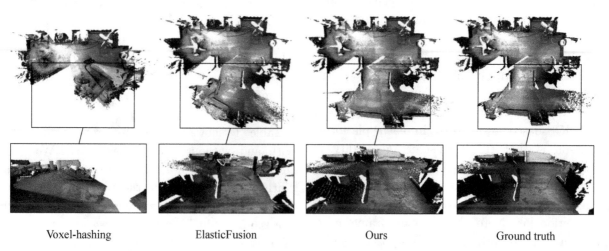

Voxel-hashing   ElasticFusion   Ours   Ground truth

Fig. 5 Reconstruction results for different methods on fr1/floor from the RGB-D benchmark [22] with frame difference 5.

a real scene, we fixed an Asus XTion depth camera on a tripod with a motor to rotate the camera with controlled speed. With this device, we firstly scanned a room by rotating the camera only around its axis (the y-axis in the camera's local coordinate frame) for several rotations with a fixed speed, and selected the RGB-D data for exactly one rotation for the test. This dataset contains 235 RGB-D frames; most of the RGB images are blurred, since it took the camera only about 5 seconds to finish the rotation. Figure 6 gives an example showing two blurred images from this RGB-D dataset. Note that our feature matching method can still match features

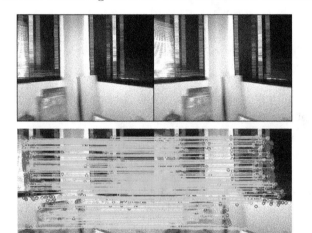

Fig. 6 Two blurred images (top) and feature matching result (bottom) from our scanned RGB-D data from a real scene using a fast-moving camera.

very well.

Figure 7 gives the reconstruction results produced by different methods on the dataset. As in Fig. 5, all reconstruction results here are also obtained using the voxel-hashing platform with camera poses pre-computed by different methods on each corresponding platform; again our method ran on the voxel-hashing platform. For the ground truth camera poses, since we scan the scene with fixed rotation speed, we simply compute the ground truth camera pose for each frame $i\,(0 \leqslant i < 235)$ as $\boldsymbol{R}_i = \boldsymbol{R}_y(\theta_i)$ with $\theta_i = (360(i-1)/235)°$ and $\boldsymbol{t}_i = 0$, where $\boldsymbol{R}_y(\theta_i)$ rotates around the y-axis by an angle θ_i. Moreover, note that ElasticFusion [9] utilizes loop closure detection and deformation graph optimization to globally optimize camera poses and global point positions in the final model. To make the comparison more reasonable, we introduce the same loop closure detection in ElasticFusion [9] into our method, and use a pose graph optimization tool [15] to globally optimize camera poses for all frames efficiently. Figure 7 shows that our optimized camera poses can determine the structure of the reconstructed model very well for the real-scene data captured by a fast-moving camera.

4.4 Justification of feature correspondence list

In our method we utilize the FCL in order to

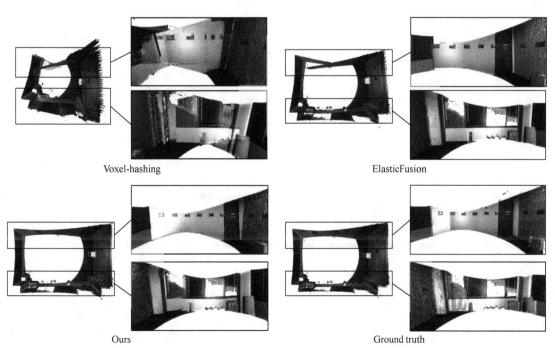

Voxel-hashing   ElasticFusion

Ours   Ground truth

Fig. 7 Reconstruction results for different methods on room data captured by a speed-controlled fast-moving camera.

reduce the impact of bad features on camera pose estimation, and also to avoid accumulating error in camera poses during scanning. Current feature-based methods always estimate the relative transformation between the current frame and the previous one using only the matched features in these two consecutive frames [12–14] and here we call this strategy *consecutive-feature estimation*.

In our framework, the consecutive-feature estimation can be easily implemented by only using steps (1) and (2) (lines 1 and 2) in Algorithm 1 for each $q_j = p_{(i-1)j}$, which is p_{ij}'s matched 3D point in the previous frame. Figure 9 gives the ATE and RPE errors for our method utilizing FCLs and the consecutive-feature method on fr1/floor, for increasing frame differences. Clearly our method with FCLs outperforms the consecutive-feature method in determining camera poses for RGB-D data with large shifts.

4.5 Performance

We have tested our method on the voxel-hashing platform on a laptop running Microsoft Windows 8.1 with an Intel Core i7-4710HQ CPU at 2.5 GHz, 12 GB RAM, and an NVIDIA GeForce GTX 860M GPU with 4 GB memory. We used the OpenSURF library and used OpenCL [30] to extract SURF features on each down-sampled 320×240 RGB image. For each frame, our camera pose optimization pipeline takes about 10 ms to extract features and finish feature matching, 1–2 ms for FCL construction, and only 5–8 ms for the camera pose optimization step, including the iterative optimization of camera poses for all relevant frames. Therefore, our method is efficient enough to run in real time. We also note that the offline pose graph optimization tool [15] used for the RGB-D data described in Section 4.3 takes only 10 ms for global pose optimization of all frames.

5 Conclusions and future work

This paper has proposed a novel feature-based camera pose optimization algorithm which efficiently and robustly estimates camera pose in online RGB-D reconstruction systems. Our approach utilizes the feature correspondences from all previous frames and optimizes camera poses across frames. We have implemented our method within two state-of-the-art online RGB-D reconstruction platforms. Experimental results verify that our method improves current online systems in estimating more accurate camera poses and generating more reliable reconstructions for RGB-D data with large shifts between consecutive frames.

Considering that our camera pose optimization method is only part of the RGB-D reconstruction system pipeline, we aim to develop a new RGB-D reconstruction system with our camera pose optimization framework in it. Moreover, we will also explore utilizing our optimized camera poses in previous frames to update the previously reconstructed model in the online system.

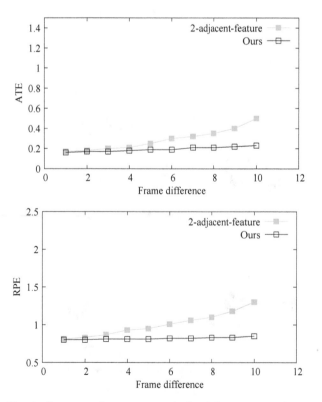

Fig. 9 Comparison between our method and the consecutive-feature method on fr1/floor for varying frame difference.

References

[1] Keller, M.; Lefloch, D.; Lambers, M.; Izadi, S.; Weyrich, T.; Kolb, A. Real-time 3D reconstruction in dynamic scenes using point-based fusion. In: Proceedings of the International Conference on 3D Vision, 1–8, 2013.

[2] Nießner, M.; Zollhöfer, M.; Izadi, S.; Stamminger, M. Real-time 3D reconstruction at scale using voxel hashing. *ACM Transactions on Graphics* Vol. 32, No. 6, Article No. 169, 2013.

[3] Zhou, Q.-Y.; Koltun, V. Color map optimization for 3D reconstruction with consumer depth cameras. *ACM Transactions on Graphics* Vol. 33, No. 4, Article No. 155, 2014.

[4] Newcombe, R. A.; Izadi, S.; Hilliges, O.; Molyneaux, D.; Kim, D.; Davison, A. J.; Kohi, P.; Shotton, J.; Hodges, S.; Fitzgibbon, A. KinectFusion: Real-time dense surface mapping and tracking. In: Proceedings of the 10th IEEE International Symposium on Mixed and Augmented Reality, 127–136, 2011.

[5] Whelan, T.; Kaess, M.; Johannsson, H.; Fallon, M.; Leonard, J.; McDonald, J. Real-time large-scale dense RGB-D slam with volumetric fusion. *The International Journal of Robotics Research* Vol. 34, Nos. 4–5, 598–626, 2015.

[6] Peasley, B.; Birchfield, S. Replacing projective data association with Lucas–Kanade for KinectFusion. In: Proceedings of the IEEE International Conference on Robotics and Automation, 638–645, 2013.

[7] Henry, P.; Krainin, M.; Herbst, E.; Ren, X.; Fox, D. RGB-D mapping: Using Kinect-style depth cameras for dense 3D modeling of indoor environments. *The International Journal of Robotics Research* Vol. 31, No. 5, 647–663, 2012.

[8] Newcombe, R. A.; Lovegrove, S. J.; Davison, A. J. DTAM: Dense tracking and mapping in real-time. In: Proceedings of the IEEE International Conference on Computer Vision, 2320–2327, 2011.

[9] Whelan, T.; Leutenegger, S.; Salas-Moreno, R.; Glocker, B.; Davison, A. ElasticFusion: Dense SLAM without a pose graph. In: Proceedings of Robotics: Science and Systems, 11, 2015.

[10] Whelan, T.; Johannsson, H.; Kaess, M.; Leonard, J. J.; McDonald, J. Robust real-time visual odometry for dense RGB-D mapping. In: Proceedings of the IEEE International Conference on Robotics and Automation, 5724–5731, 2013.

[11] Zhang, K.; Zheng, S.; Yu, W.; Li, X. A depth-incorporated 2D descriptor for robust and efficient 3D environment reconstruction. In: Proceedings of the 10th International Conference on Computer Science & Education, 691–696, 2015.

[12] Endres, F.; Hess, J.; Engelhard, N.; Sturm, J.; Cremers, D.; Burgard, W. An evaluation of the RGB-D SLAM system. In: Proceedings of the IEEE International Conference on Robotics and Automation, 1691–1696, 2012.

[13] Huang, A. S.; Bachrach, A.; Henry, P.; Krainin, M.; Maturana, D.; Fox, D.; Roy, N. Visual odometry and mapping for autonomous flight using an RGB-D camera. In: *Robotics Research*. Christensen, H. I.; Khatib, O.; Eds. Springer International Publishing, 235–252, 2011.

[14] Xiao, J.; Owens, A.; Torralba, A. SUN3D: A database of big spaces reconstructed using SfM and object labels. In: Proceedings of the IEEE International Conference on Computer Vision, 1625–1632, 2013.

[15] Kümmerle, R.; Grisetti, G.; Strasdat, H.; Konolige, K.; Burgard, W. G^{2}o: A general framework for graph optimization. In: Proceedings of the IEEE International Conference on Robotics and Automation, 3607–3613, 2011.

[16] Roth, H.; Vona, M. Moving volume KinectFusion. In: Proceedings of British Machine Vision Conference, 1–11, 2012.

[17] Zeng, M.; Zhao, F.; Zheng, J.; Liu, X. Octree-based fusion for realtime 3D reconstruction. *Graphical Models* Vol. 75, No. 3, 126–136, 2013.

[18] Whelan, T.; Johannsson, H.; Kaess, M.; Leonard, J. J.; McDonald, J. Robust tracking for real-time dense RGB-D mapping with Kintinuous. Computer Science and Artificial Intelligence Laboratory Technical Report, MIT-CSAIL-TR-2012-031, 2012.

[19] Henry, P.; Fox, D.; Bhowmik, A.; Mongia, R. Patch volumes: Segmentation-based consistent mapping with RGBD cameras. In: Proceedings of the International Conference on 3D Vision, 398–405, 2013.

[20] Chen, J.; Bautembach, D.; Izadi, S. Scalable real-time volumetric surface reconstruction. *ACM Transactions on Graphics* Vol. 32, No. 4, Article No. 113, 2013.

[21] Steinbrucker, F.; Kerl, C.; Cremers, D. Large-scale multiresolution surface reconstruction from RGB-D sequences. In: Proceedings of the IEEE International Conference on Computer Vision, 3264–3271, 2013.

[22] Sturm, J.; Engelhard, N.; Endres, F.; Burgard, W.; Cremers, D. A benchmark for the evaluation of RGB-D SLAM systems. In: Proceedings of the IEEE/RSJ International Conference on Intelligent Robots and Systems, 573–580, 2012.

[23] Stückler, J.; Behnke, S. Multi-resolution surfel maps for efficient dense 3D modeling and tracking. *Journal of Visual Communication and Image Representation* Vol. 25, No. 1, 137–147, 2014.

[24] Zhou, Q.-Y.; Koltun, V. Dense scene reconstruction with points of interest. *ACM Transactions on Graphics* Vol. 32, No. 4, Article No. 112, 2013.

[25] Zhou, Q.-Y.; Miller, S.; Koltun, V. Elastic fragments for dense scene reconstruction. In: Proceedings of the IEEE International Conference on Computer Vision, 473–480, 2013

[26] Choi, S.; Zhou, Q.-Y.; Koltun, V. Robust reconstruction of indoor scenes. In: Proceedings of the IEEE Conference on Computer Vision and Pattern Recognition, 5556–5565, 2015.

[27] Steinbrücker, F.; Sturm, J.; Cremers, D. Real-time visual odometry from dense RGB-D images. In: Proceedings of the IEEE International Conference on Computer Vision Workshops, 719–722, 2011.

[28] Hänsch, R.; Weber, T.; Hellwich, O. Comparison of 3D interest point detectors and descriptors for point cloud fusion. *ISPRS Annals of the Photogrammetry, Remote Sensing and Spatial Information Sciences* Vol. 2, No. 3, 57, 2014.

[29] Juan, L.; Gwun, O. A comparison of SIFT, PCA-SIFT and SURF. *International Journal of Image Processing* Vol. 3, No. 4, 143–152, 2009.

[30] Yan, W.; Shi, X.; Yan, X.; Wan, L. Computing openSURF on openCL and general purpose GPU. *International Journal of Advanced Robotic Systems* Vol. 10, No. 10, 375, 2013.

[31] Hartley, R.; Zisserman, A. *Multiple View Geometry in Computer Vision.* Cambridge University Press, 2003.

[32] Arun, K. S.; Huang, T. S.; Blostein, S. D. Least-squares fitting of two 3-D point sets. *IEEE Transactions on Pattern Analysis and Machine Intelligence* Vol. PAMI-9, No. 5, 698–700, 1987.

4

Decoding and calibration method on focused plenoptic camera

Chunping Zhang[1] (✉), Zhe Ji[1], and Qing Wang[1]

Abstract The ability of light gathering of plenoptic camera opens up new opportunities for a wide range of computer vision applications. An efficient and accurate method to calibrate plenoptic camera is crucial for its development. This paper describes a 10-intrinsic-parameter model for focused plenoptic camera with misalignment. By exploiting the relationship between the raw image features and the depth–scale information in the scene, we propose to estimate the intrinsic parameters from raw images directly, with a parallel biplanar board which provides depth prior. The proposed method enables an accurate decoding of light field on both angular and positional information, and guarantees a unique solution for the 10 intrinsic parameters in geometry. Experiments on both simulation and real scene data validate the performance of the proposed calibration method.

Keywords calibration; focused plenoptic camera; depth prior; intrinsic parameters

1 Introduction

The light field cameras, including plenoptic camera designed by Ng [1, 2] and focused plenoptic camera designed by Georgiev [3–5], capture both angular and spatial information of rays in space. With the micro-lens array between image sensor and main lens, the rays from the same point in the scene fall on different locations of image sensor. With a particular camera model, the 2D raw image can be decoded into a 4D light field [6, 7], which allows applications on refocusing, multiview imaging, depth estimation, and so on [1, 8–10]. To support the applications, an accurate calibration method for light field camera is necessary.

Prior work in this area has dealt with the calibration of plenoptic camera and focused plenoptic camera by projecting images into the 3D world, but their camera models are still improvable. These methods make an assumption that the geometric center of micro-lens image lies on the optical axis of its corresponding micro-lens, and do not consider the constraints on the high-dimensional features of light fields. In this paper, we concentrate on the focused plenoptic camera and analyze the variance and invariance between the distribution of rays inside the camera and in real world scene, namely the relationship between the raw image features and the depth–scale information. We fully take into account the misalignment of the micro-lens array, and propose a 10-intrinsic-parameter light field camera model to relate the raw image and 4D light fields by ray tracing. Furthermore, to improve calibration accuracy, instead of a single-planar board, we design a parallel biplanar board to provide depth and scale priors. The method is verified on simulated data and a physical focused plenoptic camera. The effects of rendered images on different intrinsic parameters are compared.

In summary, our main contributions are listed as follows:

(1) A full light field camera model taking into account the geometric relationship between the center of micro-lens image and the optical center of micro-lens, which is ignored in most literature.

(2) A loop-locked algorithm which is capable of exploiting the 3D scene prior for estimating the intrinsic parameters in one shoot with good stability and low computational complexity.

The remainder of this paper is organized as follows. Section 2 summarizes related work on

1 School of Computer Science, Northwestern Polytechnical University, Xi'an 710072, China. E-mail: C. Zhang, 724495506@qq.com (✉); Z. Ji, 1277440141@qq.com; Q. Wang, qwang@nwpu.edu.cn.

light field camera models, decoding and calibration methods. Section 3 describes the ideal model for a traditional camera or a focused plenoptic camera, and presents three theorems we utilize for intrinsic parameter estimation. In Section 4, we propose a more complete model for a focused plenoptic camera. Section 5 presents our calibration algorithm. In Section 6, we evaluate our method on both simulation and real data. Finally, Section 7 concludes with summary and future work.

2 Related work

A light field camera captures light field in a single exposure. The 4D light field data is rearranged on a 2D image sensor in accordance with the optical design. Moreover, the distribution of raw image depends on the relative position of the focused point inside the camera and the optical center of the micro-lens, as shown in Fig. 1. Figure 1(a) shows the design of Ng's plenoptic camera, where the micro-lens array is on the image plane of the main lens and the rays from the focused point almost fall on the same micro-lens image. Figure 1(b) and Fig. 1(c) show the design of Georgiev's focused plenoptic camera with a micro-lens array focused on the image plane of main lens,

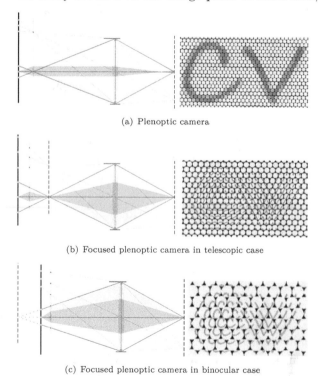

(a) Plenoptic camera

(b) Focused plenoptic camera in telescopic case

(c) Focused plenoptic camera in binocular case

Fig. 1 Different designs of light field camera and raw images that consist of many micro-lens images closely packed.

and the rays from the focused point fall on different micro-lenses.

Decoding light field is equivalent to computing multiview images in two perpendicular directions. Multiview images are reorganized by selecting a contiguous set of pixels from each micro-lens image, for example, one pixel for plenoptic camera [2] and a patch for focused plenoptic camera [3, 10] However, for a focused plenoptic camera, the patch size influences the focus depth of the rendered image. Such decoding method causes discontinuity on out-of-focus area and results in artifact of aliasing.

For decoding a 2D raw image to a 4D light field representation, a common assumption is made that the center of each micro-lens image lies on the optical axis of its corresponding micro-lens [7, 11, 12] in ideal circumstances. Perwaß et al. [7] synthesized refocused images on different depths by searching pixels from multiple micro-lens images. Georgiev et al. [13] decoded into light field using ray transfer matrix analysis. Based on this assumption, the deviation in the ray's original direction has little effect on rendering a traditional image. However, the directions of decoded rays are crucial for an accurate estimation of camera intrinsic parameters, which is particularly important for absolute depth estimation [14] or light field reparameterization for cameras in different poses [15].

The calibration of a physical light field camera aims to decode rays more accurately. Several methods are proposed for the plenoptic camera. Dansereau et al. [6] presented a 15-parameter plenoptic camera model to relate pixels to rays in 3D space, which provides theoretical support for light field panorama [15]. The parameters are initialized using traditional camera calibration techniques. Bok et al. [16] formulated a geometric projection model to estimate intrinsic and extrinsic parameters by utilizing raw images directly, including analytical solution and non-linear optimization. Thomason et al. [17] concentrated on the misalignment of the micro-lens array and estimated its position and orientation. In this work, the directions of rays may deviate due to an inaccurate solution of the installation distances among main lens, micro-lens array, and image sensor. On the other hand, Johannsen et al. [12] estimated the intrinsic and extrinsic parameters for a focused plenoptic camera by reconstructing a grid pattern from the raw image directly. The depth distortion caused by main lens was taken into account in their method. More importantly, expect for Ref. [17], these methods do not consider the deviation of the image center or the optical center for each micro-lens, which tends to cause inaccuracy in decoded light field.

3 The world in camera

The distribution of rays refracted by a camera lens is different from the original light field. In this section, we first discuss the corresponding relationship between the points in the scene and inside the camera modelled as a thin lens. Then we analyze the invariance in an ideal focused plenoptic camera, based on a thin lens and a pinhole model for the main lens and micro-lens respectively. Finally we conclude the relationship between the raw image features and the depth–scale information in the scene. Our analysis is conducted in the non-homogeneous coordinate system.

3.1 Thin lens model

As shown in Fig. 2, the rays emitted from the scene point $(x_{\text{obj}}, y_{\text{obj}}, z_{\text{obj}})^{\text{T}}$ in different directions are refracted through the lens aperture and brought to a single convergence point $(x_{\text{in}}, y_{\text{in}}, z_{\text{in}})^{\text{T}}$ if $z_{\text{obj}} > F$, where F denotes the focal length of the thin lens. The relationship between the two points is described as follows:

$$\frac{1}{|z_{\text{obj}}|} + \frac{1}{|z_{\text{in}}|} = \frac{1}{F} \tag{1}$$

$$\begin{pmatrix} x_{\text{in}} \\ y_{\text{in}} \\ z_{\text{in}} \end{pmatrix} = \frac{F}{F - z_{\text{obj}}} \begin{pmatrix} x_{\text{obj}} \\ y_{\text{obj}} \\ z_{\text{obj}} \end{pmatrix} \tag{2}$$

Equation (2) shows that the ratio on the

coordinates of the two points changes with z_{obj}. Furthermore, there is a projective relationship between the coordinates inside and outside the camera. For example, as shown in Fig. 3, the objects with the same size in different depths in the scene correspond to the objects with different sizes inside the camera. The relationship can be described as

$$\frac{T^2}{S_1 S_2} = \frac{a_1 - a_2}{b_1 - b_2} \tag{3}$$

where the focal length F satisfies:

$$F = \frac{b_2 S_1 - b_1 S_2}{S_1 - S_2} \tag{4}$$

3.2 Ideal focused plenoptic camera model

As shown in Fig. 1, there are two optical designs of the focused cameras. In this paper, we only consider the design in Fig. 1(b). The case in Fig. 1(c) is similar to the former, only with the difference in the relative position of the focus point and the optical center of the micro-lens.

In this section, the main lens and the micro-lens array are described by a thin lens and a pinhole model respectively. As shown in Fig. 4, the main lens, the micro-lens array, and the image sensor are parallel to each other and all perpendicular to the optical axis. The optical center of the main lens lies on the optical axis.

Let d_{img} and d_{lens} be the distance between two geometric centers of arbitrary adjacent micro-lens images and the diameter of the micro-lens respectively, as shown in Fig. 4(a). The ratio between them is

$$\frac{d_{\text{lens}}}{d_{\text{img}}} = \frac{L}{L + l} \tag{5}$$

where L and l are the distances among the main lens, the micro-lens array, and the image sensor respectively. We can find that the ratio L/l is

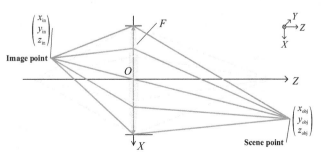

Fig. 2 Thin lens model.

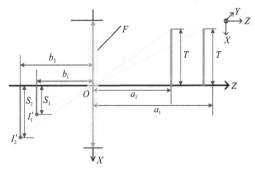

Fig. 3 Two objects with the same size of T in the scene at different depths focus inside a camera with focal length F.

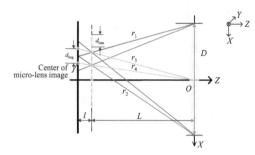

(a) Rays r_1 and r_2 intersect at the same point on image sensor to ensure the maximum size of the micro-lens image. Rays r_3 and r_4 fall on the geometric centers of two micro-lens images

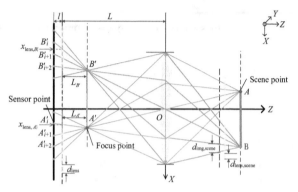

(b) The rays emitted from two scene points A and B in the scene and refracted through main lens pass through the optical centers of the micro-lenses and fall on different micro-lens images straightly. AB is perpendicular to axis Z

Fig. 4 Ideal focused plenoptic camera in telescopic case.

dependent on the raw image and the diameter of micro-lens, which is useful for our calibration model in Section 5. Moreover, there is a deviation between the optical center of micro-lens and the geometric center of its image, and d_{img} is constant in the same plenoptic camera.

Let $d_{\mathrm{lens,\ scene}}$ and $d_{\mathrm{img,\ scene}}$ be the size of micro-lens and its image refracted through the main lens into the scene respectively (Fig. 4(b)), combining Eqs. (2) and (5), the ratio between them satisfies:

$$\alpha = \frac{d_{\mathrm{lens,\ scene}}}{d_{\mathrm{img,\ scene}}} = \frac{L^2 + lL - LF}{L^2 + lL - LF - lF} \neq 1 \quad (6)$$

Equation (6) shows that though the rays are refracted through the main lens, the deviation between the geometric center of micro-lens image and the optical center of micro-lens still can not be ignored. The effect of deviations on the rendered images will be demonstrated and discussed in experiment.

In Fig. 4(b), A' and B' are the focus points of two scene points A and B respectively. The rays emitted from every focus point fall on multiple micro-lens

and focus on the image sensor, resulting in multiple images A'_i and B'_i. The distance between sensor points A'_i and A'_{i+1} is computed:

$$d_{A'} = \left| x'_{A_i} - x'_{A_{i+1}} \right| = d_{\mathrm{lens}} \frac{L_{A'} + l}{L_{A'}} \quad (7)$$

where $L_{A'}$ is the distance between focus point A' and the micro-lens array, and $|\cdot|$ denotes the absolute operator. Equation (7) indicates that the distance between arbitrary two adjacent sensor points of the same focus point inside the camera is only dependent on intrinsic parameters. Once the raw image is shot (thus $d_{A'}$ is determined), $L_{A'}$ is only dependent on l and d_{lens}. According to triangle similarity, we can get the coordinate of the focus point:

$$x_{A'} = x_{\mathrm{lens},A'_i} - \frac{L_{A'}}{l}\left(x_{A'_i} - x_{\mathrm{lens},A'_i}\right) \quad (8)$$

Based on Eq. (7), we can simplify Eq. (8) as

$$x_{A'} = \frac{d_{A'}}{d_{A'} - d_{\mathrm{lens}}} x_{\mathrm{lens},A'_i} - \frac{d_{\mathrm{lens}}}{d_{A'} - d_{\mathrm{lens}}} x_{A'_i} \quad (9)$$

According to Eq. (9), once a raw image is shot (thus d'_A and $x_{A'}$ are determined) and d_{lens} is given, $x_{A'}$ and $y_{A'}$ can be calculated and they are independent on other intrinsic parameters. Furthermore, the length of AB can be calculated using only the raw image and d_{lens}.

Imaging that there are two objects with equal size in the scene, as shown in Fig. 3, the distance between the focus point and the micro-lens array can be calculated via Eq. (7). Replacing b_1 and b_2 in Eq. (4) and simplifying via Eqs. (5) and (7), we get the relationship:

$$F = L - \frac{S_1 L_{I'_2} - S_2 L_{I'_1}}{S_1 - S_2} \quad (10)$$

where S_1, S_2, $L_{I'_1}$, and $L_{I'_2}$ are dependent on only three factors, including the raw image, d_{lens}, and l. Equation (10) shows that the value of F can be calculated uniquely once the other intrinsic parameters are determined.

In the same manner, Eq. (3) can be simplified as

$$T = \frac{b_2 S_1 - b_1 S_2}{b_1 - b_2} \quad (11)$$

From Eq. (11), the size of an object in the scene is independent on l. The size of an object which we reconstruct from the raw image can not be taken as a cost function to constrain l.

In summary, given the coordinates of micro-lens and the raw image, three theorems can be concluded as follows:

(1) The size of a reconstructed object inside the camera and its distance to the micro-lens array are constant (Eq. (9)).

(2) The unique F can be determined by the prior of the scene (Eq. (10)).

(3) The size of the reconstructed object in the scene is constant with changing L (Eq. (11)).

4 Micro-lens-based camera model

In this section we present a more complete model for a focused plenoptic camera with misalignment of the micro-lens array [17], which is capable of decoding more accurate light field. There are 10 intrinsic parameters totally to be presented in this section, including the distance between the main lens and the micro-lens array, L, the distance between the micro-lens array and the image sensor, l, the misalignment of micro-lens array, x_m, y_m, (θ, β, γ), the focal length of the main lens, F, and the shift of image coordinate, (u_0, v_0).

4.1 Distribution of micro-lens image

As shown in Fig. 5(a), every micro-lens with its unique coordinate $(x_i, y_i, 0)^\mathrm{T}$ is tangent with each other. In addition, $(x_i, y_i, 0)^\mathrm{T}$ is only dependent on d_lens. To simplify the discussion, we assume the layout of the micro-lens array is square-like. For hexagon-like configuration, it is easy to partition the whole array into two square-like ones. With the transformation shown in Fig. 5(b), the coordinate of the optical center of the micro-lens is represented as

$$\begin{pmatrix} x_\mathrm{c} \\ y_\mathrm{c} \\ z_\mathrm{c} \end{pmatrix} = \boldsymbol{R} \begin{pmatrix} x_i \\ y_i \\ 0 \end{pmatrix} + \boldsymbol{t} \qquad (12)$$

where $\boldsymbol{t} = (x_\mathrm{m}, y_\mathrm{m}, L)^\mathrm{T}$ and $\boldsymbol{R}$ is the rotation matrix with three degrees of freedom, i.e., the rotations (θ, β, γ) about three coordinate axes, which are similar to the traditional camera calibration model [18].

Although the main lens and the image sensor are parallel, the case between the micro-lens array and the image sensor is not similar (Fig. 5(c)). Each geometric center of the micro-lens image is represented as

$$\begin{pmatrix} x'_\mathrm{c} \\ y'_\mathrm{c} \\ L+l \end{pmatrix} = \frac{L+l}{z_\mathrm{c}} \begin{pmatrix} x_\mathrm{c} \\ y_\mathrm{c} \\ z_\mathrm{c} \end{pmatrix} \qquad (13)$$

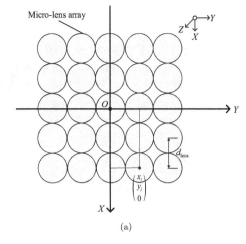

(a)

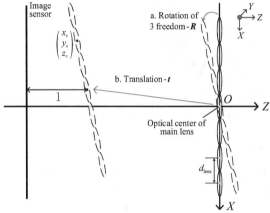

(b)

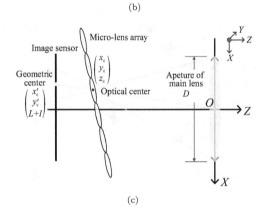

(c)

Fig. 5 The coordinate system of a focused plenoptic camera.

4.2 Projections from the raw image

Once the coordinate of a micro-lens's optical center $(x_\mathrm{c}, y_\mathrm{c}, x_\mathrm{c})^\mathrm{T}$ and its image point $(x_\mathrm{img}, y_\mathrm{img}, L+l)^\mathrm{T}$ are calculated, we can get a unique ray $\boldsymbol{r}_i$ represented as

$$\boldsymbol{r}_i = \begin{pmatrix} x_\mathrm{c} \\ y_\mathrm{c} \\ z_\mathrm{c} \end{pmatrix} + t_i \left(\begin{pmatrix} x_\mathrm{c} \\ y_\mathrm{c} \\ z_\mathrm{c} \end{pmatrix} - \begin{pmatrix} x_\mathrm{img} \\ y_\mathrm{img} \\ L+l \end{pmatrix} \right), \ t_i \in \mathbf{R} \qquad (14)$$

As shown in Fig. 4(b), the multiple images $\{(x_{A'_i}, y_{A'_i})^{\mathrm{T}} | i = 1, \cdots, n\}$ on the image sensor from the same focus point A' can be located if a proper pattern is shot, such as a grid-array pattern [12]. Thus the multiple rays emitted from point A' through different optical centers of the micro-lenses are collected to calculate the coordinate of point A':

$$\hat{\boldsymbol{t}} = \underset{\boldsymbol{t}}{\arg\min} \sum_{j=1}^{n} \left\| \boldsymbol{r}_j(t_j) - \frac{1}{n}\sum_{k=1}^{n} \boldsymbol{r}_k(t_k) \right\|_2 \quad (15)$$

$$\hat{A}' = \frac{1}{n}\sum_{i=1}^{n} \boldsymbol{r}_i(\hat{t}_i) \quad (16)$$

where $\|\cdot\|_2$ represents L_2 norm. Till now, we have accomplished the decoding process of light field inside the camera. To obtain the light field data in the scene, combining the depth-dependent scaling ratio described in Eq. (2), the representation of the focused points $\hat{A}'$ can be transformed using the focal lens F easily.

5 Calibration

Compared to the ideal focused plenoptic camera model, the shift caused by the rotations of related micro-lenses is far less than l and the difference in the numerical calculation is trivial, therefore the three theorems concluded for an ideal focused plenoptic camera still hold for our proposed model with misalignment. More importantly, when there is zero machining error, the diameter of the micro-lens d_{lens} is set, and does not need to be estimated during the calibration. Consequently, the unique solution of the intrinsic parameters $\mathscr{P} = (\theta, \beta, \gamma, x_{\mathrm{m}}, y_{\mathrm{m}}, L, l, u_0, v_0)^{\mathrm{T}}$ and F can be estimated using the two steps described in the following.

5.1 Decoding by micro-lens optical center

To locate the centers of the micro-lens images, we shoot a white scene [19, 20]. Then a template of proper size is cut out from the white image and its similarity with the original white image is calculated via normalized cross-correlation (NCC). To find the locations with subpixel accuracy, a threshold is placed on the similarity map such that all values less than 50% of the maximum intensity are set to zero. Then we take the filtered similarity map as weight and calculate the weighted coordinate of every small region. The results are shown in Fig. 6.

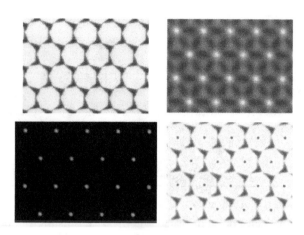

Fig. 6 The template (top-left), the crops of similarity map (top-right), the filtered similarity map (bottom-left), and the final location of the micro-lens image centers (bottom-right).

To estimate parameters $\mathscr{P}$, we minimize the cost function:

$$\hat{\mathscr{P}} = \underset{\mathscr{P}}{\arg\min} \sum_{i,j} \left\| \begin{pmatrix} x'_{\mathrm{c},i} \\ y'_{\mathrm{c},i} \end{pmatrix} + \begin{pmatrix} u_0 \\ v_0 \end{pmatrix} - \begin{pmatrix} \hat{x}'_{\mathrm{c},i} \\ \hat{y}'_{\mathrm{c},i} \end{pmatrix} \right\|_2 \quad (17)$$

where (u_0, v_0) is the offset between the camera coordinate and the image coordinate. After this optimization, $\mathscr{P}$ is used to calculate micro-lens optical centers and reconstruct the calibration points. Then the rays are obtained via Eq. (14).

According to Eq. (5), the solution of Eq. (17), changing with the initial value of L, is not unique. Moreover, the ratio L/l is almost constant with changing initial value of $\mathscr{P}$. Although there are differences between the models described in Section 3.2 and Section 4, the theorems still hold since the shift caused by the rotations can be ignored. This observation will be verified in experiment later.

In addition, the value of l influences the direction of decoded rays. Due to the coupling relationship of angle and depth, either of them can be used as the prior to be introduced to estimate the unique $\mathscr{P}$.

5.2 Reconstruction of calibration points

To reconstruct a plane in the scene, we may shoot a certain pattern in order to recognize multiple images from different scene points. A crop of the calibration board and its raw image we shoot are shown in Fig. 7. To locate the multiple images of every point on the calibration board, we preprocess the grid image by adding the inverse color of the white image to the grid image (Fig. 7). Then one of the sensor points corresponding to the focus point A', denoted by

Fig. 7 A crop of calibration board, its raw image, and the preprocessed image by white image.

$(\hat{x}_{A'_i}, \hat{y}_{A'_i})^{\mathrm{T}}$, is located by the same method described in Section 5.1. Consequently, the plane we shoot in the scene, denoted by $\hat{\Pi} = \{A_i | i = 1, \cdots, n\}$, is easy to be reconstructed using Eqs. (2) and (14).

As shown in Fig. 8, we design a parallel biplanar board with known distance between the two parallel planes and the distance between adjacent grids, which can provide depth prior Pr_{dp} and scale prior Pr_{sc}. Equivalently, we can shoot a single-plane board twice while we move the camera on a guide rail to a fixed distance.

After the sensor point $(\hat{x}_{A'_i}, \hat{y}_{A'_i})^{\mathrm{T}}$ of arbitrary scene point A is located and the intrinsic parameters $\mathscr{P}$ are determined, we can reconstruct the grid-array plane $\hat{\Pi}_1$ and $\hat{\Pi}_2$ in the scene. Then the minimum distance of arbitrary point on the two calibration board planes can be calculated, referred as $\hat{T}_1$ and $\hat{T}_2$ respectively. Finally, we can minimize the cost function to estimate the focal length F of main lens:

$$\hat{F} = \underset{F}{\arg\min} \left\| \hat{T}_1(F) - \hat{T}_2(F) \right\|_2, 0 < F < max(z) \tag{18}$$

where $\hat{T}_1$ and $\hat{T}_2$ are only dependent on F in this step. According to Eq. (10), there is an optimal solution for Eq. (18) if $\mathscr{P}$ is determined.

Note that if the values of L or l is incorrect, the distance between plane $\hat{\Pi}_1$ and $\hat{\Pi}_2$ is not equal to the prior distance. Therefore we take the distance

between plane $\hat{\Pi}_1$ and $\hat{\Pi}_2$ as the last cost function:

$$\hat{L} = \underset{L}{\arg\min} \left\| dis(\hat{\Pi}_1, \hat{\Pi}_2) - Pr_{\mathrm{dp}} \right\|_2, L > 0 \tag{19}$$

where $dis(\cdot, \cdot)$ represents the distance between two parallel planes. In practice, we take the mean distance of reconstructed points on $\hat{\Pi}_1$ to plane $\hat{\Pi}_2$ as the value of dis.

Moreover, $\hat{T}_1$ and $\hat{T}_2$ may not be equal to Pr_{sc} due to possible calculation error, so we must refine the value of depth prior to ensure the correct ratio of scale and depth.

5.3 Algorithm summary

The complete algorithm is summarized in Algorithm 1.

To make the algorithm more efficiently, the search

Algorithm 1: Calibration method for a focused camera with a parallel calibration board

Input:
Micro-lens images' centers $\{(\hat{x}'_{\mathrm{c},i}, \hat{y}'_{\mathrm{c},j})^{\mathrm{T}} | i = 1, \cdots, p, j = 1, \cdots, q\}$ extracted from a white image;
The diameter of micro-lens d_{lens};
Sensor points of P_1 extracted from grid image: $\{(\hat{x}'_{1',i}, \hat{y}'_{1',i}, \hat{z}'_{1',i})^{\mathrm{T}} | i = 1, \cdots, m_1\}$;
Sensor points of P_2 extracted from grid image: $\{(\hat{x}'_{2',i}, \hat{y}'_{2',i}, \hat{z}'_{2',i})^{\mathrm{T}} | i = 1, \cdots, m_2\}$;
The resolution of the image sensor $H * W$;
The installation parameter L_0, l_0;
$Pr_{\mathrm{dp}}, Pr_{\mathrm{sc}}$;
Output:
$\mathscr{P} = (\theta, \beta, \gamma, x_{\mathrm{m}}, y_{\mathrm{m}}, L, l, u_0, v_0)^{\mathrm{T}}$;
F.
Initialize:
$\mathscr{P}_0 = (0, 0, 0, 0, 0, L_0, l_0, H/2, W/2)^{\mathrm{T}}$;
$cnt = 1$;
for $L_0 - searchRange$ to $L_0 + searchRange$ **do**
    Optimize $\hat{\mathscr{P}}$ using Eq. (17);
    Reconstruct focus points on $\hat{\Pi}'_1$ using Eqs. (15) and (16): $\{(\hat{x}'_{1,i}, \hat{y}'_{1,i}, \hat{z}'_{1,i})^{\mathrm{T}} | i = 1, \cdots, n_1\}$;
    Reconstruct focus points on $\hat{\Pi}'_2$ using Eqs. (15) and (16): $\{(\hat{x}'_{2,i}, \hat{y}'_{2,i}, \hat{z}'_{2,i})^{\mathrm{T}} | i = 1, \cdots, n_2\}$;
    Optimize $\hat{F}$ using Eq. (18);
    Reconstruct $\hat{\Pi}_1$ and $\hat{\Pi}_2$ using Eq. (2);
    $distance(cnt) = dis(\hat{\Pi}_1, \hat{\Pi}_2)$;
    $PSet(cnt) = \hat{\mathscr{P}}$;
    $FSet(cnt) = \hat{F}$;
    $cnt = cnt + 1$;
end for
$ind = $ the index of the closest value to repaired Pr_{dp} in $distance$;
$\mathscr{P} = PSet(ind)$;
$F = FSet(ind)$.

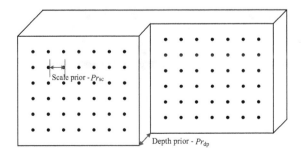

Fig. 8 The parallel biplanar board we designed to provide depth prior for calibration.

step of the loop of L should be changed with the value of $\|dis(\hat{\Pi}_1, \hat{\Pi}_2) - Pr_{dp}\|_2$ in Eq. (19). The same principle is applied to the search step of F. In addition, because of the monotonicity of $\|dis(\hat{\Pi}_1, \hat{\Pi}_2) - Pr_{dp}\|_2$ with L, and F with $\|\hat{T}_1(F) - \hat{T}_2(F)\|_2$, we can use dichotomy to search an accurate value more efficiently.

6 Experimental results

In experiments, we apply our calibration method on simulated and real world scene data. We capture three datasets of white images and grid images using a self-assembly focused plenoptic camera (Fig. 9). The camera includes a GigE camera with a CCD image sensor whose resolution is 4008×2672 pixels that are $9\,\mu m$ wide, F-mount Nikon lens with $50\,mm$ focal length, and a micro-lens array whose diameter is $300\,\mu m$ with negligible error in hexagon layout.

We use the function "fminunc" in MATLAB to complete the non-linear optimization in Eqs. (15), (17), and (18). The initial parameters are set as the installation parameters, and $\theta, \beta, \gamma, x_m, y_m$ are set to zero.

6.1 Simulated data

First we verify the calibration method on simulated images rendered in MATLAB, as shown in Fig. 1. The ground truth and the calibrated parameters are shown in Table 1. We compare the estimated angle of the ray passing through each optical center of micro-

Table 1 The parameters we estimated and the ground truth

Parameter	Ground truth	Calibration
θ (°)	0.3000	0.2998
β (°)	0.1500	0.1493
γ (°)	0.1000	0.0997
(x_m, y_m) (mm)	0.7200, 0.6300	1.5030, −4.5009
(L, l) (mm)	67.3168, 3.3162	67.1861, 3.3096
(u_0, v_0) (pixel)	−1326.0, −2000.0	−1337.4, −1999.7
F (mm)	50.0000	50.02558

lens and the one of the main lens to the ground truth, which is shown in Fig. 10. The differences are less than 1.992×10^{-3} rad.

We compare the geometric centers of the micro-lens images we locate and the ones with optimization. The error maps of 84×107 geometric centers optimized with different L are shown in Fig. 11(a). From Fig. 11(b), we find that there are 96.53% of the centers whose error is less than 0.1 pixel, which is the input for the following projection step.

The comparison of the locations of optical centers of micro-lenses with different L is illustrated in Fig. 12. The difference in x-coordinate and y-coordinate of the optical center is trivial with changing L. The maximal difference is $4.2282 \times 10^{-6}\,mm$ when L changes from 55 to $84\,mm$, which proves our observation mentioned in Section 5.1.

The values of F, $dis(\hat{\Pi}_1, \hat{\Pi}_2)$, $\hat{S}_1$, $\hat{S}_2$, $\hat{T}_1$, and $\hat{T}_2$ are shown in Fig. 13. It is obvious that $\hat{S}_1$ and $\hat{S}_2$ are almost constant when L changes, proving the correctness made in Eqs. (9) and (11). In addition, the values of $dis(\hat{\Pi}_1, \hat{\Pi}_2)$ correlate linearly with L, which testifies the reasonability of the cost function described in Eq. (18). The relationship among $\hat{T}_1$, $\hat{T}_2$, and F is shown in Fig. 14, which proves the

Fig. 9 The focused plenoptic camera we installed and its micro-lens array inside the camera.

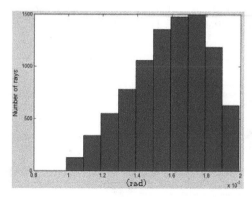

Fig. 10 The histogram of the deviation between the estimated angles of the rays and the ground truth.

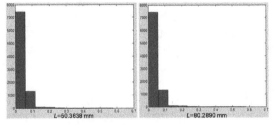

(a) Error maps with different L

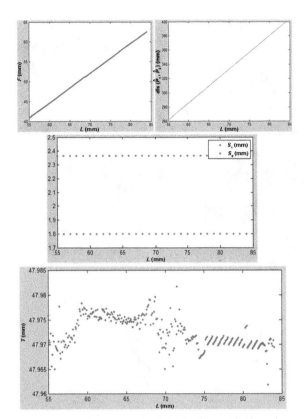

(b) The histogram of errors with different L

Fig. 11 The results of optimization on geometric centers of the micro-lens image on simulated data.

Fig. 13 The values of F, $dis(\hat{\Pi}_1, \hat{\Pi}_2)$, $\hat{S}_1$, $\hat{S}_2$, and $\hat{T}$ ($\hat{T}_2 = \hat{T}_1$) with different L on simulated data.

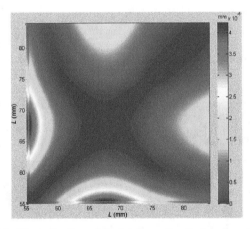

Fig. 12 The comparison of the locations of optical centers of micro-lenses with different L from 55 to 84 mm on simulated data. The value in row i and column j represents the difference in x-coordinate and y-coordinate between the results optimized in L_i and L_j.

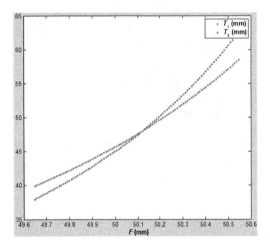

Fig. 14 The relationship of $\hat{T}_1$, $\hat{T}_2$, and F when $L = 67.3129$ mm.

analysis about Eq. (10).

6.2 Physical camera

Then we verify the calibration method on the physical focused plenoptic camera. To obtain the equivalent data of parallel biplanar board, we shoot a single-plane board twice while we move the camera on a guide rail to an accurate fixed distance, as shown in Fig. 9. The depth prior Pr_{dp} is precisely controlled to be 80.80 mm and the scale prior Pr_{sc}

is 28.57 mm. The calibration results are shown in Fig. 15.

As shown in Fig. 15(a), there is an obvious error between the computed geometric centers and the located centers on the edge of the error map, which may result from the distortion of lenses or the machining error of micro-lens. However, we find that that there are 73.00% of the centers whose error is less than 0.6 pixel, as shown in Fig. 15(b). The

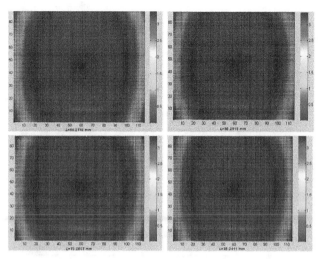

(a) Error maps with different L

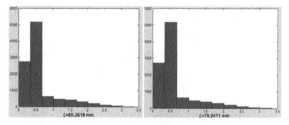

(b) The histogram of errors corresponding to (a)

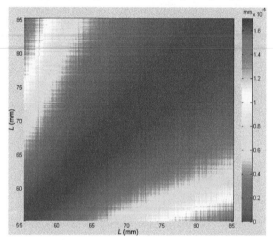

(c) The comparison of the locations of optical centers of micro-lenses with different L from 55 to 85 mm on the physical camera. The value in row i and column j represents the difference in x-coordinate and y-coordinate between the results optimized in L_i and L_j.

Fig. 15 The results of optimization on geometric centers of micro-lens image on physical data.

mean difference of geometric centers of micro-lens images optimized with different L is 1.89×10^{-4} pixel (Fig. 15(c)). The results of F, $dis(\hat{\Pi}_1, \hat{\Pi}_2)$, $\hat{S}_1$, $\hat{S}_2$, $\hat{T}$ ($\hat{T}_1 = \hat{T}_2$) with different L are similar to the results on simulated data.

Finally, to verify the stability of our algorithm, we calibrate intrinsic parameters with different poses of

calibration board. Corresponding results are shown in Table 2.

6.3 Rendering

We render the focused image with deviations between the optical center of micro-lens and the geometric center of micro-lens image.

We shoot a resolution test chart on the same depth for simulated data (Fig. 16), which indicates that the deviation surely effects the accuracy of decoded light

Table 2 Parameters estimated with calibration board with different poses. The third parameter is the angle between the calibration board and the optical axis

Parameter	Dataset 1	Dataset 2	Dataset 3
Pr_{dp} (mm)	80.80	80.80	80.80
Pr_{sc} (mm)	28.57	28.57	28.57
$Angle$ (°)	175.8386	151.9994	139.5982
θ (°)	0.3978	0.3978	0.3978
β (°)	−0.0616	−0.0615	−0.0616
γ (°)	0.1377	0.1377	0.1378
x_{m} (mm)	0.0300	0.0299	0.0302
y_{m} (mm)	−0.0341	−0.0344	−0.0343
L (mm)	67.8059	67.7860	67.8109
l (mm)	2.1215	2.1209	2.1217
u_0 (pixel)	−12.0622	−12.0623	−12.0620
v_0 (pixel)	−17.9686	−17.9689	−17.9688
F (mm)	54.1801	53.9759	54.1841

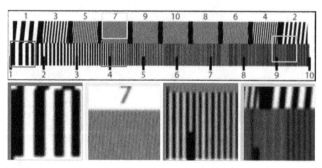

(a) Rendering without deviation of the micro-lens' optical center and its image center

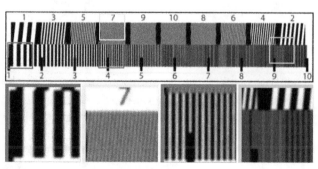

(b) Rendering with the calibrated result

Fig. 16 The rendered images from simulated data.

field. Then we shoot a chess board for simulated data to evaluate the width of every grid in the rendered images. We resize the images by setting the mean width of the grids to be 100 pixels. Then we calculate the range and the standard deviation of the grid width. The results are shown in Table 3, which indicates that the calibration contributes to the uniform scale in the same depth and reduces the distortion caused by incorrect deviations. The results on physical camera are shown in Table 4 and Fig. 17. The decoded light field with the estimated intrinsic parameters leads to more accurate refocus

Table 3 The range and variance of rendered chess board on simulated data

State	Std (pixel)	$Range$ (pixel)
No deviation	0.053281	0.38697
Calibrated	0.040079	0.25109

(a) Rendering without deviation of the micro-lens' optical center and its image center

(b) Rendering with the calibrated result

Fig. 17 The image rendered from physical camera.

Table 4 The range and variance of rendered chess board on physical camera

State	Std (pixel)	$Range$ (pixel)
No deviation	1.1145	0.042755
Calibrated	0.87151	0.034322

distance [14], which is equivalent to a correct ratio of scale and depth.

7 Conclusions and future work

In the paper we present a 10-intrinsic-parameter model to describe a focused plenoptic camera with misalignment. To estimate the intrinsic parameters, we propose a calibration method based on the relationship between the raw image features and the depth–scale information in the real world scene. To provide depth and scale priors to constrain the intrinsic parameters, we design a parallel biplanar board with grids. The calibration approach is evaluated on simulation as well as real data. Experimental results show that our proposed method is capable of decoding more accurate light field for the focused plenoptic camera.

Future work includes modelling the distortion caused by the micro-lens and main lens, optimization of extrinsic parameters, and the reparameterization of multiple and re-sampling light field data from cameras with different poses.

Acknowledgements

The work is supported by the National Natural Science Foundation of China (Nos. 61272287 and 61531014) and the research grant of State Key Laboratory of Virtual Reality Technology and Systems (No. BUAAVR-15KF-10).

References

[1] Ng, R. Digital light field photography. Ph.D. Thesis. Stanford University, 2006.

[2] Ng, R.; Levoy, M.; Bredif, M.; Duval, G.; Horowitz, M.; Hanrahan, P. Light field photography with a hand-held plenoptic camera. Stanford University Computer Science Tech Report CSTR 2005-02, 2005.

[3] Georgiev, T. G.; Lumsdaine, A. Focused plenoptic camera and rendering. *Journal of Electronic Imaging* Vol. 19, No. 2, 021106, 2010.

[4] Lumsdaine, A.; Georgiev, T. Full resolution lightfield rendering. Technical Report. Indiana University and Adobe Systems, 2008.

[5] Lumsdaine, A.; Georgiev, T. The focused plenoptic camera. In: Proceedings of IEEE International Conference on Computational Photography, 1–8, 2009.

[6] Dansereau, D. G.; Pizarro, O.; Williams, S. B. Decoding, calibration and rectification for lenselet-based plenoptic cameras. In: Proceedings of IEEE Conference on Computer Vision and Pattern Recognition, 1027–1034, 2013.

[7] Perwaß, C.; Wietzke, L. Single lens 3D-camera with extended depth-of-field. In: Proceedings of SPIE 8291, Human Vision and Electronic Imaging XVII, 829108, 2012.

[8] Bishop, T. E.; Favaro, P. Plenoptic depth estimation from multiple aliased views. In: Proceedings of IEEE 12th International Conference on Computer Vision Workshops, 1622–1629, 2009.

[9] Levoy, M.; Hanrahan, P. Light field rendering. In: Proceedings of the 23rd Annual Conference on Computer Graphics and Interactive Techniques, 31–42, 1996.

[10] Wanner, S.; Fehr, J.; Jähne, B. Generating EPI representations of 4D light fields with a single lens focused plenoptic camera. In: Lecture Notes in Computer Science, Vol. 6938. Bebis, G.; Boyle, R.; Parvin, B. et al. Eds. Springer Berlin Heidelberg, 90–101, 2011.

[11] Hahne, C.; Aggoun, A.; Haxha, S.; Velisavljevic, V.; Fernández, J. C. J. Light field geometry of a standard plenoptic camera. Optics Express Vol. 22, No. 22, 26659–26673, 2014.

[12] Johannsen, O.; Heinze, C.; Goldluecke, B.; Perwaß, C. On the calibration of focused plenoptic cameras. In: Lecture Notes in Computer Science, Vol. 8200. Grzegorzek, M.; Theobalt, C.; Koch, R.; Kolb, A. Eds. Springer Berlin Heidelberg, 302–317, 2013.

[13] Georgiev, T.; Lumsdaine, A.; Goma, S. Plenoptic principal planes. Imaging Systems and Applications, OSA Technical Digest (CD), paper JTuD3, 2011.

[14] Hahne, C.; Aggoun, A.; Velisavljevic, V. The refocusing distance of a standard plenoptic photograph. In: Proceedings of 3DTV-Conference: The True Vision—Capture, Transmission and Display of 3D Video, 1–4, 2015.

[15] Birklbauer, C.; Bimber, O. Panorama light-field imaging. Computer Graphics Forum Vol. 33, No. 2, 43–52, 2014.

[16] Bok, Y.; Jeon, H.-G.; Kweon, I. S. Geometric calibration of micro-lens-based light-field cameras using line features. In: Lecture Notes in Computer Science, Vol. 8694. Fleet, D.; Pajdla, T.; Schiele, B.; Tuytelaars, T. Eds. Springer International Publishing, 47–61, 2014.

[17] Thomason, C. M.; Thurow, B. S.; Fahringer, T. W. Calibration of a microlens array for a plenoptic camera. In: Proceedings of the 52nd Aerospace Sciences Meeting, AIAA SciTech, AIAA 2014-0396, 2014.

[18] Zhang, Z. A flexible new technique for camera calibration. IEEE Transactions on Pattern Analysis and Machine Intelligence Vol. 22, No. 11, 1330–1334, 2000.

[19] Cho, D.; Lee, M.; Kim, S.; Tai, Y.-W. Modeling the calibration pipeline of the Lytro camera for high quality light-field image reconstruction. In: Proceedings of IEEE International Conference on Computer Vision, 3280–3287, 2013.

[20] Sabater, N.; Drazic, V.; Seifi, M.; Sandri, G.; Perez, P. Light-field demultiplexing and disparity estimation. 2014. Available at https://hal.archives-ouvertes.fr/hal-00925652/document.

5

Texture image classification with discriminative neural networks

Yang Song[1] (✉), Qing Li[1], Dagan Feng[1], Ju Jia Zou[2], and Weidong Cai[1]

Abstract   Texture provides an important cue for many computer vision applications, and texture image classification has been an active research area over the past years. Recently, deep learning techniques using convolutional neural networks (CNN) have emerged as the state-of-the-art: CNN-based features provide a significant performance improvement over previous handcrafted features. In this study, we demonstrate that we can further improve the discriminative power of CNN-based features and achieve more accurate classification of texture images. In particular, we have designed a discriminative neural network-based feature transformation (NFT) method, with which the CNN-based features are transformed to lower dimensionality descriptors based on an ensemble of neural networks optimized for the classification objective. For evaluation, we used three standard benchmark datasets (KTH-TIPS2, FMD, and DTD) for texture image classification. Our experimental results show enhanced classification performance over the state-of-the-art.

Keywords   texture classification; neural networks; feature learning; feature transformation

1   Introduction

Texture is a fundamental characteristic of objects, and classification of texture images is an important

1 School of Information Technologies, the University of Sydney, NSW 2006, Australia. E-mail: Y. Song, yang. song@sydney.edu.au (✉); Q. Li, qili4463@uni.sydney. edu.au; D. Feng, dagan.feng@sydney.edu.au; W. Cai, tom.cai@sydney.edu.au.

2 School of Computing, Engineering and Mathematics, Western Sydney University, Penrith, NSW 2751, Australia. E-mail: J.Zou@westernsydney.edu.au.

component in many computer vision tasks such as material classification, object detection, and scene recognition. It is however difficult to achieve accurate classification due to the large intra-class variation and low inter-class distinction [1, 2]. For example, as shown in Fig. 1, images in the *paper* and *foliage* classes have heterogeneous visual characteristics within each class, while some images in the *paper* class show similarity to some in the *foliage* class.

Design of feature descriptors that can well accommodate large intra-class variation and low inter-class distinction has been the focus of research in most studies. Until recently, the predominant approach was based on mid-level encoding of handcrafted local texture descriptors. For example, the earlier methods use vector quantization based on clustering to encode the local descriptors into a bag-of-words [3–7]. More recent methods show that encoding using Fisher vectors is more effective than vector quantization [8, 9]. Compared to bag-of-words, the Fisher vector representation based on Gaussian mixture models (GMM) is able to better exploit the clustering structure in

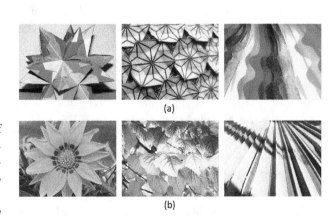

Fig. 1 Sample images from the FMD dataset in the (a) *paper* and (b) *foliage* classes.

the feature space and provide more discriminative power for images with low inter-class distinction. When designing local descriptors, feature invariance to transformations is often a key consideration. For example, the scale-invariant feature transform (SIFT) [10], local binary patterns (LBP) and their variations [11–13], basic image features [14], and fractal analysis [2, 15] are commonly used.

Recent studies in texture image classification have shown that features generated using convolutional neural networks (CNN) [16] are generally more discriminative than those from previous approaches. Specifically, the DeCAF and Caffe features, which are computed using the pretrained ImageNet models, provide better classification performance than the Fisher vector encoding of SIFT descriptors on a number of benchmark datasets [9, 17]. The current state-of-the-art [18, 19] in texture image classification is achieved using CNN-based features generated from the VGG-VD model [20]. Using the VGG-VD model pretrained on ImageNet, the FV-CNN descriptor is generated by Fisher vector (FV) encoding of local descriptors from the convolutional layer [18], and the B-CNN descriptor is computed by bilinear encoding [19]. These two descriptors have similar performance, providing significant improvement over previous approaches. By integrating FV-CNN and the descriptor from the fully-connected layer (FC-CNN), the best classification performance is obtained [18]. In all these approaches, a support vector machine (SVM) classifier with linear kernel is used for classification.

A common trait of these CNN-based features is their high dimensionality. With 512-dimensional local descriptors, the FV-CNN feature has 64k dimensions and B-CNN has 256k dimensions. Although an SVM classifier can intrinsically handle high-dimensional features, it has been noted that there is high redundancy in the CNN-based features, but dimensionality reduction using principal component analysis (PCA) has little impact on the classification performance [18]. This observation prompts the following question: is it possible to have an algorithm that can reduce the feature redundancy and also improve the classification performance?

There have been many dimensionality reduction techniques proposed in the literature and a detailed review of well-known techniques can be found in Refs. [21, 22]. Amongst them, PCA and linear discriminant analysis (LDA) are representative of the most commonly used unsupervised and supervised algorithms, respectively. With these techniques, the resultant feature dimension is limited by the number of training data or classes, and this can result in undesirable information loss. A different approach to dimensionality reduction is based on neural networks [23–25]. These methods create autoencoders, which aim to reconstruct the high-dimensional input vectors in an unsupervised manner through a number of encoding and decoding layers. The encoding layers of the network produce the reduced dimensionality features. The sizes of the layers are specified by the user and hence autoencoders provide flexibility in choosing the feature dimension after reduction. However, autoencoders tend to result in lower performance than PCA in many classification tasks [21]. In addition, to the best of our knowledge, there is no existing study that shows dimensionality reduction methods can be applied to CNN-based methods (especially FC-CNN and FV-CNN) to further enhance classification performance.

In this paper, we present a texture image classification approach built upon CNN-based features. While the FC-CNN and FV-CNN descriptors are highly effective, we hypothesize that further reducing the feature redundancy would enhance the discriminative power of the descriptors and provide more accurate classification. We have thus designed a new discriminative neural network-based feature transformation (NFT) method with this aim. Compared to existing neural network-based dimensionality reduction techniques that employ the unsupervised autoencoder model [23–25], our NFT method incorporates supervised label information to correlate feature transformation with classification performance. In addition, our NFT method involves an ensemble of feedforward neural network (FNN) models, by dividing the feature descriptor into a number of blocks and training one FNN for each block. This ensemble approach helps to reduce the complexity of the individual models and improve the overall performance. We also note that in order to avoid information loss when reducing feature redundancy, our NFT method does not greatly reduce the feature dimension, and the transformed descriptor tends to have a much higher dimensionality than those resulted from the usual dimensionality reduction techniques.

Our experiments were performed on three benchmark datasets commonly used for texture image classification: the KTH-TIPS2 dataset [26], the Flickr material dataset (FMD) [27], and the describable texture dataset (DTD) [9]. We show that improved performance is obtained over the state-of-the-art on these datasets.

The rest of the paper is organized as follows. We describe our method in Section 2. Results, evaluation, and discussion are presented in Section 3. Finally, we conclude the paper in Section 4.

2 Our approach

Our method has three components: CNN-based texture feature extraction, feature transformation based on discriminative neural networks, and classification of the transformed features using a linear-kernel SVM. Figure 2 illustrates the overall framework of our method.

2.1 CNN-based feature extraction

During texture feature extraction, we use two types of feature descriptors (FC-CNN and FV-CNN) that have recently shown state-of-the-art texture classification performance [18]. With FC-CNN, the VGG-VD model (very deep with 19 layers) pretrained on ImageNet [20] is applied to the image. The 4k-dimensional descriptor extracted from the penultimate fully-connected (FC) layer is the FC-CNN feature. This FC-CNN feature is the typical CNN descriptor when pretrained models are used instead of training a domain-specific model.

Differently from FC-CNN, FV-CNN involves Fisher vector (FV) encoding of local descriptors [28]. Using the same VGG-VD model, the 512-dimensional local descriptors from the last convolutional layer are pooled and encoded using FVs to obtain the FV-CNN feature. During this process, the dense local descriptors are extracted at multiple scales by scaling the input image to different sizes (2^s, $s = -3, -2.5, \ldots, 1.5$). A visual vocabulary of 64 Gaussian components is then generated from the local descriptors extracted from the training images, and encoding is performed based on the first and second order differences between the local descriptors and the visual vocabulary. The FV-CNN feature has dimension $512 \times 64 \times 2 = 64\text{k}$.

2.2 FNN-based feature transformation

Since the FC-CNN and FV-CNN descriptors have high dimensionality, we expect there to be some redundancy in these features, and that the discriminative power of these descriptors could be improved by reducing the redundancy. We have thus designed a discriminative neural network-based feature transformation (NFT) method to perform feature transformation; the transformed descriptors are then classified using a linear-kernel SVM. We choose to use FNN as the basis of our NFT model, since the multi-layer structure of FNN naturally provides a dimensionality reduction property using the intermediate outputs. In addition, the supervised learning of FNN enables the model to associate the objective of feature transformation with classification. In this section, we first give some preliminaries about how FNN can be considered as a dimensionality reduction technique, and then we describe the details of our method.

2.2.1 Preliminary

Various kinds of artificial neural networks can be used to classify data. One of the basic forms is

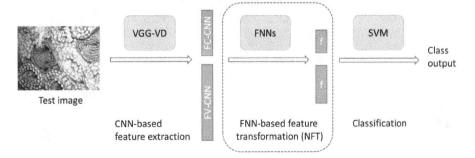

Fig. 2 Method.

the feedforward neural network (FNN) [29], which contains an input layer, multiple hidden layers, and an output layer. The interconnection between layers of neurons creates an acyclic graph, with information flowing in one direction to produce the classification result at the output layer.

Figure 3 shows a simple FNN model with one hidden layer of 4 neurons and one output layer corresponding to two classes. The functional view of this model is that first the 10-dimensional input x is transformed into a 4-dimensional vector h by multiplying a weight matrix $W \in \mathbb{R}^{4 \times 10}$ by x, adding a bias b, and passing through an activation function (typically tanh, the hyperbolic tangent sigmoid transfer function). Then similarly h is transformed to the 2-dimensional label vector y. The weight matrix and bias can be learned using backpropagation.

Here, rather than using the output y as the classification result, we can consider the intermediate vector h as a transformed representation of the input x, and h can be classified using a binary SVM to produce the classification outputs. This design forms the underlying concept of our NFT method.

2.2.2 Algorithm design

In our NFT method, the intermediate vector from the hidden layer of FNN is used as the transformed feature. There are two main design choices to make when constructing this FNN model, corresponding to the various layers of the network.

Firstly, we define the input and output layers. The output layer simply corresponds to the classification output, so the size of the output layer equals the number of image classes in the dataset. For the input layer, while it would be intuitive to use the FC-CNN and FV-CNN feature vectors directly, the high dimensionality of these features would cause difficulty in designing a suitable network architecture (i.e., the number of hidden layers and neurons). Our empirical studies furthermore showed that using the features as input does not provide enhanced classification performance. Instead, therefore, we designed a block-based approach, in which the FC-

CNN and FV-CNN features are divided into multiple blocks of much shorter vectors, and each of the blocks is used as the input: given the original feature dimension d, assume that the features are divided into blocks of n dimensions each. We create one FNN for each block with n as the size of input layer. An ensemble of d/n FNNs is thus created.

Next, the hidden layers must be determined; all d/n FNNs employ the same design. Specifically, we opt for a simple structure with two hidden layers of size h and $h/2$ respectively. We also specify $h \leqslant n$ so that the transformed feature has lower dimensionality than the original feature. The simple two-layer structure helps to enhance the efficiency of training of the FNNs, and our experiments demonstrate the effectiveness of this design. Nevertheless, we note that other variations might achieve better classification performance, especially if our method is applied to different datasets.

The intermediate vector outputs of the second hidden layer of all d/n FNNs are concatenated as the final transformed feature descriptor. Formally, define the input vector as $x \in \mathbb{R}^{n \times 1}$. The intermediate vector $v \in \mathbb{R}^{(h/2) \times 1}$ is derived as

$$v = W_2 \tanh(W_1 x + b_1) + b_2 \tag{1}$$

where $W_1 \in \mathbb{R}^{h \times n}$ and $W_2 \in \mathbb{R}^{(h/2) \times h}$ are the weight matrices at the two hidden layers, and $b_1 \in \mathbb{R}^{h \times 1}$ and $b_2 \in \mathbb{R}^{(h/2) \times 1}$ are the corresponding bias vectors. These W and b parameters are learned using the scaled conjugate gradient backpropagation method. To avoid unnecessary feature scaling, the tanh function is not applied to the second hidden layer. Instead, L2 normalization is applied to v before concatenation to form the transformed feature descriptor f, which is of size $hd/(2n)$. Since $h \leqslant n$, the dimensionality of f is at most half of that of the original feature. Figure 4 illustrates the feature transformation process using our NFT model, and Fig. 5 shows the overall information flow.

3 Experimental results

3.1 Datasets and implementation

In this study, we performed experiments using three benchmark datasets: KTH-TIPS2, FMD, and DTD. The KTH-TIPS2 dataset has 4752 images in 11 material classes such as brown bread, cotton, linen,

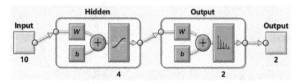

Fig. 3 A simple FNN model.

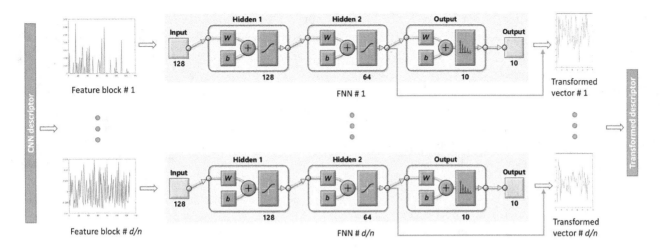

Fig. 4 How our NFT method transforms CNN-based features using an ensemble of FNNs, for the FMD dataset with 10 output classes. The CNN-based feature descriptor is divided into blocks of size $n = 128$, and one FNN is constructed for each feature block. The two hidden layers have sizes of $h = 128$ and $h/2 = 64$, respectively. The dimensionality of the final transformed descriptor f is half of that of the original CNN-based descriptor.

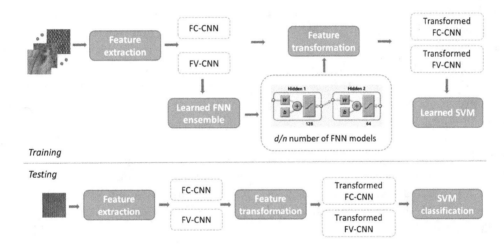

Fig. 5 Information flow. During training, an ensemble of FNN models is learned for feature transformation, and a linear-kernel SVM is learned from the transformed descriptors. Given a test image, the FC-CNN and FV-CNN descriptors are extracted and then transformed using the learned FNN ensemble, and SVM classification is finally performed to label the image.

and wool. FMD has 1000 images in 10 material classes, including fabric, foliage, paper, and water. DTD contains 5640 images in 47 texture classes including blotchy, freckled, knitted, meshed, porous, and sprinkled. These datasets present challenging texture classification tasks and have frequently been used in earlier studies.

Following the standard setup used in earlier studies [9], we perform training and testing as follows. For the KTH-TIPS2 dataset, one sample (containing 108 images) from each class was used for training and three samples were used for testing. For FMD, half of the images were selected for training and the other half for testing. For DTD, 2/3 of the images were used for training and 1/3 for testing.

Four splits of training and testing data were used for evaluation of each dataset. Average classification accuracy was computed from these tests.

Our program was implemented using MATLAB. The MatConvNet [30] and VLFeat [31] packages were used to compute the FC-CNN and FV-CNN features. The FNN model was generated using the patternnet function in MATLAB. To set the parameters n and h, we evaluated a range of possible values (1024, 512, 256, 128, and 64, with $h \leqslant n$), and selected the best performing parameters. This selection process was conducted by averaging the classification performance on two splits of training and testing data, and these splits were different from those used in performance evaluation. The selected settings were $n = 64$ and $h = 64$ for the KTH-TIPS2 and DTD datasets, and $n = 128$ and $h = 128$ for FMD. The dimensionality of the transformed feature descriptor was thus half of the original feature dimension. In addition, LIBSVM [32] was used for SVM classification. The regularization parameter C in the linear-kernel SVM was chosen based on the same split of training and testing data, and $C = 15$ was found to perform well for all datasets.

3.2 Classification performance

Table 1 shows the classification performance on the three datasets. For each dataset, we evaluated the performance using the FC-CNN descriptor, the FV-CNN descriptor, and the concatenated FC-CNN and FV-CNN descriptors. For each descriptor, we compared the performance using three classifiers, including the linear-kernel SVM, FNN, and our classification method (NFT then linear-kernel SVM). With FNN, we experimented with various network configurations of one, two, or three hidden layers and each layer containing 32 to 1024 neurons; and it was found that two layers with 128 and 64 neurons provided the best performance. The results for FNN in Table 1 were obtained using this configuration.

Overall, using FC-CNN and FV-CNN combined as the feature descriptor achieved the best classification performance for all datasets. The improvement of our approach over SVM indicates the advantage of including the feature transformation step, i.e.,

our NFT method. The largest improvement was obtained on the KTH-TIPS2 dataset, showing a 2.0% increase in average classification accuracy. For FMD and DTD, the improvement was 1.1% and 0.7%, respectively. The state-of-the-art [18] is essentially the same method as SVM but with slightly different implementation details, hence the results were similar for SVM and Ref. [18]. The results also show that NFT had more benefit when FV-CNN was used compared to FC-CNN. We suggest that this was due to the higher dimensionality of FV-CNN than that of FC-CNN, and hence more feature redundancy in FV-CNN could be exploited by our NFT method to enhance the discriminative power of the descriptors. It can also be seen that the FNN classifier resulted in lower classification performance than SVM and our method. The linear-kernel SVM classifier has regularly been used with FV descriptors in computer vision [18, 28], and our results validated this design choice. Also, the advantage of our method over FNN indicates that it is beneficial to include an ensemble of FNNs as an additional discriminative layer before SVM classification, but direct use of FNN for classifying FV descriptors is not effective.

The classification recall and precision for each image class are shown in Figs. 6–8. The results were obtained by combining the FC-CNN and FV-CNN features with our NFT method. It can be seen that the classification performance was relatively balanced on the FMD and DTD datasets. On

Table 1 Classification accuracies, comparing our method (NFT+SVM) with SVM only, FNN, and the state-of-the-art [18]

(Unit: %)

	FC-CNN			FV-CNN		
	SVM	FNN	Ours	SVM	FNN	Ours
KTH-TIPS2	75.2±1.8	74.5±2.3	75.8±1.7	81.4±2.4	80.1±2.8	82.5±2.5
FMD	77.8±1.5	72.2±3.2	78.1±1.6	79.7±1.8	76.2±2.3	80.2±1.8
DTD	63.1±1.0	58.9±1.8	63.4±0.9	72.4±1.2	67.2±1.6	72.9±0.8
	FC-CNN + FV-CNN					
	SVM	FNN	Ours	Ref. [18]		
KTH-TIPS2	81.3±1.2	81.1±2.1	**83.3±1.4**	81.1±2.4		
FMD	82.1±1.8	75.5±1.6	**83.2±1.6**	82.4±1.4		
DTD	74.8±1.0	70.2±1.8	**75.5±1.1**	74.7±1.7		

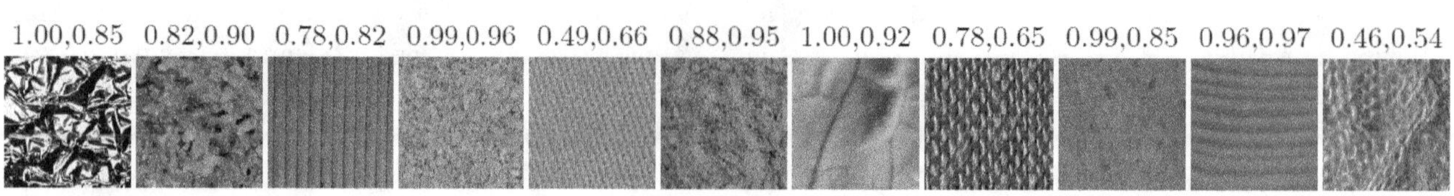

1.00,0.85   0.82,0.90   0.78,0.82   0.99,0.96   0.49,0.66   0.88,0.95   1.00,0.92   0.78,0.65   0.99,0.85   0.96,0.97   0.46,0.54

Fig. 6 Classification recall and precision for the KTH-TIPS2 dataset. Each class is represented by one image. The two numbers above the image indicate the classification recall and precision for that class, respectively.

0.89,0.85 0.95,0.92 0.85,0.79 0.82,0.88 0.69,0.71 0.81,0.81 0.80,0.80 0.85,0.86 0.88,0.89 0.81,0.81

Fig. 7 Classification recall and precision for the FMD dataset.

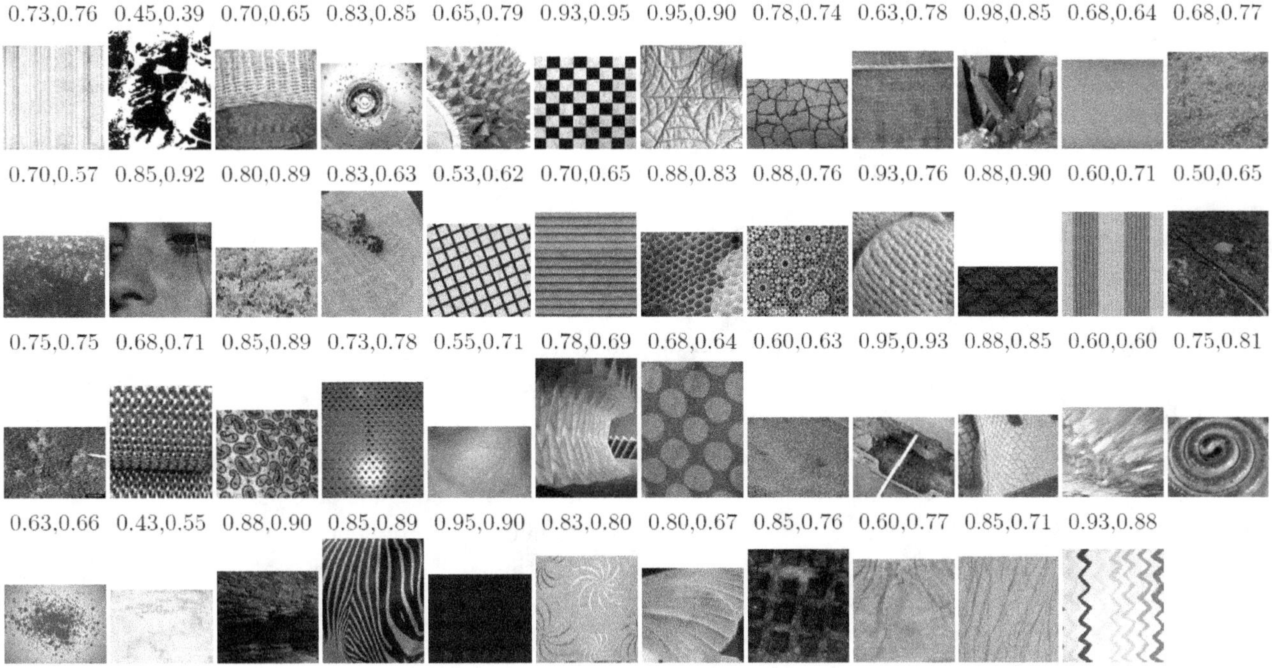

0.73,0.76 0.45,0.39 0.70,0.65 0.83,0.85 0.65,0.79 0.93,0.95 0.95,0.90 0.78,0.74 0.63,0.78 0.98,0.85 0.68,0.64 0.68,0.77

0.70,0.57 0.85,0.92 0.80,0.89 0.83,0.63 0.53,0.62 0.70,0.65 0.88,0.83 0.88,0.76 0.93,0.76 0.88,0.90 0.60,0.71 0.50,0.65

0.75,0.75 0.68,0.71 0.85,0.89 0.73,0.78 0.55,0.71 0.78,0.69 0.68,0.64 0.60,0.63 0.95,0.93 0.88,0.85 0.60,0.60 0.75,0.81

0.63,0.66 0.43,0.55 0.88,0.90 0.85,0.89 0.95,0.90 0.83,0.80 0.80,0.67 0.85,0.76 0.60,0.77 0.85,0.71 0.93,0.88

Fig. 8 Classification recall and precision on the DTD dataset.

the KTH-TIPS2 dataset, however, there was a larger variation in classification performance for different classes. In particular, misclassification often occurred between the fifth (cotton), eighth (linen), and last (wool) classes, resulting in low recall and precision for these classes. The high degree of visual similarity between these image classes explains these results. On the other hand, the characteristics of the forth (cork), seventh (lettuce leaf), and tenth (wool) classes were quite unique. Consequently, the classification recall and precision for these classes were excellent.

Figure 9 shows the classification performance with different parameter settings for n (the size of the input vector block) and h (the size of the first hidden layer). In general, larger n decreases the classification performance: it is more advantageous to divide the high-dimensional FC-CNN and FV-CNN descriptors into small blocks of vectors for feature transformation. This result validated our design choice of building an ensemble of FNNs with each FNN processing a local block within the feature descriptor. Such block-based processing can reduce

the number of variables, making it possible to build a simple FNN model with two hidden layers which fits the discriminative objective effectively.

The results also show that for a given value of n, the classification performance fluctuates with different settings of h. For the KTH-TIPS2 and DTD datasets, there was a general tendency for lower h to give higher classification accuracy. This implies that there was a relatively high degree of redundancy in the CNN-based features for these images, and reducing the feature dimensionality could enhance the discriminative capability of the features. However, for the FMD dataset, lower h tended to produce lower classification accuracy, indicating a relatively low degree of feature redundancy in this dataset. This is explained by the high level of visual complexity in the FMD images.

3.3 Dimensionality reduction

To further evaluate our NFT method, we compared it with other dimensionality reduction techniques including PCA, LDA, and autoencoders. PCA and LDA are popular dimensionality

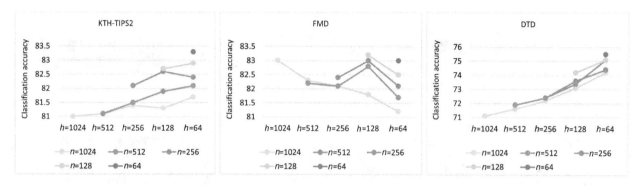

Fig. 9 Classification results using FC-CNN + FV-CNN as the feature descriptor, for varying values of parameters n and h.

reduction techniques and key representatives of the unsupervised and supervised approaches, respectively. Autoencoders are closely related to our NFT method, since they are also built on neural networks. All approaches were conducted on the same sets of training and testing data as for our method, and SVM was used as the classifier.

The main parameter in PCA and LDA was the feature size after reduction. We found that using the maximum possible dimension after reduction provided the best classification results. For autoencoders, we experimented with one to three encoding layers of various sizes ranging from 64 to 1024. Using one encoding layer provided the best classification results; the results were not sensitive to the size of this layer. We did not conduct more extensive evaluation using deeper structures or larger layers due to the cost of training. In addition, for a more comprehensive comparison with our NFT method, we also experimented with an ensemble of autoencoders. Specifically, similarly to the approach used in our NFT method, we divided the CNN-based feature descriptors into blocks and trained an autoencoder model for each block. Experiments tested each model with one or two encoding layers of various sizes (64 to 1024). The best performing

configuration was used for comparison as well.

As shown in Fig. 10, our method achieved the highest performance. It was interesting to see that besides our NFT method, only LDA was able to improve the classification performance relative to using the original high-dimensional descriptors. PCA had no effect on the classification performance if the reduced feature dimension equalled the total number of principal components, but lower performance was obtained when fewer feature dimensions were used. These results suggest that it was beneficial to use supervised dimensionality reduction with CNN-based feature descriptors. The degree of improvement provided by LDA was smaller than that for our method, demonstrating the advantage of our NFT method. The autoencoder (AE) and ensemble of autoencoders (EAE) techniques were the least effective and the resultant classification accuracies were lower than when using the original high-dimensional descriptors. EAE performed better than AE on the KTH-TIPS2 and FMD datasets but worse on the DTD dataset. Such results show that autoencoder models are unsuitable for dimensionality reduction of CNN-based features. The superiority of our method to EAE indicates

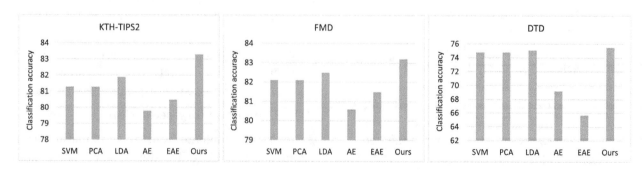

Fig. 10 Classification results using various dimensionality reduction techniques, with FC-CNN + FV-CNN as the feature descriptor. SVM classification without dimensionality reduction is also included as a baseline.

that by replacing the unsupervised reconstruction objective in autoencoders with the supervised discriminative objective in our NFT method, dimensionality reduction is better correlated with classification output and hence can enhance classification performance.

4 Conclusions

We have presented a texture image classification method in this paper. Recent studies have shown that CNN-based features (FC-CNN and FV-CNN) provide significantly better classification than handcrafted features. We hypothesized that reducing the feature redundancy of these high dimensionality of these features could lead to better classification performance. We thus designed a discriminative neural network-based feature transformation (NFT) method to transform the high-dimensional CNN-based descriptors to ones of lower dimensionality in a more discriminative feature space before performing classification. We conducted an experimental evaluation on three benchmark datasets: KTH-TIPS2, FMD, and DTD. Our results show the advantage of our method over the state-of-the-art in texture image classification and over other dimensionality reduction techniques. As a future study, we will investigate the effect of including more feature descriptors into the classification framework. In particular, we will evaluate FV descriptors based on other types of local features that are handcrafted or learned via unsupervised learning models.

Acknowledgements

This work was supported in part by Australian Research Council (ARC) grants.

References

[1] Leung, T.; Malik, J. Representing and recognizing the visual appearance of materials using three-dimensional textons. *International Journal of Computer Vision* Vol. 43, No. 1, 29–44, 2001.

[2] Varma, M.; Garg, R. Locally invariant fractal features for statistical texture classification. In: Proceedings of IEEE 11th International Conference on Computer Vision, 1–8, 2007.

[3] Malik, J.; Belongie, S.; Leung, T.; Shi, J. Contour and texture analysis for image segmentation. *International Journal of Computer Vision* Vol. 43, No. 1, 7–27, 2001.

[4] Lazebnik, S.; Schmid, C.; Ponce, J. A sparse texture representation using local affine regions. *IEEE Transactions on Pattern Analysis and Machine Intelligence* Vol. 27, No. 8, 1265–1278, 2005.

[5] Zhang, J.; Marszalek, M.; Lazebnik, S.; Schmid, C. Local features and kernels for classification of texture and object categories: A comprehensive study. *International Journal of Computer Vision* Vol. 73, No. 2, 213–238, 2007.

[6] Liu, L.; Fieguth, P.; Kuang, G.; Zha, H. Sorted random projections for robust texture classification. In: Proceedings of International Conference on Computer Vision, 391–398, 2011.

[7] Timofte, R.; Van Gool, L. A training-free classification framework for textures, writers, and materials. In: Proceedings of the 23rd British Machine Vision Conference, Vol. 13, 14, 2012.

[8] Sharma, G.; ul Hussain, S.; Jurie, F. Local higher-order statistics (LHS) for texture categorization and facial analysis. In: *Computer Vision—ECCV 2012.* Fitzgibbon, A.; Lazebnik, S.; Perona, P.; Sato, Y.; Schmid, C. Eds. Springer Berlin Heidelberg, 1–12, 2012.

[9] Cimpoi, M.; Maji, S.; Kokkinos, I.; Mohamed, S.; Vedaldi, A. Describing textures in the wild. In: Proceedings of the IEEE Conference on Computer Vision and Pattern Recognition, 3606–3613, 2014.

[10] Lowe, D. G. Distinctive image features from scale-invariant keypoints. *International Journal of Computer Vision* Vol. 60, No. 2, 91–110, 2004.

[11] Ojala, T.; Pietikainen, M.; Maenpaa, T. Multiresolution gray-scale and rotation invariant texture classification with local binary patterns. *IEEE Transactions on Pattern Analysis and Machine Intelligence* Vol. 24, No. 7, 971–987, 2002.

[12] Sharan, L.; Liu, C.; Rosenholtz, R.; Adelson, E. H. Recognizing materials using perceptually inspired features. *International Journal of Computer Vision* Vol. 103, No. 3, 348–371, 2013.

[13] Quan, Y.; Xu, Y.; Sun, Y.; Luo, Y. Lacunarity analysis on image patterns for texture classification. In: Proceedings of the IEEE Conference on Computer Vision and Pattern Recognition, 160–167, 2014.

[14] Crosier, M.; Griffin, L. D. Using basic image features for texture classification. *International Journal of Computer Vision* Vol. 88, No. 3, 447–460, 2010.

[15] Xu, Y.; Ji, H.; Fermüller, C. Viewpoint invariant texture description using fractal analysis. *International Journal of Computer Vision* Vol. 83, No. 1, 85–100, 2009.

[16] Krizhevsky, A.; Sutskever, I.; Hinton, G. E. Imagenet classification with deep convolutional neural networks. In: Proceedings of Advances in Neural Information Processing Systems, 1097–1105, 2012.

[17] Song, Y.; Cai, W.; Li, Q.; Zhang, F.; Feng, D.; Huang, H. Fusing subcategory probabilities for texture classification. In: Proceedings of the IEEE Conference on Computer Vision and Pattern Recognition, 4409–4417, 2015.

[18] Cimpoi, M.; Maji, S.; Vedaldi, A. Deep filter banks for texture recognition and segmentation. In: Proceedings of the IEEE Conference on Computer Vision and Pattern Recognition, 3828–3836, 2015.

[19] Lin, T. Y.; Maji, S. Visualizing and understanding deep texture representations. *arXiv preprint* arXiv:1511.05197, 2015.

[20] Simonyan, K.; Zisserman, A. Very deep convolutional networks for large-scale image recognition. *arXiv preprint* arXiv:1409.1556, 2014.

[21] Van der MLJP, P. E. O.; van den HH, J. Dimensionality reduction: A comparative review. Tilburg, Netherlands: Tilburg Centre for Creative Computing, Tilburg University, Technical Report: 2009-005, 2009.

[22] Cunningham, J. P.; Ghahramani, Z. Linear dimensionality reduction: Survey, insights, and generalizations. *Journal of Machine Learning Research* Vol. 16, 2859–2900, 2015.

[23] Hinton, G. E.; Salakhutdinov, R. R. Reducing the dimensionality of data with neural networks. *Science* Vol. 313, No. 5786, 504–507, 2006.

[24] Wang, W.; Huang, Y.; Wang, Y.; Wang, L. Generalized autoencoder: A neural network framework for dimensionality reduction. In: Proceedings of the IEEE Conference on Computer Vision and Pattern Recognition Workshops, 490–497, 2014.

[25] Wang, Y.; Yao, H.; Zhao, S. Auto-encoder based dimensionality reduction. *Neurocomputing* Vol. 184, 232–242, 2016.

[26] Caputo, B.; Hayman, E.; Mallikarjuna, P. Class-specific material categorization. In: Proceedings of the 10th IEEE International Conference on Computer Vision, Vol. 1, 1597–1604, 2005.

[27] Sharan, L.; Rosenholtz, R.; Adelson, E. Material perception: What can you see in a brief glance? *Journal of Vision* Vol. 9, No. 8, 784, 2009.

[28] Perronnin, F.; Sánchez, J.; Mensink, T. Improving the fisher kernel for large-scale image classification. In: *Computer Vision—ECCV 2010*. Daniilidis, K.; Maragos, P.; Paragios, N. Eds. Springer Berlin Heidelberg, 143–156, 2010.

[29] Svozil, D.; Kvasnicka, V.; Pospichal, J. Introduction to multi-layer feed-forward neural networks. *Chemometrics and Intelligent Laboratory Systems* Vol. 39, No. 1, 43–62, 1997.

[30] Vedaldi, A.; Lenc, K. Matconvnet: Convolutional neural networks for MATLAB. In: Proceedings of the 23rd ACM International Conference on Multimedia, 689–692, 2015.

[31] Vedaldi, A.; Fulkerson, B. VLFeat: An open and portable library of computer vision algorithms. In: Proceedings of the 18th ACM International Conference on Multimedia, 1469–1472, 2010.

[32] Chang, C.-C.; Lin, C.-J. LIBSVM: A library for support vector machines. *ACM Transactions on Intelligent Systems and Technology* Vol. 2, No. 3, Article No. 27, 2011.

6

Discriminative subgraphs for discovering family photos

Changmin Choi[1], YoonSeok Lee[1], and Sung-Eui Yoon[1] (✉)

Abstract We propose to use discriminative subgraphs to discover family photos from group photos in an efficient and effective way. Group photos are represented as face graphs by identifying social contexts such as age, gender, and face position. The previous work utilized bag-of-word models and considered frequent subgraphs from all group photos as features for classification. This approach, however, produces numerous subgraphs, resulting in high dimensions. Furthermore, some of them are not discriminative. To solve these issues, we adopt a state-of-the-art, frequent subgraph mining method that removes non-discriminative subgraphs. We also use TF-IDF normalization, which is more suitable for the bag-of-word model. To validate our method, we experiment in two datasets. Our method shows consistently better performance, higher accuracy in lower feature dimensions, compared to the previous method. We also integrate our method with the recent Microsoft face recognition API and release it in a public website.

Keywords image classification; subgraph mining; social context; group photographs

1 Introduction

Recent studies on image classification focus on object and scene classification. They show remarkable performance thanks to the improvement of image features such as convolutional neural network (CNN) [1]. These image features are built from pixel-level descriptors, and may be not enough to describe group photos, since classifying group photos requires to utilize more semantic information like relations, events, or activities. Interestingly,

1 Korea Advanced Institute of Science and Technology (KAIST), 291 Daehak-ro, Yuseong-gu, Daejeon, Republic of Korea. E-mail: sungeui@gmail.com (✉).

humans can classify types (e.g., friends and family) of group photos without much training, because we can estimate a variety of social contexts such as age, gender, proximity, and place, by observing face, position, clothing, and other objects.

Once we identify the social context on group photos, we can use this information for various applications. One application is to control privacy of shared images in various social websites (e.g., Facebook). People share images sometimes without much consideration on what information shared images can deliver to other people. When we identify that a shared group photo is a family photo containing children, we may wish to share that image to a small circle of persons, e.g., relatives, instead of publicly.

For classifying group photos, Chen et al. [2] proposed a method to categorize group photos into family and non-family types. This method assumes that annotations about age, gender, and face position are well-estimated beforehand by using existing face detection and statistical estimation derived from the pixel context. On top of that, they proposed to use a social-level feature named as Bag-of-Face-subGraph (BoFG) to represent group photos by graphs. For constructing BoFGs, a mining algorithm extracting frequent subgraphs is adopted. This is based on the assumption that prominent social subgroups captured in group photos can be identified by looking at frequently appearing subgraphs.

While the prior method enlightens an interesting research direction of classifying group photos, it has certain drawbacks. It first requires a user-specified threshold to determine the number of feature dimensions in a training phase. Furthermore, as we have more frequent subgraphs by having more feature dimensions, we also raise the probability as a side effect that more non-discriminative subgraphs are selected due to repetitive and redundant patterns. In other words, thresholding the number of subgraphs with the frequency criterion alone can cause a scalability problem.

Main contributions. To overcome these issues, we survey the state-of-the-art subgraph mining techniques, and propose to use a subgraph mining technique, CORK, that identifies discriminative subgraphs and culls out redundant subgraph generations. We also propose to use a TF-IDF, a widely-used feature normalization for the bag-of-word models, to our BoFG feature.

To validate benefits of our method in terms of classifying family and non-family types of group photos, we have tested the prior and our methods in two different datasets (Fig. 1) including the public dataset [3]. Overall, our method shows higher accuracy with less dimensions over the prior method. Furthermore, our method does not require a manually tunned threshold for computing dimensions of our BoFG features.

We have also integrated our method with the face

(a) Non-family (b) Siblings

(c) Single parent (d) Nuclear family

(e) Extended family

Fig. 1 We test our method against a new, extended dataset consisting of (a) non-family and (b−e) different family types. Our method achieves the highest accuracy, 79.34%, with 90 dimensions, while the state-of-the-art method achieves 76.8% with 1000 dimensions.

API[1] of Microsoft Project Oxford and released it at our demo site[2]. In this system (Fig. 2), users can test their own group images and see how well our method performs with them.

2 Related work and background

We review prior approaches that are related to our method.

2.1 Social context in photographs

Social contexts contain various information such as clothing, age, gender, absolute or relative position,

(a) Sending a query

(b) The result of the query

Fig. 2 Our demo site using the proposed classification method.

[1]https://www.projectoxford.ai/face/.
[2]http://is-fam.net/.

face angle, gesture, body direction, and so on. They have been widely used to recognize people and groups [2, 4, 5]. Several works analyzed the contexts to study the structure of scenes in group photos [3, 6, 7]. Some researchers utilized them to classify group types [2, 4, 8, 9], retrieve similar group photos [10–12], discover social relations [5, 13], or predict occupations [14].

Pixel contexts in addition to the social contexts have been used together to recognize a type of group photos [4]. Some of well-known pixel-level features include SIFT [15], GIST [16], CNN [1], etc. Social-level features can be estimated by face detection, clothing segmentation, or partial body detection.

2.2 Frequent subgraph mining

Our work is based on identifying subgraphs from a graph representing the relationship between people shown in group photos. Frequently appearing subgraphs provide important cues on understanding graph structures and similarity between different graphs. As a result, mining frequent subgraphs has been widely studied [17]. For various classification, frequent subgraph mining has been used in training and test phases to build a social-level feature, as used in classifying family and non-family photo types [2].

We have found that extracted subgraphs significantly affect classification accuracy. There are two simple strategies to explore subgraphs in a database: (1) BFS-based and (2) DFS-based approaches [17]. The BFS-based algorithm has been less used recently due to its technical challenges in generating candidates and pruning false positives. More advanced techniques focus on efficient candidate generation, since the subgraph isomorphism test is an NP-complete [18]. Recent successful algorithms proceed based on depth-first search and pattern growth [17], i.e., subgraph growing. Our method is also based on the DFS-based strategy, and uses canonical labels to avoid the scalability issue. We additionally measure the discriminative power of each subgraph during the pattern growth.

2.3 Graph-based image editing

In this work, we use graphs and histograms of their subgraphs for discovering family photos. Interestingly, there have been many graph-based approaches for image extrapolation [19],

interpolation [20], image segmentation [21], representations [22], etc. While these applications are not directly related to our classification problem, utilizing histograms of subgraphs could be useful in these applications, e.g., better graph matching for extrapolation.

3 Backgrounds on social subgraphs

In this section, we give the background of using BoFG features for group photo classification.

Chen et al. [2] proposed BoFG features for group photo classification. This method constructs face graphs (Fig. 3) and uses their subgraphs to describe various social relationships. BoFG is analogous to the bag-of-word model of text retrieval. For example, a text corpus corresponds to a group photo album, a document to an image, and a word to a subgraph in a face graph, respectively. The main difference between these models is that the bag-of-word model performs clustering over all vectors in order to obtain a codebook, whereas BoFG performs frequent subgraph mining over all the face graphs.

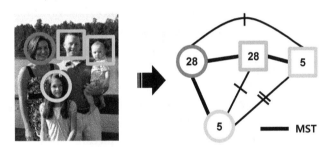

(a) Generating a group photo to a face graph

Age range	0-2	3-7	8-12	13-19	20-36	37-65	66+
Female	1	5	10	16	28	51	75
Male	1	5	10	16	28	51	75

(b) 14 types of vertices

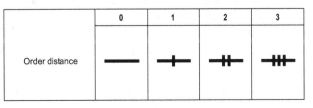

	0	1	2	3
Order distance	—	—+—	—++—	—+++—

(c) 4 types of edges

Fig. 3 (a) Representing an image as a face graph using (b) 14 vertex types and (c) 4 edge types.

Attributes of group members enable us to discriminate the type of groups, although we do not even know their names or relationships. In addition, understanding each one's position is informative to infer physical and relationship closeness among people. Chen et al. [2] showed that only knowing gender, age, and face positions as attributes of group members works effectively for a binary classification of family and non-family photos. Our approach is also based on this approach, and represents a group photo into a face graph, elaborated below.

Face graphs. Figure 3 illustrates an example of representing a group photo to a face graph. Each node of the graph corresponds to each person in the group photo, and is associated with a vertex label describing age and gender. Each edge between two nodes encodes relative position between two people.

There are 14 different types describing age and gender for each vertex label. The age ranges from 0-year-old to 75-year-old, and is categorized into seven age types. There are two gender types, male and female, and they are visualized by square and circle, respectively in Fig. 3(b). The combinations of age and gender result in 14 different types. Identifying faces and their attributes have been well studied [23, 24], and APIs of performing these operations are available, as mentioned in Section 1.

Most previous works used the Euclidean distance in image space, i.e., pixel distance, to measure the closeness between persons in group photos [3, 5, 12, 13]. Unfortunately, it has been known not to be invariant to scales of images, faces, distance to camera, or the orientation angle of a face. Instead, we use an order distance that indicates how close people stand with each other. The order distance has been demonstrated to be more stable over the pixel distance in terms of various factors [2]. The order distance is computed as the path length among vertices on a minimum spanning tree (MST) generated from a face graph. Such order distance is used for each edge label such as Fig. 3(c).

Bag-of-Face-subGraph (BoFG). Once we represent group photos into face graphs, we extract frequent subgraphs and regard them as BoFG features for classification. BoFG has been proposed to be a useful feature to compare structures of group photos. It helps to infer a type of a group by using substructures of groups. For example, in Fig. 3,

edges between two vertices of 28_f and 28_m (i.e., mother–father relationship), and between 28_f and 5_m (i.e., mother–son relationship) provide additional information on social relationship over each node of those edges; f and m represent female and male gender types, respectively.

Subgraph enumeration via gSpan. The prior work regarded frequent subgraphs as BoFG features, and generated such subgraphs by frequent subgraph mining, specifically, the gSpan method [25]. Most prior approaches of frequent subgraph mining [17] initially generate candidates of frequent subgraphs and adopt a pruning process to remove false positives. The pruning process, unfortunately, has a heavy computational cost, because it requires subgraph isomorphism testing.

gSpan adopted in the prior classification system [2] ameliorated this computational overhead issue by utilizing two techniques, DFS lexicographic order and minimal DFS code. Specifically, we first traverse an input graph, G, in a depth-first search (DFS) and assign an incrementally increasing visiting order to a newly visited vertex. Whenever we traverse an edge from v_m to v_n of the graph G, we represent the traversed edge into a 5-tuple DFS code:

$$G = (m,\ n,\ L_m,\ L_{(m,n)},\ L_n) \qquad (1)$$

where m and n are vertex indices computed by the visiting ordering during the DFS traversal, L_m and L_n are vertex labels of v_m and v_n, respectively, and $L_{(m,n)}$ is a edge label associated with the edge.

A graph, however, can have multiple DFS codes depending on traversal orders of vertices and edges. gSpan particularly allows the DFS lexicographic order computed from labels, $L_m, L_{(m,n)}, L_n$, of vertices and edges, and uses the DFS code corresponding to the minimal lexicographic order from the graph G. In this way, we can remove redundant subgraphs and maintain a subgraph among its isomorphic subgraphs.

To check the subgraph isomorphism, we simply look at the DFS code of a subgraph, G_s, to see whether the code is equal to or bigger than ones generated by prior subgraphs. If so, this indicates that G_s is a redundant subgraph, which is isomorphic to a prior subgraph. An illustration of generating DFS codes and pruning process is shown in Fig. 4.

To define frequently appearing subgraphs, gSpan requires a user defined parameter, known as

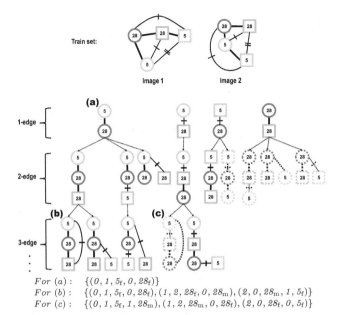

For (a) : $\{(0, 1, 5_f, 0, 28_f)\}$

For (b) : $\{(0, 1, 5_f, 0, 28_f), (1, 2, 28_f, 0, 28_m), (2, 0, 28_m, 1, 5_f)\}$

For (c) : $\{(0, 1, 5_f, 1, 28_m), (1, 2, 28_m, 0, 28_f), (2, 0, 28_f, 0, 5_f)\}$

Fig. 4 This figure shows a process of generating all the subgraphs having one edge or more in gSpan. During the enumeration of subgraphs, gSpan prunes subgraphs once their DFS codes are equal to or bigger than prior ones. We highlight three subgraphs labelled (a), (b), and (c), and their DFS codes in below. 5_f is a 5-year-old female, while 5_m is a 5-year-old male. Let the lexicographic orders of vertex and edge be $5_f < 5_m < 28_f < 28_m$ and $0 < 1 < 2$. Note that the subgraphs (b) and (c) are isomorphic to each other. However, the subgraph of (c) is not a minimal DFS code because it is bigger than that of (b). In this manner, the search space can be pruned; the dotted subgraphs are pruned during the DFS-based expansion.

minimum frequency. We consider all different subgraphs whose frequency counts are bigger than the minimum frequency to be features of the BoFG.

The aforementioned method focuses on extracting frequency-based subgraphs and has some limitations for graph classification. Extracted frequent subgraphs in this approach may not show structural differences between classes. This is a similar problem even in the text classification. For instance, "a" and "the" are most commonly appearing words, but are not discriminative words for document classification. Moreover, the minimum frequency of subgraphs for defining BoFGs should be picked through a tedious trial-and-error approach for achieving high accuracy.

To address these drawbacks of using frequently appearing subgraphs, we propose to use discriminative subgraphs, adopt a recent subgraph mining method, CORK [26], extracting such discriminative subgraphs, and apply it to our classification problem of group photos. Additionally, we further improve the classification accuracy by adopting and tailoring the TF-IDF normalization scheme to our problem.

4 Our approach

In this section, we explain our approach for classifying group photos into family and non-family types.

4.1 Overview

Figure 5 shows the overview of our method. As offline process, we first generate face graphs from group photos in a training set and extract discriminative subgraphs as Bag-of-Face-subGraph (BoFG) features from face graphs. We utilize family and non-family labels associated with training images. We then extract a BoFG feature for each photo and normalize the feature by using the TF-IDF weighting. Through discriminative learning, we finally construct an SVM classifier.

When a query image is provided, we represent it to a face graph, and extract and normalize a BoFG feature from the graph. We then estimate a query's label by utilizing the pre-trained classifier.

Our work adopts face graphs and their subgraphs as the BoFG features for the classification problem (Section 3). For achieving higher accuracy in an efficient manner, we additionally propose using discriminative subgraphs (Section 4.2) inspired by a recent near-optimal selection method [26]. We also normalize BoFG features using the term frequency and inverse document frequency, i.e., the TF-IDF weighting scheme (Section 4.3).

4.2 Discriminative subgraphs mining

We would like to identify discriminative subgraphs that are characteristic features in each category. We have identified similar issues from data mining, and found that CORK [26] works well for our problem.

CORK considers statistical significance to select discriminative subgraphs. It defines a new measurement counting the number of features that

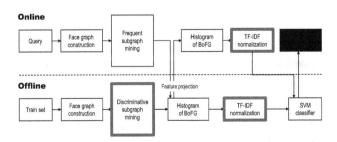

Fig. 5 The overview of our approach. The red boxes indicate the main contributions of our method.

are not helpful for classification among candidate features. This measurement can be integrated into gSpan as a culling method. It can reduce the number of features, while preserving performance in classification and can prune search space without relying upon a manually-tuned frequency threshold.

A near-optimality of CORK is obtained from a submodular quality function, $q(\cdot)$, using a greedy forward feature selection. The function $q(\cdot)$ considers presence or absence of each subgraph in each class. $q(\cdot)$ for the set containing subgraph, S, is defined as the following:

$$q(\{S\}) = -(A_{S_0} \cdot B_{S_0} + A_{S_1} \cdot B_{S_1}) \qquad (2)$$

where A and B are two classes in a dataset. A_{S_0} is the number of images of the class A that do not have the subgraph set $\{S\}$. A_{S_1} is the number of images including the subgraph set $\{S\}$ in the class A. The subscripts S_0 and S_1 are used in the same manner for another class B.

When a subgraph appears or does not appear simultaneously in both classes, it can be considered as a non-discriminative feature between two classes. To consider this observation, A_{S_0} and B_{S_0} are multiplied together; the same reasoning applies for the product of A_{S_1} and B_{S_1}. In this context, a feature becomes more discriminative, as the quality function $q(\cdot)$ becomes higher. Figure 6 shows examples of the quality function for two subgraphs in classes A and B.

While generating subgraphs, we commonly expand a subgraph S into another one, T, by adding a neighboring edge or so. During this incremental process, suppose that we already decided to include S into our feature set. We then need to check the quality of having a newly expanded feature T on top of S. As a result, we need to reevaluate $q(\{T\})$.

Unfortunately, this process can require an excessive amount of running time, since as the number of features increases to N, the number of possible feature combinations can increase exponentially to 2^N.

To accelerate this process, CORK relies on a pruning criterion. Especially, the upper bound of the quality function is derived based on three possible cases, when we consider a supergraph T from its subgraph S. One of such cases is that images from class A do not have the supergraph T, while images in the other class have the supergraph and thus their indicator values are affected. The second case is that the scenario of the first case is applied in the reverse way to classes A and B. The third case is where we do not have any changes. By considering these three different cases, the upper bound of the quality function is derived as the following [26, Theorems 2.2, 2.3]:

$$q(\{T\}) \leqslant q(\{S\}) + \max \left\{ \begin{array}{c} A_{S_1} \cdot (B_{S_1} - B_{S_0}) \\ (A_{S_1} - A_{S_0}) \cdot B_{S_1} \\ 0 \end{array} \right\} \qquad (3)$$

While expanding subgraphs, we prune the children of supergraphs T expanded from the subgraph S, when the quality function of T is equal to the one of those upper bounds. This culling criterion is adopted, since it is guaranteed that we cannot find any better supergraphs than T whose quality function is higher than the the upper bound shown in the aforementioned inequality. This approach has been proven to identify discriminative subgraphs whose quality function values are bigger than a certain lower bound [26, Theorem 2.1]. Furthermore, unlike gSpan, users do not need to provide manually-tuned parameters for identifying discriminative subgraphs.

4.3 TF-IDF normalization

Once we extract features, we normalize those features. TF-IDF [27] is one of commonly adopted normalization schemes, mainly for document classification. We apply this normalization to our feature, which resembles the bag-of-word model. Inspired by the TF-IDF normalization scheme, we give higher weights to more frequent features in each image and deemphasize features that appear in more images.

In particular, our TF-IDF weighting scheme of a subgraph s occurring in an image i given an image

| | | Dataset | | | | |
| | | Class A | | | Class B | | |
		a_1	a_2	a_3	b_1	b_2	b_3
Subgraph	S	1	1	1	1	1	0
	T	1	1	1	0	0	0

Fig. 6 A and B are two different classes in a given dataset. a_{1-3} and b_{1-3} are images in classes A and B, respectively. Each indicator is 1, if its corresponding subgraph appears in each image, otherwise 0. Referred to Eq. (2), $q(\{S\}) = -(0 \cdot 1 + 3 \cdot 2) = -6$ and $q(\{T\}) = -(0 \cdot 3 + 3 \cdot 0) = 0$. As a result, the subgraph T has a higher discriminative power than S.

database D is defined as the following:

$$\begin{cases} TF\text{-}IDF(s,i,D) = TF(s,i) \times IDF(s,D) \\ TF(s,i) = \log\left(1 + f_{s,i}\right) \\ IDF(s,D) = \log\left(\dfrac{N}{1+n_s}\right) \end{cases} \quad (4)$$

where $f_{s,i}$ is the number of the subgraph s occurring in the image i, N is the number of all images in the database D, and n_s is the number of images with the subgraph s. If $f_{s,i}$ is zero, TF term would be undefined. To prevent this case, a small constant, 1, is added. Similarly, to avoid divide-by-zero, we also add the small constant 1 to the denominator of the IDF term.

5 Results

We implemented prior and our methods for discovering family photos in a machine that has Xeon 3.47 GHz with 192 GB main memory. We evaluate the effectiveness of computing and using discriminative feature selection along with TF-IDF normalization. For classification, we use the support vector machine (SVM). The classification is conducted with linear kernel and 5-fold cross validation.

5.1 Datasets

To validate our approach, we use the existing dataset provided by Chen et al. [2]. We additionally test different methods against a new, larger, and diverse dataset, which is rearranged from the public dataset [3], as adopted also in the previous work. Based on the protocol laid out in the prior work, we obtain a "soft" ground truth containing 1613 family photos and 1890 non-family photos for our new, extended dataset. The "soft" ground truth for the new dataset is generated without any prior knowledge such as looking at labels of those images.

The new extended dataset also shares the same images to the Chen et al.'s dataset, since these two datasets are arranged from the public dataset. We also measure the common images in both or either one of two datasets (Table 1). The difference from the previous one is that the new dataset has 1073 more photos and includes wider sets of family types such as siblings, single parent, nuclear family, and extended family, as shown in Fig. 1.

Note that these images from the public dataset

Table 1 The composition of Chen et al.'s ((a)+(b)) and our datasets ((b) + (c)). (b) indicates the number of co-occurring images in both Chen et al.'s and ours. Many images of family and non-family co-occur in ours and Chen et al.'s, although we prepare the extended dataset without looking at their original labels

	(a) Images only in Chen et al.'s	(b) Images both in Chen et al.'s and ours	(c) Images only in ours
Family	66	1111	502
Non-family	136	1131	759

have labels, which are groups, wedding, and family types. Our methods independently predict family types of these images and measure accuracy by comparing their predicted labels with the original ones associated with the public dataset.

We have also considered other datasets related to group photos [4, 8]. Unfortunately, these datasets do not contain labels directly for family and non-family types. As a result, we were unable to use them for our problem.

5.2 Effects of discriminative subgraphs

We test accuracy of different methods including ours and the gSpan method [2]. We have implemented the prior method by following the guideline of the original paper [2]. For gSpan, we generate frequent subgraphs up to 10,000 subgraphs and sort them in the order of document frequency and select them as BoFG. To achieve the best accuracy for the gSpan method, it is required for users to specify the number of subgraphs. In this approach, we need to rely on many trial-and-error procedures, while our method automatically constructs a set of discriminative subgraphs.

We were unclear how the prior method uses the document frequency (DF) term, because there is an ambiguity in which the DF term is evaluated either after or during the running process of gSpan[1]. We thus experiment both cases. $gSpan + DF(1)$ and $gSpan + DF(2)$ correspond respectively to the adaption of DF *posterior to* and *during* gSpan in Table 2. In Table 2, our method finds the maximal number of subgraphs without using the minimum frequency.

Our methods w/ and w/o the TF-IDF scheme in the Chen et al.'s dataset identify a small set of discriminative subgraphs (i.e., 76 subgraphs), and achieves 80.61% and 78.65% accuracy respectively.

---

[1] We have consulted authors of the gSpan technique for faithful re-implementation of the gSpan method.

Table 2 The accuracy of different methods in Chen et al.'s and our datasets

Chen et al.'s dataset								
Dimension	76	100	500	1000	2000	3000	4000	5000	10,000
$gSpan + DF(1)$	50.00%	51.51%	52.98%	54.65%	61.92%	68.33%	69.52%	68.78%	77.76%
$gSpan + DF(2)$	78.61%	77.92%	80.12%	78.16%	77.51%	77.31%	76.49%	77.14%	77.76%
Ours + TF-IDF	**80.61%**	N/A							

Our dataset								
Dimension	90	100	500	1000	2000	3000	4000	5000	10,000
$gSpan + DF(1)$	56.00%	58.37%	62.25%	61.26%	64.51%	67.48%	69.64%	71.84%	75.61%
$gSpan + DF(2)$	74.78%	74.84%	77.43%	76.80%	76.63%	76.83%	76.49%	76.09%	75.61%
Ours + TF-IDF	**79.34%**	N/A							

Table 3 The accuracy of *DF* vs. *TF-IDF* in Chen et al.'s and our extended datasets

	Chen et al.'s dataset					Our dataset				
Dimension	76	100	1000	5000	10,000	90	100	1000	5000	10,000
$gSpan + DF(2)$	78.61%	77.92%	78.16%	77.14%	77.76%	74.78%	74.84%	76.8%	76.09%	75.61%
$gSpan + DF(2) + $ **TF-IDF**	77.67%	77.63%	81.31%	81.18%	82.04%	75.40%	75.09%	78.09%	77.55%	77.2%
Ours	78.65%	N/A				77.26%	N/A			
Ours + **TF-IDF**	80.61%	N/A				79.34%	N/A			

Our method in the extended dataset achieves 77.26%, and shows 79.34% with the TF-IDF scheme. $gSpan + DF(1)$ and $gSpan + DF(1)$ methods show inferior results over our method in most cases. Interestingly, the prior methods show even lower accuracy as they use higher dimensions. This is mainly because frequent subgraphs may not be discriminative.

5.3 Effects of TF-IDF normalization

We measure accuracy of different methods with and without TF-IDF normalization. Since $gSpan + DF(2)$ achieves higher accuracy than $gSpan + DF(1)$, we show the results of $gSpan + DF(2)$ and ours for the test.

In both $gSpan + DF(2)$ and ours, using TF-IDF over DF improves the classification accuracy in most cases. Especially, our method using TF-IDF achieves the highest accuracy, 79.34%, for the extended dataset.

5.4 Comparison of subgraphs

We check the number of subgraphs co-occurring in the BoFG features generated by both gSpan and our method. This investigation can help us to understand how many dimensions prior methods require in order to obtain discriminative features extracted by our method. Even in hundreds of thousands of dimensions extracted by gSpan, some of discriminative subgraphs extracted by our method are not identified (Table 4).

We also measure how well query images used in the test phase are represented by extracted features. For this, we measure how many query images are represented by null vector, indicating that query images are not represented by any features extracted by gSpan or our method (Table 5). As a result, we can conclude that the feature extraction of our method performs better than other tested methods ($gSpan + DF(1)$ or $gSpan + DF(2)$).

6 Conclusions and future work

We have proposed a novel classification system utilizing discriminative subgraph mining for

Table 4 The number of common subgraphs between gSpan and ours in Chen et al.'s and our datasets

Chen et al.'s dataset: **77 subgraphs** by our method									
gSpan subgraphs	78	100	500	1000	10,000	$\cdots$	111,764	$\cdots$	560,177
Number of common subgraphs	16	17	21	23	36	$\cdots$	54	$\cdots$	**59**

Our dataset: **85 subgraphs** by our method									
gSpan subgraphs	85	100	500	1000	10,000	$\cdots$	84,713	$\cdots$	326,034
Number of common subgraphs	20	21	25	26	29	$\cdots$	50	$\cdots$	**59**

Table 5 This table shows the number of query images that are represented by the null vector in Chen et al.'s and our extended data

Dimension	76	100	1000	5000	10,000
$gSpan + DF(1)$	283	283	189	82	30
$gSpan + DF(2)$	53	52	39	37	30
Ours	**26**		N/A		
Dimension	90	100	1000	5000	10,000
$gSpan + DF(1)$	351	351	236	163	43
$gSpan + DF(2)$	62	62	50	48	43
Ours	**28**		N/A		

achieving high accuracy. We represent group photos as graphs with age, gender, and face position, and then extract discriminative subgraphs and construct BoFG features. For extracting discriminative subgraphs, we proposed to use a recent discriminative subgraph mining method, CORK, that adopts a quality function with near-optimal guarantees. We additionally proposed to use the TF-IDF normalization to better support the characteristic of BoFG features. To validate benefits of our approach, we have tested different methods including ours against two different datasets including our new, extended dataset. Our method achieves higher accuracy in the same dimensionality over the prior methods. Furthermore, our method achieves higher or similar accuracy over the prior work that relies on manual turning and requires a higher dimensionality.

There are many interesting future directions. Since our work is based on the concept of social relationships, we consider subgraphs consisting of at least two nodes. However, only a single node can provide useful social cues. Incorporating single nodes in BoFGs and investigating its effects should be interesting. We would like to also investigate recent deep learning techniques that learns low-level features and classification functions. Due to the lack of sufficient training datasets, we did not consider recent deep learning techniques, but this approach should be worthwhile for achieving higher accuracy.

Acknowledgements

We are thankful to our lab members for valuable feedbacks, and to Ph.D. Yan-Ying Chen for sharing her dataset. This work was supported in part by MSIP/IITP (Nos. R0126-16-1108, R0101-16-0176) and MSIP/NRF (No. 2013-067321).

References

[1] Krizhevsky, A. Learning multiple layers of features from tiny images. Technical Report. University of Toronto, 2009.

[2] Chen, Y.-Y.; Hsu, W. H.; Liao, H.-Y. M. Discovering informative social subgraphs and predicting pairwise relationships from group photos. In: Proceedings of the 20th ACM International Conference on Multimedia, 669–678, 2012.

[3] Gallagher, A. C.; Chen, T. Understanding images of groups of people. In: Proceedings of IEEE Conference on Computer Vision and Pattern Recognition, 256–263, 2009.

[4] Murillo, A. C.; Kwak, I. S.; Bourdev, L.; Kriegman, D.; Belongie, S. Urban tribes: Analyzing group photos from a social perspective. In: Proceedings of IEEE Computer Society Conference on Computer Vision and Pattern Recognition Workshops, 28–35, 2012.

[5] Wang, G.; Gallagher, A.; Luo, J.; Forsyth, D. Seeing people in social context: Recognizing people and social relationships. In: Lecture Notes in Computer Science, Vol. 6315. Daniilidis, K.; Maragos, P.; Paragios, N. Eds. Springer Berlin Heidelberg, 169–182, 2010.

[6] Chiu, Y.-I.; Li, C.; Huang, C.-R.; Chung, P.-C.; Chen, T. Efficient graph based spatial face context representation and matching. In: Proceedings of IEEE International Conference on Acoustics, Speech and Signal Processing, 2001–2005, 2013.

[7] Gallagher, A. C.; Chen, T. Finding rows of people in group images. In: Proceedings of IEEE International Conference on Multimedia and Expo, 602–605, 2009.

[8] Choi, W.; Chao, Y.-W.; Pantofaru, C.; Savarese, S. Discovering groups of people in images. In: Lecture Notes in Computer Science, Vol. 8692. Fleet, D.; Pajdla, T.; Schiele, B.; Tuytelaars, T. Eds. Springer International Publishing, 417–433, 2014.

[9] Shu, H.; Gallagher, A.; Chen, H.; Chen, T. Face-graph matching for classifying groups of people. In: Proceedings of IEEE International Conference on Image Processing, 2425–2429, 2013.

[10] Chiu, Y.-I.; Hsu, R.-Y.; Huang, C.-R. Spatial face context with gender information for group photo similarity assessment. In: Proceedings of the 22nd International Conference on Pattern Recognition, 2673–2678, 2014.

[11] Shimizu, K.; Nitta, N.; Nakai, Y.; Babaguchi, N. Classification based group photo retrieval with bag of people features. In: Proceedings of the 2nd ACM International Conference on Multimedia Retrieval, Article No. 6, 2012.

[12] Zhang, T.; Chao, H.; Willis, C.; Tretter, D. Consumer image retrieval by estimating relation tree from family photo collections. In: Proceedings of the ACM International Conference on Image and Video Retrieval, 143–150, 2010.

[13] Singla, P.; Kautz, H.; Luo, J.; Gallagher, A. Discovery of social relationships in consumer photo

collections using Markov logic. In: Proceedings of IEEE Computer Society Conference on Computer Vision and Pattern Recognition Workshops, 1–7, 2008.

[14] Song, Z.; Wang, M.; Hua, X.-s.; Yan, S. Predicting occupation via human clothing and contexts. In: Proceedings of International Conference on Computer Vision, 1084–1091, 2011.

[15] Lowe, D. G. Distinctive image features from scale-invariant keypoints. *International Journal of Computer Vision* Vol. 60, No. 2, 91–110, 2004.

[16] Oliva, A.; Torralba, A. Modeling the shape of the scene: A holistic representation of the spatial envelope. *International Journal of Computer Vision* Vol. 42, No. 3, 145–175, 2001.

[17] Jiang, C.; Coenen, F.; Zito, M. A survey of frequent subgraph mining algorithms. *The Knowledge Engineering Review* Vol. 28, No. 1, 75–105, 2013.

[18] Cook, S. A. The complexity of theorem-proving procedures. In: Proceedings of the 3rd Annual ACM Symposium on Theory of Computing, 151–158, 1971.

[19] Wang, M.; Lai, Y.-K.; Liang, Y.; Martin, R. R.; Hu, S.-M. BiggerPicture: Data-driven image extrapolation using graph matching. *ACM Transactions on Graphics* Vol. 33, No. 6, Article No. 173, 2014.

[20] Chen, X.; Zhou, B.; Guo, Y.; Xu, F.; Zhao, Q. Structure guided texture inpainting through multi-scale patches and global optimization for image completion. *Science China Information Sciences* Vol. 57, No. 1, 1–16, 2014.

[21] Li, H.; Wu, W.; Wu, E. Robust interactive image segmentation via graph-based manifold ranking. *Computational Visual Media* Vol. 1, No. 3, 183–195, 2015.

[22] Hu, S.-M.; Zhang, F.-L.; Wang, M.; Martin, R. R.; Wang, J. PatchNet: A patch-based image representation for interactive library-driven image editing. *ACM Transactions on Graphics* Vol. 32, No. 6, Article No. 196, 2013.

[23] Taigman, Y.; Yang, M.; Ranzato, M.; Wolf, L. DeepFace: Closing the gap to human-level performance in face verification. In: Proceedings of IEEE Conference on Computer Vision and Pattern Recognition, 1701–1708, 2014.

[24] Zhao, W.; Chellappa, R.; Phillips, P. J.; Rosenfeld, A. Face recognition: A literature survey. *ACM Computing Surveys* Vol. 35, No. 4, 399–458, 2003.

[25] Yan, X.; Han, J. gSpan: Graph-based substructure pattern mining. In: Proceedings of the 2002 IEEE International Conference on Data Mining, 721–724, 2002.

[26] Thoma, M. ; Cheng, H.; Gretton, A.; Han, J.; Kriegel, H.-P.; Smola, A.; Song, L.; Yu, P. S.; Yan, X.; Borgwardt, K. M. Discriminative frequent subgraph mining with optimality guarantees. *Statistical Analysis and Data Mining: The ASA Data Science Journal* Vol. 3, No. 5, 302–318, 2010.

[27] Jones, K. S. A statistical interpretation of term specificity and its application in retrieval. *Journal of Documentation* Vol. 28, No. 1, 11–21, 1972.

7

Weighted average integration of sparse representation and collaborative representation for robust face recognition

Shaoning Zeng[1](✉)**, Yang Xiong**[1]

Abstract Sparse representation is a significant method to perform image classification for face recognition. Sparsity of the image representation is the key factor for robust image classification. As an improvement to sparse representation-based classification, collaborative representation is a newer method for robust image classification. Training samples of all classes collaboratively contribute together to represent one single test sample. The ways of representing a test sample in sparse representation and collaborative representation are very different, so we propose a novel method to integrate both sparse and collaborative representations to provide improved results for robust face recognition. The method first computes a weighted average of the representation coefficients obtained from two conventional algorithms, and then uses it for classification. Experiments on several benchmark face databases show that our algorithm outperforms both sparse and collaborative representation-based classification algorithms, providing at least a 10% improvement in recognition accuracy.

Keywords sparse representation; collaborative representation; image classification; face recognition

1 Introduction

Feature extraction and classification are two key steps in face recognition [1, 2]. Extraction of features is the basic of mathematical calculation performed in classification methods. Only if sufficient and proper features are extracted, can a classification method produce good recognition results. One prevailing paradigm is to use statistical learning approaches based on training data to determine proper features to extract and how to construct classification engines. Nowadays, many successful algorithms for face detection, alignment, and matching are learning-based algorithms. Representation-based classification methods (RBCM), such as PCA [3, 4] and LDA [5, 6], have significantly improved face recognition techniques. Such linear methods can be extended by use of nonlinear kernel techniques (kernel PCA [7] and kernel LDA [8]). The basic process in these methods is as follows: first all training samples are coded to obtain a representation matrix, then this matrix is used to evaluate each test sample and determine new lower-dimensional representation coefficients, and finally classification is performed based on these coefficients [2, 9]. Therefore, the robustness of face recognition is determined by suitability of the representation coefficients.

Sparse coding or representation has recently been proposed as an optimal representation of image samples. Sparse representation-based classification (SRC) for face recognition [2, 9, 10] first codes the test sample using a linear combination on the training samples, and then determines the differences between the test sample and all training samples using the representation coefficients. Consequently, the test sample can be classified as belonging to the class with minimal distance. SRC has been widely applied to face recognition [11–13], image categorization [14, 15], and image super-resolution [9, 16]. Indeed, SRC can be viewed as a global representation method [17], because it uses all

1 Huizhou University, Guangdong 516007, China. E-mail: S. Zeng, zsn@outlook.com (✉); Y. Xiong, xyang.2010@hzu.edu.cn.

training samples to represent the test sample. On the contrary, collaborative representation-based classification (CRC), proposed as an improvement to SRC, considers the local features in common for each class in its representation. The training samples as a whole are used to determine the representation coefficients of a test sample. CRC considers the collaboration between all classes in the representation as the underlying reason it is possible to make a powerful image classification method [18–20]. However, we believe the collaborative contribution from local classes can also be used to refine the sparse representation, and that it is possible to improve the robustness of image classification by integrating both types of representation. Zhang et al. [17] integrated the globality of SRC with the locality of CRC for robust representation-based classification, and Li et al. [21] also combined sparse and collaborative representations for hyperspectral target detection with a linear operation. Further similar integrative methods have been proposed for other domains.

In this paper, we propose to use a slightly more sophisticated mathematical operation performing weighted averaging of sparse and collaborative representations for classification, which we call WASCRC. Firstly, it determines the sparse representation coefficients β for the test sample via l_1-norm minimization on all training samples. Secondly, it determines the collaborative representation coefficients α for the same test sample via l_2-norm minimization on all training samples. Thirdly, it calculates the new representation coefficients as a weighted average of these two groups of coefficients: $\beta' = a\alpha + b\beta$. Finally, the distance between the test sample and each training sample is determined as $\text{res}_{\text{WASCRC}} = \|y - X_i\hat{\beta}'_i\|_2/(a+b)$, allowing the test sample to be classified as belonging to the nearest class. Usually, we can let $a = 1$ for simplicity and vary b appropriately to a specific application. We conducted various experiments on several benchmark face databases, which showed that our WASCRC algorithm could decrease the failure rate of classification by up to 17% and 26% relative to SRC and CRC respectively.

The rest content of this paper is organized as follows. Section 2 introduces related work on sparse representation for robust face recognition. Section 3 describes our proposed algorithm and the rationale behind it. Section 4 presents experimental results on several benchmark face databases. Section 5 gives our conclusions.

2 Related work

2.1 Sparse representation

The sparse representation-based classification (SRC) algorithm was proposed by Wright et al. [2]. The basic procedure involves two steps, first representing the test sample as a linear combination of all training samples, and then identifying the closest class based on the minimal deviation.

Assume that there are C subjects or pattern classes with n training samples $x_1, x_2, \ldots, x_n$ and the test sample is y. Let the matrix $X_i = [x_{i,1}, x_{i,2}, \ldots, x_{i,n_i}] \in I^{m \times n_i}$ denote n_i training samples from the ith class. By stacking all columns from the vector for a $w \times h$ gray-scale image, we can obtain the vector for this image: $x \in I^m$ ($m = w \times h$). Each column of A_i then represents the training images of the ith subject. Any test sample $y \in I^m$ from the same class can be described by a linear formula as

$$y = a_{i,1}x_{i,1} + a_{i,2}x_{i,2} + \cdots + a_{i,n}x_{i,n} \qquad (1)$$

where $a_{i,j} \in I, j = 1, 2, \ldots, n_i$.

The n training samples of C subjects can be denoted by a new matrix: $X = [X_1, X_2, \ldots, X_C]$. Thus, Eq. (1) can be rewritten more simply as

$$y = X\beta \in I^m \qquad (2)$$

where $\beta = [0, \ldots, 0, a_{i,1}, a_{i,2}, \ldots, 0, \ldots, 0]^{\mathrm{T}}$ is the sparse coefficient vector in which only entries for the ith class are non-zero. This vector of coefficients is the key factor which affects the robustness of classification. Note that SRC uses the entire set of training samples to find these coefficients. This is a significant difference from one-sample-at-one-time or one-class-at-one-time methods such as nearest neighbor (NN) [22] and nearest subspace (NS) [23] algorithms. These local methods can both identify objects represented in the training set and reject samples that do not belong to any of the classes present in the training set.

The next step in SRC is to perform l_1-norm minimization to solve the optimization problem to find the sparsest solution to Eq. (2). This result is used to identify the class of the test sample y. Here we use:

$$\hat{\beta} = \arg \min_{\beta} \|\beta\|_1 \tag{3}$$

Next, SRC computes the residuals for this representative coefficient vector for the ith class:

$$\text{res}_{\text{SRC}}(y) = \|y - X_i \hat{\beta}_i\|_2 \tag{4}$$

Finally the identity of y is output as

$$\text{identity}(y) = \arg \min_i \{\text{res}_{\text{SRC},i}\} \tag{5}$$

There are five prevailing fast l_1-minimization approaches: gradient projection, homotopy, iterative shrinkage-thresholding, proximal gradient, and augmented Lagrange multipliers (ALM) [15]. As we know, it is more efficient to use first order l_1-minimization techniques for noisy data, e.g., SpaRSA [9], FISTA [24], and ALM [13], while homotopy [25], ALM, and l_1_ls [26] are more suitable for face recognition because of their accuracy and speed. Other SRC algorithms are implemented using l_0-norm, l_p-norm ($0 < p < 1$), or even l_2-norm minimization. Xu et al. [26] exploited $l_{1/2}$-norm minimization to constrain the sparsity of representation coefficients; further descriptions of various norm minimizations can be seen in Ref. [22]. Yang et al. [13] proposed fast l_1-minimization algorithms called augmented Lagrangian methods (ALM) for robust face recognition. Furthermore, many researchers proposed different SRC implementations and improvements, such as kernel sparse representation by Gao et al. [15], an algorithm by Yang and Zhang [27] that uses a Gabor occlusion dictionary to significantly reduce the computational cost when dealing with face occlusion, l_1-graphs for image classification by Cheng et al. [28], sparsity preserving projections by Qiao et al. [29], combination of sparse coding with linear pyramid matching by Yang et al. [30], and a prototype-plus-variation model for sparsity-based face recognition [31]. Classification accuracy can be further improved by using virtual samples [32–34]. All these methods attempt to improve the robustness of image classification for face recognition—it is clear that sparsity plays a paramount role in robust classification for face recognition.

2.2 Collaborative representation

Collaborative representation-based classification (CRC) was proposed as an improvement to and replacement for SRC by Zhang et al. [18, 19] and Chen and Ramadge [20]. Much literature on SRC, including Ref. [2], overemphasizes the significance of l_1-norm sparsity in image classification, while the role of collaborative representation (CR) is downplayed [18]. CR involves contributions from every training sample to represent the test sample y, because different face images share certain common features helpful for classification. It is thus based on nonlocal samples. CRC can use this nonlocal strategy to output more robust face recognition results.

Setting $X = [X_1, X_2, \ldots, X_C] \in I^{m \times n}$, and the test sample $y \in I^m$ can be represented as

$$y = a_1 x_1 + a_2 x_2 + \cdots + a_n x_n \tag{6}$$

Using a regularized least square approach [35] we can collaboratively represent the test sample using X with low computational burden:

$$(\hat{\alpha}) = \arg \min_{\alpha} \{\|y - X \cdot \alpha\|_2^2 + \lambda \|\alpha\|_2^2\} \tag{7}$$

where λ is a regularization parameter, which makes the least square solution stable and introduces better sparsity in the solution than using l_1-norm. Thus, the CR in Eq. (5) now becomes:

$$\hat{\alpha} = (X^{\text{T}} \cdot X + \lambda \cdot I)^{-1} X^{\text{T}} \tag{8}$$

Let $P = (X^{\text{T}} \cdot X + \lambda \cdot I)^{-1} X^{\text{T}}$, so we can just simply project the test sample y onto P:

$$\hat{\alpha} = P \cdot y \tag{9}$$

We may then compute the regularized residuals by

$$\text{res}_{\text{CRC}} = \|y - X_i \cdot \hat{\alpha}_i\|_2 / \|\hat{\alpha}_i\|_2 \tag{10}$$

Finally, we can output the identity of the test sample y as

$$\text{identity}(y) = \arg \min_i \{\text{res}_{\text{CRC},i}\} \tag{11}$$

In this way, CRC involves all training samples to represent the test sample. We consider this collaboration to be an effective approach, giving a better sparse representation result.

3 Our method

We believe that sparse representation (SR) still makes a significant contribution to robust classification, while the real importance of collaborative representation (CR) is to refine the sparse representation but not to negate it. Recent literature has proposed novel approaches which integrate both algorithms in pursuit of more robust results. Zhang et al. [17] integrated the globality of SRC with the locality of CRC for robust representation-based classification. In this method, integration was performed in the residual calculation in the representation, rather than in the sparse vector for the test sample. Li et al. [21] proposed a method to combine sparse and collaborative representations for hyperspectral target detection. This combination also happened at the step of computing the distance after the sparse vector had been determined. We compute a weighted average of the representation coefficients produced by SRC and CRC algorithms, as well as the computation of residuals, in an approach we call WASCRC. WASCRC works as follows. In the first stage, we obtain two kinds of coefficients from SRC and CRC. We use a conventional SRC algorithm to find the sparse representation coefficients β for the test sample, using Eq. (3). We also find the collaborative representation coefficients α using a conventional CRC algorithm, as in Eq. (8).

Next, we integrate them by means of a weighted average, denoted by $y = (ax_1 + bx_2)/(a + b)$. Our algorithm obtains new coefficients by imposing different weights on the two kinds of coefficients found by the two algorithms as follows:

$$\beta' = a\alpha + b\beta \qquad (12)$$

where a and b indicate the weights of two algorithms.

Finally, we compute the residuals between the test sample and training samples with an l_2-norm operation. Unlike conventional SRC and CRC, after performing the normalization, we need to divide by the sum of the two weights:

$$\text{res}_{\text{WASCRC}} = \|y - X_i\hat{\beta}'_i\|(a + b) \qquad (13)$$

In this way, this new residual incorporates the weighted average, producing a refined solution. We can use it to identify the test sample y as

$$\text{identity}(y) = \arg\min_i\{\text{res}_{\text{WASCRC},i}\} \qquad (14)$$

In practice, we use $a = 1$ for simplicity and vary b to adjust the contribution of the two algorithms. We used two values, $b = 4$ and $b = 300$, in our experiments.

4 Results

We conducted comprehensive experiments on several mainstream benchmark face databases to compare the robustness of our WASCRC and conventional SRC and CRC algorithms. The benchmarks chosen include ORL [36], Georgia Tech [37], and FERET [38] face databases. We ran experiments with different numbers of training samples for each face database. We now explain the samples, steps, and results for each experiment, as well as an analysis and comparison of the results. The experimental results indicate that WASCRC produces a lower classification failure rate than the SCR and CRC algorithms, reaching a 10% improvement in some cases.

4.1 Experiments on the ORL face database

The ORL face database [36] is a small database that includes only 400 face images with 10 different face images taken from 40 distinct subjects. The face images were captured under different conditions for each subject at varying time, with varying lighting, facial expressions (open or closed eyes, smiling or not smiling), and facial details (glasses or no glasses). These images were captured against a dark homogeneous background while the subjects were in an upright, frontal position. To reduce the computational complexity, we resized all face images to 56 × 46 pixels. Figure 1 presents the first 20 images from the ORL database.

We calculated the improvements provided by WASCRC over both SRC and CRC in each case. We set the weighted average factor $b = 1$ in these cases. The best case for SRC was the one using two training samples, in which WASCRC diminished the classification failure by 27%. The best case for CRC reached 23% reduction in failure when using five training samples. On average, the improvements to SRC and CRC by WASCRC were 17% and 18% respectively. In the one-training-sample case, which

Fig. 1 The first two subjects in the ORL face database.

is typical of real applications, WASCRC gained 1% and 17% in accuracy, respectively.

In order to further understand the cause of these improvements, we added a step to analyze the change in representation coefficients in all three algorithms. We picked a single test sample that WASCRC succeeded in classifying for which both SRC and CRC failed. We selected the first two samples for all 40 subjects as training samples, so that 80 training samples in total were used to determine the representation coefficients for the test sample. In our experiment, we found that the 214th test sample, the 6th sample for the 26th subject, was not recognized correctly by either SRC or CRC, while WASCRC succeeded in classifying it. We thus carefully analyzed the representation coefficients of this test sample, shown in Fig. 3. It is clear that

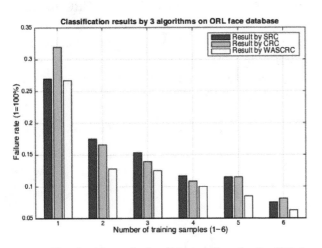

Fig. 2 Classification results for all 3 algorithms for the ORL face database.

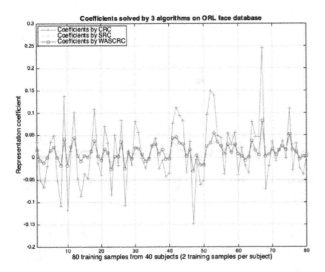

Fig. 3 Coefficients determined by the 3 algorithms for the ORL face database.

every single coefficient used by WASCRC (green) was between the values used by SRC (pink) and CRC (yellow): the new coefficients were smoother than the original ones, due to the weighted average calculation. The distance between the test sample and each class is calculated by the sum of entries for all training samples belonging to a class. We believe that if the curve is smoother, which means the values are relatively smaller and closer to zero, the resulting distances will be closer to zero and have smaller differences. On one hand, more entries close to zero produce a sparser representation vector; on the other hand, smaller differences help output a more precise comparison. Therefore, this had a positive effect on the representation and made a better sparse representation than conventional representation-based methods, leading to higher classification accuracy.

4.2 Experiments on the Georgia Tech face database

The next group of experiments used the Georgia Tech face database [37, 39]. This database has 750 face images captured from 50 individuals in several sessions; all images are in 15-color JPEG format. Each subject shows frontal and/or tilted faces as well as different facial expressions, lighting conditions, and scale. The original face images all have cluttered backgrounds, and a resolution of 640 × 480 pixels, which is too large for efficient representation. For the experiments, we programmatically removed the background and resized the images to 30 × 40 pixels to reduce computing load. However, this image preprocessing did not negatively affect on our results. Figure 4 shows the first subject with 15 samples in the face database. It is not necessary to use all three dimensions of color data in these colored images: we only used two dimensions of gray-scale data from these RGB images. Again, this did not affect our experimental results.

We successively picked the first 1 to 10 face images as training samples and the rest as test samples. In this case, we set the weighted average factor $b = 300$ and recorded the classification results for all test samples given by all three algorithms. The resulting failure rates are shown in Fig. 5. The results from the SRC algorithm (blue) unexpectedly outperformed the CRC algorithm (green), while our WASCRC algorithm (yellow) not surprisingly gave best results.

Fig. 4 The first subject, with 15 samples in the Georgia Tech face database.

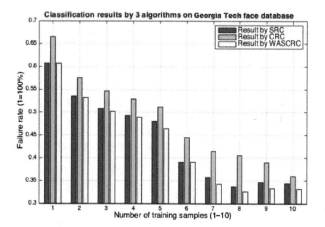

Fig. 5 Classification results for all 3 algorithms for the Georgia Tech face database.

Furthermore, as the number of training samples increased, the failure rates dropped dramatically.

We again determined the improvement by WASCRC over SRC and CRC, which were slightly lower than those for the ORL face database. The conventional SRC algorithm still performed well and the best case over SRC generated only 4% improvement when using 7 training samples. As conventional CRC algorithm underachieved, WASCRC outperformed it by up to 20% when using 8 training samples. On average, WASCRC outperformed SRC and CRC by 2% and 11% respectively. WASCRC outperformed CRC by 9% in the one-training-sample case.

4.3 Experiments on the FERET face database

The last group of experiments was performed on one of the largest public benchmark face databases, the FERET database [38]. It is much bigger than the Georgia Tech and ORL face databases. Each subject has five to eleven images with two frontal views (fa and fb) and one more frontal image with a different

facial expression. Our experiments used 200 subjects in total, with 7 samples for each. Figure 7 shows the first three subjects in the database; images 1–7 belong to the first subject, while 8–14 belong to the second subject and image 15 belongs to the third subject (who has 6 more images not shown in the figure).

We used images 1–5 as training samples and the remaining images as test samples, and again set the weighted average factor $b = 300$. The resulting classification failure rates from all three algorithms are shown in Fig. 8. As for the experiments on other databases, our WASCRC algorithm (yellow) still outperformed both SRC (blue) and CRC (green) algorithms in all test cases. Even in the one-training-sample case, WASCRC also produced the highest classification accuracy.

WASCRC outperformed SRC and CRC by up to 26% and 49% respectively when using 5 training samples. On average, WASCRC outperformed SRC and CRC by 12% and 26% respectively. WASCRC outperformed SRC and CRC by 5% and 10% in the one-training-sample case.

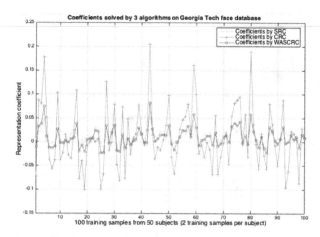

Fig. 6 Coefficients determined by the 3 algorithms for the Georgia Tech face database.

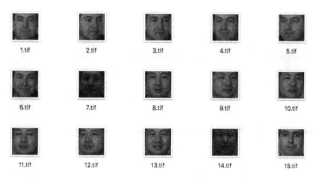

Fig. 7 The first fifteen face images from the FERET face database.

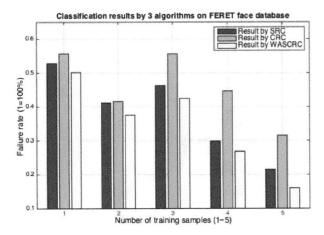

Fig. 8 Classification results for all 3 algorithms for the FERET face database.

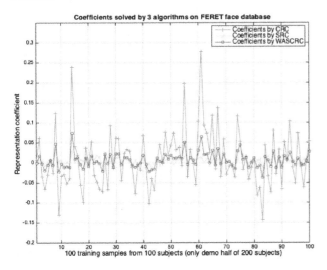

Fig. 9 Coefficients determined by the 3 algorithms for the FERET face database.

The representation coefficients used by WASCRC were always smoother, as shown in Fig. 9. The weighted average operation worked well, as expected. Figure 9 only shows the first half of all 200 training samples, from one test sample classified correctly by WASCRC and incorrectly by both SRC and CRC. This result validates that our proposed algorithm is a more robust classifier.

5   Conclusions

Sparsity of a representation is the key to successful sparse representation-based classification, while collaboration from all classes in the representation is the key to promising collaborative representation-based classification. We have shown how to integrate these approaches in a method that performs a weighted average operation on sparse

and collaborative representations for robust face recognition. Such integration can lower the failure rate in face recognition. Our experiments demonstrated that our new approach can outperform both sparse and collaborative representation-based classification algorithms for face recognition, decreasing the recognition failure rate by about 10%. It is possible to achieve higher accuracy still in some specific cases by altering the factor used for weighted averaging.

Acknowledgements

This work was supported in part by the National Natural Science Foundation of China (Grant No. 61502208), the Natural Science Foundation of Jiangsu Province of China (Grant No. BK20150522), the Scientific and Technical Program of City of Huizhou (Grant No. 2012-21), the Research Foundation of Education Bureau of Guangdong Province of China (Grant No. A314.0116), and the Scientific Research Starting Foundation for Ph.D. in Huizhou University (Grant No. C510.0210).

References

[1] Brunelli, R.; Poggio, T. Face recognition: Features versus templates. *IEEE Transactions on Pattern Analysis and Machine Intelligence* Vol. 15, No. 10, 1042–1052, 1993.

[2] Wright, J.; Yang, A. Y.; Ganesh, A.; Sastry, S. S.; Ma, Y. Robust face recognition via sparse representation. *IEEE Transactions on Pattern Analysis and Machine Intelligence* Vol. 31, No. 2, 210–227, 2009.

[3] Xu, Y.; Zhang, D.; Yang, J.; Yang, J.-Y. An approach for directly extracting features from matrix data and its application in face recognition. *Neurocomputing* Vol. 71, Nos. 10–12, 1857–1865, 2008.

[4] Turk, M.; Pentland, A. Eigenfaces for recognition. *Journal of Cognitive Neuroscience* Vol. 3, No. 1, 71–86, 1991.

[5] Park, S. W.; Savvides, M. A multifactor extension of linear discriminant analysis for face recognition under varying pose and illumination. *EURASIP Journal on Advances in Signal Processing* Vol. 2010, 158395, 2010.

[6] Lu, J.; Plataniotis, K. N.; Venetsanopoulos, A. N. Face recognition using LDA-based algorithms. *IEEE Transactions on Neural Networks* Vol. 14, No. 1, 195–200, 2003.

[7] Debruyne, M.; Verdonck, T. Robust kernel principal component analysis and classification. *Advances in Data Analysis and Classification* Vol. 4, No. 2, 151–167, 2010.

[8] Muller, K.-R.; Mika, S.; Ratsch, G.; Tsuda, K.; Scholkopf, B. An introduction to kernel-based learning

algorithms. *IEEE Transactions on Neural Networks* Vol. 12, No. 2, 181–201, 2001.

[9] Yang, J.; Wright, J.; Huang, T. S.; Ma, Y. Image super-resolution via sparse representation. *IEEE Transactions on Image Processing* Vol. 19, No. 11, 2861–2873, 2010.

[10] Xu, Y.; Zhang, D.; Yang, J.; Yang, J.-Y. A two-phase test sample sparse representation method for use with face recognition. *IEEE Transactions on Circuits and Systems for Video Technology* Vol. 21, No. 9, 1255–1262, 2011.

[11] Zhong, D.; Zhu, P.; Han, J.; Li, S. An improved robust sparse coding for face recognition with disguise. *International Journal of Advanced Robotic Systems* Vol. 9, 126, 2012.

[12] Xu, Y.; Zhu, Q.; Zhang, D. Combine crossing matching scores with conventional matching scores for bimodal biometrics and face and palmprint recognition experiments. *Neurocomputing* Vol. 74, No. 18, 3946–3952, 2011.

[13] Yang, A. Y.; Zhou, Z.; Balasubramanian, A. G.; Sastry, S. S.; Ma, Y. Fast l_1-minimization algorithms for robust face recognition. *IEEE Transactions on Image Processing* Vol. 22, No. 8, 3234–3246, 2013.

[14] Mairal, J.; Bach, F.; Ponce, J.; Sapiro, G.; Zisserman, A. Discriminative learned dictionaries for local image analysis. In: Proceedings of IEEE Conference on Computer Vision and Pattern Recognition, 1–8, 2008.

[15] Gao, S.; Tsang, I. W.-H.; Chia, L.-T. Kernel sparse representation for image classification and face recognition. In: *Computer Vision—ECCV 2010*. Daniilidis, K.; Maragos, P.; Paragios, N. Eds. Springer Berlin Heidelberg, 1–14, 2010.

[16] Yang, J.; Wright, J.; Huang, T.; Ma, Y. Image super-resolution as sparse representation of raw image patches. In: Proceedings of IEEE Conference on Computer Vision and Pattern Recognition, 1–8, 2008.

[17] Zhang, Z.; Li, Z.; Xie, B.; Wang, L.; Chen, Y. Integrating globality and locality for robust representation based classification. *Mathematical Problems in Engineering* Vol. 2014, Article No. 415856, 2014.

[18] Zhang, L.; Yang, M.; Feng, X. Sparse representation or collaborative representation: Which helps face recognition? In: Proceedings of IEEE International Conference on Computer Vision, 471–478, 2011.

[19] Zhang, L.; Yang, M.; Feng, X.; Ma, Y.; Zhang, D. Collaborative representation based classification for face recognition. *arXiv preprint* arXiv:1204.2358, 2012.

[20] Chen, X.; Ramadge, P. J. Collaborative representation, sparsity or nonlinearity: What is key to dictionary based classification? In: Proceedings of IEEE International Conference on Acoustics, Speech and Signal Processing, 5227–5231, 2014.

[21] Li, W.; Du, Q.; Zhang, B. Combined sparse and collaborative representation for hyperspectral target detection. *Pattern Recognition* Vol. 48, No. 12, 3904–3916, 2015.

[22] Feng, Q.; Pan, J.-S.; Yan, L. Restricted nearest feature line with ellipse for face recognition. *Journal of Information Hiding and Multimedia Signal Processing* Vol. 3, No. 3, 297–305, 2012.

[23] Elhamifar, E.; Vidal, R. Sparse subspace clustering: Algorithm, theory, and applications. *IEEE Transactions on Pattern Analysis and Machine Intelligence* Vol. 35, No. 11, 2765–2781, 2013.

[24] Beck, A.; Teboulle, M. A fast iterative shrinkage-thresholding algorithm for linear inverse problems. *SIAM Journal on Imaging Sciences* Vol. 2, No. 1, 183–202, 2009.

[25] Zhang, Z.; Xu, Y.; Yang, J.; Li, X.; Zhang, D. A survey of sparse representation: Algorithms and applications. *IEEE Access* Vol. 3, 490–530, 2015.

[26] Xu, Z.; Zhang, H.; Wang, Y.; Chang, X.; Liang, Y. $L_{1/2}$ regularization. *Science China Information Sciences* Vol. 53, No. 6, 1159–1169, 2010.

[27] Yang, M.; Zhang, L. Gabor feature based sparse representation for face recognition with Gabor occlusion dictionary. In: *Computer Vision—ECCV 2010*. Daniilidis, K.; Maragos, P.; Paragios, N. Eds. Springer Berlin Heidelberg, 448–461, 2010.

[28] Cheng, B.; Yang, J.; Yan, S.; Fu, Y.; Shuang, T. S. Learning with l^1-graph for image analysis. *IEEE Transactions on Image Processing* Vol. 19, No. 4, 858–866, 2010.

[29] Qiao, L.; Chen, S.; Tan, X. Sparsity preserving projections with applications to face recognition. *Pattern Recognition* Vol. 43, No. 1, 331–341, 2010.

[30] Yang, J.; Yu, K.; Gong, Y.; Huang, T. Linear spatial pyramid matching using sparse coding for image classification. In: Proceedings of IEEE Conference on Computer Vision and Pattern Recognition, 1794–1801, 2009.

[31] Deng, W.; Hu, J.; Guo, J. In defense of sparsity based face recognition. In: Proceedings of the IEEE Conference on Computer Vision and Pattern Recognition, 399–406, 2013.

[32] Xu, Y.; Zhu, X.; Li, Z.; Liu, G.; Lu, Y.; Liu, H. Using the original and 'symmetrical face' training samples to perform representation based two-step face recognition. *Pattern Recognition* Vol. 46, No. 4, 1151–1158, 2013.

[33] Xu, Y.; Zhang, Z.; Lu, G.; Yang, J. Approximately symmetrical face images for image preprocessing in face recognition and sparse representation based classification. *Pattern Recognition* Vol. 54, 68–82, 2016.

[34] Liu, Z.; Song, X.; Tang, Z. Fusing hierarchical multi-scale local binary patterns and virtual mirror samples to perform face recognition. *Neural Computing and Applications* Vol. 26, No. 8, 2013–2026, 2015.

[35] Lee, H.; Battle, A.; Raina, R.; Ng, A. Y. Efficient sparse coding algorithms. In: Proceedings of Advances in Neural Information Processing Systems, 801–808, 2006.

[36] AT&T Laboratories Cambridge. The database of faces. 2002. Available at http://www.cl.cam.ac.uk/research/

dtg/attarchive/facedatabase.html.

[37] Computer Vision Online. Georgia Tech face database. 2015. Available at http://www.computervisiononline.com/dataset/1105138700.

[38] NIST Information Technology Laboratory. Color FERET database. 2016. Available at https://www.nist.gov/itl/iad/image-group/color-feret-database.

[39] Xu, Y.; Zhang, B.; Zhong, Z. Multiple representations and sparse representation for image classification. *Pattern Recognition Letters* Vol. 68, 9–14, 2015.

8

LSTM-in-LSTM for generating long descriptions of images

Jun Song[1], Siliang Tang[1], Jun Xiao[1], Fei Wu[1](✉), and Zhongfei (Mark) Zhang[2]

Abstract   In this paper, we propose an approach for generating rich *fine-grained* textual descriptions of images. In particular, we use an LSTM-in-LSTM (long short-term memory) architecture, which consists of an inner LSTM and an outer LSTM. The inner LSTM effectively encodes the long-range *implicit* contextual interaction between visual cues (i.e., the spatially-concurrent visual objects), while the outer LSTM generally captures the *explicit* multi-modal relationship between sentences and images (i.e., the correspondence of sentences and images). This architecture is capable of producing a long description by predicting one word at every time step conditioned on the previously generated word, a hidden vector (via the outer LSTM), and a context vector of fine-grained visual cues (via the inner LSTM). Our model outperforms state-of-the-art methods on several benchmark datasets (Flickr8k, Flickr30k, MSCOCO) when used to generate *long* rich fine-grained descriptions of given images in terms of four different metrics (BLEU, CIDEr, ROUGE-L, and METEOR).

Keywords   long short-term memory (LSTM); image description generation; computer vision; neural network

1   Introduction

Automatically describing the content of an image

1   College of Computer Science and Technology, Zhejiang University, Hangzhou 310027, China. E-mail: J. Song, songjun54cm@zju.edu.cn; S. Tang, siliang@cs. zju.edu.cn; J. Xiao, junx@cs.zju.edu.cn; F. Wu, wufei@ cs.zju.edu.cn (✉).
2   Department of Computer Science, Watson School of Engineering and Applied Sciences, Binghamton University, Binghamton, NY, USA. E-mail: zhongfei@ cs.binghamton.edu.

by means of text (description generation) is a fundamental task in artificial intelligence, with many applications. For example, generating descriptions of images may help visually impaired people better understand the content of images and retrieve images using descriptive texts. The challenge of description generation lies in appropriately developing a model that can effectively represent the visual cues in images and describe them in the domain of natural language at the same time.

There have been significant advances in description generation recently. Some efforts rely on manually-predefined visual concepts and sentence templates [1–3]. However, an effective image description model should be free of hard coded templates and categories. Other efforts treat the image description task as a multi-modal retrieval problem (e.g., *image–query–text*) [4–7]. Such methods obtain a descriptive sentence of each image by retrieving similarly described images from a large database and then modifying these retrieved descriptions based on the query image. Such methods lack the ability to generate descriptions of unseen images.

Motivated by recent successes in computer vision and natural language processing, current image description generation approaches generate more reasonable descriptive sentences of given images [8–10] based on an approach of *word-by-word* generation via recurrent neural networks (RNN) (e.g., using long short-term memory (LSTM)) since these approaches store context information in a recurrent layer. Most description generation research only utilizes the image being described to the RNN at the beginning [10]. By looking at the image only once during word-by-word generation, the precision and recall of the predicted noun words (i.e., visual objects in images) decrease rapidly with their position of

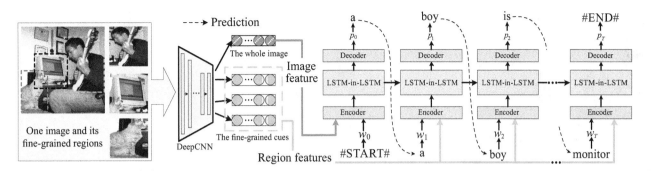

Fig. 1 Overview of our approach. The DeepCNN model projects the pixels of an image and its fine-grained regions into a 4096-dimensional feature. The encoder layer encodes the textual words, the whole image, and the visual objects as vectors. The prediction layer outputs one hidden vector at each step which is then used to predict the next word in the decoder layer. While training, the tth word in the sentence is fed into the model to predict the next word (solid lines). While testing, the word predicted at the previous step $(t-1)$ is fed into the model at step t.

occurrence in a sentence (as shown in Fig. 5), since these approaches merely preserve global semantics at the beginning and disregard the fine-grained interactions between visual cues which could be useful if we wish to generate richer, more descriptive captions.

From the point of view of the mutual utilization of visual and textual contexts during each step of word-by-word generation, image description generation methods may in general be categorized into two classes. The first class repeatedly takes advantage of the whole image at each time step of the output word sequence [9]. Such methods may identify the most interesting salient objects the words refer to; however, they may still ignore the fine-detail objects.

The second class explicitly learns the correspondences between visual objects (detected as object-like or regions of attention) and the matching words at each step of generation, and then generates the next word according to both the correspondences and the LSTM hidden vector [11, 12]. Such methods may neglect *long-range* interactions between visual cues (e.g., the spatially-concurrent visual objects).

In this paper, we develop a new neural network structure called LSTM-in-LSTM (long short-term memory) which can generate semantically rich and descriptive sentences for given images. The LSTM-in-LSTM consists of an inner LSTM (encoding the implicit long-range interactions between visual cues) and an outer LSTM (capturing the explicit multi-modal correspondences between images and sentences). This architecture is capable of producing a description by predicting one word at each time step conditioned on the previously generated word,

a hidden vector (via the outer LSTM), and the context vector of fine-grained visual cues (via the inner LSTM).

Compared with existing methods, the proposed LSTM-in-LSTM architecture, as illustrated in Fig. 1, is particularly appropriate for generating rich fine-grained *long* descriptions with appealing diversity, owing to its modeling of long-range interactions between visual cues.

2 Related work

2.1 Natural language models

Over the last few years, natural language models based on neural networks have been widely used in the natural language processing domain. Artificial neural networks have been employed to learn a distributed representation for words which better captures the semantics of words [13]. Recursive neural networks have been used to encode a natural language sentence as a vector [7]. Palangi et al. [14] use a recurrent neural network (RNN) with *long short-term memory* (LSTM) to sequentially take each word in a sentence, and encode it as a semantic vector. A recurrent neural network encoder–decoder architecture has been proposed to encode a source language sentence, and then decode it into a target language [15].

2.2 Deep model for computer vision

Methods based on deep neural networks have been adopted by a large number of computer vision applications. *Deep convolutional neural networks* (DeepCNN) have achieved excellent performance in image classification tasks (e.g., AlexNet [16],

VggNet [17]). Object detection systems based on a well trained DeepCNN outperform previous works (RCNN [18], SPPNet [19]). Girshick [20] proposed Fast-RCNN which is much faster than RCNN and SPPNet for object detection during both training and testing.

2.3 Image descriptions

There are two main categories of methods for automatically describing an image: retrieval based methods and generation based methods. Many works try to describe an image by retrieving a relevant sentence from a database. They learn the co-embedding of images and sentences in a common vector space and then descriptions are retrieved which lie close to the image in the embedding space [4, 5, 7]. Karpathy et al. [21] argue that by using a correspondence model that is based on a combination of image regions and phrases of sentences, the performance of retrieval based image description methods can be boosted. Generation based methods often use fixed templates or generative grammars [22]. Other generation methods more closely related to our method learn the probability distribution of the next word in a sentence based on all previously generated words [8–10].

3 Method

Our model comprises three layers: the encoder layer, the prediction layer, and the decoder layer. In the encoder layer, the words in sentences are encoded into different word vectors (one vector per word). For whole images and visual objects (detected as object-like regions), a deep convolutional neural network is used to encode them into 4096-dimensional visual vectors. The prediction layer outputs a single hidden vector which is then used to predict the next word in the decoder layer. The overview of our approach is illustrated in Fig. 1.

3.1 Encoder layer

First, we encode the words in sentences, the whole image, and the visual objects in the image as vectors. Given training data denoted as (S, I), which is a pair of a sentence S and its length (in words) T, and image I. The words in the sentence S are $w_1, w_2, \cdots, w_T$. We first denote each word

as a one-hot representation $w_1, w_2, \cdots, w_T$. This representation is a binary representation which has the same dimension as the vocabulary size and only one non-zero element. After that, the one-hot representation is transformed into an h-dimensional vector as follows:

$$\omega_t = W_s w_t \qquad (1)$$

W_s is a matrix of size $h \times V$, where V is the size of the vocabulary. W_s is randomly initialized and learned during the model training.

For images, we use Fast-RCNN [20] to detect the visual objects in the image. Fast-RCNN is a fast framework for object detection based on a deep convolutional neural network. This framework is trained using a multi-task loss function in a single training stage, which not only simplifies learning but also improves the detection accuracy.

A threshold τ is set to select the *valid* visual objects from all objects detected by Fast-RCNN. Visual objects with a detection score higher than τ are considered as *valid* visual objects; the rest are discarded. The number of the *valid* objects may be different in each image.

For each image I and each visual object r, we first obtain their 4096-dimensional VGGNet16 [17] fc7 features. Then these features are encoded as h-dimensional vectors as follows:

$$v_I = W_e CNN_{VGGNet16}(I) + b_e \qquad (2)$$

$$r = W_r CNN_{VGGNet16}(r) + b_r \qquad (3)$$

v_I is the vector of image I and r is the vector of visual object r. The $CNN_{VGGNet16}(\cdot)$ function projects the pixels into a 4096-dimensional VGGNet16 [17] fc7 feature. W_e and W_r are matrices with dimension $h \times 4096$; b_e and b_r are bias vectors with dimension h. W_e, W_r, b_e, and b_r are parameters learned during training.

3.2 Prediction layer

The prediction layer consists of two LSTMs, namely the outer LSTM and the inner LSTM. We call this architecture LSTM-in-LSTM.

3.2.1 Basic LSTM unit

In order to predict each word in a sentence, the recurrent net needs to store information over an extended time interval. Here we briefly introduce the basic LSTM approach [23] which has had great success in machine translation [24] and sequence generation [25].

As shown in Fig. 2, a single memory cell c is surrounded by three gates controlling whether to input new data (*input gate i*), whether to forget history (*forget gate f*), and whether to produce the current value (*output gate o*) at each time t. The memory cell in LSTM encodes information at every time step concerning what inputs have been observed prior to this step. The value of each gate is calculated according to the word vector $\boldsymbol{\omega}_t$ at step t and the predicted hidden vector $\boldsymbol{m}_{t-1}$ at step $t-1$. The definitions of the memory cell and each gate are as follows:

$$\begin{cases} \boldsymbol{x}_t = [\boldsymbol{\omega}_t; \boldsymbol{m}_{t-1}] \\ \boldsymbol{i}_t = \sigma(\boldsymbol{W}_i \cdot \boldsymbol{x}_t) \\ \boldsymbol{f}_t = \sigma(\boldsymbol{W}_f \cdot \boldsymbol{x}_t) \\ \boldsymbol{o}_t = \sigma(\boldsymbol{W}_o \cdot \boldsymbol{x}_t) \\ \boldsymbol{c}_t = \boldsymbol{f}_t \odot \boldsymbol{c}_{t-1} + \boldsymbol{i}_t \odot \phi(\boldsymbol{W}_c \cdot \boldsymbol{x}_t) \\ \boldsymbol{m}_t = \boldsymbol{o}_t \odot \boldsymbol{c}_t \end{cases} \quad (4)$$

where $\odot$ represents the element-wise product. σ and ϕ are nonlinearlity mapping functions. In our experiments, we set σ as a sigmoid function and ϕ as hyperbolic tangent. $\boldsymbol{m}_t$ is the output of the LSTM at step t. $\boldsymbol{W}_i$, $\boldsymbol{W}_f$, $\boldsymbol{W}_o$, and $\boldsymbol{W}_c$ are parameter matrices learned during training.

3.2.2 LSTM-in-LSTM unit

As previously discussed, we attempt to employ both the explicit multi-modal correspondence of sentences and images, and the implicit long-range interactions of fine-grained visual cues, during the prediction of each word. The proposed LSTM-in-LSTM has two layers of LSTM networks, namely the outer LSTM and the inner LSTM.

See Fig. 3. The outer LSTM is a basic LSTM unit. At each step t, the outer LSTM takes a word vector $\boldsymbol{\omega}_t$ (the tth word vector of the sentence in training, or the word vector of the previously predicted word in prediction), the last predicted hidden vector $\boldsymbol{m}_{t-1}$,

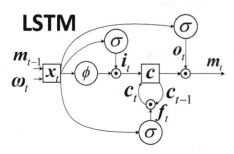

Fig. 2 The basic LSTM method.

and the context output vector of the inner LSTM $\boldsymbol{m}_t^{\text{inner}}$ as the input. In the outer LSTM, the vector $\boldsymbol{x}_t$ is defined as follows:

$$\boldsymbol{x}_t = [\boldsymbol{\omega}_t; \boldsymbol{m}_{t-1}; \boldsymbol{m}_t^{\text{inner}}] \quad (5)$$

$\boldsymbol{x}_t$ is employed to obtain the t step output of the LSTM-in-LSTM $\boldsymbol{m}_t$.

The inner LSTM is composed of stacked LSTM units. In essence, the gates of the inner LSTM learn to adaptively look up significant visual object-like regions, and encode the implicit interactions between visual cues at each step. For the kth basic LSTM in the inner LSTM, the input is the kth object vector $\boldsymbol{r}_k$ and the output vector of the previous basic LSTM ($\boldsymbol{m}_{t-1}$ for the first LSTM unit), as follows:

$$\boldsymbol{x}_k^{\text{inner}} = [\boldsymbol{m}_{k-1}^{\text{inner}}; \boldsymbol{r}_k], \quad \boldsymbol{m}_0^{\text{inner}} = \boldsymbol{m}_{t-1} \quad (6)$$

Note that the parameters of the outer LSTM (e.g., $\boldsymbol{W}_i$, $\boldsymbol{W}_f$, $\boldsymbol{W}_o$, and $\boldsymbol{W}_c$) differ from those of the inner LSTM ($\boldsymbol{W}_i^{\text{inner}}$, $\boldsymbol{W}_f^{\text{inner}}$, $\boldsymbol{W}_o^{\text{inner}}$, and $\boldsymbol{W}_c^{\text{inner}}$); however all basic LSTM units in the inner LSTM share the same parameters.

For the inner LSTM, each basic LSTM unit takes one visual object vector as an input, so the number of basic LSTM units in the inner LSTM equals the number of *valid* visual objects.

3.3 Training the model

We use a probabilistic mechanism to generate the description of each image. The training objective is to minimize the log-likelihood of the *perplexity* of each sentence in the training set using an L_2 regularization term, as shown in Eq. (7):

$$O(\theta) =$$

$$\arg \min_{\theta} \left(\frac{1}{\sum_{i=1}^{N} T_i} \sum_{i=1}^{N} \log \mathcal{PPL}(S_i | I_i, \theta) + \frac{\lambda}{2} \|\theta\|_2^2 \right) \quad (7)$$

θ denotes all training parameters in our model, N is the size of the training set, i indicates the index of each training sample, and I_i and S_i denote the image and the sentence for the ith training sample. T_i denotes the length (in words) of sentence S_i; λ is the weighting parameter for standard L_2 regularization of θ.

The *perplexity* of a sentence is calculated as the negative log-likelihood of its words according to its associated image, as follows:

$$\mathcal{PPL}(S_i | I_i, \theta) = -\sum_{t=1}^{T_i} \log_2 P(w_t^{(i)} | w_{1:t-1}^{(i)}, I_i, \theta) \quad (8)$$

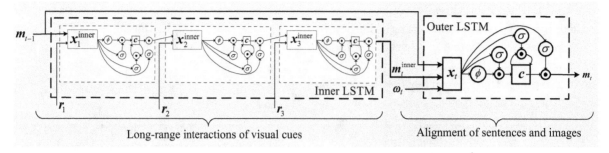

Fig. 3 LSTM-in-LSTM structure. For simplicity, we show three visual object vectors r_1, r_2, and r_3, so there are 3 LSTM units in the inner LSTM. The 3 visual objects are sequentially fed into the inner LSTM in a descending order according to their Fast-RNN detection scores. The parameters of the outer LSTM and the inner LSTM differ, but each LSTM unit in the inner LSTM shares the same parameters.

Here the probability of each word is computed based on the words in its context and the corresponding image. $w_t^{(i)}$ denotes the tth word in the ith sentence and $w_{1:t-1}^{(i)}$ denotes the words before the tth word in the ith sentence. Therefore, minimizing the *perplexity* is equivalent to maximizing the log-likelihood. Stochastic gradient descent is used to learn the parameters of our model.

Algorithm 1 summarises the training procedure for our model. outerLSTM($\cdot$) denotes the forward pass of the outer LSTM and innerLSTM($\cdot$) denotes the forward pass of the inner LSTM. We insert a start token #START# at the beginning of each sentence

---

Algorithm 1: Algorithm for training our model

Input: A batch $\mathcal{B}$ of training data, as image and sentence pairs.

for all pair $(S_i, I_i) \in \mathcal{B}$ **do**
  /* Encoder layer */
  Encode each word in sentence I_i into word vectors ω_t $(t = 0, \cdots, T_i)$.
  Detect visual objects and learn the vector of objects r_k $(k = 1, \cdots, K)$ and the image v_{I^i}.
  /* Prediction layer */
  $m_0 = \text{outerLSTM}(\omega_0, \mathbf{0}, v_{I^i})$
  for all $t \leftarrow 1$ to T_i **do**
    $m_t^{\text{inner}} = \text{innerLSTM}(r_1, r_2, \cdots, r_K)$
    $m_t = \text{outerLSTM}(\omega_t, m_{t-1}, m_t^{\text{inner}})$
  end for
  /* Decoder layer */
  for all $t \leftarrow 0$ to T_i **do**
    $p_t = \text{Softmax}(W_d m_t + b_d)$
  end for
  Calculate and accumulate the gradients.
end for
Calculate the update values $\nabla \theta$
/* Update the parameters */
$\theta = \theta - \nabla \theta$
Output: The parameters θ of the model.

---

and an end token #END# at its end. Thus the subscript t expands from 0 (#START#) to $T + 1$ (#END#). In the first step ($t = 0$), the word vector of the start token #START# ω_0 and the vector of the ith image (v_{I^i}) are fed into the outer LSTM to obtain the first predicted hidden vector m_0.

3.4 Sentence generation

Given an image, its descriptive sentence is generated in a word-by-word manner according to the predicted probability distribution at each step, until the end token #END# or some maximum length L is reached. We insert a start token #START# at the beginning of each sentence and an end token #END# at its end. Thus the subscript t goes from 0 (#START#) to $T + 1$ (#END#). In the first step ($t = 0$), the word vector of the start token #START# ω_0 and the vector of ith image (e.g., v_{I^i}) are fed into the outer LSTM to get the first predicted hidden vector m_0. We use *BeamSearch* to iteratively select the set of κ best sentences up to step t as candidates to generate sentences at step $t + 1$, and keep only the resulting best κ of them. Algorithm 2 summarises the process used to generate one sentence.

4 Experiments

4.1 Comparison methods

Since we are interested in word-by-word image-caption generation which utilizes mutual visual and textual information during each prediction step, we compare our work to three types of algorithms as follows:

- **NIC model** [10] and **Neural-Talk** [8]: NIC and Neural-Talk models only utilize whole-image

---

Algorithm 2: Generating one sentence in our model

Input: The input image I.

Detect visual objects and learn the vectors r_k ($k = 1, \cdots, K$) and v_I.

ω_0 is the word vector of $\#START\#$.

$m_0 = \text{outerLSTM}(\omega_0, \mathbf{0}, v_I)$

$t = 1$, w_t is the word with the highest probability.

while w_t is not $\#END\#$ and $t \leqslant L$ **do**

    $m_t^{\text{inner}} = \text{innerLSTM}(r_1, \cdots, r_K)$

    $m_t = \text{outerLSTM}(\omega_t, m_{t-1}, m_t^{\text{inner}})$

    $p_t = \text{Softmax}(W_d m_t + b_d)$

    $t = t + 1$

    w_t is the word with the highest probability.

end while

Output: The sentence with words in sequence: $w_1, \cdots, w_T$.

---

information at the beginning during description prediction.

- **m-RNN** [9]: the m-RNN model employs whole-image information at each prediction step.
- **attention model** [11]: this attention model uses fine-grained visual cues (regions of attention) during each prediction step.

4.2 Datasets

Three different benchmark datasets were used in the experiments; Table 1 shows the size of each dataset.

- **Flickr8k**: the Flickr8k [5] dataset comprises 8000 images from Flickr showing persons and animals. Each image has 5 descriptive sentences.
- **Flickr30k**: the Flickr30k [26] comprises 30,000 images from Flickr showing daily activities, events, and scenes. Each image has 5 descriptive sentences.
- **MSCOCO**: the Microsoft COCO [27] dataset comprises more than 120,000 images. Each image has 5 descriptive sentences.

4.3 Experimental setup

In order to perform a fair comparison, we used the same VGGNet16 fc7 feature as the visual feature for all models. For the Flickr8k and Flickr30k datasets,

Table 1 Sizes of the three benchmark datasets, and the numbers of images used for training, validation, and testing

Dataset	Size		
	Training	Validation	Testing
Flickr8k	6000	1000	1000
Flickr30k	28000	1000	1000
MSCOCO	82783	40504	5000

the dimension of the hidden vectors was $h = 512$. For MSCOCO, $h = 600$. In our experiments, we used the threshold $\tau = 0.5$ to select valid visual objects in each image.

4.4 Results

Our experiments compared the methods in three ways: (i) a qualitative analysis of long description generation performance in terms of four metrics, (ii) the predictive ability for rich fine-grained semantics in *long* descriptive sentences, and (iii) the ability to predict SVO (*subject–verb–object*) triplets.

4.4.1 Generation of long descriptions

Many metrics have been used in the image description literature. The most commonly used metrics are BLEU [28] and ROUGE [29]. BLEU is a precision-based measure and ROUGE is a recall-related measure. BLEU and ROUGE scores can be computed automatically from a number of ground truth sentences, and have been used to evaluate a number of sentence generation systems [2, 5, 30]. In this paper we use BLEU-N, ROUGE-L, CIDEr [31], and METEOR [32] to evaluate the effectiveness of our model. We used the open-source project coco-caption software[1] to calculate those metrics.

When generating descriptions, accurate generation of the sentences which consist of many words (i.e., long sentences) is difficult, as it is likely that long sentences deliver rich fine-grained semantics. We argue that the LSTM-in-LSTM architecture is capable of predicting long sentence descriptions since it implicitly learns the contextual interactions between visual cues. Thus, we divide the test data into two parts: images with *long* sentence descriptions and images with *short* sentence descriptions. Descriptions of images in the test dataset are considered to be long if they have more than 8 words (which is the average length of the sentences in the MSCOCO test dataset); the remaining images have short descriptions.

Table 2 reports the image-captioning performance of the images with long and short descriptions. **B-N** gives the BLEU-N metric. The performance of our model is comparable to that of the state-of-the-art methods on short descriptions. However, the performance of our approach is remarkably better than that for other models for long descriptions.

---

[1] coco-caption: https://github.com/tylin/coco-caption.

Table 2 Performance for image-captioning on Flickr8k, Flickr30k, and MSCOCO on *long* and *short* descriptions. The best results shown in boldface

Model	B-1	B-2	B-3	B-4	CIDEr	ROUGE-L	METEOR
	Flickr8k (short descriptions / long descriptions)						
NIC model	66.5 / 53.4	48.7 / 35.1	33.3 / 22.3	21.2 / 14.7	52.1 / 31.7	48.1 / 40.7	21.0 / 17.6
Neural-Talk	63.0 / 54.8	43.3 / 34.9	28.5 / 21.5	17.9 / 13.7	38.3 / 22.2	42.0 / 38.8	17.0 / 15.0
m-RNN	**68.2** / 53.4	**48.4** / 32.1	**31.9** / 19.9	19.7 / 12.6	46.1 / 29.3	43.6 / 38.8	17.9 / 16.4
Our model	64.1 / **58.1**	45.4 / **39.0**	30.8 / **26.2**	19.9 / **18.2**	**48.4** / **37.2**	**44.2** / **43.3**	**18.6** / **18.4**
	Flickr30k (short descriptions / long descriptions)						
NIC model	62.5 / 57.6	40.4 / 36.7	26.3 / 22.9	16.5 / 14.6	25.9 / 22.2	37.3 / 38.7	14.7 / 15.1
Neural-Talk	60.9 / 57.4	41.1 / 36.0	28.6 / 22.1	18.0 / 14.1	24.3 / 14.9	39.6 / 38.5	14.7 / 14.1
m-RNN	65.8 / 58.4	45.7 / 37.7	30.4 / 24.7	18.8 / 16.6	34.3 / 28.4	39.5 / 40.1	15.6 / 16.0
Our model	**66.7** / **61.4**	**46.9** / **40.8**	**31.3** / **27.1**	**19.7** / **18.2**	**39.9** / **29.6**	**41.0** / **41.5**	**16.3** / **16.7**
	MSCOCO (short descriptions / long descriptions)						
NIC model	68.3 / 61.7	49.4 / 43.7	35.0 / 31.5	24.9 / 23.3	68.5 / 68.8	48.1 / 46.3	20.4 / 21.3
Neural-Talk	67.6 / 57.0	48.7 / 40.2	34.5 / 29.0	24.6 / 21.0	60.8 / 55.0	47.2 / 42.4	19.0 / 19.5
m-RNN	**70.0** / 63.0	**52.1** / 45.5	**37.5** / 33.1	26.7 / 24.1	74.4 / 70.9	48.9 / 46.2	**21.3** / 20.8
Our model	69.8 / **66.3**	51.5 / **48.8**	37.3 / **35.9**	**27.0** / **26.9**	**76.5** / **80.9**	**49.2** / **49.1**	20.9 / **23.0**

Compared with the second best methods, our long descriptions of the MSCOCO data show 5.2%, 7.3%, 8.5%, 11.6%, 14.1%, 6.0%, and 8.0% average performance improvements for B-1, B-2, B-3, B-4, CIDEr, ROUGE-L, and METEOR metrics, respectively. Other methods which utilize the visual cues at each step also achieve a better performance than methods only using the visual cues at the beginning step; this observation demonstrates that appropriate utilization of visual information helps boost the performance of image-captioning with rich diverse semantics. We show some examples generated by our model for the MSCOCO dataset in Fig. 4.

4.4.2 Fine-grained semantic interaction

During image captioning, the caption is predicted

(a) A living room filled with furniture and a window

(b) A group of people riding skis down a snow covered slope

(c) A man flying through the air while riding a skateboard

(d) A man standing in a kitchen preparing food

(e) A group of young men playing a game of soccer

(f) A group of people flying kites in a field

Fig. 4 Long descriptions of images generated by our model.

word-by-word in grammatical interaction order. It is interesting to show the prediction performance of the nouns (i.e., the corresponding grounded visual objects) in order (deminstrating how the next noun word is generated). Figure 5 illustrates the average prediction performance of the first 5 noun words in sentences in terms of recall and precision for the Flick8k dataset.

As can be seen in Fig. 5(a), our model (red line with diamond) shows better performance than the other models due to taking into account long-range interactions between visual objects at each prediction step in our model.

Figure 5(b) shows that our model does not perform better than m-RNN. In m-RNN, the whole image is used at each step and therefore mRNN has a tendency to predict noun words for a large region several times. For the test images in the Flick8k dataset, the occurrence rate of one noun word appearing more than once in a sentence is 0.076. The rates of the predicted noun words occurring more than once in a sentence are 0.245 (m-RNN), 0.015 (Neural-Talk), and 0.039 (our model). This demonstrates that our model is capable of generating more diverse rich fine-grained descriptions.

4.4.3 SVO triplet prediction

We next evaluate the performance of our model in terms of predicting SVO (*subject–verb–object*) triplets. First, we found all SVO triplets in the descriptive sentences in the Flickr8k and Flickr30k test data respectively, using the Stanford Parser [33].

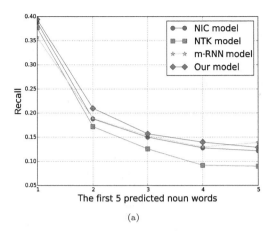

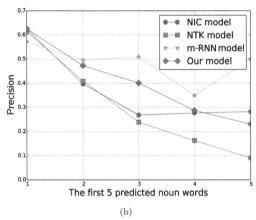

Fig. 5 Recall–precision curves in terms of the first 5 predicted noun words from NIC model, Neural-Talk (NTK) model, m-RNN model, and our model.

For example, given the sentence "a small girl in the grass plays with fingerpaints in front of a white canvas with a rainbow on it", we get the following SVO triplets: (girl, in, grass), (rainbow, on, grass), (girl, play, fingerpaint), (girl, play, rainbow). Then we remove the *object* of each triplet, and feed the visual content (the whole image and the visual objects), the *subject* and the *verb* into each method, and evaluate how well it can predict the removed *object*.

Table 3 compares the ability of different models to predict the removed *object*. R@K (Recall at K) measures whether the correct result is ranked ahead of others. We use R@K ($K = 1, 5, 10, 15, 20$) to compute the fraction of times where the correct result is found among the top K ranked items. A higher R@K means a better performance.

5 Limitations and further work

The major limitation of our model lies in the time taken to train our model. Compared to other models

Table 3 Triplet prediction performance. The best results are shown in boldface

Model	R@1	R@5	R@10	R@15	R@20
	Flickr8k				
Neural-Talk	0.50	1.80	3.00	5.01	6.11
NIC model	0.80	4.91	7.52	9.02	11.52
m-RNN	0.60	5.31	8.82	11.02	13.03
Our model	**1.20**	**6.11**	**9.42**	**12.63**	**14.73**
	Flickr30k				
Neural-Talk	0.30	1.50	2.50	3.30	4.60
NIC model	0.40	1.60	3.30	4.40	5.50
m-RNN	0.40	2.60	4.80	6.60	8.20
Our model	**0.40**	**3.00**	**6.20**	**8.50**	**10.60**

which ignoring contextual interaction between visual cues, our model spends more time for object detection and encoding the long-range implicit contextual interactions. Our model can generate rich fine-grained textual descriptions of each image; it could be further extended to generate much more detailed descriptions of visual objects in each image and much more accurate descriptions of the interactions between visual objects.

6 Conclusions

This paper proposed an LSTM-in-LSTM architecture for image captioning. The proposed model not only encodes long-range *implicit* contextual interactions between visual cues (spatially occurrences of visual objects), but also captures the *explicit* hidden relations between sentences and images (correspondence of sentences and images). The proposed method shows significant improvements over state-of-the-art methods, especially for long sentence descriptions.

Acknowledgements

This work was supported in part by the National Basic Research Program of China (No. 2012CB316400), National Natural Science Foundation of China (Nos. 61472353 and 61572431), China Knowledge Centre for Engineering Sciences and Technology, the Fundamental Research Funds for the Central Universities and 2015 Qianjiang Talents Program of Zhejiang Province. Z. Zhang was supported in part by the US NSF (No. CCF-1017828) and Zhejiang Provincial Engineering Center on Media Data Cloud Processing and Analysis.

References

[1] Farhadi, A.; Hejrati, M.; Sadeghi, M. A.; Young, P.; Rashtchian, C.; Hockenmaier, J.; Forsyth, D. Every picture tells a story: Generating sentences from images. In: *Computer Vision—ECCV 2010*. Daniilidis, K.; Maragos, P.; Paragios, N. Eds. Springer Berlin Heidelberg, 15–29, 2010.

[2] Kulkarni, G.; Premraj, V.; Ordonez, V.; Dhar, S.; Li, S.; Choi, Y.; Berg, A. C.; Berg, T. L. BabyTalk: Understanding and generating simple image descriptions. *IEEE Transactions on Pattern Analysis and Machine Intelligence* Vol. 35, No. 12, 2891–2903, 2013.

[3] Li, S.; Kulkarni, G.; Berg, T. L.; Berg, A. C.; Choi, Y. Composing simple image descriptions using web-scale n-grams. In: Proceedings of the 15th Conference on Computational Natural Language Learning, 220–228, 2011.

[4] Gong, Y.; Wang, L.; Hodosh, M.; Hockenmaier, J.; Lazebnik, S. Improving image-sentence embeddings using large weakly annotated photo collections. In: *Computer Vision—ECCV 2014*. Fleet, D.; Pajdla, T.; Schiele, B.; Tuytelaars, T. Eds. Springer International Publishing, 529–545, 2014.

[5] Hodosh, M.; Young, P.; Hockenmaier, J. Framing image description as a ranking task: Data, models and evaluation metrics. *Journal of Artificial Intelligence Research* Vol. 47, 853–899, 2013.

[6] Ordonez, V.; Kulkarni, G.; Berg, T. L. Im2text: Describing images using 1 million captioned photographs. In: Proceedings of Advances in Neural Information Processing Systems, 1143–1151, 2011.

[7] Socher, R.; Karpathy, A.; Le, Q. V.; Manning, C. D.; Ng, A. Y. Grounded compositional semantics for finding and describing images with sentences. *Transactions of the Association for Computational Linguistics* Vol. 2, 207–218, 2014.

[8] Karpathy, A.; Fei-Fei, L. Deep visual-semantic alignments for generating image descriptions. In: Proceedings of IEEE Conference on Computer Vision and Pattern Recognition, 3128–3137, 2015.

[9] Mao, J.; Xu, W.; Yang, Y.; Wang, J.; Huang, Z.; Yuille, A. Deep captioning with multimodal recurrent neural networks (m-RNN). *arXiv preprint* arXiv:1412.6632, 2014.

[10] Vinyals, O.; Toshev, A.; Bengio, S.; Erhan, D. Show and tell: A neural image caption generator. In: Proceedings of the IEEE Conference on Computer Vision and Pattern Recognition, 3156–3164, 2015.

[11] Jin, J.; Fu, K.; Cui, R.; Sha, F.; Zhang, C. Aligning where to see and what to tell: Image caption with region-based attention and scene factorization. *arXiv preprint* arXiv:1506.06272, 2015.

[12] Xu, K.; Ba, J.; Kiros, R.; Cho, K.; Courville, A.; Salakhutdinov, R.; Zemel, R. S.; Bengio, Y. Show, attend and tell: Neural image caption generation with visual attention. In: Proceedings of the 32nd International Conference on Machine Learning, 2048–2057, 2015.

[13] Bengio, Y.; Schwenk, H.; Senécal, J.-S.; Morin, F.; Gauvain, J.-L. Neural probabilistic language models. In: *Innovations in Machine Learning*. Holmes, D. E.; Jain, L. C. Eds. Springer Berlin Heidelberg, 137–186, 2006.

[14] Palangi, H.; Deng, L.; Shen, Y.; Gao, J.; He, X.; Chen, J.; Song, X.; Ward, R. Deep sentence embedding using the long short term memory network: Analysis and application to information retrieval. *IEEE/ACM Transactions on Audio, Speech, and Language Processing* Vol. 24, No. 4, 694–707, 2016.

[15] Bahdanau, D.; Cho, K.; Bengio, Y. Neural machine translation by jointly learning to align and translate. *arXiv preprint* arXiv:1409.0473, 2014.

[16] Krizhevsky, A.; Sutskever, I.; Hinton, G. E. Imagenet classification with deep convolutional neural networks. In: Proceedings of Advances in Neural Information Processing Systems, 1097–1105, 2012.

[17] Simonyan, K.; Zisserman, A. Very deep convolutional networks for large-scale image recognition. *arXiv preprint* arXiv:1409.1556, 2014.

[18] Girshick, R.; Donahue, J.; Darrell, T.; Malik, J. Rich feature hierarchies for accurate object detection and semantic segmentation. In: Proceedings of IEEE Conference on Computer Vision and Pattern Recognition, 580–587, 2014.

[19] He, K.; Zhang, X.; Ren, S.; Sun, J. Spatial pyramid pooling in deep convolutional networks for visual recognition. In: *Computer Vision—ECCV 2014*. Fleet, D.; Pajdla, T.; Schiele, B.; Tuytelaars, T. Eds. Springer International Publishing, 346–361, 2014.

[20] Girshick, R. Fast r-cnn. In: Proceedings of the IEEE International Conference on Computer Vision, 1440–1448, 2015.

[21] Karpathy, A.; Joulin, A.; Li, F. F. F. Deep fragment embeddings for bidirectional image sentence mapping. In: Proceedings of Advances in Neural Information Processing Systems, 1889–1897, 2014.

[22] Elliott, D.; Keller, F. Image description using visual dependency representations. In: Proceedings of the Conference on Empirical Methods in Natural Language Processing, 1292–1302, 2013.

[23] Sutton, R. S.; Barto, A. G. *Reinforcement Learning: An Introduction*. The MIT Press, 1998.

[24] Sutskever, I.; Vinyals, O.; Le, Q. V. Sequence to sequence learning with neural networks. In: Proceedings of Advances in Neural Information Processing Systems, 3104–3112, 2014.

[25] Graves, A. Generating sequences with recurrent neural networks. *arXiv preprint* arXiv:1308.0850, 2013.

[26] Young, P.; Lai, A.; Hodosh, M.; Hockenmaier, J. From image descriptions to visual denotations: New similarity metrics for semantic inference over event descriptions. *Transactions of the Association for Computational Linguistics* Vol. 2, 67–78, 2014.

[27] Lin, T.-Y.; Maire, M.; Belongie, S.; Hays, J.; Perona,
      P.; Ramanan, D.; Dollár, P.; Zitnick, C. L. Microsoft
      COCO: Common objects in context. In: *Computer
      Vision—ECCV 2014*. Fleet, D.; Pajdla, T.; Schiele, B.;
      Tuytelaars, T. Eds. Springer International Publishing,
      740–755, 2014.

[28] Papineni, K.; Roukos, S.; Ward, T.; Zhu, W.-J.
      BLEU: A method for automatic evaluation of machine
      translation. In: Proceedings of the 40th Annual
      Meeting on Association for Computational Linguistics,
      311–318, 2002.

[29] Lin, C.-Y. ROUGE: A package for automatic
      evaluation of summaries. In: Text Summarization
      Branches Out: Proceedings of the ACL-04 Workshop,
      Vol. 8, 2004.

[30] Kuznetsova, P.; Ordonez, V.; Berg, A. C.; Berg,
      T. L.; Choi, Y. Collective generation of natural
      image descriptions. In: Proceedings of the 50th
      Annual Meeting of the Association for Computational
      Linguistics: Long Papers, Vol. 1, 359–368, 2012.

[31] Vedantam, R.; Zitnick, C. L.; Parikh, D. CIDEr:
      Consensus-based image description evaluation. In:
      Proceedings of the IEEE Conference on Computer
      Vision and Pattern Recognition, 4566–4575, 2015.

[32] Denkowski, M.; Lavie, A. Meteor universal: Language
      specific translation evaluation for any target language.
      In: Proceedings of the 9th Workshop on Statistical
      Machine Translation, 2014.

[33] De Marneffe, M.-C.; Manning, C. D. The Stanford
      typed dependencies representation. In: Proceedings of
      the Workshop on Cross-Framework and Cross-Domain
      Parser Evaluation, 1–8, 2008.

9

Robust camera pose estimation by viewpoint classification using deep learning

Yoshikatsu Nakajima[1] (✉), Hideo Saito[1]

Abstract Camera pose estimation with respect to target scenes is an important technology for superimposing virtual information in augmented reality (AR). However, it is difficult to estimate the camera pose for all possible view angles because feature descriptors such as SIFT are not completely invariant from every perspective. We propose a novel method of robust camera pose estimation using multiple feature descriptor databases generated for each partitioned viewpoint, in which the feature descriptor of each keypoint is almost invariant. Our method estimates the viewpoint class for each input image using deep learning based on a set of training images prepared for each viewpoint class. We give two ways to prepare these images for deep learning and generating databases. In the first method, images are generated using a projection matrix to ensure robust learning in a range of environments with changing backgrounds. The second method uses real images to learn a given environment around a planar pattern. Our evaluation results confirm that our approach increases the number of correct matches and the accuracy of camera pose estimation compared to the conventional method.

Keywords pose estimation; augmented reality (AR); deep learning; convolutional neural network

1 Introduction

Since augmented reality (AR) toolkit [1] introduced the superimposition of virtual information onto planar patterns in images by real-time estimation of camera pose, technologies for markerless camera-tracking technology have become mainstream [2, 3]. Markerless tracking needs to find a point of correspondence between the input image and the planar pattern for any camera pose.

Lowe's SIFT [4] is one of the most famous algorithms in computer vision for detecting keypoints and describing local features in images. SIFT detects keypoints using differences of Gaussians to approximate a Laplacian of Gaussian filter and describes them using a 128-dimensional feature vector. Then, keypoint correspondences are obtained using Euclidean distances between feature vectors. Although SIFT is robust in the face of scaling and rotation [5], when the input image is distorted due to projection distortion of the planar pattern, we cannot find keypoint correspondences. *Randomised trees* (RT) [6] improve the problem by training a variety of descriptors for each keypoint using affine transformations, and generating a tree structure [7] based on the resulting brightness values, for real-time recognition of keypoint identity. *Viewpoint generative learning* (VGL), developed by Yoshida et al. [8], extends this idea to train various descriptors for every keypoint by generating images as if they were taken from various viewpoints using a projection transformation, and generating a database of keypoints and features from the images.

However, methods based on training feature descriptors of keypoints, such as RT and VGL, trade robustness of the various descriptors against computation time when searching for matched keypoints. For example, VGL compresses the database of training descriptors using k-means clustering [9] for fast search, but this sometimes results in wrong keypoint matching, especially when the camera angle is shallow. Because feature descriptors of keypoints change significantly at a

---

1 Department of Science and Technology, Keio University, Japan. E-mail: Y. Nakajima, nakajima@hvrl.ics.keio.ac.jp (✉); H. Saito, saito@hvrl.ics.keio.ac.jp.

shallow angle, weak compression of the database is required to allow such shallow camera angles, but this increases the computation for keypoint search.

In this paper, we propose a novel method for camera pose estimation based on two-stage keypoint matching to solve the trade-off problem. The first stage is viewpoint classification using a *convolutional neural network* (CNN) [10–12], so that the feature descriptors of every keypoint are similar from the classified viewpoints. The second stage is camera pose estimation based on accurate keypoint matching, which is achieved in the classified viewpoint using a nearest neighbor (NN) search for the descriptor. To achieve this two-stage camera pose estimation, in pre-processing, our method generates the uncompressed descriptor databases of a planar pattern for each partitioned viewpoint, including a shallow angle, and trains a CNN to classify the viewpoint of the input image.

A CNN can perform stable classification against variations of a property for the same class by learning from a large amount of data with variations for each class. For instance, object recognition which is stable under viewpoint changes can be performed by learning from many images taken from various viewpoints for each object class [13]. This stable performance against viewpoint change is not achieved by just the structure of the CNN, but through the capability of a CNN to learn from variable data for each class. For example, Agrawal et al. [14] applied a CNN to estimate egomotion by constructing a network model with two inputs comprising two images whose viewpoints slightly differ. In this paper, we apply a CNN to a viewpoint classification for a single object.

Additional reasons for using a CNN for viewpoint classification are as follows. Firstly, a CNN is robust to occlusion. This is very important, as it widens

the range of applications. Secondly, computation time is unchanged as the number of viewpoint classes increases, enabling us to easily analyze the trade-off relationship between accuracy and size.

We introduce two methods for generating a database and preparing the images for deep learning, under the assumption that those methods might be used in different ways. The first one is robust for a range of environments and is used to initialize camera pose estimation, etc. The second method learns the entire environment around the planar pattern and is used in a learned environment.

The NN search in the second stage is not time-consuming, because little variety is necessary in the descriptors in the classified viewpoint in the first stage. The camera pose of the input image is computed based on correspondences between matched keypoints.

2 Method

Figure 1 shows the flow of our proposed method, which consists of three parts. The first part generates databases of features for every viewpoint class, which are partitioned into viewing angles from the entire viewing angle range ($-90° < \theta < 90°$, $-180° < \phi < 180°$) with respect to a target planar pattern, as shown in Fig. 2. The second part trains the CNN to classify the viewpoint of the input image. The last part estimates the camera pose of the input image. We now explain each part in detail.

In particular, during database generation (Section 2.1) and CNN training (Section 2.2), we use two methods to prepare images for database generation and deep learning by the CNN, with the assumption that these methods are to be used in different ways.

The first method uses only one image of the planar pattern and generates many images by use

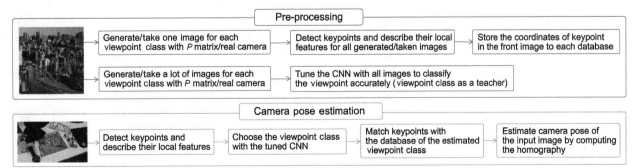

Fig. 1 Flow of proposed method. Top: database generation, middle: deep learning by the CNN, bottom: camera pose estimation.

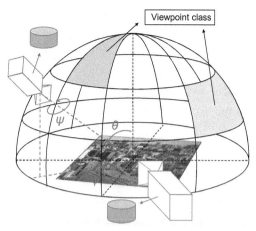

Fig. 2 Generating databases: viewpoint class, virtual camera, and angle definitions.

of projection matrices (P matrices). This reduces the learning cost because it only uses a single image and P matrices. Moreover, this enables the CNN to be robust with changes in background of the input image, because we can vary the backgrounds of the images generated for deep learning. Viewpoint class estimation will not be extremely accurate; however, because the CNN only uses the appearance of the planar pattern in the input image, so this first method is not suitable for movies. On the other hand, it can manage shallow angles better than the conventional method, so it is useful for the initialization of the camera pose, etc. From now on, we call this method *learning based on generated viewpoints*.

The second method uses real images by fixing the planar pattern within the environment and taking pictures with a camera. The CNN can learn not only about the appearance of the planar pattern but also the environment around it, including the background, the lighting, and so on. Therefore, the viewpoint class of the input image can be estimated with almost perfect precision, so this method is suitable for movies. However, the CNN can be only used in the environment in which the planar pattern is fixed when images for deep learning are taken. In contrast to the first method, we call this method *learning based on example viewpoints*.

2.1 Database generation

In this part, we generate one feature database per viewpoint class. Each database is generated from one image because features sampled from a certain viewpoint are almost identical in the viewpoint

class, so one image is enough. As mentioned in the introduction, we use two methods for preparing images for database generation. Firstly, we will explain the method using one image and a P matrix, which is robust in various environments. Secondly, we will explain the method using real images taken by a camera, which is more robust in the particular environment in which the pre-processing is performed. This flow is shown in the upper part of Fig. 1.

2.1.1 Learning based on generated viewpoints

Firstly, we partition the entire range of viewing angles of the camera's viewpoint with respect to a target pattern. We call each partitioned viewpoint a viewpoint class (see Fig. 2). Secondly, we compute the projection matrices that transform the frontal image to images which appear to have been taken from the center of each viewpoint class, using Eq. (1). From now on, we will denote the number of viewpoint classes by N, the viewpoint classes by V_i ($i = 1, \ldots, N$), and the projection matrix for each viewpoint class V_i by $\boldsymbol{P}_i$. In Eq. (1), let the intrinsic parameters of the virtual camera, the rotation matrix for viewpoint class V_i, and the translation vector, be $\boldsymbol{A}$, $\boldsymbol{R}_i$, and $\boldsymbol{t}$, respectively. The matrix $\boldsymbol{R}_i$ is given by Eq. (2), using θ, ϕ, and ψ defined as in Fig. 2.

$$\boldsymbol{P}_i = \boldsymbol{A}(\boldsymbol{R}_i | \boldsymbol{t}) \tag{1}$$

$$\boldsymbol{R}_i = \begin{pmatrix} \cos\psi & -\sin\psi & 0 \\ \sin\psi & \cos\psi & 0 \\ 0 & 0 & 1 \end{pmatrix} \begin{pmatrix} \cos\phi & \theta & \sin\phi \\ 0 & 1 & 0 \\ -\sin\phi & 0 & \cos\phi \end{pmatrix} \begin{pmatrix} 1 & 0 & 0 \\ 0 & \cos\theta & -\sin\theta \\ 0 & \sin\theta & \cos\theta \end{pmatrix} \tag{2}$$

Using the projection matrix $\boldsymbol{P}_i$, we obtain an image I_i for each viewpoint class V_i. Next, we detect keypoints and describe their local features for each image I_i, using the appropriate algorithm. We denote the number of detected keypoints by M_i, each keypoint by p_{ij}, and each feature by d_{ij} ($j = 1, \ldots, M_i$). Then we compute a homography matrix $\boldsymbol{H}_i$ that transforms the image I_i, which represents the viewpoint class V_i, to the frontal image. We also generate the database in which the described features d_{ij} and their coordinates p'_{ij} in the frontal image are stored. The coordinates p'_{ij} are found by transforming the coordinates of each detected keypoint p_{ij} to the frontal image using the equation $p'_{ij} = \boldsymbol{H}_i p_{ij}$. By performing this process on all images that represent each viewpoint class, we obtain one uncompressed descriptor database per viewpoint class.

2.1.2 Learning based on example viewpoints

For this method, we first use the camera to take multiple viewpoints of the planar pattern that is fixed in the environment. Next, for each image I_i, we compute a homography matrix $\boldsymbol{H}_i$ that transforms the image I_i to the frontal image. In this computation, we use four points whose coordinates in the frontal image are easily determined, like corners. Equation (3) can be used to compute the homography matrix $\boldsymbol{H}_i$:

$$\tilde{\boldsymbol{x}}' \sim \boldsymbol{H}\tilde{\boldsymbol{x}} \qquad (3)$$

Here, we denote the coordinates in the frontal image of the planar pattern by $\tilde{\boldsymbol{x}}' \sim (x', y', 1)^{\mathrm{T}}$ and the coordinates in the taken image as $\tilde{\boldsymbol{x}} \sim (x, y, 1)^{\mathrm{T}}$. Then, we detect keypoints and describe their local features in the image I_i using the appropriate algorithm. We denote the number of detected keypoints by M_i, each keypoint by p_{ij}, and each feature by d_{ij} $(j = 1, \ldots, M_i)$. The keypoint p_{ij} can be projected into p'_{ij}, which represents the coordinates in the frontal image, using $p'_{ij} = \boldsymbol{H}_i p_{ij}$. Finally, we generate the database for each image; multiple sets of p'_{ij} and d_{ij} are stored. By judging whether the coordinates of p'_{ij} are on the planar pattern or not, we can eliminate features belonging to the environment when we store features belonging to the planar pattern in the database.

2.2 Deep learning by the CNN

We train a CNN for the purpose of classifying the viewpoint of the input image. A CNN is a deep neural network mainly used for object recognition. We apply a CNN to viewpoint classification of a single planar pattern. In this step, we only use images, and do not use features for deep learning, because we employ a CNN that only receives images as input. As we do with database generation, we will explain the two methods of preparing images for deep learning. However, the deep learning processing explained below should use the same method as that used for the database generation step. This process is illustrated in the middle row of Fig. 1.

2.2.1 Learning based on generated viewpoints

Firstly, we generate multiple images for each viewpoint class V_i using Eq. (1). Then we randomly change the background of every image and the position and scale of the planar pattern. By using these images for deep learning, the weight of the background part is reduced and the CNN can classify the viewpoint robustly. Here, we employ a softmax function as the activation function of the output layer and make its number of units coincide with the number of viewpoint classes—this is the CNN design recommended for classification problems. Finally, we perform deep learning by teaching the CNN the correct viewpoint class for each generated image using the techniques of back-propagation [15], pre-training [16], and drop-out [17]. In general, it is a problem for deep learning to prepare images for training, but our method uses images synthesized from a single planar pattern, enabling us to reduce the learning cost.

2.2.2 Learning based on example viewpoints

For each image I_i, we take multiple images of the planar pattern for deep learning from the same viewpoint as that used for image I_i. We then change the scale and the rotation to help ensure that the CNN is robust. Deep learning is performed as in Section 2.2.1, i.e., we employ a softmax function in the output layer, we make its number of units coincide with the number of the viewpoint classes, and we teach the CNN the correct viewpoint class for every image.

2.3 Camera pose estimation

In this section, we explain the details of camera pose estimation given the input image. This process is shown at the bottom of Fig. 1. We detect keypoints and describe their local features in the image using the same algorithm as that used to generate the databases. Next, we input the image to the CNN, which has been tuned by deep learning. Because the activation function of the output layer is a softmax function, the percentage informs us which viewpoint class the image belongs to (see Fig. 3). We select the viewpoint class with the highest percentage and compare keypoints in the database for that viewpoint class with keypoints in the input image in terms of the Euclidean distance of their feature descriptors. Then we search for the nearest keypoint and the next nearest as suggested by Mikolajczy et al. [18], so that we can use the ratio to reduce mismatches between keypoints. Only when the Euclidean distance to the nearest keypoint is sufficiently smaller than the Euclidean distance to the second one, there is a match. Thus, D_{A} and D_{B} are matched only when

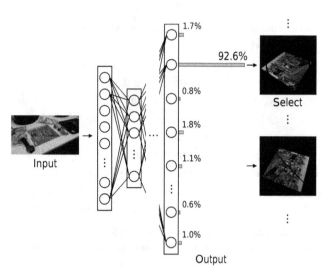

Fig. 3 Viewpoint class estimation using CNN.

Eq. (4) is satisfied:

$$\frac{\|D_A - D_B\|}{\|D_A - D_C\|} < t \qquad (4)$$

Here, D_A, D_B, and D_C represent the feature descriptor of the input image, the feature descriptor of the nearest keypoint in the database, and the feature descriptor of the second nearest, respectively. If we set the threshold t large, the number of matches increases as well as the number of mismatches; conversely, if we set the threshold t small, the number of matches reduces as well as the number of mismatches.

By matching keypoints between the database and the input image, we can obtain corresponding points in the input image and the frontal image, as feature descriptors and their coordinates in the frontal image are stored in each database. After mismatches are reduced by RANSAC [19], we estimate the camera pose of the input image by computing the homography that transforms the frontal image to the input image using the coordinates of those correspondinge points.

3 Experimental evaluation

In this section, we demonstrate the validity of our method through experiments. In Section 2, we introduce two methods of preparing images for database generation and deep learning. Because those methods have different uses, we evaluate them with different datasets. We use VGL [8] as a basis for comparison. Conventional methods of camera pose estimation with CNN are typified by

PoseNet, as described by Kendall et al.; however, such a method does not use SIFT-like point-based features, while VGL does use point-based matching. Furthermore, VGL is more robust than other conventional methods that use point-based matching like ASIFT [20] and *random ferns* [21]. Thus, we compare our method to VGL.

3.1 Experimental setup

The evaluation environment was as follows. CPU: Intel Core i7-4770K 3.5 GHz, GPU: GeForce GTX760, and RAM: 16 GB. The definition of viewpoint class and the datasets are different for the two methods, and will be explained separately. The deep learning framework used in this evaluation experiment was Chainer [22].

3.1.1 Learning based on generated viewpoints

For this method, we defined the viewpoint class V_i by splitting the viewpoints for observing the planar pattern as shown in Table 1. As features change more at a shallow angle, we subdivided the viewpoint more as angle θ increased. Thus, the number of viewpoint classes was $4 + 8 + 12 + 12 = 36$ in this experiment.

As for ψ, due to use of rotation invariant features including SIFT, we obtained many keypoint matches between the input image and the database for every values of camera pose angle ψ for the input image.

Next, we generated images I_i to represent each viewpoint class V_i using Eq. (1), using angles θ and ϕ at the center of each viewpoint class V_i. We used SIFT to detect keypoints p_{ij} and describe their local features d_{ij}. We used *network-in-network* (NIN) [23] to constitute the CNN. NIN is useful for reducing classification time by reducing the number of parameters while maintaining high accuracy. To tune the parameters of the CNN by deep learning, we generated about three thousand images for each viewpoint class V_i. The background images were prepared by capturing each frame from a movie taken indoors. Furthermore, we randomly changed the radius of the sphere (see Fig. 2) and the angle ψ when we generated the images for deep learning. Doing so allows estimation of the viewpoint class with the trained CNN even if the camera distance and the

Table 1 Viewpoint class definition

Range of θ	0°–19°	20°–39°	40°–59°	60°–79°
Partitions of ϕ	4	8	12	12

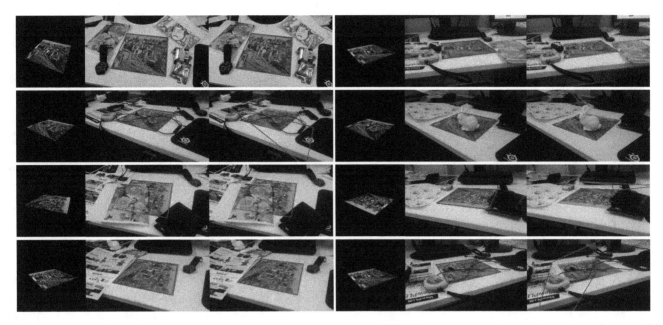

Fig. 4 Viewpoint class and camera pose estimation results using our method and VGL [8], using evaluation images. Left: estimated viewpoint class, center: our method, right: VGL [8].

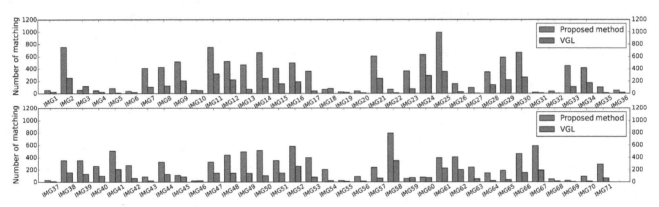

Fig. 5 Number of keypoint matches.

camera orientation with respect to the input image change.

We prepared 71 images of the planar pattern, including ones taken from a shallow angle and ones in which the planar pattern was occluded. Using those images, we compared the accuracy of camera pose estimation, the number of correct matches, and the processing time with the corresponding values for VGL. For VGL, we generated a database using the same images as in our method and set the number of clusters to five and the number of stable keypoints to 2000.

3.1.2 Learning based on example viewpoints

In this method, we took 22 images I_i ($N = 22$) of a planar pattern from multiple viewpoints after fixing the planar pattern onto a desk. These images define the viewpoint class V_i (see Fig. 2), so

there were 22 viewpoint classes in this experiment. Using those images I_i, we generated 22 feature databases containing the coordinates p'_{ij} of all detected keypoints and their local features d_{ij}. We employed SIFT as a keypoint detector and a feature descriptor, and used the coordinates of four corners to compute $\boldsymbol{H}_i$ used to transform coordinates p_{ij} to coordinates p'_{ij}. We again employed NIN as the network model for the CNN. Next, we generated about 600 images for each viewpoint class V_i by clipping every frame of movies that we took from around the viewpoint of each of the 22 images I_i. By teaching the correct viewpoint class for every prepared image to the CNN using deep learning, the CNN became able to estimate the viewpoint class for each input image. Again in this method, we randomly changed the camera distance and the angle

ψ when we prepared the images for deep learning to make the CNN robust to changes in scale and rotation.

For the evaluation experiment, we prepared a movie of the fixed planar pattern, including frames taken from a shallow angle, in the same environment as the one used for database generation and image preparation for deep learning.

In this experiment, we evaluated the estimated camera pose from the re-projection error of the corners of the planar pattern. Denoting the coordinates of the corners observed in the test image by P_k, and the coordinates of the corners re-projected using the estimated homography $\boldsymbol{H}$ by Q_k, the re-projection error E is given by the following equation:

$$E = \sqrt{\frac{1}{4} \sum_{k=1}^{4} \|P_k - Q_k\|^2} \qquad (5)$$

E represents the average Euclidean distance of the four corners between the ground-truth coordinates and the estimated coordinates. Minimising E gives the camera pose estimation.

To compare VGL with this method, we generated a database with the same 22 images used for our method and set the number of clusters to five and the number of stable keypoints to 2000.

3.2 Results

We now describe the results of the experimental evaluation of each method.

3.2.1 Learning based on generated viewpoints

Figure 4 shows the results of viewpoint class estimation by the CNN, and camera pose estimation using our method and VGL. The left image indicates the viewpoint class estimated by the CNN for the input image, the center image shows the result of camera pose estimation by our method, and the right image is the result from VGL. We visualize camera pose estimation by re-projecting coordinates of the four corners of the frontal image using the computed homography and connecting them with red lines. Images without red lines indicate lacked sufficient matches to compute the homography. Figure 5 gives the number of keypoint matches used to compute the homography for each of the 71 images.

As Fig. 4 shows, our method estimated camera pose more robustly for shallow angles than the conventional method. Figure 5 shows that the number of matches was higher for our method than for the conventional method, for almost all images. Because our method matches keypoints between the input image and a database that was generated using an image similar to the input image, matching was more accurate with our method. Although the planar pattern is occluded in some images in Fig. 4, our method estimated the viewpoint class and camera pose accurately. Because deep CNNs give robust results in the presence of occlusion [13], and the uncompressed descriptor databases of the planar pattern are generated for each viewpoint class, our method was robust to occlusion.

Regarding the accuracy of viewpoint classification, 7 of 71 images were incorrectly classified. However, 4 of these 7 images were successfully classified into the adjacent viewpoint class, so that keypoint matching works well enough, and the camera pose is estimated reasonably precisely. Features in the adjacent viewpoint class are similar to features in the correct one since the database for the next viewpoint class is generated from an image taken from a viewpoint next to the correct viewpoint. This allows the second step of accurate localization to still have a chance to correct the errors, making the algorithm robust. In contrast, 3 of 7 images were classified into a completely different viewpoint class, so camera pose estimation failed. Overall, viewpoint class estimation was about 90% accurate because the CNN only uses the appearance of the planar pattern in the input image. Therefore, this method is not suitable for movies. On the other hand, it copes with shallow angles (see Fig. 4), so it is useful for initialization of the camera pose and similar tasks. Furthermore, when using our method in applications, we can easily combine it with a conventional tracking method. By doing that, we can estimate camera pose continuously while coping with shallow angles.

Next, we consider processing time. Table 2 shows the average processing time for our method and VGL for all images, for each stage of camera pose estimation, and in total.

The overhead for viewpoint class estimation in our method is small. Detecting keypoints and describing feature descriptors using SIFT account for the most of the processing time. We could easily apply our method to a binary algorithm

Table 2 Average time spent on each processing stage

(Unit: ms)

	Our method	VGL
SIFT	201	214
Viewpoint class estimation	9	—
Matching	35	28
Homography computation	10	2
Total	255	244

like AKAZE [24] because it generates uncompressed descriptor databases. Thus, we could reduce the processing time spent on detecting keypoints and describing features in our method.

3.2.2 Learning based on example viewpoints

Figure 6 shows some results of camera pose estimation using our method and VGL, for a movie that we prepared for this evaluation. The camera pose was estimated using the method described in Section 3.2.1. Figure 7 shows the re-projection error computed with Eq. (5) for each frame of the movie. The ground-truth coordinates of the corners were detected manually. Figure 8 shows the number of keypoint matches between the input image and the estimated ones used for computation of the homography.

As shown in Fig. 6, this method also estimated camera pose for shallow angles more robustly than the conventional method. In Fig. 8, the number of matches fluctuates because the database used for keypoint matching was changed by the CNN every few frames. As shown by Figs. 6–8, the accuracy of camera pose estimation using VGL decreased for shallow angles and the features changed drastically, because VGL compresses features using k-means for fast computation. On the other hand, our method estimates the camera pose more robustly because the database that contains all features sampled from images similar to the input image is appropriately selected by the CNN.

With this method, viewpoint class estimation accuracy is almost 100% (see Fig. 7), because the CNN can learn not only the appearance of the planar

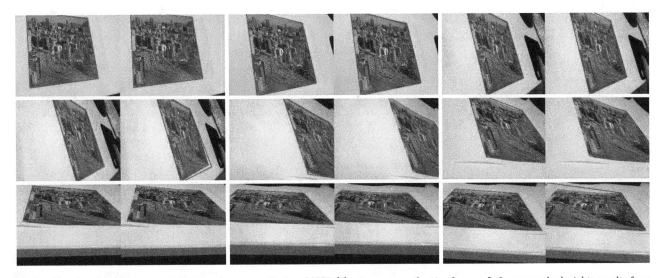

Fig. 6 Results of camera pose estimation using our method and VGL [8] using some evaluation frames. Left: our method, right: results from VGL [8].

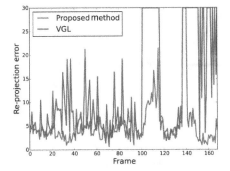

Fig. 7 Re-projection errors.

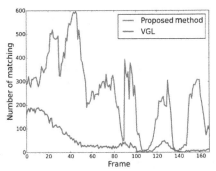

Fig. 8 Number of matches.

pattern but also the environment around it: the background, the lighting, and so on. However, the CNN can be only used in the same environment as the one in which the planar pattern was given and deep learning has been performed.

We next discuss processing time. Figure 9 shows the processing frame rate. Again, the overhead for viewpoint class estimation in the proposed method is sufficiently small.

3.2.3 Number of viewpoint classes

The number of viewpoint classes affects the results of camera pose estimation and the size of the databases. Therefore, we generated 100 test images with homographies and evaluated how the number of viewpoint classes affected the results for the method of learning based on generated viewpoints. Table 3 shows the re-projection error calculated by Eq. (5) and the database size when changing the number of viewpoint classes.

The re-projection error decreases with an increasing number of viewpoint classes since the input image and the matching image in the database become closer by splitting the viewpoint more finely. However, the size of the database is also increased as the number of generated databases is also increased. Thus, accuracy and size must be traded-off according to the particular application.

4 Conclusions

We have proposed a method for robust camera pose estimation using uncompressed descriptor databases

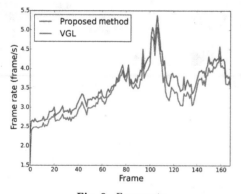

Fig. 9 Frame rate.

Table 3 Re-projection error and database size with respect to the number of viewpoint classes

Viewpoint classes	12	36	52
Re-projection error	1.21	0.90	0.81
Database size	16.6 MB	49.4 MB	67.9 MB

generated for each viewpoint class. Our method classifies the viewpoint of each input image using a CNN that is trained by deep learning so that keypoints of the input image can be matched almost perfectly with the database. We gave two ways of generating these databases and preparing the images for deep learning. These methods have different applications. The first is robust in a changing environment, while the second allows the CNN to learn the entire environment around the planar pattern. We have experimentally confirmed that the number of keypoint matches was higher, and the accuracy of camera pose estimation was better, than with a conventional method.

The application of our method to three-dimensional objects is our future work.

References

[1] Kato, H.; Billinghurst, M. Marker tracking and HMD calibration for a video-based augmented reality conferencing system. In: Proceedings of the 2nd IEEE and ACM International Workshop on Augmented Reality, 85–94, 1999.

[2] Lee, T.; Hollerer, T. Hybrid feature tracking and user interaction for markerless augmented reality. In: Proceedings of IEEE Virtual Reality Conference, 145–152, 2008.

[3] Maidi, M.; Preda, M.; Le, V. H. Markerless tracking for mobile augmented reality. In: Proceedings of IEEE International Conference on Signal and Image Processing Applications, 301–306, 2011.

[4] Lowe, D. G. Distinctive image features from scale-invariant keypoints. *International Journal of Computer Vision* Vol. 60, No. 2, 91–110, 2004.

[5] Mikolajczyk, K.; Schmid, C. A performance evaluation of local descriptors. *IEEE Transactions on Pattern Analysis and Machine Intelligence* Vol. 27, No. 10, 1615–1630, 2005.

[6] Lepetit, V.; Fua, P. Keypoint recognition using randomized trees. *IEEE Transactions on Pattern Analysis and Machine Intelligence* Vol. 28, No. 9, 1465–1479, 2006.

[7] Breiman, L. Random forests. *Machine Learning* Vol. 45, No. 1, 5–32, 2001.

[8] Yoshida, T.; Saito, H.; Shimizu, M.; Taguchi, A. Stable keypoint recognition using viewpoint generative learning. In: Proceedings of the International Conference on Computer Vision Theory and Applications, Vol. 2, 310–315, 2013.

[9] Hartigan, J. A.; Wong, M. A. Algorithm AS 136: A *k*-means clustering algorithm. *Journal of the Royal Statistical Society. Series C (Applied Statistics)* Vol. 28, No. 1, 100–108, 1979.

[10] Fukushima, K.; Miyake, S. Neocognitron: A new algorithm for pattern recognition tolerant of

deformations and shifts in position. *Pattern Recognition* Vol. 15, No. 6, 455–469, 1982.

[11] Hubel, D. H.; Wiesel, T. N. Receptive fields, binocular interaction and functional architecture in the cat's visual cortex. *The Journal of Physiology* Vol. 160, No. 1, 106–154, 1962.

[12] LeCun, Y.; Boser, B.; Denker, J. S.; Henderson, D.; Howard, R. E.; Hubbard, W.; Jackel, L. D. Backpropagation applied to handwritten zip code recognition. *Neural Computation* Vol. 1, No. 4, 541–551, 1989.

[13] Russakovsky, O.; Deng, J.; Su, H.; Krause, J.; Satheesh, S.; Ma, S.; Huang, Z.; Karpathy, A.; Khosla, A.; Bernstein, M.; Berg, A. C.; Fei-Fei, L. ImageNet large scale visual recognition challenge. *International Journal of Computer Vision* Vol. 115, No. 3, 211–252, 2015.

[14] Agrawal, P.; Carreira, J.; Malik, J. Learning to see by moving. In: Proceedings of IEEE International Conference on Computer Vision, 37–45, 2015.

[15] Rumelhart, D. E.; Hintont, G. E.; Williams, R. J. Learning representations by back-propagating errors. *Nature* Vol. 323, 533–536, 1986.

[16] Hinton, G. E.; Srivastava, N.; Krizhevsky, A.; Sutskever, I.; Salakhutdinov, R. Improving neural networks by preventing co-adaptation of feature detectors. *arXiv preprint* arXiv:1207.0580, 2012.

[17] Krizhevsky, A.; Sutskever, I.; Hinton, G. E. ImageNet classification with deep convolutional neural network. In: Proceedings of Advances in Neural Information Processing Systems, 1097–1105, 2012.

[18] Mikolajczyk, K.; Tuytelaars, T.; Schmid, C.; Zisserman, A.; Matas, J.; Schaffalitzky, F.; Kadir, T.; GooL, L. V. A comparison of affine region detectors. *International Journal of Computer Vision* Vol. 65, No. 1, 43–72, 2005.

[19] Fischler, M. A.; Bolles, R. C. Random sample consensus: A paradigm for model fitting with applications to image analysis and automated cartography. *Communications of the ACM* Vol. 24, No. 6, 381–395, 1981.

[20] Yu, G.; Morel, J.-M. ASIFT: An algorithm for fully affine invariant comparison. *Image Processing On Line* Vol. 1, 1–28, 2011.

[21] Ozuysal, M.; Calonder, M.; Lepetit, V.; Fua, P. Fast keypoint recognition using random ferns. *IEEE Transactions on Pattern Analysis and Machine Intelligence* Vol. 32, No. 3, 448–461, 2009.

[22] Tokui, S.; Oono, K.; Hido, S.; Clayton, J. Chainer: A next-generation open source framework for deep learning. In: Proceedings of Workshop on Machine Learning Systems (LearningSys) in the 29th Annual Conference on Neural Information Processing Systems, 2015.

[23] Lin, M.; Chen, Q.; Yan, S. Network in network. *arXiv preprint* arXiv:1312.4400, 2013.

10

EasySVM: A visual analysis approach for open-box support vector machines

Yuxin Ma[1], Wei Chen[1](✉), Xiaohong Ma[1], Jiayi Xu[1], Xinxin Huang[1], Ross Maciejewski[2], and Anthony K. H. Tung[3]

Abstract Support vector machines (SVMs) are supervised learning models traditionally employed for classification and regression analysis. In classification analysis, a set of training data is chosen, and each instance in the training data is assigned a categorical class. An SVM then constructs a model based on a separating plane that maximizes the margin between different classes. Despite being one of the most popular classification models because of its strong performance empirically, understanding the knowledge captured in an SVM remains difficult. SVMs are typically applied in a black-box manner where the details of parameter tuning, training, and even the final constructed model are hidden from the users. This is natural since these details are often complex and difficult to understand without proper visualization tools. However, such an approach often brings about various problems including trial-and-error tuning and suspicious users who are forced to trust these models blindly.

The contribution of this paper is a visual analysis approach for building SVMs in an open-box manner. Our goal is to improve an analyst's understanding of the SVM modeling process through a suite of visualization techniques that allow users to have full interactive visual control over the entire SVM training process. Our visual exploration tools have been developed to enable intuitive parameter tuning, training data manipulation, and rule extraction as part of the SVM training process. To demonstrate the efficacy of our approach, we conduct a case study using a real-world robot control dataset.

Keywords support vector machines (SVMs); rule extraction; visual classification; high-dimensional visualization; visual analysis

1 Introduction

A support vector machine (SVM) [1] is a supervised learning method widely used in a variety of application areas, such as text analysis [2], computer vision [3], and bioinformatics [4, 5]. An SVM model is a discriminative model which tries to split the training data into two classes by creating a *separating hyper-plane* at the place where the two classes are furthest apart. The class of a new data point is predicted by determining which side of the hyper-plane it lies on.

While SVMs have been shown to have high accuracy in classification [6], they also face a variety of challenges when we want to use them for data analytics. First, conventional SVM approaches are *black-box* schemes in which details of the model construction and prediction processes are hidden from the user. The user simply provides the SVM with a training dataset and relevant input parameters, and a model is constructed for making predictions from unlabelled data. Other outputs that can be retrieved from the trained SVM model are a vector that represents the feature weights, and a set of training data instances called *support vectors*. These outputs are unable to provide any insights for domain users who want to better understand

1 State Key Lab of CAD&CG, Zhejiang University, Hangzhou, 310058, China. E-mail: Y. Ma, mayuxin@zju.edu.cn; W. Chen, chenwei@cad.zju.edu.cn (✉); X. Ma, maxiao1112@foxmail.com; J. Xu, jiayi.xu64@gmail.com; X. Huang, huangxinxin07@gmail.com.

2 Arizona State University, USA. E-mail: rmacieje@asu.edu.

3 National University of Singapore, Singapore. E-mail: atung@comp.nus.edu.sg.

the reasoning behind certain classification results. Thus, while the automatic black-box model releases the user from laborious interaction, it may hinder the user in terms of understanding and insight. Previous work by Tzeng and Ma [7] indicates that users can gain much insight if allowed to apply function-based techniques that can be explained and validated. Such function-based methods enable the interpretation of the classification process with respect to the application domain. The importance of gaining such insight has motivated data mining algorithms [8, 9] that try to extract *if-then-structured* rules from the classification model.

Another issue that makes gaining insight from SVMs difficult is the use of non-linear kernels [10] which typically improve the classification accuracy. There is, however, a lack of systematic, effective methods to select appropriate kernel functions and input parameters to give good classification results [11]. Thus, tuning parameters in this black-box environment can be extremely difficult and time-consuming for the user. In addition, the non-linear characteristic further complicates the difficulties of interpreting the classification process. While recently developed local model techniques [11, 12] have effectively reduced the complexity of non-linear SVMs by approximating the boundaries with multiple local linear planes, interpreting the complex patterns and data distributions at the boundaries remains complicated.

In order to overcome these challenges, we have designed an open-box approach where the user is embedded in the modeling process and equipped with tools to explore and study complex circumstances. We believe the key to shifting from a *black-box* to an *open-box* approach is to empower the user with a visual analytics interface which will enable a better understanding of SVMs, the underlying dataset, and the classification process. Specifically, our interface design focuses on these three questions:

- Q1: How can we help the user to be better informed about the training dataset and the model building process of SVMs?
- Q2: How can we enable the user to effectively understand non-linear decision boundaries and build local models that fit the boundaries?
- Q3: How can we help the user to interpret and manipulate the prediction results in a user-friendly

way?

This paper presents our efforts in opening the black box of model building and knowledge extraction from SVMs. In this paper, we propose our design and implementation of a web-based visual analysis system that supports model building using SVMs. To the best of our knowledge, this paper is the first to address the issues of open-box analysis of SVMs in the visual analytics literature. The main contributions include:

- an interactive visualization method for exploring data instances, linear SVMs, and their relationships;
- a visual analysis approach for building local linear SVM models that overcomes the non-linearity of the underlying dataset;
- a visual rule extraction method that allows the user to extract rules that best interpret the models.

The remaining sections are organized as follows. Related work is covered in Section 2. Section 3 presents an introduction to SVMs. The next section describes our visual analysis solutions for three tasks: model building and explanation, local SVM building, and rule extraction. Section 5 demonstrates the effectiveness of our solution through a case study on robot control, and is followed by a discussion in Section 6 and conclusions in Section 7.

2 Related work

The work presented in this paper is related to three broad topics: (i) support vector machines, (ii) visual exploration of high-dimensional data, and (iii) visual classification.

2.1 Support vector machines

SVMs are currently regarded as a state-of-the-art classification technique [6], and studies have revealed that SVMs perform well when compared to other classification techniques [13]. This performance can be partly attributed to the use of non-linear kernels which unfortunately make it difficult to interpret the models. In addition, the production of the boundary function is often quite difficult. Work by Wahba [14] explored the use of SVM functionals to produce classification boundaries, exploring tradeoffs between the size of the SVM functional and the smoothing parameters.

In practice, it is very difficult for non-experienced

users to tune an SVM [15]. However, recently, a set of methods were developed to simplify model complexity while managing non-linearity [16, 17]. One representative scheme is to build multiple local models to approximate the global one [11, 18, 19]. Local modeling methods train a series of linear SVM models near decision boundaries by using training data instances in the corresponding local regions. Unlabelled instances are then classified by the nearest local models in the prediction stage. This method is able to approximate the non-linear boundaries by a series of local linear ones. No intuitive indications are given by the local models about how complex the local regions are, or what kinds of patterns are represented in the regions.

Rule extraction is an important component for the interpretation of SVMs or other classification techniques [20, 21]. Martens et al. [8] provided a comprehensive study of rule extraction from SVMs. These methods commonly employ an automatic optimization process and result in an axis-parallel representation. However, the targets and interests may vary according to the user and analysis task. It is likely that a visual analysis process can enable the user to explore both the input parameter space and the classification boundaries.

Unfortunately, there is little work dedicated to visualizing SVMs. Caragea et al. [22] applied a projection method to transform data instances into 2D space. The separating hyper-plane is sampled in the data space, and projected onto the 2D plane. The work by Aragon et al. [23] utilized SVMs as part of a visual analysis system for astrophysics, but provided no general support for SVM exploration. In Ref. [24], we presented an interactive visualization system for visualizing SVMs and providing interactions for users to perform exploration in the dataset.

2.2 Visual exploration of high-dimensional data

One key challenge in opening up SVMs is the need for high-dimensional data exploration methods. Recent work in this area has utilized multi-dimensional projections to map data instances in high-dimensional data space to the low-dimensional (2D) space. The key issue is how to explore the underlying dataset with informative projections. Previous works, such as grand tour [25]

and projection pursuit [26], generate a series of projections that allow the user to dynamically explore various lower-dimensional projections of the data in a systematic way in order to find a preferred projection. Other exploration techniques help the user by giving controls for the projection matrix (e.g., Refs. [27, 28]). Nam and Mueller [29] proposed a projection navigation interface, where the exploration and navigation activities are decomposed into five major tasks: sight identification, tour path planning, touring, looking around & zooming into detail, and orientation & localization. Additionally, an N-dimensional touchpad polygon is provided to navigate in high-dimensional space by adjusting the combination of projection weights on each dimension.

Alternatively, high-dimensional data can be visualized with a scatterplot matrix [30], a parallel coordinate plot (PCP) [31, 32], or radar charts [33]. Previous work has also employed interactive exploration and navigation within scatterplots to fill the gap between projections and axis-based visualization techniques. Elmqvist et al. [34] presented an interactive method to support visualization and exploration of relations between different 2D scatterplots in high-dimensional space. Similarly, 3D navigation [35] on the basis of rigid body rotation can be employed for viewing 3D scatterplot matrices. 3D rotation interaction improves the user's ability to perceive corresponding points in different scatterplots for comparison.

2.3 Visual classification

Some visual classification approaches, such as decision and rule-based classifiers [36, 37], employ so-called *white-box* models, in which the detailed process is easy to understand. Teoh and Ma [38] considered the process of building decision trees as a knowledge discovery method, and argued that visualization of the decision tree model can reveal valuable information in the data. Van den Elzen and van Wijk [39] presented a system for interactive construction and analysis of decision trees with operations including growing, pruning, optimization, and analysis.

Another category of work focuses on designing model-transparent frameworks in which the user is allowed to provide training datasets and view the results. Thus, low-level classification techniques can be directly employed without modification of the analytical process. Heimerl et al. [40] proposed to tightly integrate the user into the labelling process and suggested an interactive binary classifier training approach for text analysis. Höferlin et al. [41] presented a system to build cascades of linear classifiers for image classification.

For open-box visual analysis approaches, one of the most similar works to our approach is from Tzeng and Ma [7]. It combines several visualization designs for artificial neural networks to open the black box of underlying dependencies between the input and output data. Unlike our interactive visual analysis approach, their open-box scheme is limited to presenting a static visualization of the model structure and does not provide a means of data exploration and interpretation of the classification process.

3 An introduction to SVM classification

Given a set of training data points each with m attributes and an associated class label, the SVM attempts to separate these points using an $(m-1)$-dimensional hyper-plane. In this section, we will briefly describe this process with the help of Fig. 1.

Suppose that $\boldsymbol{x}_i \in \mathbb{R}^m, i = 1, \ldots, n$, are n training data instances in two different classes, and $y_i \in \{-1, +1\}, i = 1, \ldots, n$, are their corresponding class labels. A linear support vector machine aims to construct a hyper-plane:

$$\boldsymbol{w}^{\mathrm{T}}\boldsymbol{x} + b = 0 \qquad (1)$$

in the m-dimensional data space $\mathbb{R}^m$ that has the largest distance to the nearest training data instances of each class (the *functional margin*).

Equation (1) can be solved by solving the following optimization problem:

$$\min_{\boldsymbol{w}, b, \xi} \frac{1}{2}\boldsymbol{w}^{\mathrm{T}}\boldsymbol{w} + C \sum_{i=1}^{n} \xi_i \qquad (2)$$

subject to $y_i(\boldsymbol{w}^{\mathrm{T}}\boldsymbol{x}_i + b) \geqslant 1 - \xi_i, \xi_i \geqslant 0, \ i = 1, \ldots, n$ where C is a user-adjustable parameter to control the relative importance of maximizing the margin or satisfying the constraint of partitioning each training data instance into the correct half-space. The dual problem to Eq. (2) is derived by introducing Lagrange multipliers α_i:

$$\max \frac{1}{2} \sum_{i,j=1}^{n} \alpha_i \alpha_j y_i y_j K(\boldsymbol{x}_i, \boldsymbol{x}_j) - \sum_{i=1}^{n} \alpha_i \qquad (3)$$

subject to $\sum_{i=1}^{n} \alpha_i y_i = 0, 0 \leqslant \alpha_i \leqslant C, \ i = 1, \ldots, n$

Here, $K(\boldsymbol{x}_i, \boldsymbol{x}_j) = \Phi(\boldsymbol{x}_i)\Phi(\boldsymbol{x}_j) = \langle \Phi(\boldsymbol{x}_i)\Phi(\boldsymbol{x}_j) \rangle$ is called the *kernel function*. For a linear SVM, its kernel is the dot product of $\boldsymbol{x}_i$ and $\boldsymbol{x}_j$, i.e., $K(\boldsymbol{x}_i, \boldsymbol{x}_j) = \boldsymbol{x}_i^{\mathrm{T}}\boldsymbol{x}_j$. Support vectors are those training data instances $\boldsymbol{x}_{\mathrm{s}}$ whose corresponding Lagrange multipliers are above zero. Finally, the decision function for classifying a new data instance $\hat{\boldsymbol{x}}$ is

$$\hat{y} = \mathrm{sgn}(\sum_{i=1}^{n} y_i \alpha_i K(\boldsymbol{x}_i, \hat{\boldsymbol{x}}) + b) \qquad (4)$$

4 EasySVM: Open-box visual modeling of SVMs

As previously stated, the shortcomings of SVMs lie primarily in the fact that they are difficult to interpret and explore. A general visual modeling approach for a linear SVM has two requirements: (i) visualization of the training data instances, the SVM model, and interaction between data instances and model, and (ii) user-guided construction of the SVM model. These basic operations underpin the entire analysis process. Figure 2 shows the analytical

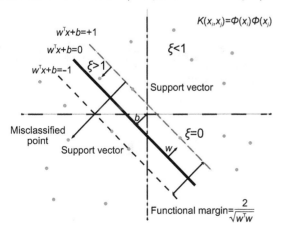

Fig. 1 A linear support vector machine.

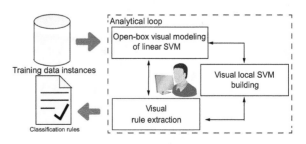

Fig. 2 Overview of our approach.

scheme for our solution which consists of three components:

Open-box visual modeling for SVMs. To enable the user to quickly determine item relationships, we map the data instances and SVM models into a 2D plane with an orthogonal projection. We have designed an interactive projection control scheme to support flexible exploration of the dataset and the model in different ways.

Local SVM building through visualization. Once the data instances and models have been visualized, the user may recognize non-linearities within the model space. The underlying SVM model can then be progressively approximated with a sequence of linear localized SVM models. An integrated suite of visual linkage and comparison operations enable analysts to explore relations between data instances and SVM models as well as to manipulate local models.

Visual rule extraction. Rule extraction is interactively performed along each axis. The user can either select segments on the axes or select regions from the projected results of data instances and the SVM models. Each extracted rule can be represented using a hierarchical tree structure.

This scheme is encapsulated in our EasySVM system, a web-based interactive visualization system depicted in Fig. 3. The system consists of four main views: a scatterplot view, a projection management view, a dimension selection view, and a rule extraction view.

4.1 Open-box visual modeling of linear SVM

The traditional SVM model building process can be summarized as the following fours steps: (i)

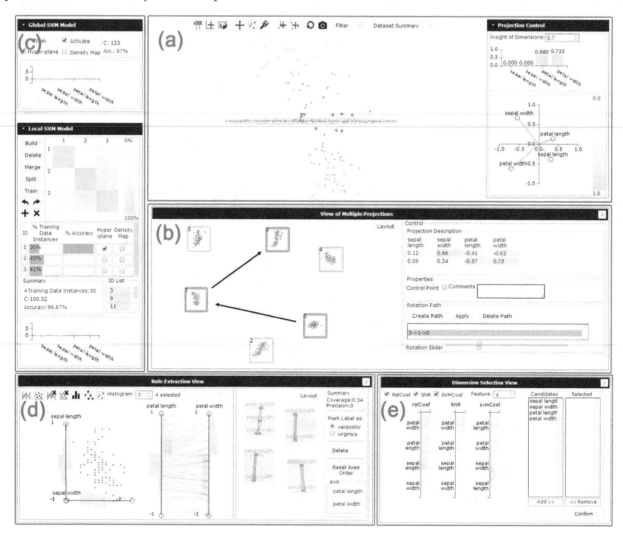

Fig. 3 Interface of EasySVM: (a) the data view, (b) the view of multiple projections, (c) the SVM model building view, (d) the rule extraction view, and (e) the dimension selection view.

preprocess the data, (ii) select parameters, (iii) train the model, and (iv) validate the training result [15]. If the validation result does not pass the test (i.e., gives low prediction accuracy on the test dataset), the process is restarted from step (ii) again until it meets the user's requirements. In our visual model building process, each of these model building steps is enhanced by interactive visualization and visual exploration methods to facilitate understanding during the model building process. Meanwhile, additional data exploration and manipulation can be performed during any model building step. Figure 4(a) shows our iterative visual model building process.

Data exploration and initial training. The user can explore the training dataset to approximate the classification boundaries. Then a global model is trained with all training data instances using

an initial parameter C in the global SVM model building panel (Fig. 3(c)). After this initial step, the user can perform analysis and operations iteratively using the following two steps.

Visual model exploration and validation. For a trained model, an initial projection is generated in the direction of the side view. The user can evaluate the model starting from the side view to locate misclassified instances, check their distributions and patterns with projections, view the boundaries near the separating hyper-plane, and make decisions on data operations. Compared with the traditional machine learning procedure, the visual exploration of the training result provides insight into the reasons why the training result is as it is. Meanwhile, the prediction accuracy on the training dataset is computed and displayed as another reference for model validation.

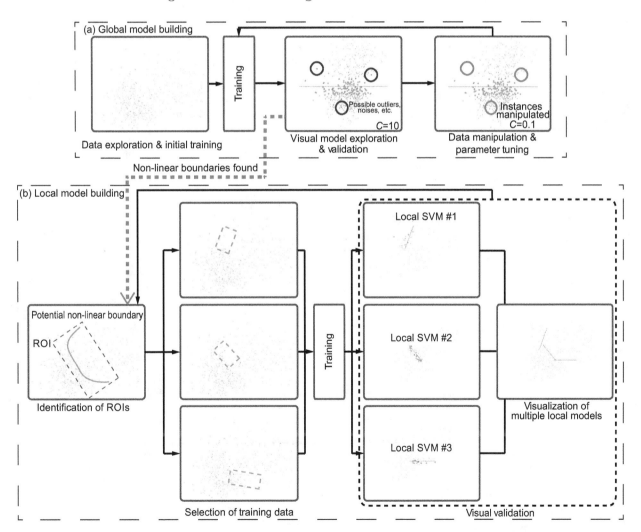

Fig. 4 (a) Global SVM model building process. If a non-linear decision boundary is found, the user can enter the local model building process (b).

Data manipulation and parameter tuning. After exploration, some training data instances that affect model building can be modified by changing their labels or deleting them from the dataset if they are considered to be noise or instances with invalid values. In addition, the parameter C can be tuned in this step to balance the trade-off between margins of the hyper-plane and prediction accuracy on the training dataset. It is required to re-train the model after these two operations to update the model and classification results. The model building process stops when the validation result satisfies the user's requirements, such as prediction accuracy on a test dataset. It should be noted that for a dataset with non-linear, complex decision boundaries, local linear models are needed.

4.1.1 Visualization of training data and the SVM model

The data view (see Fig. 3(a)) in our system is based on a scatterplot in which data instances are projected into a low-dimensional subspace. We use an orthogonal projection to embed high-dimensional data instances and the SVM model in a 2D plane. This view features two panels: a top menubar that contains exploration tools for the scatterplot, and a projection control panel that provides visualization of the dimension axes and control methods for interactive projection control. Two reasons for providing this are: (i) it is a powerful technique for visualizing the training dataset, and (ii) it simultaneously makes clear the geometrical relations between data instances and the hyper-plane, like relative positions and distances between each other that are essential for the user to understand the structure of SVM models.

Orthogonal projection. Given an orthogonal projection matrix $\boldsymbol{A}_{m \times 2} = [\boldsymbol{f}_1, \boldsymbol{f}_2]$, two m-dimensional vectors $\boldsymbol{f}_1, \boldsymbol{f}_2$ span a 2D plane in the m-dimensional data space onto which all data instances are projected. Applying it to a high-dimensional data instance yields a corresponding data point on the 2D plane, i.e., the coordinates of the data point in the scatterplot view $\boldsymbol{x}'_i = \boldsymbol{x}_i \boldsymbol{A}$. It should be noted that the 2D projection formula of the separating hyper-plane is very hard to find. We first sample a set of points on the separating hyper-plane, and then project sample points onto the 2D plane to approximate the hyper-plane. Specifically,

the sample procedure contains the following four steps:

1. project all training data instances onto the separating hyper-plane;
2. calculate a bounding-box of the projections in step (1);
3. uniformly sample N_{sample} points in the bounding-box on the separating hyper-plane;
4. project the N_{sample} sample points onto the 2D plane with $\boldsymbol{A}$.

Visual encoding. To encode the data instances, three visual channels are employed as illustrated in Fig. 5. The input label of each data instance is encoded with a filled color. If the predicted label by the SVM is different from its input label, a border color other than the filled color is employed. The shape represents whether a data instance is a support vector; we use a rectangle for a support vector and a circle otherwise. Furthermore, the opacity of a data instance encodes the distance from the corresponding separating plane.

For the separating hyper-plane of the SVM model, the sample points are drawn on the view as dots in grey with a smaller size than the data points (shown in Fig. 6(a)). Additionally, to visualize the density of training data instances, a density map is computed and rendered. For each class, the density maps of two colors are generated separately, then the two maps are composed on the view. Figure 6(b) shows the result.

4.1.2 Visual exploration of the projected scatterplot

In our visual exploration, an interactive projection control method is provided for manipulating the direction of the selected projection. Our method is based on Ref. [28], where the control is similar to the trackball control in a high-dimensional data

Channel	Description	Example
Filled color	The input label of a training data instance	Input label = -1 Input label = +1
Border color (optional)	If the label assigned by the SVM is different from the input label	Classified as +1 (with the input label = -1) Classified as -1 (with the input label = +1)
Shape	Whether it is a support vector	No → Yes
Opacity	Distance to the corresponding separating plane	Near Far

Fig. 5 Our visual encoding scheme.

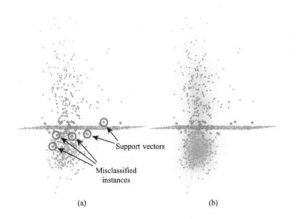

Fig. 6 Examples of projections: (a) visual encoding applied to data points, (b) a density map composition.

space. A weight is specified first for each dimension to determine which one is going to be manipulated, then the user can rotate the projection plane by dragging the mouse in the scatterplot view. Finally the user's mouse action is translated into a rotation matrix and applied to the projection matrix, thus changing the scatterplot. However, a gimbal lock problem exists in the method, which limits the rotation at the singular point. We improve their method by using quaternions to compute the rotation to avoid this issue.

To assist the user in the exploration of the relationships between multiple projections, we offer a view of multiple projections (Fig. 3(b)). Each projection glyph holds a snapshot of the interesting scatterplot inside the glyph with the projection matrix. We define the similarity between two projection glyphs as the Euclidean distance between two corresponding projection matrices, i.e., $\|A_1 - A_2\|_2$. Thus, the layout of the glyphs is determined using a local affine multi-dimensional projection algorithm [42]. The user can plan a rotation path containing a sequence of projection glyphs among the multiple projection glyphs, then a rotation animation is generated based on interpolation between adjacent projections along the path [27] with a slider to control the position of the animation.

Two categories of exploration actions can be performed to extract knowledge from the dataset and SVM model.

Data distributions, clusters, or outliers. Data distributions and patterns in the projections indicate the potential location and direction of a separating plane. The exploratory discovery of

distributions and patterns can be performed at each stage of the analytical process. For example, before training any SVM models, the user can explore the training dataset to inspect boundaries between two classes; after an SVM model is trained, data distributions along the separating hyper-plane and specific patterns in support vectors, such as outliers, may illuminate the direction of further exploration, label manipulation, or parameter tuning.

Side views of the separating hyper-plane. When one of the basis vectors f_1, f_2 is equal to the weight vector w of the SVM model, all the sample points will be projected into a line in the view. This can be easily proved: let $f_1 = w$, for all sample points with $w^T x + b = 0$; the coordinates of f_1 are constant. We call a view under this kind of projection matrix a *side view*. Figure 7 shows some examples of a side view. Side views are useful when investigating or validating a trained model, because:

- the boundaries of each class and gaps between them are shown clearly in the projection;
- the distance from each data point to the hyper-plane on a 2D plane and the actual distance in high-dimensional data space are in the same proportion, leading to an intuitive illustration of the spatial relations between training data instances and the separating hyper-plane.

A useful exploration strategy is to start from the side view of the separating hyper-plane. The user can rotate the projection through a small range of angles using interactive projection control, allowing data distributions near the hyper-plane to be displayed and explored.

Orthogonal projection is unable to show high-dimensional data separation which may cause profound visual clutter. A dimension selection view (Fig. 3(e)) is provided for filtering out non-informative dimensions in the classification task. In

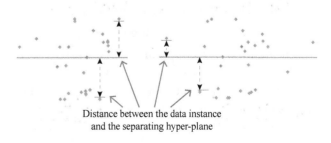

Distance between the data instance
and the separating hyper-plane

Fig. 7 Examples of a side view.

this view, three bar charts rank all the dimensions of the training data instances according to three measures: correlation coefficients between the dimension and the class labels, signal-to-noise ratio, and weighting by a linear SVM [43]. The user can select the most informative dimensions, which will be highlighted in the candidate list. After the selection is confirmed, the projected scatterplot will be updated to apply the changes. Dimensions that are filtered out will not take part in the projection process and the future model building process.

4.2 Visual local SVM building

For clarity, we use the term *global model* to represent the SVM model built with the process described in Section 4.1, which covers all the training data instances in the dateset. A *local model*, on the contrary, is trained on a selected subset of training data instances.

4.2.1 Visual exploration of decision boundaries

Before building local SVM models, it is necessary to perform a preliminary exploration of the decision boundary and an evaluation of complexity. First, it is necessary to explore the data distributions, because the data distribution near the decision boundaries is a strong indication of the boundary complexity. The user can control the projection interactively and inspect the patterns of boundaries between pairs of classes of data points. Additionally, the user can explore the decision boundaries guided by the global SVM model. Although not applicable to low prediction accuracy in complex circumstances, the separating hyper-plane of the global SVM model can act as a guide to the decision boundary. Training data instances lying on opposite sides of the hyper-plane always imply local regions containing non-linear boundaries, or even non-classifiable areas with mixed distributions of a pair of classes. The user can locate the regions in the projected scatterplot, check the patterns visually, and make further analysis.

4.2.2 Visual local model building process

Our visual local model building process extends the previous global one in Section 4.1. The key issues are to (i) locate regions-of-interest, and (ii) select proper subsets of training data instances for each local SVM model. We propose the following four steps to build local models iteratively (see Fig. 4(b)).

Identification of regions-of-interest. The target regions are located using the visual exploration methods given in Section 4.2.1. It should be pointed out that when some local models have been created, any of them, not just the global model, can be considered as a starting point for visual exploration and location. Local models with different numbers of training data instances and ranges of coverage in high-dimensional data spaces will provide diverse levels of details. The user can select the starting point as desired.

Selection of training data instances. The training data instances of a new local model can be selected directly by user interaction in the projection view. Moreover, we propose a hierarchical model creation method based on split-and-merge operations on the models created. A local model can be split into two new ones by dividing its corresponding training dataset into two subsets and training two new models on each subset. The training data instances from several models can also be merged together. A new local model is trained on the merged dataset to replace the existing ones. Both operations change the level of detail, in opposite directions. When a model is split into several multiple ones, the details of the decision boundary can be made more precise, while in merging, a set of models carrying much detailed information is replaced by a generalized model. Such level-of-detail exploration and incremental model creation allow the user to determine the decision boundaries and understand the distributions.

Training. Once the parameter C is set for each model, the newly created or updated local models are re-trained in this step.

Validation. In this step, the training result is validated in two ways. For a single local model, the same validation methods for the global model are applied; for checking relations and coverage between multiple models, the projection rotations between multiple models can be considered as indications of their positions and directions.

After the local model building process is done, the models can be employed for predicting new data instances. A prediction algorithm is provided based on the set of local models, where the query instances are labeled by the nearest local SVM. Algorithm 1 gives the prediction process.

Algorithm 1   Prediction procedure of local SVMs

Input:

The decision functions of n local SVMs, $H_i(\boldsymbol{x}), i = 1,\ldots,n$;

The training dataset of n local SVMs, $\boldsymbol{X}_i, i = 1,\ldots,n$;

The query instance, $\hat{\boldsymbol{x}}$.

Output:

Label of $\hat{\boldsymbol{x}}$, $\hat{y}_i$.

1: $\boldsymbol{X}_{k\mathrm{nn}} = k$ nearest neighbors of $\hat{\boldsymbol{x}}$ in $\bigcup_{i=1}^{n} \boldsymbol{X}_i$

2: $i_{\mathrm{nearest}} = \arg\max_i |\boldsymbol{X}_{k\mathrm{nn}} \cap \boldsymbol{X}_i|$

3: $\hat{y}_i = H_i(\hat{\boldsymbol{x}})$

4.2.3   Visualization and interactions of multiple models

Statistical information about existing local SVM models is displayed. In particular, a matrix is used to encode the similarity between all models in terms of the number of shared training data instances. Each matrix cell (i, j) is defined as

$$\mathrm{similarity}(i,j) = \frac{\#(\mathrm{TrSet}(H_i) \cap \mathrm{TrSet}(H_j))}{\#(\mathrm{TrSet}(H_i))}$$

where $\mathrm{TrSet}(H_i)$ is the training dataset of the ith local model. The matrix is visualized with an opacity-modulated color (green in our system), as shown in Fig. 3(c). The opacity of each cell is set to its similarity.

Note that the side view best depicts the structure of a linear SVM model, while rotating from the side view of a local model to another can depict the spatial relations between different models. This is done by taking side view snapshots for each model and creating a rotation path through multiple projections.

4.3   Visual rule extraction

By a rule we mean a small-sized canonical subspace of the input high-dimensional data space that may encapsulate some domain knowledge. The subspace is bounded by a set of dimension intervals, each of which refers to one or several ranges of a dimension. Thus, determining a rule is identical to specifying one or several intervals in each dimension. Each rule denotes a class and assigns the corresponding class label automatically to the data instances in the rule.

As shown in the rule extraction view (see Fig. 3(d)), we apply the flexible linked axes method [44] to visualize the training data instance. The positions and orientations of the dimension axes can be arranged freely. Between pairs of axes, the data instances are represented by parallel coordinate

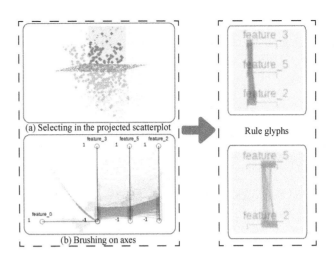

(a) Selecting in the projected scatterplot

Rule glyphs

(b) Brushing on axes

Fig. 8   Two ways of constructing rules.

plot-styled edges or scatterplot-styled dots. The reason is that this allows the user to choose desired dimensions based on their importance, and visualize the data distributions in one dimension (on axis), two dimensions (in a scatterplot), or multiple dimensions (in a parallel coordinate plot).

The following two interaction methods are provided for specifying classification rules.

Brushing line plots. The user directly brushes the axis to select a range. Note that the number of training data instances included in a range should be maximized, as more training data instances lead to higher confidence in the rule when classifying new instances.

Selecting points in the projected scatterplot. Selection of data points in the projected scatterplot is linked in the rule extraction view. When selecting an interesting cluster of data instances in the projected scatterplot, the corresponding dots or edges are highlighted, as well as the range of their bounding-box on each axis.

After the set of selected ranges is committed, a new rule glyph that represents the set of ranges, i.e., the rule, is displayed. In the rule glyph, a parallel coordinate plot is provided to summarize the dimension intervals. The background color of the rule glyph encodes its expected class with a unique color. Next the user is given the option to explore the relations between different rules for further optimization. To express the similarity between two rules, we use the force-direct layout based on the Jaccard index between the sets of training data instances in two separate rules as the similarity measure. This layout enables a better understanding of their intersecting areas. For instance, the glyphs that are close to each other may be redundant.

5 Case study

5.1 System implementation

EasySVM is primarily implemented in *JavaScript* for its front-end UI, employing *D3.js* as graphic rendering library, the *jQuery* UI for user interface components, and *Backbone.js* as the MVC framework. For back-end computational support, we designed a RESTful interface for communication built on the *Django* Web Framework, and apply *scikit-learn* as the SVM implementation.

5.2 Wall-following Robot Navigation dataset

For the Wall-following Robot Navigation dataset [45], four moving actions (*Move-Forward*, *Slight-*

Right-Turn, *Sharp-Right-Turn*, and *Slight-Left-Turn*) are to be determined based on the input values from 24 ultrasound sensors (US0–US23). Given a series of sensor values, a classifier is supposed to be trained for predicting the best action. We only use the data instances in *Move-Forward* and *Sharp-Right-Turn* in our binary classification (4302 instances in total) and divide the dataset into two parts: 50 percent as the training set, and the other 50 percent as the test set.

Data exploration. See Fig. 9(a). By default, the initial projected scatterplot is the same as the 2D scatterplot with only the first two dimensions (US0, US1). The user starts from this initial projection and performs interactive projection control by selecting each of the other dimensions (US2–US23). While manipulating dimension US14, a coarse gap appears on a large branch on the right side, which indicates a potential linear boundary. However, training data

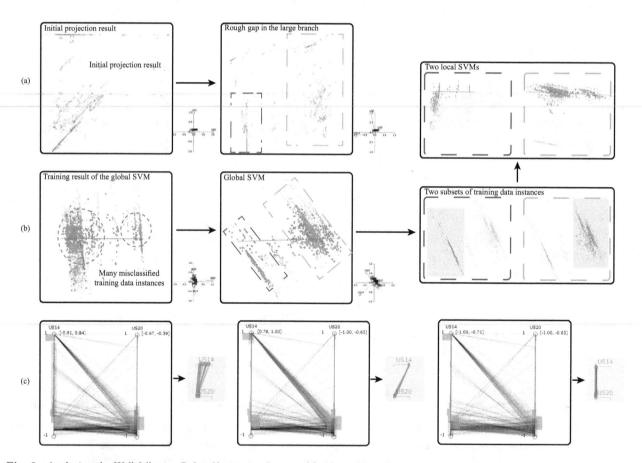

Fig. 9 Analyzing the Wall-following Robot Navigation dataset. (a) After adding the weight of projection for dimension US14, the dataset is approximately separated into two branches in the blue and green boxes. A coarse gap appears in the large branch on the right side. (b) The result of a global SVM model is not acceptable because too many data instances are misclassified (marked in the two red circles). When increasing the projection weight on dimension US14, the projection result shows that the separating hyper-plane of the global SVM model is located in a different direction to the gap found in the previous step. Two separate local models are created based on the two branches. (c) Three classification rules are extracted based on the result of the local model built on the large branch.

instances of different classes in a smaller branch on the left side are overlapping, which seem impossible to linearly separate. A snapshot is taken to support further investigation.

Global SVM model building. See Fig. 9(b). After preliminary data exploration, the user trains a global SVM model with all training data instances. However, the accuracy on the training dataset is around 80% for various settings of parameter C, meaning that the dataset is not linearly separable. In the side view, a set of wrongly-classified instances is observed, scattered near the separating hyper-plane.

Local SVM model building. See Fig. 9(b). The user manipulates dimension US14 again to investigate the probable boundary found earlier, while the separating hyper-plane is located in a different direction. Now the user decides to build two separate models for the two branches. After training two local SVM models, two side views show that the two corresponding separating hyper-planes are in different directions and give better separation in the regions near their training datasets, which is also indicated by the two accuracy values (around 91% for the model on the smaller branch and 94% for the one on the larger branch). Animated rotation between the side views of the global model and the two local models partially depicts the relations between three separating hyper-planes. Thus, the global SVM model is replaced by the two local linear ones.

Rule extraction. See Fig. 9(c). Rule extraction operations are assisted by the two local models. The user chooses to extract rules for the local model on the large branch. From the weight vector of the local model, it is obvious that dimensions US14 and US20 dominate the direction of the separating hyper-plane. Thus the user constructs a parallel coordinate plot linking US14 and US20. The user brushes three combinations of ranges on the two axes and generates three rules.

Prediction accuracy. The global linear SVM achieves $81\% \pm 1.0\%$ prediction accuracy on the test set, while the local SVM models achieve $88\% \pm 3.0\%$.

6   Discussion

In terms of non-linear SVM model building, our approach presents an approximation method using multiple linear models, which can be utilized as an interpretation tool of the original training dataset and a prediction tool for future unlabelled instances. For example, each local linear SVM interprets the boundary in a local area with its separating hyper-plane, while a prediction can also be made with the k-NN prediction algorithm.

The trade-off between complexity and interpretability is important for building local SVMs. Increasing the number of local linear models will help to approximate the non-linear decision boundary more accurately. However, it increases the difficulty for the user to understand the decision boundary at the same time. Meanwhile, some local models may be redundant because they hold almost the same information as other local models. In addition, for a training dataset containing noise around the decision boundary, over-fitting may happen if some local models represent detailed information from the noise.

One promising extension of our approach is to improve its scalability, including the number of training data instances as well as the number of dimensions. For massive amounts of data, clustering methods can be adopted before projection to reduce the visual clutter caused by too many data points in the 2D plane. For the dimensionality issue, we need to design a more scalable visual dimension selection procedure to reduce the number of dimension candidates before projection is performed.

7   Conclusions

In this paper, we have proposed a novel open-box visual analysis approach for building SVM models. The user can perform visual exploration of the dataset and the relations between data instances and SVM models. Meanwhile, a visually-enhanced local linear model building approach is dedicated to expanding the traditional linear SVM to deal with non-linear decision boundaries. Finally we provide a visual rule extraction method to enable the user to retrieve classification rules from the model building results.

Acknowledgements

This work was supported in part by the National Basic Research Program of China (973 Program, No. 2015CB352503), the Major Program of

National Natural Science Foundation of China (No. 61232012), and the National Natural Science Foundation of China (No. 61422211).

References

[1] Cortes, C.; Vapnik, V. Support-vector networks. *Machine Learning* Vol. 20, No. 3, 273–297, 1995.

[2] Tong, S.; Koller, D. Support vector machine active learning with applications to text classification. *Journal of Machine Learning Research* Vol. 2, 45–66, 2001.

[3] Osuna, E.; Freund, R.; Girosi, F. Training support vector machines: An application to face detection. In: Proceedings of the IEEE Computer Society Conference on Computer Vision and Pattern Recognition, 130–136, 1997.

[4] Furey, T. S.; Cristianini, N.; Duffy, N.; Bednarski, D. W.; Schummer, M.; Haussler, D. Support vector machine classification and validation of cancer tissue samples using microarray expression data. *Bioinformatics* Vol. 16, No. 10, 906–914, 2000.

[5] Hasenauer, J.; Heinrich, J.; Doszczak, M.; Scheurich, P.; Weiskopf, D.; Allgöwer, F. A visual analytics approach for models of heterogeneous cell populations. *EURASIP Journal on Bioinformatics and Systems Biology* Vol. 2012, 4, 2012.

[6] Abe, S. *Support Vector Machines for Pattern Classification*. Springer London, 2010.

[7] Tzeng, F.-Y.; Ma, K.-L. Opening the black box— Data driven visualization of neural networks. In: Proceedings of the IEEE Visualization, 383–390, 2005.

[8] Martens, D.; Baesens, B. B.; van Gestel, T. Decompositional rule extraction from support vector machines by active learning. *IEEE Transactions on Knowledge and Data Engineering* Vol. 21, No. 2, 178–191, 2009.

[9] Núñez, H.; Angulo, C.; Català, A. Rule extraction from support vector machines. In: Proceedings of the European Symposium on Artificial Neural Networks, 107–112, 2002.

[10] Schölkopf, B.; Smola, A. J. *Learning with Kernels: Support Vector Machines, Regularization, Optimization, and Beyond*. MIT Press, 2002.

[11] Ladicky, L.; Torr, P. Locally linear support vector machines. In: Proceedings of the 28th International Conference on Machine Learning, 985–992, 2011.

[12] Ganti, R.; Gray, A. Local support vector machines: Formulation and analysis. *arXiv preprint* arXiv:1309.3699, 2013.

[13] Baesens, B.; Gestel, T. V.; Viaene, S.; Stepanova, M.; Suykens, J.; Vanthienen, J. Benchmarking state-of-the-art classification algorithms for credit scoring. *Journal of the Operational Research Society* Vol. 54, No. 6, 627–635, 2003.

[14] Wahba, G. Support vector machines, reproducing kernel Hilbert spaces, and randomized GACV. In: *Advances in Kernel Methods*. Schölkopf, B.; Burges, C. J. C.; Smola, A. J. Eds. Cambridge, MA, USA: MIT Press, 69–88, 1999.

[15] Hsu, C.-W; Chang, C.-C; Lin, C.-J. A practical guide to support vector classification. 2016. Available at http://www.csie.ntu.edu.tw/~cjlin/papers/guide/guide.pdf.

[16] Mangasarian, O. L.; Wild, E. W. Proximal support vector machine classifiers. In: Proceedings of KDD-2001: Knowledge Discovery and Data Mining, 77–86, 2001.

[17] Maji, S.; Berg, A. C.; Malik, J. Classification using intersection kernel support vector machines is efficient. In: Proceedings of the IEEE Conference on Computer Vision and Pattern Recognition, 1–8, 2008.

[18] Blanzieri, E.; Melgani, F. An adaptive SVM nearest neighbor classifier for remotely sensed imagery. In: Proceedings of the IEEE International Symposium on Geoscience and Remote Sensing, 3931–3934, 2006.

[19] Yin, C.; Zhu, Y.; Mu, S.; Tian, S. Local support vector machine based on cooperative clustering for very large-scale dataset. In: Proceedings of the 8th International Conference on Natural Computation, 88–92, 2012.

[20] Barakat, N. H.; Bradley, A. P. Rule extraction from support vector machines: A sequential covering approach. *IEEE Transactions on Knowledge and Data Engineering* Vol. 19, No. 6, 729–741, 2007.

[21] Fung, G.; Sandilya, S.; Rao, R. B. Rule extraction from linear support vector machines. In: Proceedings of the 11th ACM SIGKDD International Conference on Knowledge Discovery in Data Mining, 32–40, 2005.

[22] Caragea, D.; Cook, D.; Wickham, H.; Honavar, V. Visual methods for examining SVM classifiers. In: *Visual Data Mining*. Simoff, S. J.; Böhlen, M. H.; Mazeika, A. Eds. Springer Berlin Heidelberg, 2007.

[23] Aragon, C. R.; Bailey, S. J.; Poon, S.; Runge, K. J.; Thomas, R. C. Sunfall: A collaborative visual analytics system for astrophysics. In: Proceedings of the IEEE Symposium on Visual Analytics Science and Technology, 219–220, 2007.

[24] Ma, Y.; Chen, W.; Ma, X.; Xu, J.; Huang, X.; Maciejewski, R.; Tung, A. K. H. EasySVM: A visual analysis approach for open-box support vector machines. In: Proceedings of the IEEE VIS 2014 Workshop on Visualization for Predictive Analytics, 2014.

[25] Asimov, D. The grand tour: A tool for viewing multidimensional data. *SIAM Journal on Scientific and Statistical Computing* Vol. 6, No. 1, 128–143, 1985.

[26] Friedman, J. H.; Tukey, J. W. A projection pursuit algorithm for exploratory data analysis. *IEEE Transactions on Computers* Vol. C-23, No. 9, 881–890, 1974.

[27] Buja, A.; Cook, D.; Asimov, D.; Hurley, C. Computational methods for high-dimensional rotations in data visualization. In: *Handbook of Statistics, Volume 24: Data Mining and Data Visualization*. Rao, C. R.; Wegman, E. J.; Solka, J.

L. Eds. Amsterdam, the Netherlands: North-Holland Publishing Co., 391–413, 2005.

[28] Cook, D.; Buja, A. Manual controls for high-dimensional data projections. *Journal of Computational and Graphical Statistics* Vol. 6, No. 4, 464–480, 1997.

[29] Nam, J. E.; Mueller, K. TripAdvisor^{N-D}: A tourism-inspired high-dimensional space exploration framework with overview and detail. *IEEE Transactions on Visualization and Computer Graphics* Vol. 19, No. 2, 291–305, 2013.

[30] Cleveland, W. C.; McGill, M. E. *Dynamic Graphics for Statistics*. Boca Raton, FL, USA: CRC Press, 1988.

[31] Inselberg, A. The plane with parallel coordinates. *The Visual Computer* Vol. 1, No. 2, 69–91, 1985.

[32] Inselberg, A.; Dimsdale, B. Parallel coordinates: A tool for visualizing multi-dimensional geometry. In: Proceedings of the 1st Conference on Visualization, 361–378, 1990.

[33] Chambers, J. M.; Cleveland, W. S.; Kleiner, B.; Tukey, P. A. *Graphical Methods for Data Analysis*. Duxbury Press, 1983.

[34] Elmqvist, N.; Dragicevic, P.; Fekete, J. D. Rolling the dice: Multidimensional visual exploration using scatterplot matrix navigation. *IEEE Transactions on Visualization and Computer Graphics* Vol. 14, No. 6, 1539–1148, 2008.

[35] Sanftmann, H.; Weiskopf, D. 3D scatterplot navigation. *IEEE Transactions on Visualization and Computer Graphics* Vol. 18, No. 11, 1969–1978, 2012.

[36] Liu, B.; Ma, Y.; Wong, C. K. Improving an association rule based classifier. In: *Principles of Data Mining and Knowledge Discovery*. Zighed, D. A.; Komorowski, J.; Żytkow, J. Eds. Springer Berlin Heidelberg, 504–509, 2000.

[37] Quinlan, J. R. Induction of decision trees. *Machine Learning* Vol. 1, No. 1, 81–106, 1986.

[38] Teoh, S. T.; Ma, K.-L. PaintingClass: Interactive construction, visualization and exploration of decision trees. In: Proceedings of the 9th ACM SIGKDD International Conference on Knowledge Discovery and Data Mining, 667–672, 2003.

[39] Van den Elzen, S.; van Wijk, J. J. BaobabView: Interactive construction and analysis of decision trees. In: Proceedings of the IEEE Conference on Visual Analytics Science and Technology, 151–160, 2011.

[40] Heimerl, F.; Koch, S.; Bosch, H.; Ertl, T. Visual classifier training for text document retrieval. *IEEE Transactions on Visualization and Computer Graphics* Vol. 18, No. 12, 2839–2848, 2012.

[41] Höferlin, B.; Netzel, R.; Höferlin, M.; Weiskopf, D.; Heidemann, G. Inter-active learning of ad-hoc classifiers for video visual analytics. In: Proceedings of the IEEE Conference on Visual Analytics Science and Technology, 23–32, 2012.

[42] Joia, P.; Coimbra, D.; Cuminato, J. A.; Paulovich, F. V.; Nonato, L. G. Local affine multidimensional projection. *IEEE Transactions on Visualization and Computer Graphics* Vol. 17, No. 12, 2563–2571, 2011.

[43] Guyon, I.; Elisseeff, A. An introduction to variable and feature selection. *Journal of Machine Learning Research* Vol. 3, 1157–1182, 2003.

[44] Claessen, J. H. T.; van Wijk, J. J. Flexible linked axes for multivariate data visualization. *IEEE Transactions on Visualization and Computer Graphics* Vol. 17, No. 12, 2310–2316, 2011.

[45] Freire, A. L.; Barreto, G. A.; Veloso, M.; Varela, A. T. Short-term memory mechanisms in neural network learning of robot navigation tasks: A case study. In: Proceedings of the 6th Latin American Robotics Symposium, 1–6, 2009.

11

Robust facial landmark detection and tracking across poses and expressions for in-the-wild monocular video

Shuang Liu[1], Yongqiang Zhang[2] (✉), Xiaosong Yang[1], Daming Shi[2], and Jian J. Zhang[1]

Abstract   We present a novel approach for automatically detecting and tracking facial landmarks across poses and expressions from in-the-wild monocular video data, e.g., YouTube videos and smartphone recordings. Our method does not require any calibration or manual adjustment for new individual input videos or actors. Firstly, we propose a method of robust 2D facial landmark detection across poses, by combining shape-face canonical-correlation analysis with a global supervised descent method. Since 2D regression-based methods are sensitive to unstable initialization, and the temporal and spatial coherence of videos is ignored, we utilize a coarse-to-dense 3D facial expression reconstruction method to refine the 2D landmarks. On one side, we employ an in-the-wild method to extract the coarse reconstruction result and its corresponding texture using the detected sparse facial landmarks, followed by robust pose, expression, and identity estimation. On the other side, to obtain dense reconstruction results, we give a face tracking flow method that corrects coarse reconstruction results and tracks weakly textured areas; this is used to iteratively update the coarse face model. Finally, a dense reconstruction result is estimated after it converges. Extensive experiments on a variety of video sequences recorded by ourselves or downloaded from YouTube show the results of facial landmark detection and tracking under various lighting conditions, for various head poses and facial expressions. The overall performance and a comparison with state-of-art methods demonstrate the robustness and effectiveness of our method.

Keywords   face tracking; facial reconstruction; landmark detection

1   Introduction

Facial landmark detection and tracking is widely used for creating realistic face animations of virtual actors for applications in computer animation, film, and video games. Creation of convincing facial animation is a challenging task due to the highly nonrigid nature of the face and the complexity of detecting and tracking the facial landmarks accurately and efficiently in uncontrolled environments. It involves facial deformation and fine-grained details. In addition, the *uncanny valley* effect [1] indicates that people are extremely capable of identifying subtle artifacts in facial appearance. Hence, animators need to make a tremendous amount of effort to localize high quality facial landmarks. To reduce the amount of manual labor, an ideal face capture solution should automatically provide the facial shape (landmarks) with high performance given reasonable quality input videos.

As a key role in facial performance capture, robust facial landmark detection across poses is still a hard problem. Typical generative models including active shape models [2], active appearance models [3], and their extensions [4–6] mitigate the influence of illumination and pose, but tend to fail when used *in the wild*. Recently, discriminative models have shown promising performance for robust facial landmark detection, represented by cascaded regression-based

1   Bournemouth University, Poole, BH12 5BB, UK. E-mail: S. Liu, sliu@bournemouth.ac.uk; X. Yang, xyang@bournemouth.ac.uk; J. J. Zhang, jzhang@bournemouth.ac.uk.

2   Harbin Institute of Technology, Harbin, 150001, China. E-mail: Y. Zhang, seekever@foxmail.com (✉); D. Shi, damingshi@hotmail.com.

methods, e.g., explicit shape regression [7], and the supervised descent method [8]. Many recent works following the cascaded regression framework consider how to improve efficiency [9, 10] and accuracy, taking into account variations in pose, expression, lighting, and partial occlusion [11, 12]. Although previous works have produced remarkable results on nearly frontal facial landmark detection, it is still not easy to locate landmarks across a large range of poses under uncontrolled conditions. A few recent works [13–15] have started to consider multi-pose landmark detection, and can deal with small variations in pose. How to solve the multiple local minima issue caused by large differences in pose is our concern.

On the other hand, facial landmark detection and tracking can benefit from reconstructed 3D face geometry based on existing 3D facial expression databases. Remarkably, Cao et al. [16] extended the 3D dynamic expression model to work with even monocular video, with improved performance of facial landmark detection and tracking. Their methods work well with indoor videos for a range of expressions, but tend to fail for videos captured *in the wild* (ITW) due to uncontrollable lighting, varying backgrounds, and partial occlusions. Many researchers have made great efforts on dealing with ITW situations and have achieved many successes [16–18]. However, the expressiveness of captured facial landmarks from these ITW approaches is limited since most pay little attention to very useful details not represented by sparse

landmarks. Additionally, optical flow methods have been applied to track facial landmarks [19]. Such a method can take advantage of fine-grained detail, down to pixel level. However, it is sensitive to shadows, light variations, and occlusion, which makes it difficult to apply in noisy uncontrolled environments.

To this end, we have designed a new ITW facial landmark detection and tracking method that employs optical flow to enhance the expressiveness of captured facial landmarks. A flowchart of our work is shown in Fig. 1. First, we use a robust 2D facial landmark detection method which combines canonical correlation analysis (CCA) with a global supervised descent method (SDM). Then we improve the stability and accuracy of the landmarks by reconstructing 3D face geometry in a coarse to dense manner. We employ an ITW method to extract a coarse reconstruction and corresponding texture via sparse landmark detection, identity, and expression estimation. Then, we use a face tracking flow method that exploits the coarsely reconstructed model to correct inaccurate tracking and recover details of the weakly textured area, which is used to iteratively update the face model. Finally, after convergence, a dense reconstruction is estimated, thus boosting the tracked landmark result. Our contributions are three fold:

- A novel robust 2D facial landmark detection method which works across a range of poses, based on combining shape-face CCA with SDM.
- A novel 3D facial optical flow tracking method for

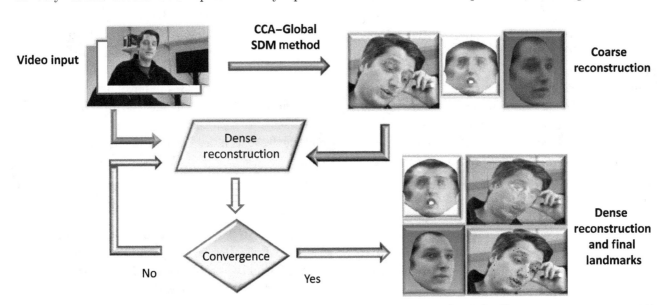

Fig. 1 Flowchart of our method.

robustly tracking expressive facial landmarks to enhance the location result.

- Accurate and smooth landmark tracking result sequences due to simultaneously registering the 3D facial shape model in a coarse-to-dense manner.

The rest of the paper is structured as follows. The following section reviews related work. In Section 3, we introduce how we detect 2D landmarks from monocular video and create the coarsely reconstructed landmarks. Section 4 describes how we refine landmarks by use of optical flow to achieve a dense reconstruction result.

2 Literature review

To reconstruct the 3D geometry of the face, facial landmarks first have to be detected. Most facial landmark detection methods can be categorized into three groups: constrained local methods [20, 21], active appearance models (AAM) [3, 22, 23], and regressors [24–26]. The performance of constrained local methods is limited in the wild because of the limited discriminative power of their local experts. Since the input is uncontrolled in ITW videos, person specific facial landmark detection methods such as AAM are inappropriate. AAM methods explicitly minimize the difference between the synthesized face image and the real image, and are able to produce stable landmark detection results for videos in controlled environments. However, conventional wisdom states that their inherent facial texture appearance models are not powerful enough for ITW problems. Although in recent literature [18] efforts have been made to address this problem, superior results to other ITW methods have not been achieved. Regressor-based methods, on the other hand, work well in the face of ITW problems and are robust [27], efficient [28], and accurate [24, 29].

Most ITW landmark detection methods were originally designed for processing single images instead of videos [8, 24, 30]. On image facial landmark detection datasets such as 300-W [31], Helen [32], and LFW [33], existing ITW methods have achieved varying levels of success. Although they provide accurate landmarks for individual images, they do not produce temporally or spatially coherent results because they are sensitive to the bounding box provided by face detector. ITW methods can only produce semantically correct but inconsistent landmarks, and while these facial landmarks might seem accurate when examined individually, they are poor in weakly textured areas such as around the face contour or where a higher level of detail is required to generate convincing animation. One could use sequence smoothing techniques as post processing [16, 17], but this can lead to an oversmoothed sequence with a loss of facial performance expressiveness and detail.

It is only recently that an ITW video dataset [34] was introduced to benchmark landmark detection in continuous ITW videos. Nevertheless, the number of facial landmarks defined in Ref. [34] is limited and does not allow us to reconstruct the person's nose and eyebrow shape. Since we aim to robustly locate facial landmarks from ITW videos, we collected a new dataset by downloading YouTube videos and recording video with smartphones, as a basis for comparing our method to other existing methods.

In terms of 3D facial geometry reconstruction for the refinement of landmarks, recently there has been an increasing amount of research based on 2D images and videos [19, 35–41]. In order to accurately track facial landmarks, it is important to first reconstruct face geometry. Due to the lack of depth information in images and videos, most methods rely on *blendshape* priors to model nonrigid deformation while structure-from-motion, photometric stereo, or other methods [42] are used to account for unseen variation [36, 38] or details [19, 37].

Due to the nonrigidness of the face and depth ambiguity in 2D images, 3D facial priors are often needed for initializing 3D poses and to provide regularization. Nowadays consumer grade depth sensors such as Kinect have been proven successful, and many methods [43–45] have been introduced to refine its noisy output and generate high quality facial scans of the kind which used to require high end devices such as laser scanners [46]. In this paper we use the FaceWarehouse [43] as our 3D facial prior. Existing methods can be grouped into two categories. One group aims to robustly deliver coarse results, while the other one aims to recover fine-grained details. For example, methods such as those in Refs. [19, 37, 40] can reconstruct details such as wrinkles, and track subtle facial movements, but are affected by shadows and occlusions. Robust methods such as Refs. [35, 36, 39] can track facial performance in the presence of noise but often miss subtle details such as small eyelid and mouth movements, which are important in conveying the target's emotion and to generate convincing animation. Although we use a 3D optical flow approach similar to that in Ref. [19] to track facial performance, we also deliver stable results even in noisy situations or when the quality of the automatically reconstructed coarse model is poor.

3 Coarse landmark detection and reconstruction

An example of coarse landmark detection and reconstruction is shown in Fig. 2. To initialize our method, we build an average shape model from the input video. First, we run a face detector [47] on the input video to be tracked. Due to the uncontrolled nature of the input video, it might fail in challenging frames. In addition to filtering out failed frames, we also detect the blurriness of remaining ones by thresholding the standard deviation of their Laplacian filtered results. Failed and blurry frames are not used in coarse reconstruction as they can contaminate the reconstructed average shape.

3.1 Robust 2D facial landmark detection

Next, inspired by Refs. [28, 48], we use our robust 2D facial landmark detector which combines shape-face CCA and global SDM. It is trained on a large multi-pose, multi-expression face dataset, FaceWarehouse [16], to locate the position of 74 fiducial points. Note that our detector is robust in the wild because the input videos for shape model reconstruction are from uncontrolled environments.

Using SDM, for one image $\boldsymbol{d}$, the locations of p landmarks $\vec{x} = [x_1, y_1, \ldots, x_p, y_p]$ are given by

Fig. 2 Example of detected coarse landmarks and reconstructed facial mesh for a single frame.

a feature mapping function $\vec{h}(\boldsymbol{d}(\vec{x}))$, where $\boldsymbol{d}(\vec{x})$ indexes landmarks in the image $\boldsymbol{d}$. The facial landmark detection problem can be regarded as an optimization problem:

$$f(\vec{x}_0 + \Delta\vec{x}) = \|\vec{h}(\boldsymbol{d}(\vec{x}_0 + \Delta\vec{x})) - \phi_*\|_2^2 \quad (1)$$

where $\phi_* = \vec{h}(\boldsymbol{d}(\vec{x}_*))$ represents the feature extracted according to correct landmarks $\vec{x}_*$, which is known in the training images, but unknown in the test images. A general descent mapping can be learned from training dataset. The supervised descent method form is

$$\vec{x}_k = \vec{x}_{k-1} - \boldsymbol{R}_{k-1}(\phi_{k-1} - \phi_*) \quad (2)$$

Since ϕ_* for a test image is unknown but constant, SDM modifies the objective to align with respect to the average of $\overline{\phi}_*$ over the training set, and the update rule is then modified:

$$\Delta\vec{x} = \boldsymbol{R}_k(\overline{\phi}_* - \phi_k) \quad (3)$$

Instead of learning only one $\boldsymbol{R}_k$ over all samples during one updating step, the global SDM learns a series of $\boldsymbol{R}^t$, each for a subset of samples S^t, where the whole set of samples is divided into T subsets $S = \{S^t\}_1^T$.

A generic descent method exists under these two conditions: (i) $\boldsymbol{R}\vec{h}(\vec{x})$ is a strictly locally monotone operator anchored at the optimal solution, and (ii) $\vec{h}(\vec{x})$ is locally Lipschitz continuous anchored at $\vec{x}_*$. For a function with only one minimum, these normally hold. But a complicated function may have several local minima in a relatively small neighborhood, so the original SDM tends to average conflicting gradient directions. Instead, the global SDM ensures that if the samples are properly partitioned into subsets, there is a descent method in each of the subsets. $\boldsymbol{R}_t$ for subset S_t can be solved as a constrained optimization problem:

$$\min_{S,R} \sum_{t=1}^{T} \sum_{i \in S^t} \|\Delta\vec{x}_* - \boldsymbol{R}_t \Delta\phi^{i,t}\|^2 \quad (4)$$

such that $\Delta\vec{x}_*^i \boldsymbol{R}_t \Delta\phi^{i,t} > 0, \quad \forall\, t, i \in S^t \quad (5)$

where $\Delta\vec{x}_*^i = \vec{x}_*^i - \vec{x}_k^i$, $\Delta\phi^{i,t} = \overline{\phi}_*^t - \phi^i$, and where $\overline{\phi}_*^t$ averages all ϕ_* over the subset S^t. Equation (5) guarantees that the solution satisfies descent method condition (i). It is NP-hard to solve Eq. (4), so we use a deterministic scheme to approximate the solution. A set of sufficient conditions for Eq. (5) is given:

$$\Delta\vec{x}_*^{i\mathrm{T}} \Delta\boldsymbol{X}_*^t > \vec{0}, \quad \forall\, t, i \in S^t \quad (6)$$

$$\Delta\boldsymbol{\Phi}^{t\mathrm{T}} \Delta\phi^{i,t} > \vec{0}, \quad \forall\, t, i \in S^t \quad (7)$$

where $\Delta \boldsymbol{X}_*^t = [\Delta \vec{x}_*^{1,t}, \ldots, \Delta \vec{x}_*^{i,t}, \ldots]$, each column is $\Delta \vec{x}_*^{i,t}$ from the subset S^t; $\Delta \Phi^t = [\Delta \phi^{1,t}, \ldots, \Delta \phi^{i,t}, \ldots]$, and each column is $\Delta \phi^{i,t}$ from the subset S^t.

It is known that $\Delta \vec{x}$ and $\Delta \phi$ are embedded in a lower dimensional manifold for human faces, so dimension reduction methods (e.g., PCA) on the whole training set $\Delta \vec{x}$ and $\Delta \phi$ can be used for approximation. The global SDM authors project $\Delta \vec{x}$ onto the subspace spanned by the first two components of the $\Delta \vec{x}$ space, and project $\Delta \phi$ onto the subspace spanned by the first component of the $\Delta \phi$ space. Thus, there are 2^{2+1} subsets in their work. This is a very naive scheme and unsuitable for face alignment. Correlation-based dimension reduction theory can be introduced to develop a more practical and efficient strategy for low dimensional approximation of the high dimensional partition problem.

Considering the low dimensional manifold, the $\Delta \vec{x}$ space and $\Delta \phi$ space can be projected onto a medium-low dimensional space with projection matrices $\boldsymbol{Q}$ and $\boldsymbol{P}$, respectively, which keeps the projected vectors $\vec{v} = \boldsymbol{Q} \Delta \vec{x}$, $\vec{u} = \boldsymbol{P} \Delta \phi$ sufficiently correlated: (i) $\vec{v}$, $\vec{u}$ lie in the same low dimensional space, and (ii) for each jth dimension, $\text{sign}(v_j, u_j) = 1$. If the projection satisfies these two conditions, the projected samples $\{\vec{u}^i, \vec{v}^i\}$ can be partitioned into different hyperoctants in this space simply according to the signs of $\vec{u}^i$, due to condition (ii). Since samples in a hyperoctant are sufficiently close to each other, this partition can carry small neighborhoods better. It is also a compact low dimensional approximation of the high dimensional hyperoctant-based partition strategy in both $\Delta \vec{x}$ space and $\Delta \phi$ space, which is a sufficient condition for the existence of a generic descent method, as mentioned above.

For convenience, we re-denote $\Delta \vec{x}$ as $\vec{y} \in \Re^n$, re-denote $\Delta \phi$ as $\vec{x} \in \Re^m$, $\boldsymbol{Y}_{s \times n} = [\vec{y}^1, \ldots, \vec{y}^i, \ldots, \vec{y}^s]$ collects all $\vec{y}^i$ from the training set, and $\boldsymbol{X}_{s \times m} = [\vec{x}^1, \ldots, \vec{x}^i, \ldots, \vec{x}^s]$ collects all $\vec{x}^i$ from the training set. The projection matrices are:

$$\boldsymbol{Q}_{r \times n} = [\vec{q}_1, \ldots, \vec{q}_j, \ldots, \vec{q}_r]^{\mathrm{T}}, \quad \vec{q}_j \in \Re^n$$
$$\boldsymbol{P}_{r \times m} = [\vec{p}_1, \ldots, \vec{p}_j, \ldots, \vec{p}_r]^{\mathrm{T}}, \quad \vec{p}_j \in \Re^m$$

The projection vectors are $\vec{v} = \boldsymbol{Q} \vec{y}$ and $\vec{u} = \boldsymbol{P} \vec{x}$. We denote the projection vectors along the sample space by $\vec{w}_j = \boldsymbol{Y} \vec{q}_j = [v_j^1, \ldots, v_j^i, \ldots, v_j^s]^{\mathrm{T}}$, and $\vec{z}_j = \boldsymbol{X} \vec{p}_j = [u_j^1, \ldots, u_j^i, \ldots, u_j^s]^{\mathrm{T}}$. This problem can be formulated as a constrained optimization problem:

$$\min_{\boldsymbol{P},\boldsymbol{Q}} \sum_{j=1}^r \| \boldsymbol{Y} \vec{q}_j - \boldsymbol{X} \vec{p}_j \|^2 = \min_{\boldsymbol{P},\boldsymbol{Q}} \sum_{j=1}^r \sum_{i=1}^s (v_j^i - u_j^i)^2 \quad (8)$$

such that $\sum_{j=1}^r \sum_{i=1}^s \text{sign}(v_j^i, u_j^i) = sr$ $\quad (9)$

After normalizing the samples $\{\vec{y}^i\}_{i=1:s}$ and $\{\vec{x}^i\}_{i=1:s}$ (removing means and dividing by the standard deviation), the sign-correlation constrained optimization problem can be solved by standard canonical correlation analysis (CCA). The CCA problem for the normalized $\{\vec{y}^i\}_{i=1:s}$ and $\{\vec{x}^i\}_{i=1:s}$ is:

$$\max_{\vec{p}_j, \vec{q}_j} \vec{q}_j^{\mathrm{T}} \text{cov}(\boldsymbol{Y}, \boldsymbol{X}) \vec{p}_j \quad (10)$$

such that

$$\vec{q}_j^{\mathrm{T}} \text{var}(\boldsymbol{Y}, \boldsymbol{Y}) \vec{q}_j = 1, \quad \vec{p}_j^{\mathrm{T}} \text{var}(\boldsymbol{X}, \boldsymbol{X}) \vec{p}_j = 1 \quad (11)$$

Following the CCA algorithm, the max sign-correlation pair $\vec{p}_1$ and $\vec{q}_1$ are solved first. Then one seeks $\vec{p}_2$ and $\vec{q}_2$ by maximizing the same correlation subject to the constraint that they are to be uncorrelated with the first pair of canonical variables $\vec{w}_1$, $\vec{z}_1$. This procedure is continued until $\vec{p}_r$ and $\vec{q}_r$ are found.

After all $\vec{p}_j$ and $\vec{q}_j$ have been computed, we only need the projection matrix $\boldsymbol{P}$ in $\Delta \vec{x}$ space. We then project each $\Delta \vec{x}^i$ into the sign-correlation subspace to get the reduced feature $\vec{u}^i = \boldsymbol{P} \Delta \vec{x}^i$. Then we partition the whole sample space into independent descent domains by considering the sign of each dimension of $\vec{u}^i$ and group it into the corresponding hyperoctant. Finally, in order to solve Eq. (4) at each iterative step, we learn a descent mapping for every subset at each iterative step with the ridge regression algorithm. When testing a face image, we also use the projection matrix $\boldsymbol{P}$ to find its corresponding descent domain and predict its shape increment at each iterative step.

Regressor-based methods are sensitive to initialization, and sometimes require multiple initializations to produce a stable result [24]. Generally, the obtained results of the landmark positions are accurate and visually plausible when inspected individually, but they may vary drastically on weakly textured areas when the face initialization changes slightly, since in these methods the temporally and spatially coherent nature of videos is not considered. Since we are reconstructing faces from input videos recorded in an uncontrolled environment, the bounding box generated by the face detector can be unstable. The unstable initialization and the sensitive nature of the landmark detector on missing and blurry frames lead to jittery and unconvincing results.

Nevertheless, the set of unstable landmarks is enough to reconstruct a rough facial geometry and texture model of the target person. As in Ref. [17], we first align a generic 3D face mesh to the 2D landmarks. The corresponding indices of the facial landmarks of the nose, eye boundaries, lips, and eyebrow contours are fixed, whereas the vertex indices of the face contour are recomputed with respect to frame specific poses and expressions. To generate uniformly distributed contour points we selectively project possible contour vertices onto the image and sample its convex hull with uniform 2D spacing.

The facial reconstruction problem can be formulated as an optimization problem in which the *pose*, *expression*, and *identity* of the person are determined in a coordinate descent manner.

3.2 Pose estimation

Following Ref. [49] we use a pinhole camera model with radial distortion. Assuming the pixels are square and that the center of projection is coincident with the image center, the projection operation $\prod$ depends on 10 parameters: the 3D orientation R (3×1 vector), the translation t (3×1 vector), the focal length f (scalar), and the distortion parameter k (3×1 vector). We assume the same distortion and focal length for the entire video, and initialize the focal length to be the pixel width of the video and distortion to zero. First, we apply a direct linear transform [50] to estimate the initial rotation and translation then optimize them via the Levenberg–Marquardt method with a robust loss function [51].

The 3D rotation matrix is constructed from the orientation vector R using:

$$\omega \leftarrow R/\sigma, \; \sigma \leftarrow \|R\| \tag{12}$$

$$\cos(\sigma)\mathbb{I} + (1-\cos(\sigma))\mathcal{K} + \sin(\sigma) \begin{vmatrix} 0 & -R_0 & R_1 \\ R_2 & 0 & -R_0 \\ -R_1 & R_0 & 0 \end{vmatrix} \tag{13}$$

whose derivative is computed via forward accumulation automatic differentiation [52].

3.3 Expression estimation

In the pose estimation stage, we used a generic face model for initialization, but to get more accurate results we need to adjust the model according to the expression and identity. We use the FaceWarehouse dataset [43], which contains the performances of 150 people with 47 different expressions. Since we are only tracking facial expressions, we select only the frontal facial vertices because the nose and head shape are not included in the detected landmarks. We flatten the 3D vertices and arrange them into a 3 mode data tensor. We compress the original tensor representing 30k vertices $\times$ 150 identities $\times$ 47 expressions into a 4k vertices $\times$ 50 identities $\times$ 25 expression coefficients core using higher order singular value decomposition [53]. Any facial mesh in the dataset can be approximated by the product of its core $B_{\text{exp}} = C \times U_{\text{id}}$ or $B_{\text{id}} = C \times U_{\text{exp}}$, where U_{id} and U_{exp} are the identity and expression orthonormal matrices respectively; B_{exp} is a person with different facial expressions, B_{id} is the same expression performed by different individuals.

For efficiency we first determine the identity with the compressed core and prevent over-fitting with an early stopping strategy. To generate plausible results we need to solve for the uncompressed expression coefficients with early stopping and box constrain them to lie within a valid range, which in the case of FaceWarehouse is between 0 and 1. We do not optimize identity and camera coefficients for individual frames. They are only optimized jointly after expression coefficients have been estimated.

We group the camera parameters into a vector $\theta = [R, t, f]$. We generate a person specific facial mesh B_{id} with this person's identity coefficient I, which results in the same individual performing the 47 defined expressions. The projection operator is defined as $\prod([x, y, z]^{\text{T}}) = r[x, y, z]^{\text{T}} + t$, where r is the 3×3 rotation matrix constructed from Eq. (13) and the radial distortion function $\mathbb{D}$ is defined as

$$\mathbb{D}(X', k) = f \times X'(1 + k_1 r^2 + k_2 r^4) \tag{14}$$

$$\mathbb{D}(Y', k) = f \times Y'(1 + k_1 r^2 + k_2 r^4) \tag{15}$$

$$r^2 = X'^2 + Y'^2, \quad X' = X/Z, \quad Y' = Y/Z \tag{16}$$

$$[X, Y, Z]^{\text{T}} = \prod([x, y, z]^{\text{T}}) \tag{17}$$

We minimize the squared distance between the 2D landmarks L after applying radial distortion while fixing the identity coefficient and pose parameters $\mathbb{D}$:

$$\min_E \frac{1}{2}|L - \mathbb{D}(\prod(B_{\text{id}} \cdot E, \theta), k)|^2 \qquad (18)$$

To solve this problem efficiently, we apply the reverse distortion to L, then rotate and translate the vertices. By denoting the projected coordinates by p, the derivative of E can be expressed efficiently as

$$(L - f \cdot p)\left(f \cdot \frac{B_{\text{id}(0,1)}^{(i)} + B_{\text{id}(2)}^{(i)} \cdot p}{Z}\right) \qquad (19)$$

We use the Levenberg–Marquardt method for initialization and perform line search [54] to constrain E to lie within the valid range.

3.4 Identity adaption

Since we cannot apply a generic B_{id} to different individuals with differing facial geometry, we solve for the subject's identity in a similar fashion to the expression coefficient. With the estimated expression coefficients from the last step, we generate facial meshes of different individuals performing the estimated expressions. Unlike expression coefficient estimation, we need to solve identity coefficient jointly across I frames with different poses and expressions. We denote the nth facial mesh by B_{exp}^n and minimize the distance:

$$\min_I \sum_n \frac{1}{2}|L^n - \mathbb{D}(\prod(B_{\text{exp}}^n \cdot I, \theta), k)|^2 \qquad (20)$$

while fixing all other parameters. Here it is important to exclude inaccurate single frames from being considered otherwise they lead to erroneous identity.

3.5 Camera estimation

Some videos may be captured with camera distortions. In order to reconstruct the 3D facial geometry as accurately as possible, we undistort the video by estimating its focal length and distortion parameters. All of the following dense tracking is performed in undistorted camera space. To avoid local minima caused by over-fitting the distortion parameters, we solve for focal length analytically using:

$$f = \frac{\sum_n L^n}{\sum_n \mathbb{D}(\prod(B_{\text{exp}}^n \cdot I, \theta), k)} \qquad (21)$$

then use nonlinear optimization to solve for radial distortion. We find the camera parameters by jointly minimizing the difference between the selected 2D landmarks L and their corresponding projected vertices:

$$\min_k \sum_n \frac{1}{2}|L^n - \mathbb{D}(\prod(B_{\text{exp}}^n \cdot I, \theta), k)|^2 \qquad (22)$$

3.6 Average texture estimation

In order to estimate an average texture, we extract per pixel color information from the video frames. We use the texture coordinates provided in FaceWarehouse to normalize the facial texture onto a flattened 2D map. By performing visibility tests we filter out invisible pixels. Since the eyeball and inside of the mouth are not modeled by facial landmarks or FaceWarehouse, we consider their texture separately. Although varying expressions, pose, and lighting conditions lead to texture variation across different frames, we use their summed average as a low rank approximation. Alternatively, we could use the median pixel values as it leads to sharper texture, but at the coarse reconstruction we choose not to because computing the median requires all the images to be available whereas the average can be computed on-the-fly without additional memory costs. Moreover, while the detected landmarks are not entirely accurate, robustness is more important than accuracy. Instead, we selectively compute the median of high quality frames from dense reconstruction to generate better texture in the next stage.

The idea of tracking the facial landmarks by minimizing the difference between synthesized view and the real image is similar to that used in active appearance models (AAM) [3]. The texture variance can be modeled and approximated by principle component analysis, and expression–pose specific texture can be used for better performance. Experimental results show that high rank approximation leads to unstable results because of the landmark detection in-the-wild issues. Moreover, AAM typically has to be trained on manually labeled images that are very accurate. Although it is able to fit the test image with better texture similarity, it is not suitable for robust automated landmark detection. A comparison of our method with traditional AAM method is shown later and examples of failed detections are shown in Fig. 3.

Up to this point, we have been optimizing the 3D coordinates of the facial mesh and the camera parameters. Due to the limited expressiveness of the facial dataset, which only contains 150 persons, the

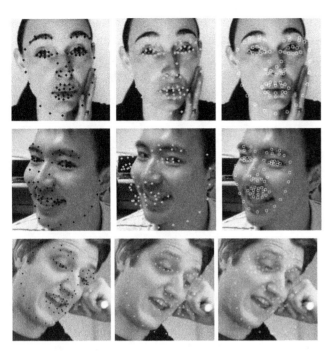

Fig. 3 Landmark tracking comparison. From left to right: ours, in-the-wild, AAM.

fitted facial mesh might not exactly fit the detected landmarks. To increase the expressiveness of the reconstructed model and add more person specific details, we use the method in Ref. [55] to deform the facial mesh reconstructed for each frame. We first assign the depth of the 2D landmarks to that of their corresponding 3D vertices, then unproject them into 3D space. Finally, we use the unprojected 3D coordinates as anchor points to deform the facial mesh of every frame.

Since the deformed facial mesh may not be represented by the original data, we need to add them into the person specific facial meshes B_{exp} and keep the original expression coefficients. Given an expression coefficient E we could reconstruct its corresponding facial mesh $F = B_{exp}E$. Thus the new deformed mesh base should be computed via $F_d = B_d E_d$. We flatten the deformed and original facial meshes using B_{exp}, then concatenate them together as $B_c = [B; B_d]^T$. We concatenate coefficients of the 47 expressions in FaceWarehouse and the recovered expressions from the video frames as $E_c = [E; E_d]^T$. The new deformed facial mesh base is computed from $B_d = E_c^{-1}B_c$.

We simply compute for each pixel the average color value and run the k-means algorithm [56] on the extracted eyeball and mouth interior textures,

saving a few representative k-means centers for fitting different expressions and eye movements. An example of the reconstructed average face texture is shown in Fig. 4(a).

4 Dense reconstruction to refine landmarks

4.1 Face tracking flow

In the previous step we reconstructed an average face model with a set of coarse facial landmarks. To deliver convincing results we need to track and reconstruct all of the vertices even in weakly textured areas. To robustly capture the 3D facial performance in each frame, we formulate the problem in terms of 3D optical flow and solve for dense correspondence between the 3D model and each video frame, optimally deforming the reference mesh to fit the seen image. We use the rendered average shape as initialization and treat it as the previous frame; we use the real image as the current frame to densely compute the displacement of all vertices. Assuming the pixel intensity does not change by the displacement, we may write:

$$I(x,y) = C(x + u, y + v) \qquad (23)$$

where I denotes the intensity value of the rendered image, C the real image, and x and y denote pixel coordinates. In addition, the gradient value of each pixel should also not change due to displacement because not only the pixel intensity but also the texture stay the same, which can be expressed as

$$\nabla I(x,y) = \nabla C(x + u, y + v) \qquad (24)$$

Finally, the smoothness constraint dictates that pixels should stay in the same spatial arrangement

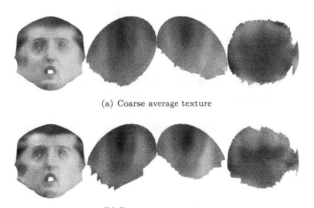

(a) Coarse average texture

(b) Dense average texture

Fig. 4 Refined texture after robust dense tracking.

to their original neighbors to avoid the aperture problem, especially since many facial areas are weakly textured, i.e., have no strong gradient. We search for $f = (u, v)^{\mathrm{T}}$ that satisfies the pixel intensity, gradient, and smoothness constraints.

By denoting each projected vertex of the face mesh by $p = \mathbb{D}(\prod(B_{\mathrm{id}}^n \cdot E, \theta), k)$, we formulate the energy as

$$E_{\mathrm{flow}}(f) = \sum_v |I(p+f) - C(p)|^2 + \alpha(|\nabla f|^2) + \beta(|\partial f|^2) \tag{25}$$

Here $|\nabla f|^2$ is a smoothness term and $\beta(|\partial f|^2)$ is a piecewise smooth term. As this is a highly nonlinear problem we adopt the numerical approximation in Ref. [57] and take a multi-scale approach to achieve robustness. We do not use the additional match term Eq. (26) in Ref. [58], where $\gamma(p)$ is the match weight: although we have the match from the landmarks to the vertices, we cannot measure the quality of the landmarks, as well as the matches, so:

$$E_{\mathrm{match}}(f) = \sum_p \mu(p)|p_I + f - p_C|^2 \mathrm{d}p \tag{26}$$

4.2 Robust tracking

Standard optical flow suffers from drift, occlusion, and varying visibility because of lack of explicit modeling. Since we already have a rough prior of the face from the coarse reconstruction step, we use it to correct and regularize the estimated optical flow.

We test the visibility of each vertex by comparing its transformed value to its rendered depth value. If it is larger than a threshold then it is considered to be invisible and not used to solve for pose and expression coefficient. To detect partially occluded areas we compute both the forward flow (rendered to real image f_{f}) and backward flow (real image to rendered f_{b}), and compute the difference for each of the vertices' projections:

$$\sum_p |f_{\mathrm{f}}(p) + f_{\mathrm{b}}(p + f_{\mathrm{f}}(p))|^2 \tag{27}$$

We use the GPU to compute the flow field whereas the expression coefficient and pose are computed on the CPU. Solving them for all vertices can be expensive when there is expression and pose variation, so to reduce the computational cost, we also check the norm of $f_{\mathrm{f}}(p)$ to filter out pixels with negligible displacement.

Because of the piecewise smoothness constraint, we consider vertices with large forward and backward flow differences to be occluded and exclude them

from the solution process. We first find the rotation and translation, then the expression coefficients after putative flow fields have been identified. The solution process is similar to that used in the previous section with the exception that we update each individual vertex at the end of the iterations to fit the real image as closely as possible. To exploit temporal and spatial coherence, we use the average of a frame's neighboring frames to initialize its pose and expression, then update them using coordinate descent. If desired, we reconstruct the average face model and texture from the densely tracked results and use the new model and texture to perform robust tracking again. An example of updated reconstructed average texture is shown in Fig. 4, which is *sharper* and *more accurate* than the coarsely reconstructed texture. Filtered vertices and the tracked mesh are shown in Fig. 5, where putative vertices are color coded and filtered out vertices are hidden. Note that the color of the actress' hand is very close to that of her face, so it is hard to mask out by color difference thresholding without piecewise smoothness regularization.

4.3 Texture update

Finally, after robust dense tracking results and the validity of each vertex have been determined, each valid vertex can be optionally optimized individually to recover further details. This is done in a coordinate descent manner with respect to the pose parameters. Updating all vertices with

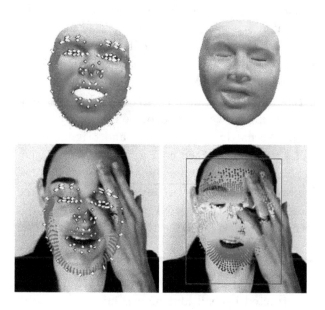

Fig. 5 Example of reconstruction with occlusion.

a standard nonlinear optimization routine might be inefficient because of the computational cost of inverting or approximating a large second order Hessian matrix, which is sparse in this case because the points do not have influence on each other. Thus, instead, we use the Schur complement trick [59] to reduce the computational cost. The whole pipeline of our method is summarized in Algorithm 1. Convergence is determined by the norm of the optical flow displacement. This criterion indicates whether further vertex adjustment is possible or necessary to minimize the difference between the observed image and synthesized result.

Compared to the method in Ref. [19], which also formulates the face tracking problem in an optical flow context, our method is more robust. In videos with large pose and expression variation, inaccurate coarse facial landmark initialization and partial occlusion caused by texturally similar objects, our method is more accurate and expressive and generates smoother results than the coarse reconstruction computed with landmarks from in-the-wild methods in Ref. [30].

Algorithm 1:   Automatic dense facial capture

Input: Video
CCA-GSDM landmark detection
Solve **Pose** on landmarks
Solve **Expression** using Eq. (18) on landmarks
Solve **Identity** using Eq. (20) on landmarks
Solve **Focal** using Eq. (21) on landmarks
Solve **Distortion** using Eq. (22) on landmarks
while not converged **do**
  while norm(flow) > threshold **do**
    Determine vertex validity using depth check
    Determine vertex validity using Eq. (27)
    Determine vertex validity using norm of flow displacement
    Solve **Pose** on optical flow
    Solve **Expression** using Eq. (18) on optical flow
    if Inner max iteration reached **then**
      break
    end if
  end while
  Update camera
  Update vertex
  Update texture
  if Outer max iteration reached **then**
    break
  end if
end while
Output: Facial meshes, poses, expressions

---

5   Experiments

Our proposed method aims to deliver smooth facial performances and landmark tracking in uncontrolled in-the-wild videos. Although recently a new dataset has been introduced designed for facial landmark tracking in the wild [34], it is not adequate for this work since we aim to deliver *smooth* tracking results rather than just locating landmark positions. In addition, we also concentrate on capturing detail to reconstruct realistic expressions. Comparison of the expression norm between the coarse landmarks and dense tracking is shown in Fig. 6.

In order to evaluate the performance of our robust method, AAM [3, 22], and an in-the-wild regressor-based method [28, 30] working as *fully automated* methods, we collected 50 online videos with frame counts ranging from 150 to 897 and manually labeled them. Their resolution is 640×360. There are a wide range of different poses and expressions in these videos, and heavy partial occlusion as well. Being *fully automated* means that given any in-the-wild video no more additional effort is required to tune the model. We manually label landmarks for a quarter of the frames sampled uniformly throughout the entire video to train a person specific AAM model then use the trained model to track the landmarks. Note that doing so *disqualifies* the AAM approach as a *fully automated* method. Next we manually correct the tracked result to generate a smooth and visually plausible landmark sequence. We treat such sequences as ground truth and test each method's accuracy against it. We also use these manually labeled landmarks to build corresponding coarse facial models and texture in a similar way to the approach used in Section 3. The result is shown in Table 1. Each numeric column represents the error between the ground truth and the method's output. Following standard practice [24, 28, 60], we use the inter-pupillary distance normalized landmark error. Mesh reconstruction error is measured by the average L_2 distance between the reconstructed meshes. Texture error is measured by the average of per-pixel color difference between the reconstructed textures.

We mainly compare our method to appearance-based methods [3, 22] and in-the-wild methods [28, 30] because they are appropriate for in-the-wild video and have similar aims to minimize texture

(a) Smoothness evaluation of in-the-wild

(b) Smoothness evaluation of AAM

(c) Smoothness evaluation of our method

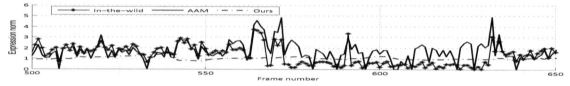

(d) Overall smoothness evaluation

Fig. 6 Example tracking results.

Table 1 Whole set error comparison

Method	Mesh	Texture	Landmark
Ours 1 iteration	**13.3**	**29.2**	**4.4**
Ours 2 iteration	**10.3**	**25.4**	**3.2**
Kazemi and Sullivan [30]	33.2	95.4	9.7
Ren et al. [28]	37.8	114.3	7.4
Donner et al. [22]	23.3	67.7	15.2
Cootes et al. [3]	24.3	86.5	24.4
Low	41.3	136.8	35.4
High	54.3	186.5	32.2

discrepancy between synthetic views and real images. We have also built a CUDA-based face tracking application using our method; it can achieve real-time tracking. The tested video resolution is 640 × 360, for which ir achieves more than 30 fps, benefiting from CUDA speed up. The dense points (there are 5760 of them) are from the frontal face of a standard blendshape mesh.

For completeness we also used the detected landmarks obtained from in-the-wild methods to train the AAM models, then used these to detect landmarks in videos. Doing so *qualifies* them as *fully automated* methods again. Due to the somewhat inconsistent results produced by in-the-wild landmark detectors, we use both high and

low rank texture approximation thresholds when training the AAM. Note that although Donner et al. [22] propose use of regression relevant information which may be discarded by purely generative PCA-based models, they also use an approximate texture variance model. Models trained with low rank variance are essentially the same as our approach of just taking the average of all images. While low rank AAM can accurately track the pose of the face most of the time when there is no large rotation, it fails to track facial point movements such as closing and opening of eyes, and talking, because the low rank model limits its expressiveness. High rank AAM, on the other hand, can track facial point movements but produces unstable results due to the instability of the training data provided by the in-the-wild method. Experimental results of training AAM with landmarks detected by the method in Ref. [30] are shown in the *Low* and *High* columns of Table 1

We also considered spearately a challenging subset of the videos, in which there is more partial occlusion, large head rotation or exaggerated facial expression. The performance of each method is given in Table 2. A comparison of our method to AAM and the in-the-wild method is shown in Fig. 6, where

Table 2 Challenging subset error comparison

Method	Mesh	Texture	Landmark
Ours 1 iteration	**41.7**	**59.1**	**7.2**
Ours 2 iteration	**15.1**	**35.2**	**4.1**
Kazemi and Sullivan [30]	92.3	95.4	19.2
Ren et al. [28]	88.1	114.3	11.4
Donner et al. [22]	97.3	142.7	21.9
Cootes et al. [3]	87.9	136.2	21.3
Low	114.3	146.5	25.3
High	134.7	186.2	33.4

the x axis is the frame count and the y axis is the norm of the expression coefficient. Compared to facial performance tracking with only coarse and inaccurate landmarks, our method is very stable and has a lower error rate than the other two methods. Further landmark tracking results are shown in Fig. 7. Additional results and potential applications are shown in the Electronic Supplementary Material.

6 Conclusions

We have proposed a novel fully automated method for robust facial landmark detection and tracking across poses and expressions for in-the-wild monocular videos. In our work, shape-face canonical correlation analysis is combined with a global supervised descent method to achieve robust coarse 2D facial landmark detection across poses. We perform coarse-to-dense 3D facial expression reconstruction with a 3D facial prior to boost tracked landmarks. We have evaluated its performance with respect to state-of-the-art landmark detection methods and empirically compared the tracked results to those of conventional approaches. Compared to conventional tracking methods that are able to capture subtle facial movement details, our method is fully automated, just as expressive and robust in noisy situations. Compared to other robust in-the-wild methods, our method delivers smooth tracking results and is able to capture small facial movements even for weakly textured areas. Moreover, we can accurately compute the possibility of a facial area being occluded in a particular frame, allowing us to avoid erroneous results. The 3D facial geometry and performance reconstructed and captured by our method are not only accurate and visually convincing, but we can also extract 2D landmarks from the mesh and use them in other methods that depend on 2D facial landmarks, such as facial editing, registration, and recognition.

Currently we are only using the average texture model for all poses and expressions. To further improve the expressiveness, we could adopt a similar approach to that taken for active appearance models, where after we have robustly built an average face model, texture variance caused by different lighting conditions, pose and expression variation could also be modeled to improve the expressiveness and accuracy of the tracking results.

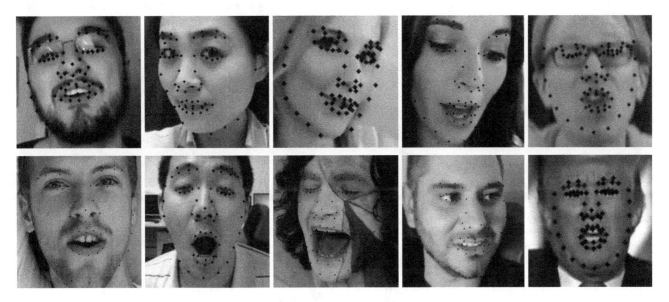

Fig. 7 Landmark tracking results.

Acknowledgements

This work was supported by the Harbin Institute of Technology Scholarship Fund 2016 and the National Centre for Computer Animation, Bournemouth University.

References

[1] Mori, M.; MacDorman, K. F.; Kageki, N. The uncanny valley [from the field]. *IEEE Robotics & Automation Magazine* Vol. 19, No. 2, 98–100, 2012.

[2] Cootes, T. F.; Taylor, C. J.; Cooper, D. H.; Graham, J. Active shape models—Their training and application. *Computer Vision and Image Understanding* Vol. 61, No. 1, 38–59, 1995.

[3] Cootes, T. F.; Edwards, G. J.; Taylor, C. J. Active appearance models. *IEEE Transactions on Pattern Analysis and Machine Intelligence* Vol. 23, No. 6, 681–685, 2001.

[4] Cristinacce, D.; Cootes, T. F. Feature detection and tracking with constrained local models. In: Proceedings of the British Machine Conference, 95.1–95.10, 2006.

[5] Gonzalez-Mora, J.; De la Torre, F.; Murthi, R.; Guil, N.; Zapata, E. L. Bilinear active appearance models. In: Proceedings of IEEE 11th International Conference on Computer Vision, 1–8, 2007.

[6] Lee, H.-S.; Kim, D. Tensor-based AAM with continuous variation estimation: Application to variation-robust face recognition. *IEEE Transactions on Pattern Analysis and Machine Intelligence* Vol. 31, No. 6, 1102–1116, 2009.

[7] Cao, X.; Wei, Y.; Wen, F.; Sun, J. Face alignment by explicit shape regression. U.S. Patent Application 13/728,584. 2012-12-27.

[8] Xiong, X.; De la Torre, F. Supervised descent method and its applications to face alignment. In: Proceedings of the IEEE Conference on Computer Vision and Pattern Recognition, 532–539, 2013.

[9] Xing, J.; Niu, Z.; Huang, J.; Hu, W.; Yan, S. Towards multi-view and partially-occluded face alignment. In: Proceedings of the IEEE Conference on Computer Vision and Pattern Recognition, 1829–1836, 2014.

[10] Yan, J.; Lei, Z.; Yi, D.; Li, S. Z. Learn to combine multiple hypotheses for accurate face alignment. In: Proceedings of the IEEE International Conference on Computer Vision Workshops, 392–396, 2013.

[11] Burgos-Artizzu, X. P.; Perona, P.; Dollár, P. Robust face landmark estimation under occlusion. In: Proceedings of the IEEE International Conference on Computer Vision, 1513–1520, 2013.

[12] Yang, H.; He, X.; Jia, X.; Patras, I. Robust face alignment under occlusion via regional predictive power estimation. *IEEE Transactions on Image Processing* Vol. 24, No. 8, 2393–2403, 2015.

[13] Feng, Z.-H.; Huber, P.; Kittler, J.; Christmas, W.; Wu, X.-J. Random cascaded-regression copse for robust facial landmark detection. *IEEE Signal Processing Letters* Vol. 22, No. 1, 76–80, 2015.

[14] Yang, H.; Jia, X.; Patras, I.; Chan, K.-P. Random subspace supervised descent method for regression problems in computer vision. *IEEE Signal Processing Letters* Vol. 22, No. 10, 1816–1820, 2015.

[15] Zhu, S.; Li, C.; Loy, C. C.; Tang, X. Face alignment by coarse-to-fine shape searching. In: Proceedings of the IEEE Conference on Computer Vision and Pattern Recognition, 4998–5006, 2015.

[16] Cao, C.; Hou, Q.; Zhou, K. Displaced dynamic expression regression for real-time facial tracking and animation. *ACM Transactions on Graphics* Vol. 33, No. 4, Article No. 43, 2014.

[17] Liu, S.; Yang, X.; Wang, Z.; Xiao, Z.; Zhang, J. Real-time facial expression transfer with single video camera. *Computer Animation and Virtual Worlds* Vol. 27, Nos. 3–4, 301–310, 2016.

[18] Tzimiropoulos, G.; Pantic, M. Optimization problems for fast AAM fitting in-the-wild. In: Proceedings of the IEEE International Conference on Computer Vision, 593–600, 2013.

[19] Suwajanakorn, S.; Kemelmacher-Shlizerman, I.; Seitz, S. M. Total moving face reconstruction. In: *Computer Vision–ECCV 2014*. Fleet, D.; Pajdla, T.; Schiele, B.; Tuytelaars, T. Eds. Springer International Publishing, 796–812, 2014.

[20] Cootes, T. F.; Taylor, C. J. Statistical models of appearance for computer vision. 2004. Available at http://personalpages.manchester.ac.uk/staff/timothy.f.cootes/Models/app_models.pdf.

[21] Yan, S.; Liu, C.; Li, S. Z.; Zhang, H.; Shum, H.-Y.; Cheng, Q. Face alignment using texture-constrained active shape models. *Image and Vision Computing* Vol. 21, No. 1, 69–75, 2003.

[22] Donner, R.; Reiter, M.; Langs, G.; Peloschek, P.; Bischof, H. Fast active appearance model search using canonical correlation analysis. *IEEE Transactions on Pattern Analysis and Machine Intelligence* Vol. 28, No. 10, 1690–1694, 2006.

[23] Matthews, I.; Baker, S. Active appearance models revisited. *International Journal of Computer Vision* Vol. 60, No. 2, 135–164, 2004.

[24] Cao, X.; Wei, Y.; Wen, F.; Sun, J. Face alignment by explicit shape regression. *International Journal of Computer Vision* Vol. 107, No. 2, 177–190, 2014.

[25] Dollár, P.; Welinder, P.; Perona, P. Cascaded pose regression. In: Proceedings of IEEE Computer Society Conference on Computer Vision and Pattern Recognition, 1078–1085, 2010.

[26] Zhou, S. K.; Comaniciu, D. Shape regression machine. In: *Information Processing in Medical Imaging*. Karssemeijer, N.; Lelieveldt, B. Eds. Springer Berlin Heidelberg, 13–25, 2007.

[27] Burgos-Artizzu, X. P.; Perona, P.; Dollár, P. Robust face landmark estimation under occlusion. In: Proceedings of the IEEE International Conference on Computer Vision, 1513–1520, 2013.

[28] Ren, S.; Cao, X.; Wei, Y.; Sun, J. Face alignment

at 3000 fps via regressing local binary features. In: Proceedings of the IEEE Conference on Computer Vision and Pattern Recognition, 1685–1692, 2014.

[29] Cootes, T. F.; Ionita, M. C.; Lindner, C.; Sauer, P. Robust and accurate shape model fitting using random forest regression voting. In: *Computer Vision–ECCV 2012*. Fitzgibbon, A.; Lazebnik, S.; Perona, P.; Sato, Y.; Schmid, C. Eds. Springer Berlin Heidelberg, 278–291, 2012.

[30] Kazemi, V.; Sullivan, J. One millisecond face alignment with an ensemble of regression trees. In: Proceedings of the IEEE Conference on Computer Vision and Pattern Recognition, 1867–1874, 2014.

[31] Sagonas, C.; Tzimiropoulos, G.; Zafeiriou, S.; Pantic, M. 300 faces in-the-wild challenge: The first facial landmark localization challenge. In: Proceedings of the IEEE International Conference on Computer Vision Workshops, 397–403, 2013.

[32] Zhou, F.; Brandt, J.; Lin, Z. Exemplar-based graph matching for robust facial landmark localization. In: Proceedings of the IEEE International Conference on Computer Vision, 1025–1032, 2013.

[33] Huang, G. B.; Ramesh, M.; Berg, T.; Learned-Miller, E. Labeled faces in the wild: A database for studying face recognition in unconstrained environments. Technical Report 07-49, University of Massachusetts, Amherst, 2007.

[34] Shen, J.; Zafeiriou, S.; Chrysos, G. G.; Kossaifi, J.; Tzimiropoulos, G.; Pantic, M. The first facial landmark tracking in-the-wild challenge: Benchmark and results. In: Proceedings of the IEEE International Conference on Computer Vision Workshop, 1003–1011, 2015.

[35] Cao, C.; Bradley, D.; Zhou, K.; Beeler, T. Realtime high-fidelity facial performance capture. *ACM Transactions on Graphics* Vol. 34, No. 4, Article No. 46, 2015.

[36] Cao, C.; Wu, H.; Weng, Y.; Shao, T.; Zhou, K. Real-time facial animation with image-based dynamic avatars. *ACM Transactions on Graphics* Vol. 35, No. 4, Article No. 126, 2016.

[37] Garrido, P.; Valgaerts, L.; Wu, C.; Theobalt, C. Reconstructing detailed dynamic face geometry from monocular video. *ACM Transactions on Graphics* Vol. 32, No. 6, Article No. 158, 2013.

[38] Ichim, A. E.; Bouaziz, S.; Pauly, M. Dynamic 3D avatar creation from hand-held video input. *ACM Transactions on Graphics* Vol. 34, No. 4, Article No. 45, 2015.

[39] Saito, S.; Li, T.; Li, H. Real-time facial segmentation and performance capture from RGB input. *arXiv preprint* arXiv:1604.02647, 2016.

[40] Shi, F.; Wu, H.-T.; Tong, X.; Chai, J. Automatic acquisition of high-fidelity facial performances using monocular videos. *ACM Transactions on Graphics* Vol. 33, No. 6, Article No. 222, 2014.

[41] Thies, J.; Zollhöfer, M.; Stamminger, M.; Theobalt, C.; Nießner, M. Face2face: Real-time face capture and reenactment of RGB videos. In: Proceedings of the IEEE Conference on Computer Vision and Pattern

Recognition, 1, 2016.

[42] Furukawa, Y.; Ponce, J. Accurate camera calibration from multi-view stereo and bundle adjustment. *International Journal of Computer Vision* Vol. 84, No. 3, 257–268, 2009.

[43] Cao, C.; Weng, Y.; Zhou, S.; Tong, Y.; Zhou, K. FaceWarehouse: A 3D facial expression database for visual computing. *IEEE Transactions on Visualization and Computer Graphics* Vol. 20, No. 3, 413–425, 2014.

[44] Newcombe, R. A.; Izadi, S.; Hilliges, O.; Molyneaux, D.; Kim, D.; Davison, A. J.; Kohi, P.; Shotton, J.; Hodges, S.; Fitzgibbon, A. KinectFusion: Realtime dense surface mapping and tracking. In: Proceedings of the 10th IEEE International Symposium on Mixed and Augmented Reality, 127–136, 2011.

[45] Weise, T.; Bouaziz, S.; Li, H.; Pauly, M. Realtime performance-based facial animation. *ACM Transactions on Graphics* Vol. 30, No. 4, Article No. 77, 2011.

[46] Blanz, V.; Vetter, T. A morphable model for the synthesis of 3D faces. In: Proceedings of the 26th Annual Conference on Computer Graphics and Interactive Techniques, 187–194, 1999.

[47] Yan, J.; Zhang, X.; Lei, Z.; Yi, D.; Li, S. Z. Structural models for face detection. In: Proceedings of the 10th IEEE International Conference and Workshops on Automatic Face and Gesture Recognition, 1–6, 2013.

[48] Xiong, X.; De la Torre, F. Global supervised descent method. In: Proceedings of the IEEE Conference on Computer Vision and Pattern Recognition, 2664–2673, 2015.

[49] Snavely, N. Bundler: Structure from motion (SFM) for unordered image collections. 2010. Available at http://www.cs.cornell.edu/~snavely/bundler/.

[50] Chen, L.; Armstrong, C. W.; Raftopoulos, D. D. An investigation on the accuracy of three-dimensional space reconstruction using the direct linear transformation technique. *Journal of Biomechanics* Vol. 27, No. 4, 493–500, 1994.

[51] Moré, J. J. The Levenberg–Marquardt algorithm: Implementation and theory. In: *Numerical Analysis*. Watson, G. A. Ed. Springer Berlin Heidelberg, 105–116, 1978.

[52] Rall, L. B. *Automatic Differentiation: Techniques and Applications*. Springer Berlin Heidelberg, 1981.

[53] Kolda, T. G.; Sun, J. Scalable tensor decompositions for multi-aspect data mining. In: Proceedings of the 8th IEEE International Conference on Data Mining, 363–372, 2008.

[54] Li, D.-H.; Fukushima, M. A modified BFGS method and its global convergence in nonconvex minimization. *Journal of Computational and Applied Mathematics* Vol. 129, Nos. 1–2, 15–35, 2001.

[55] Igarashi, T.; Moscovich, T.; Hughes, J. F. As-rigid-as-possible shape manipulation. *ACM Transactions on Graphics* Vol. 24, No. 3, 1134–1141, 2005.

[56] Hartigan, J. A.; Wong, M. A. Algorithm AS 136: A K-means clustering algorithm. *Journal of the Royal Statistical Society. Series C (Applied Statistics)* Vol. 28, No. 1, 100–108, 1979.

[57] Brox, T.; Bruhn, A.; Papenberg, N.; Weickert, J. High accuracy optical flow estimation based on a theory for warping. In: *Computer Vision–ECCV 2004*. Pajdla, T.; Matas, J. Eds. Springer Berlin Heidelberg, 25–36, 2004.

[58] Brox, T.; Malik, J. Large displacement optical flow: Descriptor matching in variational motion estimation. *IEEE Transactions on Pattern Analysis and Machine Intelligence* Vol. 33, No. 3, 500–513, 2011.

[59] Agarwal, S.; Snavely, N.; Seitz, S. M.; Szeliski, R. Bundle adjustment in the large. In: *Computer Vision–ECCV 2010*. Daniilidis, K.; Maragos, P.; Paragios, N. Eds. Springer Berlin Heidelberg, 29–42, 2010.

[60] Belhumeur, P. N.; Jacobs, D. W.; Kriegman, D. J.; Kumar, N. Localizing parts of faces using a consensus of exemplars. *IEEE Transactions on Pattern Analysis and Machine Intelligence* Vol. 35, No. 12, 2930–2940, 2013.

View suggestion for interactive segmentation of indoor scenes

Sheng Yang[1] (✉), Jie Xu[2], Kang Chen[1], and Hongbo Fu[3]

Abstract Point cloud segmentation is a fundamental problem. Due to the complexity of real-world scenes and the limitations of 3D scanners, interactive segmentation is currently the only way to cope with all kinds of point clouds. However, interactively segmenting complex and large-scale scenes is very time-consuming. In this paper, we present a novel interactive system for segmenting point cloud scenes. Our system automatically suggests a series of camera views, in which users can conveniently specify segmentation guidance. In this way, users may focus on specifying segmentation hints instead of manually searching for desirable views of unsegmented objects, thus significantly reducing user effort. To achieve this, we introduce a novel view preference model, which is based on a set of dedicated view attributes, with weights learned from a user study. We also introduce support relations for both graph-cut-based segmentation and finding similar objects. Our experiments show that our segmentation technique helps users quickly segment various types of scenes, outperforming alternative methods.

Keywords point cloud segmentation; view suggestion; interactive segmentation

1 Introduction

With the prevalence of consumer-grade depth sensors (e.g., Microsoft Kinect), scanning our living environments is becoming easier. However, the resulting 3D point clouds are often noisy, incomplete, and distorted, posing various challenges to traditional point cloud processing algorithms. Thus, in recent years, growing attention has been paid to low-quality point cloud processing problems. Amongst them, semantic segmentation, which aims to provide a decomposition of a 3D point cloud into semantically meaningful objects, is one of the most fundamental problems, and is important for many subsequent tasks such as object detection [1], object recognition [2], scene understanding [3], etc.

Semantic segmentation of 3D point clouds has been extensively studied, resulting in various techniques, based for instance on region growing [4, 5], graph-cut [6–8], learning [9–11], etc. Most of those approaches attempted to achieve semantic segmentation with little or even no user intervention. However, due to the complexity of real-world scenes and the limitations of 3D scanners, manual intervention is often inevitable [12].

Previous interactive segmentation work (e.g., Refs. [13, 14]) typically focuses on improving segmentation results given the same amount of user input (e.g., provided by a commonly used stroke-based interface). We observed that when interactively segmenting scenes at a moderate or large scale, finding appropriate views to provide segmentation hints is very time-consuming. For example, for a scene with multiple rooms containing objects of various types, shapes, and sizes, objects can easily occlude each other, requiring careful selection of viewpoints for interactive segmentation. In addition, due to the discrete nature of point clouds, the distances between viewpoint and objects need to be carefully chosen to ensure the desired point density and that contextual information is in view.

Based on these observations, we present a new interactive system for segmenting cluttered point

---

1 Tsinghua University, Beijing, China. E-mail: S. Yang, shengyang93fs@gmail.com (✉); K. Chen, chenkangnobel@hotmail.com.

2 Massachusetts Institute of Technology, Cambridge, USA. E-mail: eternal_answer@126.com.

3 City University of Hong Kong, Hong Kong, China. E-mail: fuplus@gmail.com.

Fig. 1   Given an input scene represented as a 3D point cloud (left), our system automatically suggests a series of reasonable views (middle) for easily inputting segmentation hints for semantic segmentation of the entire scene (right).

clouds of large real-world scenes. Our system is able to automatically suggest a series of camera views, in which users can conveniently specify segmentation guidance, i.e., 2D strokes in our case. To reduce user effort, we aim to optimize the suggestions, i.e., to provide views that both contain plenty of undetermined objects and can clearly display them. To achieve this, we introduce a novel view preference model, which is based on a set of dedicated view attributes, whose weights are learned from a user study. Given a new scene, our system uses the learned view preference model to find the next best views one by one. In this way, users may focus on specifying segmentation hints, instead of manually searching for desired views for segmentation of unsegmented objects.

To further reduce user effort in interactive segmentation, we incorporate support relations in a graph-cut-based segmentation framework, to find similar objects for segmentation propagation. We have compared the performance of interactive point cloud segmentation with and without view suggestion, and interactive segmentation of RGB-D images. The experiments show that our segmentation technique with view suggestion helps users quickly segment various types of scenes, and outperforms alternative methods.

2   Related work

2.1   Point cloud segmentation

Semantic segmentation of 3D point clouds or RGB-D images has long been an active research topic in the communities of computer graphics, vision, and robotics (see an insightful survey by Nguyen and Le [12]). Below we discuss the most relevant works, and categorize them into supervised, unsupervised, and interactive techniques.

With the growing availability of free 3D datasets

(e.g., the *NYU Depth Dataset* [11, 15], the *SUN3D* dataset [16], and ShapeNet [17]), supervised-learning-based segmentation algorithms typically exploit high-level semantic information from labeled datasets, and use the learned knowledge to help detect, recognize, and thus semantically separate object regions from backgrounds. Training data for supervised methods mainly come from two sources: CAD models and RGB-D images. High-quality CAD models are ideal training data as they provide full 3D a priori knowledge about geometric shapes [10, 18] and even contextual relationships [19], but the number and diversity of high-quality digital models are far from enough to cover everything; creating these models is expensive. Since RGB-D images are much easier to acquire, numerous methods (e.g., Refs. [1, 3, 20, 21]) learn various features from labeled RGB-D images. However, despite ease of acquisition, the labeling of RGB-D images is still labor intensive. Our system can be used as a convenient and robust segmentation tool to help produce high-quality training data.

Unsupervised semantic segmentation methods often rely on regular patterns (i.e., symmetry and repetition) observed from input data itself, and work extremely effectively on outdoor building facades [22, 23]. However, interior scenes present much more complex structures. To simplify the problem, previous works (e.g., Refs. [9, 24]) focus on large-scale working environments containing limited types of objects (e.g., office desk, office chair, monitor), each repeated many times. However, real-world scenes often contain unique objects. Thus, manual intervention is often still required to refine segmentation results produced by such automatic methods.

Since automatic segmentation methods are far from perfect, in practice interactive methods are more frequently used for segmenting both indoor scenes [13, 25] and outdoor scenes [14]. The most commonly used interactive scheme is to let users specify representative foreground and background regions (typically via a stroke-based interface), which are then used to construct a probabilistic inference model (using, e.g., conditional random fields) and optimized using graph-cut [7, 8], or simply used as seeds for region growing [4, 5, 26]. However, such an interactive scheme is designed for segmenting an individual image frame, and thus requires carefully selected views of 3D scene contents for projection to screen space. While the view selection process is time-consuming, especially for large-scale and complex scenes, it has gained little attention. Thus, our work is largely complementary to existing interactive and automatic segmentation techniques.

2.2 Camera control

Finding feasible views to display 3D graphics on a 2D screen is a fundamental problem, which in computer graphics is generally referred to as the camera control problem [27, 28]. According to the camera mode and the scale of the 3D contents, existing solutions to this problem can be divided into two categories: *fly-around* and *walk-through*. We adapt these existing ideas to a new context for interactive point cloud segmentation, and tackle unique challenges such as the handling of cluttered point clouds, and dynamic selection of a series of good views for easy labeling of objects.

A *fly-around* camera allows complete contents rendered to the screen, and is often used when displaying single objects or small-scale scenes. The core problem is best view selection, which aims to automatically select the most representative view of a 3D model. Various low-level view attributes (e.g., projected area, viewpoint entropy, silhouette length, and depth distribution) have been proposed [29, 30] as a basis for solving this problem. The state of the art is probably the work by Secord et al. [29], which learns how to combine low-level view attributes based on an extensive user study of human preferences. Our work differs from the existing best view selection techniques in terms of both inputs (cluttered point clouds versus clean surface or volume models) and outputs (a series of viewpoints looking at different parts of a scene versus a set of independent good views looking at the same target).

Walk-through camera mode is thus more relevant

to our problem; it is often used to navigate within large-scale virtual scenes [31, 32]. This problem essentially comprises two sub-problems: viewpoint selection [30] and path planning [33, 34]. Unlike the criteria used for fly-around cameras, measuring the quality of viewpoints within a scene is mainly based on *viewpoint entropy* [30]. Path planning is needed to avoid penetrating objects or walls and to present smooth scene roaming. In contrast, our problem demands essentially discrete views for labeling, although smooth transition is weakly considered. Again, existing walk-through methods often take clean scenes as input. Additionally, their extracted walk-through paths can be pre-generated, while in our case the selection of the next best view depends on the segmentation progress and needs to be determined on the fly. We have also found that top views are very useful for our application, but they are seldom used for the walk-through applications.

3 System overview

The main contribution of our work is automatic suggestion of good views for easy labeling of objects in indoor scenes represented as 3D point clouds. We implement view suggestion in an interactive segmentation system, which takes an unsegmented scan of an indoor scene as input. However, our interactive system can be helpful for interactively refining automatically generated segmentation results.

As shown in Fig. 2, our system contains three components: preprocessing, view suggestion, and interactive segmentation. In the preprocessing step (Section 4) the system automatically aligns an input scene with Manhattan directions, extracts storeys (levels), and clusters the points into patches which should be treated as indivisible units in segmentation.

Afterwards our system automatically finds candidate viewpoints and sample views for presenting as suggestions (Section 5.1). To evaluate the quality of a view, we introduce a view preference model (Section 5.2), which involves several attributes such as point density, projected area, and viewpoint entropy. The weights of these attributes are learned by conducting a user study of human preferences for views of scenes. At runtime, each view is evaluated using the learned view preference model, with

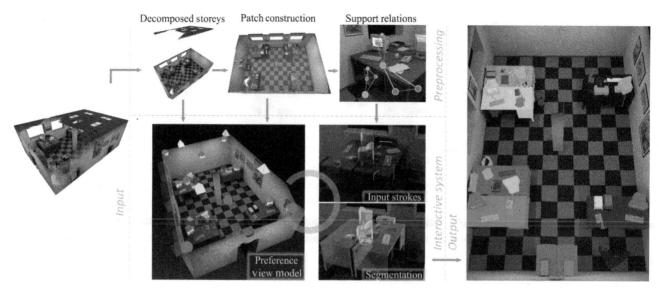

Fig. 2   System overview.

segmentation status and smooth transitions taken into account. The best view is then suggested to the user for interactive segmentation. The user may reject the current suggestion, and our system then updates the strategy for suggesting another view.

Given a view, the user provides segmentation hints on unsegmented, over-segmented, or under-segmented objects that are in view, using a classic stroke-based interface. The patches corresponding to these strokes are used as seeds to trigger a graph-cut-based segmentation optimization. We extract support relations between patches in the preprocessing step, and incorporate them into the segmentation optimization (Section 6.1). To further reduce the amount of user intervention, we find similar objects to already-segmented objects for segmentation propagation (Section 6.2). The above steps of automatic view suggestion and interactive segmentation of scenes in the selected suggested view are repeated until all objects have been labeled. For multi-storey cases, our system provides view suggestions storey by storey.

4   Preprocessing

In this section we briefly introduce our preprocessing step, which generates essential information for later use. Our system takes as input a 3D point cloud of an indoor scene, which can be acquired using different types of scanning devices such as LiDAR or Microsoft Kinect. For example, for RGB-D streams, they can be registered to form a point cloud using

KinectFusion or its variants [35, 36]. Like many other point cloud processing pipelines [37], we downsample the data, estimate point normals, and transform the input scene into Manhattan coordinates [38] with the z-axis pointing upwards. Then we extract horizontal planes (by RANSAC) as floors and an optional ceiling. As illustrated in Fig. 3, we decompose a multiple-storey building into individual storeys, with the ceiling of each storey removed to achieve top views of rooms.

4.1   Constructing representative patches

Over-segmentation has often been used in existing works for preprocessing point clouds [7, 14, 24]. We are interested in over-segmenting an input scene into semantic patches, instead of patches with similar sizes but with no semantics [7]. Such patches not only help reduce computational costs but also serve as integral semantic units to analyze the importance of views and support relations.

Fig. 3   Decomposition of one-storey (left) and two-storey (right) buildings into individual storeys, with the removal of ceilings (if any).

Our solution is an extension of the region growing approach by Ref. [24]. Since the original approach does not consider any color information, it might not split objects with similar shape but different colors (e.g., causing objects on the table in Fig. 4(c) to disappear). In addition, their approach has been shown to be effective only on good-quality scenes acquired by LiDAR devices, and can lead to numerous tiny patches for point clouds of low quality (e.g., those acquired by Kinect). To address these problems, we improve their approach by appropriately adding a new color condition and performing two rounds of growing, the first on the input point cloud and the second on the patches resulting from the first round.

The first round of region growing is applied to the input points. Specifically, let $G_0 = \langle V_0, E_0 \rangle$ denote a graph, with V_0 representing the input points and E_0 the edges generated by k-nearest neighborhoods ($k = 15$ in our implementation). As points in different colors more likely belong to different objects or parts, as well as the basic normal and position conditions (with the default parameters t_0 and t_1) for patch growing in Ref. [24], we add a color condition as follows:

$$\max \left(||R_i^{\mathrm{HS}} - R_j^{\mathrm{HS}}||, |C_i^{\mathrm{V}} - C_j^{\mathrm{V}}| \right) < t_2 \qquad (1)$$

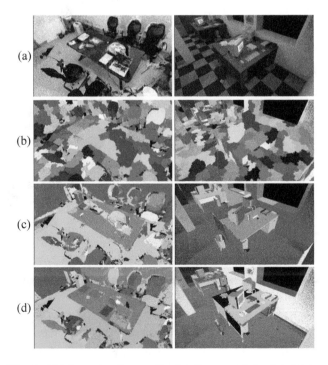

where i and j are two colors. $C_i^{\mathrm{H}} \in [0, 2\pi)$ and $C_i^{\mathrm{S}}, C_i^{\mathrm{V}} \in [0, 1]$ denote normalized HSV color values for i. $R_i^{\mathrm{HS}} = (C_i^{\mathrm{S}} \cos C_i^{\mathrm{H}}, C_i^{\mathrm{S}} \sin C_i^{\mathrm{H}})$ denotes the 2D coordinate values of i in the Hue–Saturation color disk. Intuitively, we allow two colors to be merged when their Euclidean distance in the Hue–Saturation color disk and intensity value difference are both within a small threshold t_2 ($= 0.05$ in our implementation).

This region growing process results in a set of merged patches. However, in our experiments we found that by adding the color condition, individual points might be isolated as individual patches, especially when the quality of the input point cloud is poor. To address this problem, we perform a second round of region growing on the merged patches from the first pass, but with relatively looser rules. Like G_0 is constructed over points, $G_1 = \langle V_1, E_1 \rangle$ is constructed over patches. For merging, we sort the patches in descending order of the number of contained points. For each patch, we find the normal of the best-fit plane and its centroid to check the respective normal and position conditions (the corresponding parameters are denoted t_3, t_4). The color condition is based on the color distribution and is more specifically defined using the χ-squared distance [39] between the HSV color histograms of two patches P_i and P_j in V_1:

$$\chi^2(I_i, I_j) < t_5 \qquad (2)$$

where I_i denotes the normalized HSV color histogram of points in P_i. Specifically, H, S, and V channels are discretized into 16, 16, and 8 bins respectively. We discretize V values into fewer bins to reduce the influence of different lighting conditions. The threshold t_5 is set to 1.6 in our system. The above patch-based region growing procedure is repeated multiple times (5 times in our implementation). After each iteration, the thresholds are relaxed by 20% to merge small isolated patches into larger patches. In our system, we set $t_0 = 0.8$, $t_1 = 0.05$, $t_3 = 0.75$, and $t_4 = 0.2$ for all input scenes.

5 View suggestion

In this section we first discuss view sampling, then perceptual assessment of views, and finally how to automatically suggest views for interactive segmentation.

Fig. 4 Patch construction results. (a) Downsampled point clouds from different datasets. (b) By Ref. [7]. (c) By Ref. [24]. (d) Our result.

5.1   View sampling

View sampling simplifies our problem, since it results in a discrete set of views for assessment. A view is basically determined by three vectors: the camera position, view direction, and up direction.

Inspired by previous works on urban city reconstruction using both airborne and street-borne data [40], we consider two types of views: *interior perspectives* and *top views*. Top views provide a good summary of a scene or its parts, since objects often lie on flat surfaces (e.g., tables, floors) and are thus easily separable from a top view. In contrast, interior perspectives enable a more detailed examination of a scene from a closer distance, and are useful for dealing with objects of small size or objects that are blocked in top views (e.g., objects in bookshelves). Thus these two types of views are largely complementary to each other. Next we explain how we sample these two types of views.

For interior perspectives, we fix the orientation of a view so that its up vector in image space is aligned with the upright orientation of a scene [29]. An interior perspective can then be characterized by (x, y, z, θ, ϕ), where x, y, and z define the camera position, and θ and ϕ control the view direction. A possible viewpoint should meet the following requirements: it must stay inside a room (above the floor, away from the walls, below the ceiling if any) and avoid hitting objects. Objects are approximately detected as columns using the column representation proposed by Fisher et al. [41]. We then perform uniform sampling in the space of a storey excluding the space occupied by the columns to get possible camera positions (x, y, z), each of which is associated with a view sphere parameterized by (θ, ϕ) (see Fig. 2). Both θ and ϕ are sampled every 15°, resulting in 266 views at each viewpoint.

For every top view, its view direction is fixed and always points downward along the negative z-axis. Lean view directions are not used since objects in such resulting views would often be severely blocked by vertical walls. Hence, θ is fixed at π for all top views in our implementation. We thus use (x, y, z, ϕ) for mapping the camera position of a view and its up direction. We uncover the ceiling of a room or storey and uniformly sample the viewpoints and poses inside its bounding box. It can be easily seen that higher viewpoints produce wider-range views

but fewer details. In the case of a multiple-storey building, we decompose it into multiple storeys (Section 4), and sample interior perspectives and top views for individual storeys.

5.2   View preference model

For simplicity here we assume no object has been segmented in a view; we discuss how to incorporate the segmentation status in Section 5.3. The simplified problem is similar to the problem of best view selection for a single object; the latter is often represented as a polygonal mesh. In contrast we need to deal with scenes of objects, represented as cluttered point clouds. We observe that good views have at least the following properties. First, objects in such views should be easy to recognize. Second, such views should contain as many *unsegmented* objects as possible so that only a small set of views are needed to cover every object in a scene. These two properties are somewhat conflicting. For example, a bird's eye view of a scene might include many objects in the view, but individual objects might not be easily recognizable. Thus there is no single definition to describe whether a given view is good or not.

We explored various attributes to describe the quality of a view from different perspectives; some are based on previous work while others were designed by us. A key challenge is to evaluate the impact of each attribute when combining them together into a unified view preference model. This is achieved by learning from view preferences of human viewers in a user study. Below we first describe the important attributes indicated by the user study and then give the details of the study itself.

In a preprocessing step, we pre-compute a *supplementary mesh* from the point cloud using a greedy projection triangulation algorithm [42]. This supplementary mesh greatly facilitates visibility checking. In addition, observing that people tend to focus more on objects located at the center of a view, we add weights to pixels in the *supplementary mesh* view: each pixel p_i corresponds to a projected point; its weight is defined as $w_i = 1 - \lambda_w d_i^2$, where d_i is the normalized Euclidean distance between p_i and the center of the view, while λ_w is a small factor to help emphasize the central areas ($\lambda_w = 0.2$ in our system).

Our attributes are:

A_{pa}: *projected area.* This is a rather basic attribute and has been proved effective in previous works like Ref. [29]. Let $\mathcal{P} = \{P_n\}$ denote the set of *visible* patches in a view. Visibility is checked using the pre-computed supplementary mesh. A_{pa}, the sum of the projected areas of visible patches in view, is then defined as

$$A_{\mathrm{pa}} = S_{\mathcal{P}} = \sum_{P_n \in \mathcal{P}} S_n, \quad \text{with } S_n = \sum_{p_i \in P_n} w_i \quad (3)$$

where S_n is the projected area of a visible patch, where each pixel is weighted by the focus-attention weight w_i.

A_{ve}: *viewpoint entropy.* To estimate the richness of a view, we follow Vázquez et al. [30], and calculate view entropy on the supplementary mesh.

A_{pd}: *point density.* Due to the discrete nature of our point clouds, the distance between viewpoint and objects must be carefully set to provide the desired point density and contextual information in the view. We perform such a view-related density measurement by comparing the difference of views between the point cloud and the supplementary mesh. Let p_i' be a pixel of the point cloud view, and S_i' be the weighted areas that the pixels in the point cloud view and the mesh view belong to, for the same patch i. A_{pd} representing the average density of patches in view is then defined as

$$A_{\mathrm{pd}} = \frac{\sum\limits_{P_n \in \mathcal{P}} \Omega(S_n'/S_n) S_n}{S_{\mathcal{P}}}, \quad \text{with } S_n' = \sum_{p_i' = p_i, \ p_i' \in P_n} w_i \tag{4}$$

where $\Omega(x) = 1/(1 + \mathrm{e}^{-\lambda_\Omega \cdot (x - t_6)})$ is a sigmoid function for evaluating the density of one patch. Intuitively, if S_n'/S_n exceeds a threshold t_6, the density is acceptable and allows users to recognize objects. In our system, we set $\lambda_\Omega = 16$ and $t_6 = 0.3$.

Besides the attributes listed above, we also explored additional attributes considering aesthetic perception, including: *depth information* ($A_{\mathrm{dd}}, A_{\mathrm{dc}}$), *object layout* ($A_{\mathrm{op}}, A_{\mathrm{od}}, A_{\mathrm{ov}}$), and *radial patches* (A_{rp}). Please refer to the Electronic Supplementary Material (ESM) for detailed formulations of these attributes. However, according to the user study, they are relatively dispensable.

User study. In order to analyze the importance of these attributes to our view preference model, we conducted a user study. We chose three scenes captured by different types of devices (Kinect V2 and LiDAR) to alleviate the influence of different input qualities. For each scene, we randomly sampled 60 views (using the sampling approach described in Section 5.1), including both top views (5%) and interior perspectives (95%). 16 participants with basic knowledge of computer graphics were recruited to manually evaluate the quality of each view. To ensure a proper comparative evaluation, each time, each participant was given a group of views from the same scene (6 views per group, randomly selected from 60 views) and was asked to rate each view on a scale from 1 (worst) to 5 (best). They were also told that views containing easily recognizable and multiple objects without severe occlusion should be given high scores. Representative views are shown in Fig. 5. Please refer to the ESM for other scenes and results.

Learning weights of attributes. After collecting the scores for each view, we studied the importance of attributes. We normalized the observed attributes and adopted lasso regression [43] to determine the weights β_i of the attributes: it is

(a) 4.813   (b) 4.250

(c) 3.563   (d) 2.688

(e) 1.000   (f) 1.563

Fig. 5 Representative views from the user study. (a) High-score top view. (b, c) High-score interior views. (d) Low-score interior view (the tree seriously blocks the objects behind). (e, f) Low-score interior views.

able to perform variable selection in order to enhance the accuracy of the predictions by the statistical model it produces. The learned model by lasso regression is simply formulated as

$$\widehat{Y} = \sum_i \beta_i \widehat{A}_i + \beta_0 \tag{5}$$

where $\widehat{A}_i$ is the normalized attribute of a view, β_i is the learned weight for each attribute, and $\widehat{Y}$ is the average score for the view.

Lasso regression shows that among all the attributes included in the regression testing, *view entropy* and *point density* played the most significant roles, while other attributes were dispensable. Thus, we discarded these other attributes and performed lasso regression again. The final weights provided for *view entropy* and *point density* were 2.11 and 3.05, respectively. Detailed information about the regression process can be found in the ESM.

5.3 View suggestion

Given an input scene, we first sample views (see Section 5.1) in the preprocessing step. At runtime, we use the learned view preference model (Eq. (5)) to automatically suggest views. Specifically, we generate a set of candidate views, denoted by $\mathcal{V}$, by picking views with $A_{\mathrm{pa}} > 0.6$. The view in $\mathcal{V}$ with the highest score ($V_0 = \operatorname*{argmax}_{V_i \in \mathcal{V}} Y_i$) is suggested as the first view.

Given a suggested view, the user may perform interactive segmentation (see Section 6) and then request another view. To avoid repetitive suggestions, each time a view is suggested, we lower its score by a scale factor 0.7. We also allow users to reject a current view. In this case our system will suggest new views. We suggest new views according to the following principles:

- View suggestions should respect the current segmentation status. Views with many already-segmented objects should have lower priority.
- A smooth transition between the current and the new views is preferred.
- View suggestion should take into account user rejection of suggested views.

To satisfy the first guideline, we update the score of each candidate view according to the current segmentation status. More specifically, we replace A_{ve} with the residual entropy A'_{ve}, which is calculated by removing the terms corresponding to already-labeled patches in A_{ve}, since such labeled patches provide little information. In contrast, A_{pd} remains unchanged because intuitively this term is used to clearly display point clouds to the screen, and thus is somewhat independent of labeling.

To encourage a smooth transition from V_n to V_{n+1}, we pick V_{n+1} according to the following rule:

$$V_{n+1} = \operatorname*{argmax}_{V_i \in \mathcal{V}} Y'_i \mathrm{e}^{-D(K_i, K_n)} \tag{6}$$

where Y'_x is the online score of view V_x, and $D(K_i, K_n)$ is the horizontal Euclidean distance between the current camera position K_n and the candidate position K_i. We use an exponential decay of preference to favor nearby rather than distant view candidates.

If a user rejects a suggested view, it generally means that unlabeled patches in this view are less important, and thus, their priority should be lowered when assessing subsequent suggestions. To do so, we lower the residual entropy A_{ve} of unlabeled patches in rejected views by a scale factor 0.8.

For multi-storey cases, our system begins with the highest storey and suggests views related to the current storey until the labeling progress of the current storey surpasses 90%. Once surpassed, our system will suggest the best view for the next lower storey and continue.

6 Interactive segmentation

We adopt a stroke-based interface similar to that in Ref. [14] for interactive segmentation. Given a view, users draw different strokes on unsegmented regions to indicate different objects (see Fig. 6(left)). Graph-cut-based optimization [44] is then used to achieve the desired segmentation results. Our work contributes to this paradigm by introducing support relations into graph-cut, and finding similar objects to further reduce the amount of user intervention.

6.1 Support relations for graph-cut

Previous graph-cut-based point cloud segmentation techniques (e.g., Refs. [7, 14]) mainly focus on the

Fig. 6 Graph-cut without (middle) and with (right) support relations. Left: input strokes on unsegmented objects in a given view.

use of low-level geometric features (e.g., position, normal, color) to propagate the segmentation information from the user-specified seeds to the rest of the scene. Since man-made objects often exhibit box-like shapes, due to the sharp change in normal between different faces of such objects, multiple strokes (one for each face) may be needed to segment a single object (e.g., a desk or monitor in Fig. 6(middle)).

To reduce the amount of user intervention, we introduce *support relations* as an additional measurement of distance between patches in the graph-cut formulation. This helps the reduction of both the number of user-specified strokes and the number of needed views. For example, with our support relations considered (see Fig. 6(right)), the user only needs to input strokes on the top faces of a desk and monitor in a top view to segment the objects. Without, the user would need to switch to different views to input further strokes.

Support relations are common in indoor scenes because of the influence of gravity. There are two levels of support relations: support between objects and support between primitive shapes which constitute an object. The former requires the availability of object-level segmentation (the output of our system) [11]. Our focus is on the second type of support relations to guide object-level segmentation.

We take the patches constructed in Section 4.1 as input. First we classify all patches into two types: quasi-vertical Q_v and quasi-horizontal Q_h according to the angles between the planes fitted to them and the ground plane (relative to $45°$). Then we concentrate on two common relationships: a quasi-vertical patch supporting an quasi-horizontal patch Q_vh above it, and a quasi-vertical patch being supported by a quasi-horizontal patch Q_hv below it, as shown in Fig. 7.

For each pair of an adjacent quasi-vertical patch P_i and a quasi-horizontal patch P_j (above P_i), the likelihood that patches P_i and P_j have a Q_vh

relationship is defined as follows:

$$Q_\mathrm{vh}\langle P_i, P_j\rangle = 1 - \lambda_Q^{U(P_i, P_j)} \qquad (7)$$

where $U(P_i, P_j)$ is the number of quasi-vertical patches within the neighborhood of P_i (including P_i) which have P_j as an upper patch and $\lambda_Q = 0.2$ is a fixed parameter. Intuitively, more quasi-vertical patches supporting the same quasi-horizontal patch lead to higher likelihood of having the Q_vh relationship.

Similarly, for each pair of an adjacent quasi-vertical patch P_i and a quasi-horizontal patch P_j (below P_i), the likelihood that patches P_i and P_j have a Q_hv relationship is defined as follows:

$$Q_\mathrm{hv}\langle P_i, P_j\rangle = \begin{cases} 0, & U(P_i, P_k) = 0, P_k \in Q_\mathrm{h} \\ \frac{\min(W_i, W_j)}{\max(W_i, W_j)}, & \text{otherwise} \end{cases} \qquad (8)$$

where W_i is the area of the convex hull of points in patch P_i. We consider a Q_hv relationship for a quasi-vertical patch P_i only when there is no Q_vh relationship involving P_i. Consider Fig. 7(middle): the laptop lid has Q_hv relationship with the table, the laptop base, and the keyboard, while the laptop base leads to the highest likelihood since they have about the same size.

Then we define $\mathcal{T}_\mathrm{S}(P_i, P_j)$, the likelihood for patches P_i and P_j to belong to the same object using inference from the support map, as follows:

$$\mathcal{T}_\mathrm{S}(P_i, P_j) = \begin{cases} Q_x\langle P_i, P_j\rangle, & P_i \in Q_\mathrm{v}, P_j \in Q_\mathrm{h} \\ Q_x\langle P_j, P_i\rangle, & P_i \in Q_\mathrm{h}, P_j \in Q_\mathrm{v} \\ \max_k (Q_x\langle P_i, P_k\rangle \cdot Q_x\langle P_j, P_k\rangle), & P_{i,j} \in Q_\mathrm{v}, P_k \in Q_\mathrm{h} \end{cases} \qquad (9)$$

where Q_x can be either Q_vh or Q_hv, decided by the spatial relationship between two concerning patches. The top two conditions are essentially Q_vh or Q_hv, respectively, and the third indicates co-support relations between patches in Q_v, which exist if and only if two vertical patches have the same type of support relations (Q_x) with the same horizontal patch (see the example in Fig. 7(left)). Since support relations between patches are irrelevant to the segmentation status, in our system, they are computed during the preprocessing step.

Graph-cut. Given a set of user-specified strokes, only pixels with the same patch indices on both the point cloud view and the supplementary mesh view are regarded as valid, to avoid penetration

● Quasi-vertical

● Quasi-horizontal

— H support V

— V support H

— V co-support

Fig. 7 Automatically detected support relations. Left: the quasi-vertical patches co-support the top quasi-horizontal patches.

labeling. We then formulate support relations as well as distances, colors, and normals in the graph-cut formulation. Please refer to the ESM for details.

6.2 Finding similar objects

Duplicate objects often exist in a scene. It is redundant for a user to label them one by one. Our system employs a simple algorithm to automatically retrieve candidate objects similar to a given object in the scene. If the found objects are in fact not similar, users can delete the automatically generated labels.

Several methods for finding similar objects in point cloud scenes have already been proposed. For example, Kim et al. [9] introduced a method by first learning models of frequently occurring objects and then performing real-time matching. Mattausch et al. [24] took patch similarity and spatial consistency into account and automatically found all similar objects in a scene by clustering, which, however, takes dozens of seconds for large-scale indoor scenes.

We aim for a simple and efficient tool that can perform in real time, without pre-trained models or clustering. Our approach is based on the key assumption that similar objects should contain similar support structures, i.e., both the support relations and the accompanying patches should be similar. This assumption allows us to identify similar objects by straightforwardly comparing all unlabeled candidate support structures with a given object, based on patch similarity and support relations.

More specifically, given an already segmented object, denoted by $\mathcal{C}_0$, we first identify all candidate patches which have not been segmented and have a high similarity ($t_7 = 0.3$ in our implementation) to at least one patch in $\mathcal{C}_0$. For efficiency, we slightly change the similarity metric in Ref. [24] to define our similarity $\mathcal{A}_{i,j}$ for a given pair of patches P_i and P_j (see the ESM).

Then we group these candidate patches by connectedness to form patch constellations. For each pair of patches $\langle P_i, P_j \rangle$ in each constellation $\mathcal{C}_n$, we search for a corresponding pair $\langle P_k, P_l \rangle \in \mathcal{C}_0$ with the same type of support relation. Based on our key assumption, we compute the similarity likelihood $\text{Sim}(\mathcal{C}_n, \mathcal{C}_0)$ between $\mathcal{C}_n$ and $\mathcal{C}_0$ as follows:

$$\text{Sim}(\mathcal{C}_n, \mathcal{C}_0) = 1 - \prod_{P_i, P_j \in \mathcal{C}_n} (1 - \mathcal{I}_{i,j}) \quad (10)$$

where $\mathcal{I}_{i,j}$ is the *isomorphism likelihood* of the support structure between $\langle P_i, P_j \rangle$ and $\langle P_k, P_l \rangle$,

calculated as $\mathcal{I}_{i,j} = (\min_{k,l} \mathcal{A}_{i,k}) \mathcal{A}_{j,l} \mathcal{T}_{\text{S}}(P_i, P_j) \mathcal{T}_{\text{S}}(P_k, P_l)$. Here $\mathcal{A}_{i,k}$ and $\mathcal{A}_{j,l}$ represent the similarity between P_i and P_k and between P_j and P_l respectively.

If the similarity likelihood $\text{Sim}(\mathcal{C}_n, \mathcal{C}_0)$ exceeds a threshold t_8 (= 0.25 in our implementation), we take it as a candidate similar object. We then use all patches in the found isomorphic support structures as seeds for a new object to perform another round of graph-cut.

As shown in Fig. 8 our algorithm manages to find several similar objects in two cases. In the left example, each chair is composed of different numbers of patches, but the algorithm is still able to find such similar isomorphic parts and perform graph-cut. The right example shows our ability to find different types of objects: tables (*green*), monitors (*cyan*), telephones (*yellow*), and keyboards (*purple*). Note that objects adjacent to some keyboards are mistaken by graph-cut, demanding additional strokes for refinement.

7 Results and evaluation

We have tested our system on different qualities of datasets from different sources. We also performed a user study to evaluate the performance of view suggestion. Please see the accompanying video in the ESM for interactive demos. Some representative suggested views and segmentation results are shown in Fig. 9.

Datasets. In order to test our performance of view suggestion and segmentation, we chose middle- or large-scale scenes with rich sets of objects. Specifically, we used 2 out of 3 scenes (office2, office3) in the room detection datasets of UZH [24], 1 of 5 scenes (office1) in the Floored Panorama dataset [37], and 2 of 2 synthetic scenes (office-room, living-room) with ground-truth trajectory in the ICL-NUIM dataset [45]. The ICL-NIUM data

Fig. 8 Results of finding similar objects (shown in the same color).

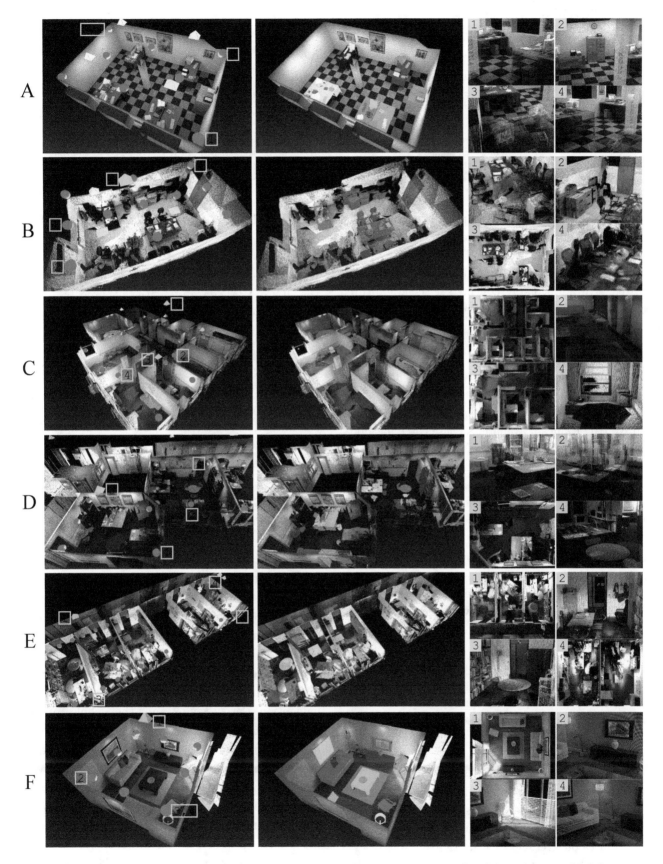

Fig. 9 Examples of results of our system. Left: view score map. Right: high score examples when no objects are labeled.

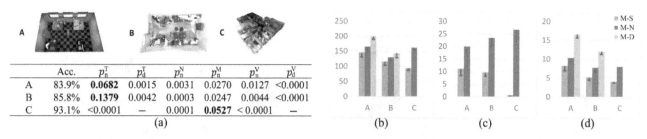

	Acc.	p_n^T	p_d^T	p_n^N	p_n^M	p_n^V	p_d^V
A	83.9%	**0.0682**	0.0015	0.0031	0.0270	0.0127	<0.0001
B	85.8%	**0.1379**	0.0042	0.0003	0.0247	0.0044	<0.0001
C	93.1%	<0.0001	–	0.0001	**0.0527**	< 0.0001	–

(a)   (b)   (c)   (d)

Fig. 10 Results of user study. Top, left: scenes with pre-defined target segmentations. (a) Acceptance rate of suggestions and hypothesis test results. The p-values are from paired sample t-tests between our method and no suggestion (n) or RGB-D (d), giving full time (T), the time spent on manual navigation (N), the counts of minimap navigation (M) and used views (V). Right: average and standard deviation of the means of observed values. (b) Time spent on the whole process in second. (c) Time spent on manual navigation in second. (d) The count of used views.

was generated by sampling point on surfaces of existing 3D mesh-based models, while others were acquired with LiDAR (with color information). Figure 9 illustrates all scenes tested. We additionally collected a scene captured by Microsoft Kinect2 to test for poor-quality scans.

7.1 Validity of view suggestion

To evaluate the effectiveness of view suggestion, we compared the performance of interactive segmentation with and without view suggestion. We also compared to stroke-based segmentation directly on RGB-D frames if available. These three methods, denoted as **M-S**, **M-N**, and **M-D**, were compared in a user study. Please refer to the accompanying video in the ESM to see how each method works.

Interfaces. For each of the methods compared, we provided a minimap for easy navigation. For **M-D**, while interactive segmentation was done on RGB-D images, we provided an additional point cloud viewer for examining the segmentation status. The only difference between **M-S** and **M-N** was the availability of view suggestion. For **M-S**, we encouraged the participants to use the view suggestion feature as much as possible, though minimap navigation and common 3D browsing were still allowed. All methods were tested in full-screen mode (1080 p) to eliminate the influence of window size. For fair comparison, we used the same preprocessing, graph-cut, and similar-object-finding algorithms for all methods.

Participants and apparatus. We recruited 12 university students, who had basic knowledge of graphics but different levels of experience in 3D browsing. In a training session, which lasted nearly 15 minutes on average, each participant was briefed and trained how to use the three methods. The entire user study was conducted on the same PC with

i7 2.10 GHz CPU, a GTX 660Ti GPU, and 16 GB RAM.

Tasks. We prepared 3 scenes with target segmentations. Scene A in Fig. 10(a) came from the ICL-NUIM dataset with 42 objects and 35 RGB-D key-frames. Scene B was our own recorded Kinect2 data, including 22 objects and 33 key-frames. Scene C was a large-scale multiple-room scene with 21 objects but no associated RGB-D images. These scenes are given in rows 1–3, respectively, in Fig. 9. The participants were asked to interactively segment these scenes using the three methods, whose presentation was counterbalanced to alleviate bias due to familiarity with the scenes. For Scene C, we tested **M-S** and **M-N** only, due to its lack of RGB-D frames. We pre-defined a ground-truth segmentation for each scene with manually labeled objects and required the participants to reproduce the ground-truth segmentations (shown on another monitor simultaneously) as closely as possible. Since it was difficult to reproduce the segmentations exactly, each scene was considered as completed if the similarity (ratio of patches) between the current and target segmentations reached 90%.

Measures. Our system recorded the following information for comparison: time spent on manual navigation, processing, and the whole progress (including planning, drawing, processing, and navigation); number of uses of view suggestion and minimap navigation operations; number of views used; number of executions of graph-cut and similar-object-finding algorithms; number and total length of input strokes. Additionally, we also recorded the acceptance ratio of view suggestion. We conducted a questionnaire survey at the end of the study.

Results. The acceptance rates of our suggested

views for Scenes A, B, and C were 83.9%, 85.8%, and 93.1%, respectively, indicating the good quality of suggested views. Figures 10(b)–10(d) show the statistics of some observed values. The table in Fig. 10(a) gives evaluation and hypothesis testing results, where p is the p-value calculated through student's t-test [46], which is helpful for evaluating statistically significant differences among small-scale paired-samples.

Using one-way analysis of variance (ANOVA), we found a significant difference in the average total time between the tested methods ($p = 0.0288$ for all methods on Scenes A and B, $p = 0.0058$ for **M-S** and **M-N** on all the scenes). In all tested scenes, our method significantly outperformed **M-D** ($p < 0.005$ from t-test) in both the number of views used and the total time. In Scene C, our method was significantly faster than **M-N** ($p < 0.001$), although they achieved comparable performance on minimap navigation ($p = 0.0527$). We observed that minimap navigation is crucial for large-scale scenes. In Scenes A and B, compared to **M-N**, our method significantly reduced the time for camera manipulation ($p < 0.005$) and the usage of minimap navigation ($p < 0.03$), but achieved comparable performance in total time ($p > 0.05$). This might be because the expense of manual navigation in such single-room scenes is relatively low. Our method also used significantly fewer views than **M-N** ($p < 0.02$) when segmenting all the tested scenes.

Our participants reported that with **M-D**, the RGB-D image views were more useful for object recognition due to their dense views, but (re-) checking the labeled objects, either through back-and-forth traversal or with the help of the auxiliary point cloud view, was not convenient. Worse, the number of RGB-D key-frames can significantly increase as scenes get bigger. Some participants also reported that they subconsciously referred to the good RGB-D views or results of view suggestion to improve labeling efficiency when using **M-N**. In fact, the performance of interactive segmentation without view suggestion can be easily affected by familiarity with the scenes and the proficiency of 3D browsing.

7.2 Robustness and efficiency

Parameters. In the preprocessing step for extracting storeys and sampling viewpoints, we used different sets of parameters for different datasets due to their different data quality and scene scale. The other parameters for patch construction, view suggestions, and interactive segmentation, remained unchanged for all the tested scenes.

Timing. On the same machine used in the user study, the preprocessing stage can cost dozens of minutes for the tested scenes. For a 140 m^2 one-floor room with 16 million points, it took about 1 minute per viewpoint to traverse through scenes to get the descriptors and 30 minutes in total; this could potentially be made faster by switching to quicker rendering tools. Since the score of each view can be calculated separately, we can also easily accelerate the method by parallelization. In the online stage, it only cost 50 ms to suggest an appropriate view, the graph-cut process only took 100 ms, and finding similar objects took 200 ms with respect to a labeled object. In summary, the online processing costs meet the requirement of real-time response.

Limitations. In some scenes with complicated objects such as plants or trees, our system may "prefer" to suggest views involving such objects (Fig. 11(left)), since they are taken as fragmentary patches (each including several leaves or stems) in patch construction, leading to high residual entropy on these views. However, once such objects are labeled, their influence will disappear. Since patches are indivisible in our implementation, if two or more objects are gathered into one patch (e.g., due to similar color and depth), it is impossible to segment the individual objects. Also the boundaries of objects may not be accurate if the points on boundaries are ambiguous. This might be addressed by introducing an interactive repair tool for boundary refinement. In addition, our proposed support relations and the algorithm for finding similar objects may fail if objects are combined as multiple discrete components (see Fig. 11(right)). Fortunately, users can modify the labeling by providing additional

Fig. 11 Less successful cases. Left: an example view with a tree with a high score. Right: failure to find similar objects in isolated patches (the chair in red).

inputs for segmentation.

8 Conclusions and future work

We have presented a novel system for interactive segmentation of large-scale indoor scenes, represented as cluttered point clouds. The key contributions of our work are the problem and solution of automatic view suggestion for interactive segmentation. Other contributions include support relations for graph-cut-based segmentation and finding similar objects. Our extensive evaluations show the advantages of our approach over alternative methods. In future, besides addressing the discussed limitations, we are also interested in applying a similar idea of view suggestion for other applications, e.g., interactive editing of large-scale scenes.

Acknowledgements

This work was supported by the Joint NSFC–ISF Research Program (Project No. 61561146393), the National Natural Science Foundation of China (Project No. 61521002), the Research Grant of Beijing Higher Institution Engineering Research Center, and the Tsinghua–Tencent Joint Laboratory for Internet Innovation Technology. The work was partially supported by grants from the Research Grants Council of the Hong Kong Special Administrative Region, China (Project Nos. CityU113513 and CityU11300615).

References

[1] Lai, K.; Bo, L.; Ren, X.; Fox, D. Detection-based object labeling in 3D scenes. In: Proceedings of the IEEE International Conference on Robotics and Automation, 1330–1337, 2012.

[2] Johnson, A. E.; Hebert, M. Using spin images for efficient object recognition in cluttered 3D scenes. *IEEE Transactions on Pattern Analysis and Machine Intelligence* Vol. 21, No. 5, 433–449, 1999.

[3] Zheng, B.; Zhao, Y.; Yu, J. C.; Ikeuchi, K.; Zhu, S. C. Beyond point clouds: Scene understanding by reasoning geometry and physics. In: Proceedings of the IEEE Conference on Computer Vision and Pattern Recognition, 3127–3134, 2013.

[4] Holz, D.; Behnke, S. Fast range image segmentation and smoothing using approximate surface reconstruction and region growing. In: *Intelligent Autonomous Systems 12*. Lee, S.; Cho, H.; Yoon, K.-J.; Lee, J. Eds. Springer Berlin Heidelberg, 61–73, 2013.

[5] Rabbani, T.; van den Heuvel, F. A.; Vosselmann, G. Segmentation of point clouds using smoothness constraint. *International Archives of Photogrammetry, Remote Sensing and Spatial Information Sciences* Vol. 36, No. 5, 248–253, 2006.

[6] Boykov, Y.; Funka-Lea, G. Graph cuts and efficient N-D image segmentation. *International Journal of Computer Vision* Vol. 70, No. 2, 109–131, 2006.

[7] Golovinskiy, A.; Funkhouser, T. Min-cut based segmentation of point clouds. In: Proceedings of the IEEE 12th International Conference on Computer Vision Workshops, 39–46, 2009.

[8] Sedlacek, D.; Zara, J. Graph cut based point-cloud segmentation for polygonal reconstruction. In: *Advances in Visual Computing*. Bebis, G.; Boyle, R.; Parvin, B.; Koracin, D. et al. Eds. Springer Berlin Heidelberg, 218–227, 2009.

[9] Kim, Y. M.; Mitra, N. J.; Yan, D.-M.; Guibas, L. Acquiring 3D indoor environments with variability and repetition. *ACM Transactions on Graphics* Vol. 31, No. 6, Article No. 138, 2012.

[10] Nan, L.; Xie, K.; Sharf, A. A *search-classify* approach for cluttered indoor scene understanding. *ACM Transactions on Graphics* Vol. 31, No. 6, Article No. 137, 2012.

[11] Silberman, N.; Hoiem, D.; Kohli, P.; Fergus, R. Indoor segmentation and support inference from RGBD images. In: *Computer Vision–ECCV 2012*. Fitzgibbon, A.; Lazebnik, S.; Perona, P.; Sato, Y.; Schmid, C. Eds. Springer Berlin Heidelberg, 746–760, 2012.

[12] Nguyen, A.; Le, B. 3D point cloud segmentation: A survey. In: Proceedings of the 6th IEEE Conference on Robotics, Automation and Mechatronics, 225–230, 2013.

[13] Shao, T.; Xu, W.; Zhou, K.; Wang, J.; Li, D.; Guo, B. An interactive approach to semantic modeling of indoor scenes with an RGBD camera. *ACM Transactions on Graphics* Vol. 31, No. 6, Article No. 136, 2012.

[14] Yuan, X.; Xu, H.; Nguyen, M. X.; Shesh, A.; Chen, B. Sketch-based segmentation of scanned outdoor environment models. In: Proceedings of the Eurographics Workshop on Sketch-Based Interfaces and Modeling, 19–26, 2005.

[15] Silberman, N.; Fergus, R. Indoor scene segmentation using a structured light sensor. In: Proceedings of the IEEE International Conference on Computer Vision Workshops, 601–608, 2011.

[16] Xiao, J.; Owens, A.; Torralba, A. SUN3D: A database of big spaces reconstructed using SfM and object labels. In: Proceedings of the IEEE International Conference on Computer Vision, 1625–1632, 2013.

[17] Chang, A. X.; Funkhouser, T.; Guibas, L.; Hanrahan, P.; Huang, Q.; Li, Z.; Savarese, S.; Savva, M.; Song, S.; Su, H.; Xiao, J.; Yi, L.; Yu, F. ShapeNet: An information-rich 3D model repository. *arXiv preprint* arXiv:1512.03012, 2015.

[18] Hinterstoisser, S.; Lepetit, V.; Ilic, S.; Holzer, S.; Bradski, G. R.; Konolige, K.; Navab, N. Model based training, detection and pose estimation of texture-less 3D objects in heavily cluttered scenes. In: *Computer Vision–ACCV 2012*. Lee, K. M.; Matsushita, Y.; Rehg, J. M.; Hu, Z. Eds. Springer Berlin Heidelberg, 548–562, 2012.

[19] Chen, K.; Lai, Y.-K.; Wu, Y.-X.; Martin, R.; Hu, S.-M. Automatic semantic modeling of indoor scenes from low-quality RGB-D data using contextual information. *ACM Transactions on Graphics* Vol. 33, No. 6, Article No. 208, 2014.

[20] Silberman, N.; Sontag, D.; Fergus, R. Instance segmentation of indoor scenes using a coverage loss. In: *Computer Vision–ECCV 2014*. Fleet, D.; Pajdla, T.; Schiele, B.; Tuytelaars, T. Eds. Springer International Publishing, 616–631, 2014.

[21] Chen, K.; Lai, Y. K.; Hu, S.-M. 3D indoor scene modeling from RGB-D data: a survey. *Computational Visual Media* Vol. 1, No. 4, 267–278, 2015.

[22] Shen, C.-H.; Huang, S.-S.; Fu, H.; Hu, S.-M. Adaptive partitioning of urban facades. *ACM Transactions on Graphics* Vol. 30, No. 6, Article No. 184, 2011.

[23] Zhang, H.; Xu, K.; Jiang, W.; Lin, J.; Cohen-Or, D.; Chen, B. Layered analysis of irregular facades via symmetry maximization. *ACM Transactions on Graphics* Vol. 32, No. 4, Article No. 121, 2013.

[24] Mattausch, O.; Panozzo, D.; Mura, C.; Sorkine-Hornung, O.; Pajarola, R. Object detection and classification from large-scale cluttered indoor scans. *Computer Graphics Forum* Vol. 33, No. 2, 11–21, 2014.

[25] Valentin, J.; Vineet, V.; Cheng, M.-M.; Kim, D.; Shotton, J.; Kohli, P.; Nießner, M.; Criminisi, A.; Izadi, S.; Torr, P. SemanticPaint: Interactive 3D labeling and learning at your fingertips. *ACM Transactions on Graphics* Vol. 34, No. 5, Article No. 154, 2015.

[26] Wong, Y.-S.; Chu, H.-K.; Mitra, N. J. SmartAnnotator an interactive tool for annotating indoor RGBD images. *Computer Graphics Forum* Vol. 34, No. 2, 447–457, 2015.

[27] Christie, M.; Olivier, P. Camera control in computer graphics: Models, techniques and applications. In: Proceedings of the ACM SIGGRAPH ASIA 2009 Courses, Article No. 3, 2009.

[28] Scott, W. R.; Roth, G.; Rivest, J.-F. View planning for automated three-dimensional object reconstruction and inspection. *ACM Computing Surveys* Vol. 35, No. 1, 64–96, 2003.

[29] Secord, A.; Lu, J.; Finkelstein, A.; Singh, M.; Nealen, A. Perceptual models of viewpoint preference. *ACM Transactions on Graphics* Vol. 30, No. 5, Article No. 109, 2011.

[30] Vázquez, P.-P.; Feixas, M.; Sbert, M.; Heidrich, W. Viewpoint selection using viewpoint entropy. In: Proceedings of the Vision Modeling and Visualization Conference, 273–280, 2001.

[31] Andújar, C.; Vázquez, P.; Fairén, M. Way-Finder: Guided tours through complex walkthrough models. *Computer Graphics Forum* Vol. 23, No. 3, 499–508, 2004.

[32] Li, T.-Y.; Lien, J.-M.; Chiu, S.-Y.; Yu, T.-H. Automatically generating virtual guided tours. In: Proceedings of the Computer Animation, 99–106, 1999.

[33] Christie, M.; Languénou, E. A constraint-based approach to camera path planning. In: *Smart Graphics*. Butz, A.; Krüger, A.; Olivier, P. Eds. Springer Berlin Heidelberg, 172–181, 2003.

[34] Salomon, B.; Garber, M.; Lin, M. C.; Manocha, D. Interactive navigation in complex environments using path planning. In: Proceedings of the Symposium on Interactive 3D Graphics, 41–50, 2003.

[35] Choi, S.; Zhou, Q.-Y.; Koltun, V. Robust reconstruction of indoor scenes. In: Proceedings of the IEEE Conference on Computer Vision and Pattern Recognition, 5556–5565, 2015.

[36] Newcombe, R. A.; Izadi, S.; Hilliges, O.; Molyneaux, D.; Kim, D.; Davison, A. J.; Kohli, P.; Shotton, J.; Hodges, S.; Fitzgibbon, A. KinectFusion: Real-time dense surface mapping and tracking. In: Proceedings of the 10th IEEE International Symposium on Mixed and Augmented Reality, 127–136, 2011.

[37] Ikehata, S.; Yang, H.; Furukawa, Y. Structured indoor modeling. In: Proceedings of the IEEE International Conference on Computer Vision, 1323–1331, 2015.

[38] Furukawa, Y.; Curless, B.; Seitz, S. M.; Szeliski, R. Manhattan-world stereo. In: Proceeding of the IEEE Conference on Computer Vision and Pattern Recognition, 1422–1429, 2009.

[39] Asha, V.; Bhajantri, N. U.; Nagabhushan, P. GLCM-based chi-square histogram distance for automatic detection of defects on patterned textures. *International Journal of Computational Vision and Robotics* Vol. 2, No. 4, 302–313, 2011.

[40] Früh, C.; Zakhor, A. Constructing 3D city models by merging aerial and ground views. *IEEE Computer Graphics and Applications* Vol. 23, No. 6, 52–61, 2003.

[41] Fisher, M.; Savva, M.; Li, Y.; Hanrahan, P.; Nießner, M. Activity-centric scene synthesis for functional 3D

scene modeling. *ACM Transactions on Graphics* Vol. 34, No. 6, Article No. 179, 2015.

[42] Marton, Z. C.; Rusu, R. B.; Beet, M. On fast surface reconstruction methods for large and noisy point clouds. In: Proceedings of the IEEE International Conference on Robotics and Automation, 3218–3223, 2009.

[43] Tibshirani, R. Regression shrinkage and selection via the lasso. *Journal of the Royal Statistical Society* Vol. 58, No. 1, 267–288, 1996.

[44] Boykov, Y.; Veksler, O.; Zabih, R. Fast approximate energy minimization via graph cuts. *IEEE Transactions on Pattern Analysis and Machine Intelligence* Vol. 23, No. 11, 1222–1239, 2001.

[45] Handa, A.; Whelan, T.; McDonald, J.; Davison, A. J. A benchmark for RGB-D visual odometry, 3D reconstruction and SLAM. In: Proceedings of the IEEE International Conference on Robotics and Automation, 1524–1531, 2014.

[46] Gosset, W. S. The probable error of a mean. *Biometrika* Vol. 6, No. 1, 1–25, 1908.

13

Rethinking random Hough Forests for video database indexing and pattern search

Craig Henderson[1] (✉), Ebroul Izquierdo[1]

Abstract Hough Forests have demonstrated effective performance in object detection tasks, which has potential to translate to exciting opportunities in pattern search. However, current systems are incompatible with the scalability and performance requirements of an interactive visual search. In this paper, we pursue this potential by rethinking the method of Hough Forests training to devise a system that is synonymous with a database search index that can yield pattern search results in near real time. The system performs well on simple pattern detection, demonstrating the concept is sound. However, detection of patterns in complex and crowded street-scenes is more challenging. Some success is demonstrated in such videos, and we describe future work that will address some of the key questions arising from our work to date.

Keywords Hough Forests; pattern detection; pattern search; machine learning

1 Introduction

Randomised Hough Forests were introduced in 2009 and demonstrated to detect instances of an object class, such as cars or pedestrians [1]. This, and subsequent works, have shown that Hough Forests can perform effectively in object detection tasks, and we see potential to translate their use to exciting opportunities in pattern search in large-scale data corpora.

Current systems are, however, incompatible with

the scalability and performance requirements of an interactive visual search system. Contemporary research trains a forest using variants of an object and regression is performed using an unseen image in which instances of the pattern are probabilistically identified. We propose to conceptually invert the use of the forest by using the corpus data that is *to be searched* as training data, and a query image of an unseen pattern to be *searched for* (Fig. 1). The new schema results in a very fast search of a large set of data whereby a single pass of a small query image through the forest yields probabilistic hypotheses of pattern detection in every image in the training data. Conventionally, regression is performed on each image and while each one can take only a few hundred milliseconds, the time to run over a large corpus invalidates its use for search at large scale.

We make the following contributions:

1. a new approach to Hough Forests training and pattern detection is described, suitable for large-scale pattern search in an interactive system;
2. a technique to train forests without explicit negative training images, eliminating the need for an otherwise arbitrary set of negative training images to be used to counter positive training images;
3. a method to select positive and negative training patches to filter noise from the background of images;
4. a flexible and scalable pattern search index that data can be added to or removed from at any time without need for any re-training of the existing forests.

1.1 Motivation

We are interested in the problem of searching a large corpus of video and still images for a previously

1 Multimedia and Vision Research Group, School of Electronic Engineering and Computer Science, Queen Mary University of London, London, E1 4NS, UK. E-mail: C. Henderson, c.d.m.henderson@qmul.ac.uk (✉); E. Izquierdo, e.izquierdo@qmul.ac.uk.

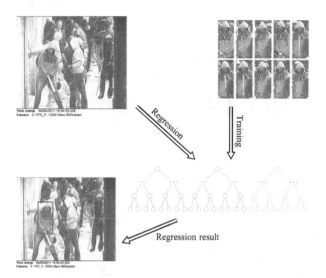

(a) A typical forest training and regression schema. The forest is trained using random patches from images depicting an object or pattern and a regression is run on a query image to detect the object or pattern.

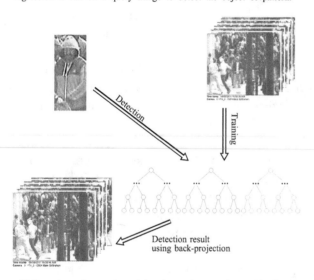

(b) Our schema inverts the training data and pattern image. The forest is trained using random patches from frames of a video sequence, and testing is run on a query image containing the object or pattern to be searched for. Using back-projection, one pass of the pattern through the forest simultaneously identifies the pattern in all frames of the video.

Fig. 1 (a) A typical forest training and regression process and (b) our novel process for video indexing.

unknown distinctive pattern such as a fashion or corporate logo, tattoo, or bag for left-luggage search. The genericity of the problem definition eliminates the opportunity to restrict the search, for example, by reducing the problem using a person detector to first find a suitable search area. The mixture of video and still images in the database also restricts the general use of spatio-temporal information available only in the video subset of data. We therefore seek a generic solution to a search problem that is flexible and fast

enough to be an interactive search with user input defining a previously unknown pattern for which to search.

1.2 Nomenclature

Literature to date describe Hough Forests used in *object detection*. We are interested in a more general *pattern detection* regardless of the structure of the pattern, and therefore refer to *pattern* where it can be referred to an object in the case of other literature.

Our data corpus consists of video sequences and collections of related still images. Each video or collection of images is treated as a unit of data for indexing. For brevity, we refer to the unit as a *video*, where it can also mean a collection of images.

2 Background

Hough Forests [2] use a random forest framework [3] that is trained to learn a mapping from densely-sampled D-dimensional feature *cuboids* in the image domain to their corresponding votes in a Hough space $\mathcal{H} \subseteq \mathbb{R}^H$. The Hough space accumulates votes for a hypothesis $\boldsymbol{h}(c, \boldsymbol{x}, s)$ of an object belonging to class $c \in C$ centred on $\boldsymbol{x} \in \mathbb{R}^D$ and with size s. Object hypotheses are then formed by local maxima in the Hough space when voting is complete. Votes contributing to a hypothesis are called *support*. The term *cuboid* refers to a local image patch ($D = 2$) or video spatio-temporal neighbourhood ($D = 3$) depending on the task. Introduced in 2009 [1], Hough Forests have gained interest in many areas such as object detection ($D = 2$) [4–8], object tracking [9], segmentation [5, 10], and feature grouping [7]. With $D = 3$, action recognition is an active research area that has used Hough Forests [11, 12], and in Ref. [13], more general randomised forests were used as part of a solution to index short video sequences using spatio-temporal interest points.

Hough Forests have shown to be effective in class-specific object detection [1], multi-class object detection [14], tracking object instances [2], and pattern detection [15], and their performance is suitable for real-time tasks with sub-second regression time on 800×600 dimension images. The high performance and effective accuracy make Hough Forests an attractive proposition for large-scale video database pattern searching. However, the conventional use of forests in object detection tasks does not scale well; a forest is trained with example images of the object or class of object to be found, and then a regression is run on unseen image to detect the object. In an interactive search system, the query *pattern* is unknown until runtime, when it is specified by the user. In this paper, we seek to address this conflict, rethink the method, and use of a randomised Hough forest for high-performance visual search.

3 Rethinking forests

In a departure from the established method, we conceptually invert the use of the forest and consider the image domain to consist not of instances of an object class or variations of the pattern to be detected, but the corpus to be *searched*. In our case, a forest's image domain is a set of frame images from a single video within the corpus.

We use a collection of forests to build a complete index of our video and image corpus. Each forest is trained using a single video (Fig. 2)—which can be just a few frames or 90,000 frames for one hour sequence at 25 fps—and can therefore be considered a sub-index of the database relating exclusively to a single video. Each forest $\mathcal{F} = \{\mathcal{T}_1, \mathcal{T}_2, \mathcal{T}_3, \ldots, \mathcal{T}_N\}$ consists of N trees where each tree $\mathcal{T}_i$ is independent of all other trees for training and testing.

Forests are trained using a novel scheme to identify positive and negative training samples (Section 3.2) from the frames of a video, thus removing the usual need for an explicit set of negative training images. Training is the most time-consuming function, and can be done as an offline activity for each video, independently of all other videos in the index. Training each forest is therefore consistent with building a video index in a more conventional retrieval system. A trained forest provides fast access to the patterns contained within the video such that it is searchable on-demand for unseen patterns of any size and dimension.

To perform a search, patches are extracted from a query image (or sub-image defined by a query region) using a sliding window, and passed through the forest. Rather than accumulating votes in the two dimensions of the query image, we accumulate votes in three dimensions of width and height of the training dataset and depth of the number of training images. The *support* of the leaf is used to trace the contributing vote back to the source frames, and the vote is accumulated in each of them (Section 3.3).

The independence of the components within a collection of forests is important for large-scale searching, providing scalability and flexibility.

Scalability. To support large video database search, the index must be highly scalable. The independence of components in the forest collection means that it is massively scalable and processing can be extended across many cores, processors, and machines. Training trees can be performed in parallel as there is no dependence between individual trees. Pattern search is less time-consuming, but similarly scalable—each forest can pass the query image patches through all of its trees simultaneously and accumulate the results as they complete.

Flexibility. New videos can be added easily without need for any re-training of existing forests. A new forest is simply created, trained with the new

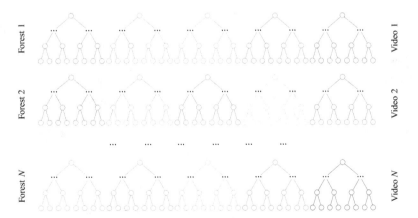

Fig. 2 The video database index is a collection of independent forests. Each row represents a forest of five independent trees, trained using frames from single video sequence.

data and then added to the collection. If a video is no longer required to be searched, then the relevant forest can simply be removed from the collection and will no longer be included in future searches. No re-training is necessary. Where available, the date of the video can be added as a property of the forest to further increase performance and search result relevance. A user can specify a time frame and forests containing videos from outside of the date range can easily be excluded from the search.

3.1 Hough Forests algorithm

We make some small amendments to the Hough Forests algorithm to achieve our goals. First, an *offset vector* is used [14] to translate the centre of the object in the training set to the centre in the regression step. With the inversion of training and query data, voting is accumulated at the patch position in the original frame dimension (Section 3.2) and the centre point offset into 2D Hough space of dimension of the query is not used, so we omit storing vector. Second, we do not scale images such that the longest spatial dimension of the bounding box is a known length. We work in the original frame dimensions of the video to avoid image data loss caused by resizing. Third, at each leaf, we record the training image to which each patch belongs, and finally, voting weights are accumulated in a multi-dimensional Hough space that includes the frame number.

3.2 Training the forest

A forest is trained using sets of *patches* that are extracted from the training images at random positions. Two sets of training images are conventionally used: a *positive* set of images containing examples of the object class or pattern to be detected, and a *negative* training set consisting images that do not contain any examples. Patches are extracted from each set yielding positive and negative *training patches*, respectively. The original authors of Hough Forests object detection [1] and subsequent research use a pre-determined patch size of 16×16 pixels, and extract 50 patches from each training image (resized such that the longest side is 100 pixels) to use in training the forest.

From each image, 32 feature channels are created: three colour channels of the Lab colour space, the absolute values of the first- and second-order derivatives in the x- and y-directions, and nine

HOG [16] channels. Each HOG channel is obtained as the soft bin count of gradient orientations in a 5×5 neighbourhood around a pixel. To increase the invariance under noise and articulations of individual parts these 16 channels are processed by applying the min and the max filtration with 5×5 filter size, yielding 32 feature channels (16 for the min filter and 16 for the max filter).

Patches are extracted from random positions within a training image, overlapping to build up a patchwork representation of the image (Fig. 4(b)). It therefore follows that the quantity and size of patches as well as the size of the training image determine the coverage. Our recent study [15] demonstrated some increase in detection accuracy can be achieved by dynamically selecting the size and quantity of training patches without resizing the training images. A large number of patches in a small training image will cause a lot of overlap, leading to redundancy in the forest. Although random forests do not suffer from over-training [3], bloating the trees with excessive patches does impede runtime performance. In an image of dimension 704×625, a saturated coverage using 16×16 dimension patches with one patch in each position on a grid would require ρ patches, with some patches overlapping because the height is not divisible by the patch height.

$$\rho = \left\lceil \frac{704}{16} \right\rceil \times \left\lceil \frac{625}{16} \right\rceil$$
$$= 44 \times 40$$
$$= 1760 \tag{1}$$

where $\lceil \cdot \rceil$ represents the *ceiling* function that maps a real number to the smallest following integer. Training time increases 1256% with this 3420% increase in the number of patches from $\rho = 50$.

However, saturated coverage with little or no overlap is a poor solution for us; the pattern is unlikely to align neatly to a grid and with each patch casting a single weighted vote, the accumulation to indicate the presence of the pattern will be weak. Positioning patches is therefore a critical step in the algorithm.

Randomness is used extensively in computer science as a means to avoid bias. Consider the training images stacked one on top of another. If patches were always placed in the same position, then each patch would represent a tunnel view through the images. All image data outside of these tunnels would be ignored. Furthermore, algorithms are usually trained using a corpus of images containing objects that contain neatly cropped and centred views of the objects. In such cases, if the position of the patch extracted from every image was in the same position, then the model would be trained only on a subset of tunnel-vision views of an object, resulting in *over-training* and ineffective detection. Variation is therefore important, and randomness is used to achieve variation, in this case to avoid over-training. However, randomness is non-deterministic, and repeated execution of the same algorithm will produce different results, which makes measuring the effect and change in accuracy of incremental adjustments impossible to compare. To overcome this, the random number generator can be seeded to a fixed value, to yield a repeatable sequence of psuedo-random numbers. This is the approach adopted in experiments in this paper.

Selecting patches. Patches are extracted from training images at random positions, thus leaving to chance the amount of coverage of the image that is used for training. If the number and size of patches are large relative to the dimensions of the training images, and the random number generator has a uniform distribution, then the chances of the coverage being spread evenly over the image and sufficient to capture the image detail are increased.

We are interested in indexing video sequences from street-scenes such as closed circuit television (CCTV) images, often filmed from high in the air and, although cluttered with respect to large crowds, still containing non-distinct areas for which searching is unlikely. Random sampling from the image is too hit-and-miss (Fig. 3) to be reliable in extracting patches of use for a search system. Patches are therefore selected based on a statistical measure of how distinctive they may be in any subsequent search. The *grey-level co-occurrence matrix* (GLCM) is a well-known statistical method of examining texture that considers the spatial relationship of pixels. We use the derived *GLCM-Contrast* statistic that measures the local variations within the matrix. For brevity, we refer to *GLCM-Contrast* simply as the *contrast* of a patch. For each of the randomly positioned 16×16 patches, the normalised contrast τ_i of the patch is calculated. A patch is selected as a positive training patch if $\tau_i > \lambda$, otherwise the patch is considered too low-contrast for positive training. This selection restricts the random placement of positive training patches to be within high-contrast areas which are

Time stamp 08/08/2011 17:35:46.072
Camera 0: HTH_2 - C087 Wilton Way

Fig. 3 Extracting patches at random is unreliable for selecting sufficient training patches to yield a good search results. Only 1 of 200 randomly placed patches will extract any of the Adidas® logo on the black hoodie.

more distinctive and therefore more searchable (see green patches in Fig. 4(b)).

Training the forest with the corpus leaves no sensible choice for negative training images to counter the positive training images. However, the use of the contrast measure has rejected a number of random patches that will not be used for positive training. We therefore use these rejected patches as negative training patches, and overcome a significant problem by providing a contextual set of negative training patches. Each patch is therefore selected as a *positive* or *negative* training patch based on the normalised GLCM-Contrast of the patch, thus:

$$\text{patch} = \begin{cases} \text{positive training,} & \text{if } \tau_i > \lambda \\ \text{negative training,} & \text{otherwise} \end{cases} \quad (2)$$

where $\lambda := 0.015$ for 16×16 patches in our experiments.

Figure 4 shows extracted patch regions that are selected positive (green) and negative (red) in the example image of Fig. 3, when searching for 200 (Fig. 4(a)) and 1760 (Fig. 4(b)) positive patches. The positive patches are clustered in the high-contrast areas of the image, which are those that contain searchable distinctive patterns. Light clothing is selected because the patch contrast is affected by shadows caused by creases, etc. Low-contrast areas are ignored as they are not distinctive patterns. The high density of 1760 patches in Fig. 4(b) shows so much overlapping of patches that the low-contrast

(a)

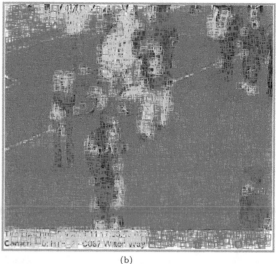
(b)

Fig. 4 Positive and negative training patches. Green patches are positive training patches and red patches are selected as negative training patches because the GLCM-Contrast is very low (Section 3.2). (a) Left, 200 positive patches are selected, and (b) right, 1760 positive patches are selected (Eq. (1)) and show the low- and high-contrast areas of the image. In each case the number of negative patches is determined by the search for positive patches—negative patches are discarded by low-contrast considerations.

and high-contrast regions become visible.

3.3 Detection

A forest, trained from all of the frames from a video, is synonymous with an index of patterns for searching the video. A single pass of patches from the query image through the tree finds a probabilistic hypothesis for the pattern's occurrence in *each frame*. The interactive visual search is therefore very fast. A given query region is defined by the user by drawing a rubber band around a pattern of interest—for example, a distinctive pattern or logo on a piece of clothing. A sliding window of size 16×16 (the same as the training patch size) is then passed over the query image and votes are accumulated for each image in the training set.

To visualise the results, we back-project votes to the *support*. Back-projection is an established method of tracing the leaves of a forest backwards through the tree to establish the source data contributing to the leaf, and has previously been used for verification [17], meta-data transfer [18], and visualisation [19]. Back-projected votes are aggregated at the patch positions to create a heat-map of votes overlaid onto the image domain (Fig. 8). This is not an integral part of the algorithm, but enables a visual inspection of the accuracy of the pattern detection.

4 Experiments

We ran four experiments to examine the feasibility

and accuracy performance of the new Hough Forests video database index. Three experiments were conceived to validate the concept without being distracted by the complexity of the search domain. In these, very simple synthetic images were constructed to train a forest and perform pattern detection in uncluttered images. We feel this is important as, although a toy example in pattern detection terms, it is used as a proof of concept for the new method of training a forest using the search domain and detection of an unseen query image. First is a very simple anti-aliased black text on a white background. Patches extracted from all the images shown in Fig. 5(a) were used as positive training samples and negative training images came from cartoon images from the *Garfield* and *Snoopy* categories of Ref. [20] and *104.homer-simpson* from Ref. [21]. Second, using the same images (Fig. 5(a)) training patches were extracted from all frames and selected as positive or negative training samples based on our algorithm (Eq. (2)). No additional negative training images were used. Third, a simple anti-aliased black text on a red-and-white high-contrast checkerboard background (Fig. 6(a)). While the first three experiments demonstrate the viability of the new use of Hough Forests and negative training method, using synthetic images, the fourth experiment tests a real-world use case. The forest is trained with 256 frames of a video sequence and detection of a pattern—an Adidas® logo on a jumper (Fig. 7)—during the

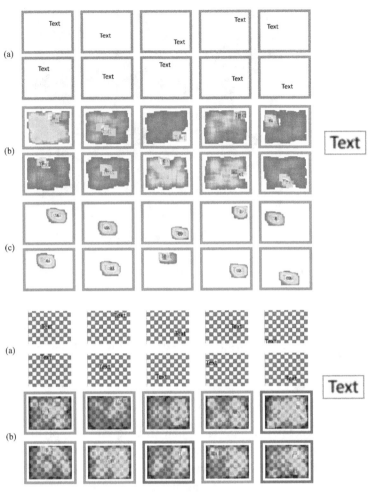

Fig. 5 (a) 10 images in the search corpus; (b) detection results using random patches through the image and negative training images from Refs. [20] and [21]; (c) detection results using a forest trained with random patches from the images and GLCM-Contrast selected positive/negative patches. Right, query image (shown with a border).

Fig. 6 (a) 10 images in the search corpus; (b) pattern detection results using a forest of five trees, each with a maximum depth of five. The coloured bordered represent successful (green) and unsuccessful (red) detection of the pattern. All patterns are detected successfully if the forest shape is changed to twenty trees, each with a maximum depth of ten.

Fig. 7 The video frame (left) from which a query region (right, actual size) is selected to perform our fourth experiment.

Fig. 8 Two frames of a video showing correctly identified positions of the search pattern. The offset hot-spot may be related to the training of the forest (see text).

London riots of 2011.

For each experiment, a forest of five trees was trained using the dataset as positive training images, extracting 200 positive training patches per image. The efficacy of pattern detection was then assessed by using a pattern that is known to be in the training data. This protocol mirrors our motivating use case.

5 Empirical results

In each of our result figures, coloured squares highlight the patch positions that contribute to a vote in favour of a pattern position. The colour reflects the accumulated vote from the patch, or series of overlaid patches, from blue (few votes) to red (many votes) on a heat map scale.

Detection of a piece of text on a plain white background is a simple enough task, but valuable as a baseline experiment for a novel method such as ours. Figure 5(b) shows the correct detection of the text with some noise in the background (a perfect detection is a hot-spot in the centre of the text). We repeat the exercise using our low-contrast filtering method to select negative training patches from low-contrast areas of the images without using arbitrary negative training images, and the result is improved considerably (Fig. 5(c)) with hot-spots more central and no votes at all accumulated in the background away from the pattern area.

Results from the third test are shown in Fig. 6. The red-and-white checker-board background is high-contrast and the background is therefore not eliminated using our patch selection technique. Accuracy is measured by the position of the most intense red region, not by the size of the region. The intensity represents the number of votes cast, so a small intense red region depicts a higher probability of the centre of the pattern than a larger, less intense colour. This is evident in the first result image (top-left). A larger red/orange area has accumulated to the north-east of the pattern ground truth, but a smaller, more intense region shows on the right-hand edge of the letter **x**. The result is therefore determined a successful detection. In total, the pattern has been detected in seven out of the ten images. A successful detection in ten out of the ten images is achieved when the number of trees in the forest is increased to twenty, and the maximum depth of each tree is ten.

Figure 8 shows the successful detection of a sportswear company logo on clothing in two frames of a video sequence, from a realistically trained forest. The images have been darkened to highlight the results. The scatter of patches is restricted to high-contrast regions because of the training patch selection algorithm. The hot-spot (intensity red) is the algorithm's predicted centre of the logo. In both frames, the centre point is within the logo, but off-centre. However, consider the patch positions of the training image in Fig. 4(a); these randomly positioned patches only cover the top-left of the logo that was searched for. Although this is only one training frame, it indicates that the detection algorithm has not received enough good training patches for the selected query, and this is affecting the detection performance. Detection in some other frames performed less well (Fig. 9). The voting hot-spot is outside the ground truth position, accumulating on a different jumper's

Fig. 9 An example of a false detection in an image where the query pattern is clearly visible. The voting hot-spot is on a jumper of another person, but the accumulated vote is lower showing less confidence in this detection.

logo. Patches in the ground truth area are very sparse indicating that the forest has not been trained sufficiently.

6 Conclusions

This paper reports on new techniques for applying an established framework of randomised Hough Forests to large-scale pattern detection. By rethinking how a forest is trained and used in pattern detection, we have shown some initial results that validate the approach, and show promise of future success in applying the problem not only at large scale, but also to sequences of videos of complex scenes.

Training the forest effectively is an open research area to achieve good general pattern detection accuracy in cluttered street-scene images. Training with negative patches from low-contrast areas of the image works well in our experiments to date, but experience from textual retrieval systems suggest this may not always hold.

Studies of [textual] *retrieval effectiveness show that all terms should be indexed … any visible component of a page might reasonably be used as a query term … Even stopwords—which are of questionable value for bag-of-words queries— have an important role in phrase queries* [22].

Relating this experience to the image search domain may suggest that low-contrast, and even background patches, should be included in the searchable forest and therefore used as positive patches for training.

Further experimentation is needed in this area. Open questions remain:

1. *How can the shape of the forest (number of trees, maximum depth, etc.) be determined per-video to maximise pattern detection accuracy?*

   All our experiments in this paper have used a consistent forest structure of five trees with a maximum depth of 5 levels, each trained using 200 positive training patches from each image. This structure generally performs well, but could theoretically be optimised based on the video image contents [15]. For example, videos containing more complex scenes should benefit from a larger forest (more trees) or more complex trees (greater depth) as experiment four demonstrates. The balance of runtime complexity, memory consumption and accuracy will be a trade-off consideration.

2. *Can a Hough Tree be learned incrementally without visibility of all its training data together?*

   One aspect of the scalability of the system to very large videos remains an open research area; To train a forest, the patches for all training data has to be accessible. This is by algorithm design and could present a scalability limit for videos with a large number of frame. The Hoeffding algorithm [23] describes a method to train a tree without visibility of all data, which may benefit our system. Some recent work has been published on incremental learning of forests for classification [24], and an opportunity exists to extend this to the problem of pattern detection.

3. *Can the granularity of forest and training data be better chosen to improve pattern detection accuracy?*

   Thus far we have used one forest per video in the corpus. This choice is made with the prior knowledge of properties of street-scene CCTV videos, for example that a video will be a sequence from a single camera without any shot change that temporally changes significantly between two consecutive frames of video [25]. While this choice is valid, in our view, it may not be optimal. We would like to investigate whether a single forest can be used to index multiple (perhaps related) videos, or if any videos can be temporally segmented and distributed to multiple forests. In such a system, each forest then becomes an index for a pre-classified set of video segments which may yield better detection performance.

As well as investigating these questions, a full assessment of the system, measuring accuracy against a ground truth is required in future work to produce a quantitative evaluation of our method.

Acknowledgements

This work is funded by the European Union's Seventh Framework Programme, specific topic "framework and tools for (semi-) automated exploitation of massive amounts of digital data for forensic purposes", under grant agreement number 607480 (LASIE IP project). The authors extend their thanks to the Metropolitan Police at Scotland Yard, London, UK, for the supply of and permission to use CCTV images.

References

[1] Gall, J.; Lempitsky, V. Class-specific Hough forests for object detection. In: Proceedings of IEEE Conference on Computer Vision and Pattern Recognition, 1022–1029, 2009.

[2] Gall, J.; Yao, A.; Razavi, N.; Van Gool, L.; Lempitsky, V. Hough forests for object detection, tracking, and action recognition. *IEEE Transactions on Pattern Analysis and Machine Intelligence* Vol. 33, No. 11, 2188–2202, 2011.

[3] Breiman, L. Random forests. *Machine Learning* Vol. 45, No. 1, 5–32, 2001.

[4] Barinova, O.; Lempitsky, V.; Kholi, P. On detection of multiple object instances using Hough transforms. *IEEE Transactions on Pattern Analysis and Machine Intelligence* Vol. 34, No. 9, 1773–1784, 2012.

[5] Payet, N.; Todorovic, S. Hough forest random field for object recognition and segmentation. *IEEE Transactions on Pattern Analysis and Machine Intelligence* Vol. 35, No. 5, 1066–1079, 2013.

[6] Razavi, N.; Alvar, N. S.; Gall, J.; Van Gool, L. Sparsity potentials for detecting objects with the Hough transform. In: Proceedings of British Machine Vision Conference, 11.1–11.10, 2012.

[7] Srikantha, A.; Gall, J. Hough-based object detection with grouped features. In: Proceedings of IEEE International Conference on Image Processing, 1653–1657, 2014.

[8] Yokoya, N.; Iwasaki, A. Object detection based on sparse representation and Hough voting for optical remote sensing imagery. *IEEE Journal of Selected Topics in Applied Earth Observations and Remote Sensing* Vol. 8, No. 5, 2053–2062, 2015.

[9] Godec, M.; Roth, P. M.; Bischof, H. Hough-based tracking of non-rigid objects. *Computer Vision and Image Understanding* Vol. 117, 1245–1256, 2013.

[10] Rematas, K.; Leibe, B. Efficient object detection and segmentation with a cascaded Hough Forest ISM. In: Proceedings of IEEE International Conference on Computer Vision Workshops, 966–973, 2011.

[11] Waltisberg, D.; Yao, A.; Gall, J.; Van Gool, L. Variations of a Hough-voting action recognition system. In: *Lecture Notes in Computer Science, Vol. 6388.* Ünay, D.; Çataltepe, Z.; Aksoy, S. Eds. Springer Berlin Heidelberg, 306–312, 2010.

[12] Yao, A.; Gall, J; Van Gool, L. A Hough transform-based voting framework for action recognition. In: Proceedings of IEEE Conference on Computer Vision and Pattern Recognition, 2061–2068, 2010.

[13] Yu, G.; Yuan, J.; Liu, Z. Unsupervised random forest indexing for fast action search. In: Proceedings of IEEE Conference on Computer Vision and Pattern Recognition, 865–872, 2011.

[14] Gall, J.; Razavi, N.; Van Gool, L. An introduction to random forests for multi-class object detection. In: Proceedings of the 15th International Conference on Theoretical Foundations of Computer Vision: Outdoor and Large-scale Real-world Scene Analysis, 243–263, 2012.

[15] Henderson, C.; Izquierdo, E. Minimal Hough forest training for pattern detection. In: Proceedings of International Conference on Systems, Signals and Image Processing, 69–72, 2015.

[16] Dalal, N.; Triggs, B. Histograms of oriented gradients for human detection. In: Proceedings of IEEE Computer Society Conference on Computer Vision and Pattern Recognition, Vol. 1, 886–893, 2005.

[17] Leibe, B.; Leonardis, A.; Schiele, B. Robust object detection with interleaved categorization and segmentation. *International Journal of Computer Vision* Vol. 77, No. 1, 259–289, 2008.

[18] Thomas, A.; Ferrari, V.; Leibe, B.; Tuytelaars, T.; Van Gool, L. Using multi-view recognition and metadata annotation to guide a robot's attention. *The International Journal of Robotics Research* Vol. 28, No. 8, 976–998, 2009.

[19] Razavi, N.; Gall, J.; Van Gool, L. Backprojection revisited: Scalable multi-view object detection and similarity metrics for detections. In: *Lecture Notes in Computer Science, Vol. 6311.* Daniilidis, K.; Maragos, P.; Paragios, N. Eds. Springer Berlin Heidelberg, 620–633, 2010.

[20] Li, F.-F.; Fergus, R.; Perona, P. Learning generative visual models from few training examples: An incremental Bayesian approach tested on 101 object categories. *Computer Vision and Image Understanding* Vol. 106, No. 1, 59–70, 2007.

[21] Griffin, G.; Holub, A.; Perona, P. Caltech-256 object category dataset. Technical Report. California Institute of Technology, 2007. Available at http://authors.library.caltech.edu/7694/1/CNS-TR-2007-001.pdf.

[22] Zobel, J.; Moffat, A. Inverted files for text search engines. *ACM Computing Surveys* Vol. 38, No. 2, Article No. 6, 2006.

[23] Domingos, P.; Hulten, G. Mining high-speed data streams. In: Proceedings of the 6th ACM SIGKDD International Conference on Knowledge Discovery and Data Mining, 71–80, 2000.

[24] Ristin, M.; Guillaumin, M.; Gall, J.; Van Gool, L. Incremental learning of random forests for large-scale image classification. *IEEE Transactions on Pattern Analysis and Machine Intelligence* DOI: 10.1109/TPAMI.2015.2459678, 2015.

[25] Henderson, C.; Blasi, S. G.; Sobhani, F.; Izquierdo, E. On the impurity of street-scene video footage. In: Proceedings of the 6th International Conference on Imaging for Crime Prevention and Detection, 1–7, 2015.

14

VideoMap: An interactive and scalable visualization for exploring video content

Cui-Xia Ma[1,3] (✉), Yang Guo[2], and Hong-An Wang[1,3]

Abstract Large-scale dynamic relational data visualization has attracted considerable research attention recently. We introduce dynamic data visualization into the multimedia domain, and present an interactive and scalable system, VideoMap, for exploring large-scale video content. A long video or movie has much content; the associations between the content are complicated. VideoMap uses new visual representations to extract meaningful information from video content. Map-based visualization naturally and easily summarizes and reveals important features and events in video. Multi-scale descriptions are used to describe the layout and distribution of temporal information, spatial information, and associations between video content. Firstly, semantic associations are used in which map elements correspond to video contents. Secondly, video contents are visualized hierarchically from a large scale to a fine-detailed scale. VideoMap uses a small set of sketch gestures to invoke analysis, and automatically completes charts by synthesizing visual representations from the map and binding them to the underlying data. Furthermore, VideoMap allows users to use gestures to move and resize the view, as when using a map, facilitating interactive exploration. Our experimental evaluation of VideoMap demonstrates how the system can assist in exploring video content as well as significantly reducing browsing time when trying to understand and find events of interest.

1 State Key Lab of Computer Science, Institute of Software, Chinese Academy of Sciences, Beijing 100190, China. E-mail: cuixia@iscas.ac.cn (✉).

2 School of Computer and Control Engineering, University of Chinese Academy of Sciences, Beijing 100080, China.

3 Beijing Key Lab of Human–Computer Interaction, Institute of Software, Chinese Academy of Sciences, Beijing 100080, China.

Keywords map metaphor; video content visualization; sketch-based interaction; association analysis

1 Introduction

Large-scale dynamic relational data visualization and interaction has attracted considerable attention recently. Many works have focused on visualization of dynamic relational data, such as social media data including music and TV viewing trends [1], streaming text data [2], web trends [3], etc. Maps are one of the typical methods used to visualize large-scale dynamic relational data as they preserve the mental map perceived by users [1]. Inspired by Ref. [1], we visualize video content by taking advantage of the map metaphor. Videos can be considered to be a type of large-scale dynamic relational data. In particular, a lengthy video (such as a movie or surveillance video data, which integrates several video clips) contains a wealth of information, containing various characters, different scenes, and complex connections between each scene. The movie *The Matrix*, an example that will be used throughout this paper, includes about 14 main characters and 76 characters in all (one character appears repeatedly in different scenes), 14 main events, and 83 kinds of connections between scenes. The detailed content and complicated relationships between this varied data make the process of browsing and analyzing video content a laborious and time consuming task for users. Efficient visualization and interaction are important in reducing the exploratory burden for users. Image a scenario. Fans of *The Matrix* do not tire of watching it over and over. If they had a video map for this movie, they would be excited to be able to access information of interest in depth, just like following

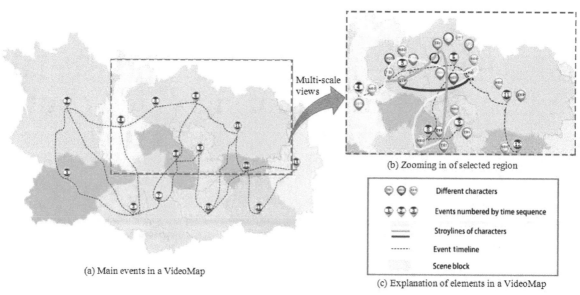

(a) Main events in a VideoMap

(b) Zooming in of selected region

(c) Explanation of elements in a VideoMap

Fig. 1 Our proposed method, VideoMap, visualizes relations in video data by taking advantage of the geographic map metaphor, providing an intuitive and effective way to explore video content. Such content as characters, scenes, events, and relationships in videos are made available through map elements, including objects (dots), scenes (blocks), and roads (lines), as shown in (c). Main events in different scenes (blocks) are represented in (a). Events involving the same characters are connected using an event timeline. VideoMap can zoom in from a very large scale to a small scale of fine-detailed representation of video data by selecting a region of interest—see (b). Users can quickly explore video content and its associated trajectories (roads) to locate items of interest.

the steps in a treasure map hunt. In this paper, we propose a tool, VideoMap, which can display multi-scale views of video content, serving as an efficient video exploration tool.

Various solutions have been provided to facilitate browsing and exploration of video data by summarizing or visualizing the video content. Traditional methods focus on extracting salient frames and displaying them in different forms, like video cubes in 3D [4], volume visualization for video sequences [5], keyframe posters [6], panorama excerpts [7], video booklets [8], video storyboarding frameworks [9], and so on. Other methods extract and visualize important information such as moving objects or movement trajectories [10, 11]. These video summarization and visualization methods rarely consider the overall layout when integrating different scenes and interaction. Ma et al. [12] proposed a sketch-based interactive video authoring tool with sketch summarization for video content, but this method was limited to visualizing content and relationships in video data using a line drawing format. In particular, most traditional approaches focus on depicting specific events and do not account for associations between events, characters, or scenes.

The purpose of visualizing video data is to develop appropriate approaches for processing large amounts

of video data with the assistance of computers, which can extract semantic associations and patterns contained within video data. Maps are a familiar way to present an overview, show connections, and allow a shift from large scale down to a precise representation of video data (cf. semantic zooming in a map). Massive video data can be processed to generate dots (representing characters or objects), graphical patterns (associations), and regions (scenes) on a map to allow intelligent judgment and provide recommendations for information analysis and retrieval. For example, on a map of video data, by sketching circles around two dots (representing characters or events of interest), related paths can be interactively synthesized and recommended using existing visualized elements. Furthermore, traditional map interaction methods of zooming and panning make them easy to use when exploring data. Thus, maps offer a promising way to visualize video data.

Few visualization techniques have been adequately utilized to help users effectively analyze associations in video content. Video summarization can help users obtain overview information from a target video sequence in limited time. Video exploration offers efficient interfaces to access video content, but integrating these two approaches so as to satisfy user demands, with user-friendly interaction, is a major challenge.

This paper proposes VideoMap, an interactive visualization system that summarizes multi-scale video content using the map metaphor, extracting characters, scenes, events, and associations. VideoMap facilitates exploration of video data. Our contributions comprise the following: (1) We provide a novel video visualization approach for exploration of video data. The system provides a multi-scale visualization that contains information from different views. (2) Our approach incorporates intuitive sketch-based interaction that facilitates association analysis through visual inspection of video data on the map, translating previously unseen video data into its most likely description. Possible examples of queries are "what happened between *Trinity* in *the Matrix* and *Cypher* in reality", or "what are the relations between these two selected events". Such complex tasks are possible primarily by exploring the different paths between the two characters by use of sketch-based interaction.

2   Related work

Our research is closely related to work on video visualization, video visual analysis, and content-based video interaction. We first review current analytical visualization techniques for video content, then recent work on content-based video interaction, and finally, work on map metaphors.

Video visual analysis has become an important technique. Exploring video data simply by watching it is inappropriate for large databases. This problem is particularly obvious in video surveillance [13, 14]. Höferlin and Weiskopf [15] propose an approach for fast identification of relevant objects based on properties of their trajectories. Meghdadi and Irani [16] present a novel video visual analytics system which considers each object's moving path, and provides analysts with various views of information related to moving objects in a video. Though the power of the system is due to its ability to summarize movements individually and apply spatiotemporal filters to limit the search results, other aspects are also considered, such as the attributes of moving objects and relations between them. Walton et al. [17] present an efficient solution

to mitigate the undesirable distortion of re-targeted vehicle objects in traffic video visualization by a series of automated algorithmic steps, including vehicle segmentation, vehicle roof detection, and non-uniform image deformation by applying a second homography. They concentrate only on aerial views; the challenges include intelligent removal of existing vehicles in an aerial view to provide more sophisticated background models. Video visual analytics addresses scalable and reliable analysis of video data to help decision making. Höferlin et al. [18] propose a video visual analytics method that combines the complementary strengths of human recognition and machine processing. Most studies focus on analyzing surveillance videos containing specific events that occur in fixed environments. For general movies, they depict a story more dramatically, which happens in variable scenes.

There are also many works in movie and video summarization and visualization which enable users to understand video content without the burden of viewing videos. A summary of video can be given by generating still images [19] or short video clips that focus on the moving objects [20]. Slit-tear visualization extracts a scan line from a video frame and adds the line to a composite image to help with video analysis and exploration [21]. Tanahashi and Ma [22] use a storyline to depict the temporal dynamics of social interaction, as well as to build a storyline for every character. Crossed lines represent interactions between characters. However, the storyline only includes one dimension, time, does not support association, and hardly considers interaction. Our work provides a 2D representation to visualize video data through a map metaphor, allowing analysis of video content by exploring the generated map.

Interaction with video content is important to access video data. Besides the traditional interaction method of using markers on a timeline to navigate through video content [23], new natural sketch-based interaction has been used in video authoring [12, 24] by operating on a sketch summary. Visual feedback is also important for efficient interaction, following user preferences [25]. Interaction with a map by zooming or drawing freely on it is familiar to all, and easy. Semantic zooming adjusts the scale of content, as in Google maps. A multi-scale interface allows users to use zooming tools to manipulate content by viewing different representations at different scales [26]. In our study, sketches and a multi-scale interface are appropriate for controlling the VideoMap via a map metaphor.

Using maps to visualize non-cartographic data in visualization systems has been studied. McCarthy and Meidel [27] build a visualization tool for location awareness by mapping offices, using badges that transmit infrared identification signals. This allows them to seek out colleagues for informal, face-to-face interactions. Their way of using the map metaphor just updates dynamic location information and represents it in an efficient way. However, this tool does not focus on how to show development of events and does not use a geographic map metaphor. Nesbitt [28] uses the metro map metaphor to summarize the ideas in a complex thesis, to communicate a business plan, to help university students understand a course structure, and so on. They simply use lines and points to represent information in a way more aking to a DAG (directed acyclic graph) than a map. Mashima et al. [1] describe a map-based visualization system to visualize user traffic on the Internet radio station last.fm and TV-viewing patterns from an IPTV service. It works well for visualizing large-scale dynamic relational data, but it limits users from interacting effectively. Gansner et al. [29] propose a method of visualizing and analyzing streaming packets viewed as a dynamic graph, and use it to visualize Twitter messages. Though its interface and algorithmic components are novel and attractive, its visualization capacity would be challenged in the presence of large-scale data.

In this paper, we use maps to visualize video data, providing user-friendly interaction to analyze video content. The system provides a special way of viewing video information. In addition, to the best of our knowledge, our work is the first to use map metaphor to visualize video data while integrating user cognition.

3 Multi-scale structure design

3.1 Cognition-based video representation

The mismatch of computing ability of machines and humans leads to inefficient processing, leading for example to the fundamental scientific question "can computers process and understand video content to the same extent as human beings?" By expanding in-depth understanding and knowledge in related subject areas, including human computer interaction, cognitive modeling, visual analysis, and computational perception, we provide a multi-scale representation of video content based on the cognition processes used by human beings.

The cognitive processes of the human brain have attracted much research attention from philosophers, psychologists, and computer scientists for a long time. Many studies into neurophysiology and neurology over the past decades have provided useful results and experimental data which can help the computer scientists to find computation models for cognitive processes that enhance the processing of information. Fu et al. [30] explore the cognitive mechanisms and computation models of visual media based on neurophysiology, cognitive psychology, and computational modeling, and propose a computational cognition model of perception, memory, and judgment (PMJ model) which corresponds to the calculation processes of analysis, modeling, and decision-making. We use the PMJ model. People usually deal with presentation in a hierarchical way at different levels of abstraction [26]. Cognition consists of a series of complex processes, with multiple processing pathways between the various stages of cognition [30]. The cognitive system chooses pathways depending on the difficulty and the goal of the information processing task [30, 31]. During the process of understanding video content, we consider three levels of video content representation: fast recognition, pattern understanding, and association deduction.

When people watch video, the human visual system can detect and quickly respond to visual stimuli. The brain extracts obvious visual features and identifies basic content such as objects, people, actions, etc., relying on the special "feature map" in the human brain. This process corresponds to the "fast process" (①+⑧) of the PMJ model (Fig. 2(a)). We define the process as "fast recognition", and the content extracted from videos in this process as "basic entities". The content is then kept in short-term memory before proceeding to the next step.

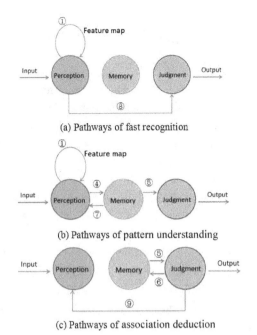

Fig. 2 Pathways for different levels of a perception, memory, and judgment model.

While watching videos, some content which appears frequently or is connected to existing knowledge we have already learned results in strong stimuli which causes this content to be kept in long-term memory. At the same time, the brain reprocesses the information to understand the patterns linking basic entities, such as who is doing what where. This process corresponds to the "meticulous process" (④+⑤ and ⑦) of the PMJ model (Fig. 2(b)). In this process, the brain determines events and patterns linking the basic entities. We call this process "pattern understanding", and its output is "pattern structure information".

As the video continues, we get more information and understand the development of the entire video and relation between sub-events. This is the third process. For example, some videos show the development of the events in incorrect time sequence, while the above two processes can only understand independent parts of the whole event. The more information the brain obtains, the greater the chance it can determine the potential associations in the correct order of sub-events. Occasionally, the brain will modify some information in memory which is incorrect. This process corresponds to the "feedback process" (⑥+⑤ or ⑨) of the PMJ model (Fig. 2(c)). We define this process as "association deduction", and its output as "abstract semantics".

From the three processes above, we conclude that cognition of video content is based on a multi-scale representation. We represent the video content as four layers, as shown in Fig. 3. In particular this helps to address the mismatch of human effort, and the need to effectively navigate and reuse rich video data.

3.2 Multi-scale description for video content

We can segment video content into four layers, each of which represents different information scales. As Fig. 3 shows, these information layers are correlated rather than independent. Usually, videos are segmented into scenes, clips, shots, and key frames based on visual features, rather than the semantics of video content. Here, we combine this usual segmentation with our cognition analysis and define the multi-scale video content elements as follows:

$< Videos >:=< Title >< Describe >< Time >$
$\{< Event >\}$
$< Association >:=< Association\_type > \text{"}Id\text{"}$
$< Value >$
$< Association\_type >:= \text{"}Event\text{"}|\text{"}Scene\text{"}|\text{"}Object\text{"}|$
$\text{"}Co-occurrence\text{"}$
$< Event >:= \text{"}Event\_id, < Association >,$
$< Video\_clips >, < Time\_duration >$
$| < Annotate >$
$< Value >:= \text{"}Number\text{"}|\text{"}Text\text{"}$
$< Scene >:= \text{"}Scene\_id\text{"} < Location >< Frame\_id >$
$< Object\_list > [< Annotate >][Association]$
$< Object >:= \text{"}Object\_id\text{"} < Picture >< Object\_describe >$
$< Time\_duration > \{(Scene\_id, < Time >)\}[< Association >]$
$< Similarity\_list > [< Annotate >]$
$< Frame >:= \text{"}Frame\_id\text{"} < Time >< Picture >$
$< Picture >:= \text{"}Pic\_id\text{"} < Path > \{< Feather >\}$
$< Video\_clips >:=< Video >< Start\_time >< End\_time >$
$< Similarity\_list >:= \{(\text{"}Object\_id\text{"}, \text{"}Object\_id\text{"}, \text{"}Value\text{"})\}$
$< Feather >= \text{"}Color_{histogram}\text{"}\text{"}Outline\text{"}\text{"}Textural\text{"}\text{"}Sift\text{"}$
$< Annotate >:= \text{"}Text\text{"}|\text{"}Sketch\text{"}|\text{"}Graph\text{"}$

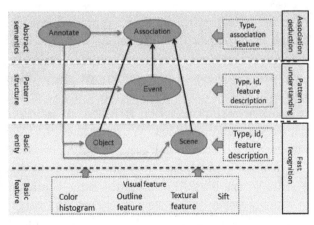

Fig. 3 Representation of video content.

4   Visualization

4.1   Data preprocessing

The form of video data used in this visualization is a chronological list of events that happen in different scenes in which characters are involved. Those events can be separated into a series of video clips, where each clip represents a time span of the corresponding part of the video, depicting details of the event. We use the video data of the movie *The Matrix* to evaluate the methods. Our datasets were manually extracted from the movie and other publicly available information.

We define an event as a unit that consists of five parts: <Start time, End time, Characters involved, Scene, Summary>. Start time is when the event begins to happen. End time refers when the event is completed. Characters involved are those characters appearing in the event. Scene corresponds to those main video shots in which the event happened. We cluster scenes into classes, and allocate a color to each kind of scene. Scenes located in different spots may be the same scene if they share the same color, but if one scene block only contains one event dot, it does not mean that only one event happened—it is just a representation. Summary relates what happens in the event using words extracted from the movie. Each event represents a time slot in the data where its members interact. We denote the data as a set of events $E = \{e_1, \cdots, e_n\}$, where for $1 < k < n$ we have a corresponding start time st_k, end time et_k, involved characters $C_k = \{c_i, \cdots, c_m\}$, scene S_k representing the scene in which the event happens, and a summary of a few words describe the event's content.

Based on the design principles previously discussed, dots with numbers represent events. We set up a map with width w and height h, and give all event dots a random initial coordinate, then use a layout algorithm to get their final positions. Afterwards, we place them on the map by using a method based on Ref. [29], to generate blocks surrounding events representing S_k. We put character dots around event dots according to C_k, to show which characters are involved in the event. We use lines to connect the same character when involved in different events according to their occurence in st_k, et_k, C_k; we also use lines to connect events to represent characters transferring between

them. Thus, the more characters involved, the thicker the lines are (Fig. 4).

4.2   Algorithm overview

Before giving the layout algorithm, the clustering algorithm used to classify the scenes is introduced. We use the RGB color matrix of images as their characteristic value and the K-means method to cluster data, as follows:

1) To extract key frames from the video, the number of key frames is set in accordance with the lengths of the scenes.

2) We choose the first key frame and use its RGB color matrix as the centroid matrix. They are R_1, G_1, B_1 of size $w \times h$, where w, h are the width and height of the keyframe respectively.

3) We choose another key frame. The distance D between this frame and the first key frame is calculated:

$$D = |R_1 - R_2| + |G_1 - G_2| + |B_1 - B_2|$$

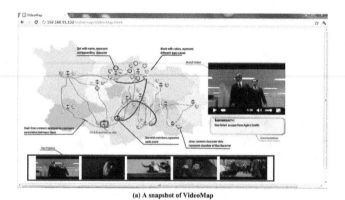

(a) A snapshot of VideoMap

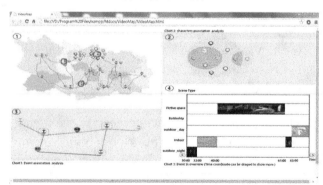

(b) Association analysis example among three selected events

Fig. 4   Top: exploring video content using VideoMap to navigate video content of interest, e.g., an event is selected, the corresponding video clip is played, and related key frames are represented. Bottom: statistical information is provided for three selected events allowing the user to understand and explore video content. View 1 shows the operating interface. View 2 presents characters involved in the events. View 3 presents relationships with other events. View 4 shows keyframes belonging to different events in different scenes.

We compare the distance matrix D with a preset threshold matrix T that also has size $w \times h$, and we compute the variation c:

$$c = \sum_i^w \sum_j^h \text{sign}(T_{i,j} - D_{i,j})$$

where

$$\text{sign}(x) = \begin{cases} 1, & \text{if } x \geqslant 0 \\ 0, & \text{otherwise} \end{cases}$$

If $c < wh/2$, we put the second frame and first frame into the same class, then a new centroid matrix ,which is the average RGB color matrix of all key frames, is calculated. Otherwise, we take the second frame as a new class. The RGB color matrix of the second key frame is used as the centroid matrix of the new class. When processing the next key frame, we compare it with the centroid matrixes of each class, and assign it into the closest, or assign it to a new class.

4) Finally, the scene is assigned to the class to which its key frames belong. Scenes are shown in different colors according to their type in the map.

Our layout algorithm is based on a genetic algorithm after expressing the layout problem in terms of function optimization. Design of the objective function to produce a layout in line with our expectations is the key issue. We thus next introduce the design principles of the objective function.

To follow aesthetic principles, and to make effective use of space, the objective function should satisfy the following conditions: (a) vertices should cover each other and edges should be crossed as infrequently as possible, and (b) the distance between two points should be proportional to the weight on the edge joining them.

The final objective function is thus:

$$f = \sum_i^E \sum_j^E \text{Cross}(e_i, e_j) + \sum_i^N \sum_j^N (kw_{ij} - |p_i - p_j|)^2$$

$$(1)$$

where E is the total number of edges, N is the total number of vertices, $\text{Cross}(e_i, e_j)$ returns 1 if edge e_j intersects e_j and 0 otherwise, w_{ij} is the weight of the edge between points $p_i(x_i, y_i)$ and $p_j(x_j, y_j)$, $x \in (0, w), y \in (0, h)$. The value of w_{ij} means the correlation between character points p_i and p_j which depends on the time they spend

together. The longer the time is, the larger w_{ij} is. If there is no edge between two points then the weight is given a large value. k is a proportionality coefficient manually. $|p_i - p_j|$ is the distance between two points on the map. Minimizing $(kw_{ij} - |p_i - p_j|)^2$ causes the distance between p_i and p_j to be proportional to the weight. The first term ensures that condition (a) is satisfied; the second term enforces condition (b). The layout problem is thus turned into a search for the minimum value of Eq. (1).

A genetic algorithm (GA) is used to solve this problem. First, for every possible solution $p_1(x_1, y_1), \cdots, p_n(x_n, y_n)$ for Eq. (1), we use a real number string $(x_1, y_1, \cdots, x_n, y_n)$ to represent a chromosome. n is the number of points. We randomly generate initial population of 15 chromosomes. Because we wish to minimise Eq. (1) while a GA maximises fitness, we choose a constant number G which is greater than maximum value of Eq. (1), then set the fitness function $F(x_1, y_1, \cdots, x_n, y_n) = G - f$. We use single point crossover and set the crossover probability $P_m = 0.8$. The roulette selection strategy is used. The probability of being selected for crossover depends on the value of the fitness function of each chromosome. For mutation, we use the following non-uniform mutation operator: Set the father to $A = (x_1, y_1, \cdots, x_n, y_n)$ and mutate the k-th gene. Assuming that gene k is an x coordinate in $[w, h]$, the new chromosome after mutation is

$$A = (x_1, y_1, \cdots, x_k{}^*, y_k, \cdots, x_n, y_n)$$

where

$$x_k{}^* = \begin{cases} x_k + \text{mut}(t, w - x), & \text{if rand(2)} = 0 \\ x_k - \text{mut}(t, x), & \text{otherwise} \end{cases} \quad (2)$$

where rand(2) is a random function which returns 0 or 1 with equal probability. $\text{mut}(t, x) = x(1 - t/T)^3$; t is the current generation number, and T is the maximum evolution generation number. mut lies in $[0, x]$ and when t is close to T, mut is close to 0. Early in evolution, the mutation operator searches within a larger range; later, the mutation operator leads to fine-tuning. The algorithm terminates either after a maximum number of generations, or a satisfactory fitness level has been reached for the population, giving the final layout.

Figure 4 shows a typical VideoMap interface. We obtained the relative positions of each event using our layout algorithm. Event dots are numbered by time sequence. Each event dot was taken as a center, and a random curve was generated around it as a block. The layout events are represented in temporal sequence in such a way as to reduce crossing intersections. The size of each block is proportional to the scene's duration. Clusters based on similarity are represented by different blocks with different or similar colors. Different types of lines represent different associations.

4.3   Visual form for association

A lengthy video such as a movie contains much video data. It is tedious to discover the relationships between characters, scenes, and events. VideoMap offers an intuitive overview of video content which supports analysis of the relationship in video data, helping users understand the content of video more easily and quickly. VideoMap's elements mainly comprise dots, lines, and blocks, which correspond to the sites, roads, and regions in a geographical map respectively, as shown in Fig. 4(a). Blocks represent different kinds of scenes in which events happened. We number event dots in time order. Lines represent temporal correlations between character dots in the VideoMap. We arrange the event dots on the map using our layout algorithm (see Section 4.2), then spread the character dots around corresponding event points to represent those characters involved in the event. We use blocks surrounding the event dots to indicate the events that happen in this scene.

Association analysis on VideoMap helps overcome the limited processing capacity of the human brain when faced with complex video data. For instance, in Fig. 4(b), VideoMap provides various statistics, for example, how many shared characters they contain (Fig. 4(b) View 2), the associations which are not included in the selected events (Fig. 4(b) View 3), and the keyframes in the selected events (Fig. 4(b) View 4).

Association analysis is useful for discovering interesting relationships hidden in the VideoMap. Following preprocessing and multi-scale data representation, uncovered relationships appear in the form of association paths. Such paths suggest that a relationship exists between the points selected on the map. For example, more than one path may exist connecting two characters on the map such as *Neo* and *Cypher*. To find paths in VideoMap:

1) Select two objects in the VideoMap (e.g., two dots on map), (e_i, c_m) and (e_j, c_n).

2) Define the adjacency matrix E as follows:

If c_m in both c_a and c_b corresponds to e_a and e_b, then $E(a,b) = 1 \quad (a < b)$;

if c_n in both c_a and c_b corresponds to e_a and e_b, then $E(a,b) = 1 \quad (a < b)$;

otherwise $E(a,b) = 0$.

3) Given G with vertices $\{e_1, e_2, \cdots\}$ and adjacency matrix E, use DFS (depth first search) or BFS (breadth first search) to find all paths from source e_i to destination e_j.

Figure 5 shows the pathfinding support in

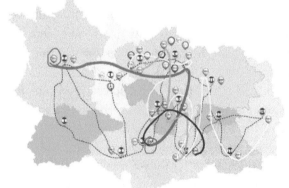

(a) The selected objects by circling them in red

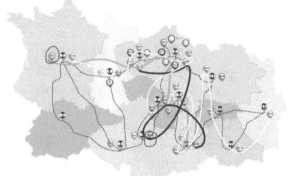

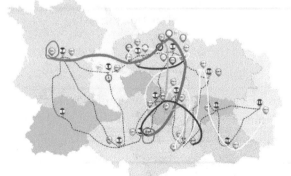

(b) In this case, two paths (in red) are given to show the different relationship between two objects

Fig. 5   Pathfinding in VideoMap.

VideoMap. On one hand, when the user picks two character dots, for example, character A in event M and character B in event N, it is just like choosing start and end points on a real map. It returns several accessible paths to show the different possible associations between the selected characters. On the other hand, however, when the user picks more than one event dot, various hidden statistical information is provided in visual analytics form (as shown in Fig. 4(b)). Other functions further support video content exploring, allowing the user to choose some specific event or character dots. VideoMap only displays related elements corresponding to what has been chosen. You can play specific video content by clicking the corresponding event point. Meanwhile it also gives a brief summary of this event to help the user to see the details. When the user chooses a character point, the association with other characters is displayed. All these functions provide users with association analysis, helping them better understand video content. Sketch-based annotation is also supported in VideoMap, which helps users to write down their ideas conveniently, facilitating later operations.

4.4 Sketch interaction

4.4.1 Interactivity through expressive gestures

The sketch-based interface provides a tradeoff between expressiveness and naturalness during interaction with the map. It allows users to draw editable sketches freely on the map to facilitate exploration and visual analysis of video contents. The interface to VideoMap provides sketch gestures (Figs. 6 and 7) and allows annotation. VideoMap recognizes sketched gestures and automatically completes different operations on the map, such as zooming, panning, or other methods of association analysis.

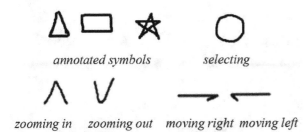

Fig. 6 Sketch gestures used in VideoMap.

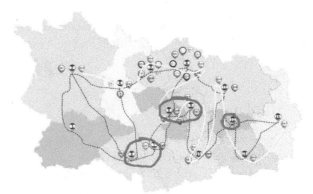

Fig. 7 Selection operation on the VideoMap.

4.4.2 Freeform annotation

Annotations can provide valuable semantic information for understanding video content. VideoMap supports freeform annotation anywhere on the map as it is useful for explanation and emphasis. Manual annotations are particularly useful for allowing users to create personalized annotations of videos. For example, users can write down their analysis or thoughts to add new associations between objects (Fig. 8). During later retrieval to find paths, the new association can be obtained. Users may draw sketches to annotate video, using symbols and hand-drawn illustrations with freeform strokes, enriching and extending the

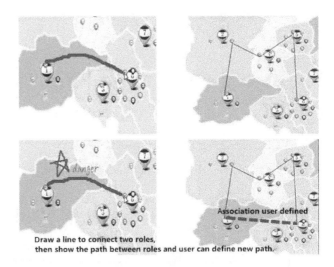

Fig. 8 Defining and adding an association in VideoMap by free annotation. Top: drawing a line connecting two objects gets the existing paths between them. Bottom: inputing freeform annotation creates an association and a new path (dashed line) is generated. The path representing the new association can be obtained during later pathfinding processes.

video content. These sketches are organized into the data structure to develop a narrative description and can be used to facilitate indexing or retrieval later.

5   Implementation

The system architecture is depicted in Fig. 9, which shows the main modules which implement the interface. There are four main modules in the system, concerned with data pre-processing, layout generation, video to map projection, and interaction. The system is implemented in d3.js. The data pre-processing module is responsible for keyframe and scene clustering, event selection, and video segmentation according to events. Data pre-processing puts the data into the required form. The data is then used to generate the layout of events, mapping video elements to map elements according to rules. Map elements and layout information generate the framework of the VideoMap, allowing interactive functions to operate on the relevant dataset. The interaction module offers several interactive functions, such as circling two character dots to find their connection and customized display of specific information. These functions permit visualization of video content and facilitate the users' understanding and browsing. Users can provide visual feedback to, e.g., correct the definitions

of events or change the associations between characters. Users also can customize associations, add them as required, and annotate details to things they are interested in.

6   Evaluation

VideoMap aims to serve as an efficient and intuitive tool for exploring video content. It has been tested in devices with diverse display sizes, including a tabletop (see Fig. 10(a)), and a Fujitsu tablet PC (see Fig. 10(b)). We conducted a study to evaluate VideoMap, which demonstrated how the system can facilitate exploration of video content and significantly reduce browsing time needed to understand and find events of interest. Firstly, we compared VideoMap to two state-of-the-art video visualization and interaction methods: Storyline [22] and the Sketch Graph method [24].

Participants. Eighteen participants from a

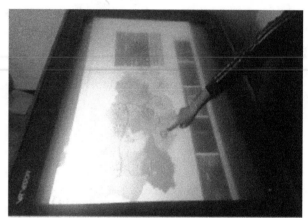

(a) Interaction on a 70-inch tabletop

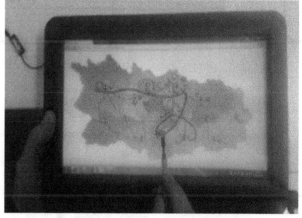

(b) Interaction on a 10-inch tablet PC

Fig. 10   Instances of VideoMap on interactive devices.

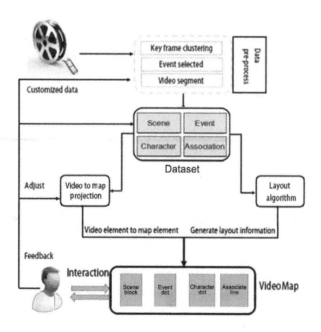

Fig. 9   System architecture.

university were recruited, including 10 females and 8 males, with ages ranginge from 20 to 35. They were divided into three groups of equal size.

Methods. Visualization of *The Matrix* movie using Storyline, Sketch Graph, and VideoMap, was presented to the participants (see Fig. 11). Each of the three groups was required to carry out the tasks below using one of the three methods:

Task 1: Find events in which *Neo* was involved.

Task 2: Find events in which *Neo* and *Morpheus* were involved.

Task 3: Find and describe the relationship between *Trinity*, who helped *Neo* back to reality, and *Cyber*, who colluded with *Smith*.

To ensure consistent evaluation, all the tasks were performed on Fujitsu Limited LIFEBOOK T Series (Intel Core i3 U380 1.33 GHZ) running Windows 7 (see Fig. 10(b)). Half an hour's training in using the three methods was taken with a tutorial before the test. At the end of experiment, the participants were required to complete the questionnaire in Table 1.

Results and discussion. We recorded the total time participants used to complete the tasks. The time spent completing Tasks 1, 2, and 3 for the three groups using three different methods are summarized in Fig. 12. It can be seen that the VideoMap method required the least time. A one-way ANOVA test

Table 1 Questionnaire. Each question was answered on a scale 1–5, as follows: 1. strongly disagree, 2. disagree, 3. neutral, 4. agree, 5. strongly agree

(1) VideoMap is an efficient and intuitive system for exploring video content.
(2) I would like to use this means of exploring video content frequently.
(3) I thought this visualization method is easy to use.
(4) I thought the multi-scale views are convenient and useful.
(5) Most people would learn to use this method quickly.
(6) I need to learn a lot of things before I could get going with this method.
(7) I though path finding is interesting and useful for association analysis.
(8) The sketch interaction on VideoMap is efficient.
(9) I felt very confident using VideoMap.

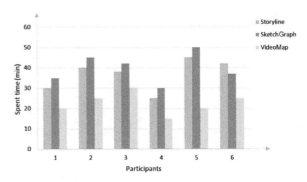

Fig. 12 Implementation time of tasks using three methods.

showed that the main effect of the different methods is significant ($F(2, 15) = 11.086, p < 0.01$). There was also a significant difference between VideoMap ($M = 22.5$ min, $SD = 5.2$) and Storyline ($M = 36.7$ min, $SD = 7.6$) ($p < 0.05$). Results of the questionnaire are summarized below:

- 94% of participants (17/18) gave positive feedback about VideoMap.
- 83% of participants (15/18) thought the multi-scale views in VideoMap are useful, and a convenient method for exploring video content and finding interesting goals.
- 89% of participants (16/18) thought the pathfinding in VideoMap is interesting and useful for facilitating association analysis and understanding video content.
- 83% of participants (15/18) gave positive feedback about the sketch interaction in VideoMap.

We also asked participants for their feedback on how well our design meets their expectations when exploring the video content. For example,

(a) A storyline visualization of the movie *The Matrix* used in Ref. [24]

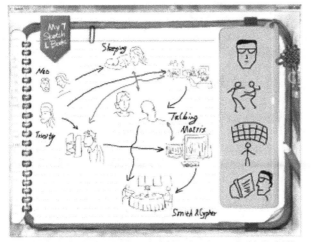

(b) Part of Sketch Graph generated following the method in Ref. [1]

Fig. 11 Storyline and Sketch Graph used in the experiment.

during Task 2, in Storyline, participants had to follow the two lines representing *Neo* and *Morpheus*. In VideoMap, participants can select *Neo* or *Morpheus* in any scene in which they appear, and the related events and association lines are highlighted. Afterwards, participants could inspect the results and play a clip that provided more detailed understanding of the content. VideoMap helps participants locate the region of interest. In Storyline and Sketch Graph, participants did not think it is easy to find these associations. They indicated that because of the many lines and detailed information, VideoMap is slightly difficult at first. However, after 30 minutes of experience with the system, the participants found it useful. They felt the process of understanding and exploring video content using VideoMap is similar to a treasure-hunting process, indicating that understanding the associations between characters or scenes by finding paths on VideoMap is an interesting experience. Some particular comments by participants included: "VideoMap gave me an unprecedented feeling of efficient access to video...", "I'm extremely satisfied with this way of viewing video...".

VideoMap still has some limitations. The multi-scale data description is critical to the performance of VideoMap. Currently the proposed multi-scale environment only supports three levels of video content description. It is difficult to achieve a precise understanding and description of complicated video semantics. Fully automated video analysis methods are difficult to achieve. The tradeoff between human cognition, computer-supported visualization, and interaction tools is important to consider when detecting events of interest. Current events represent time sequences by numbering which is not very intuitive, although it also helped users explore video content in the study. Future work will consider optimization of event visualization.

7 Conclusions

In this paper, we presented VideoMap, which can help users explore a video and find targets in an intuitive and efficient way. VideoMap extracts meaningful information from a video and conveys the extracted information to users in the form of a visual map. Association analysis by visualizing connections within a video is not intended to fully provide automatic solutions to the problem of making decisions about the contents of a video, but aims to assist users in their intelligent reasoning while reducing the burden of viewing videos. Automated video analysis methods are not fully reliable particularly when the search criteria are subjective or vaguely defined. VideoMap addresses this problem, and offers a solution to issues related to the limited processing capacity of the human brain in the face of enormous video data requirements. Operations in VideoMap are based on sketch gestures. A user study showed that VideoMap offers a promising tool for helping users to efficiently explore video content with an intuitive and natural interaction. In our future work, we intend to improve the multi-scale data description based on human cognition, and to optimize the layout algorithm. More advanced analysis methods of exploring video content are potentially possible through data descriptions and freeform sketch interaction.

Acknowledgements

This work was supported by the National Natural Science Foundation of China (Project Nos. U1435220, 61232013).

References

[1] Mashima, D.; Kobourov, S.; Hu, Y. Visualizing dynamic data with maps. *IEEE Transactions on Visualization and Computer Graphics* Vol. 18, No. 9, 1424–1437, 2012.

[2] Gansner, E. R.; Hu, Y.; North, S. Visualizing streaming text data with dynamic graphs and maps. In: *Lecture Notes in Computer Science, Vol. 7704.* Didimo, W.; Patrignani, M. Eds. Springer Berlin Heidelberg, 439–450, 2013.

[3] Information on https://ia.net/know-how/ia-trendmap-2007v2.

[4] Fels, S.; Mase, K. Interactive video cubism. In: Proceedings of the 1999 Workshop on New Paradigms in Information Visualization and Manipulation in Conjunction with the 8th ACM International Conference on Information and Knowledge Management, 78–82, 1999.

[5] Daniel, G.; Chen, M. Video visualization. In: Proceedings of IEEE Visualization, 409–416, 2003.

[6] Yeung, M. M.; Yeo, B.-L. Video visualization for compact presentation and fast browsing of pictorial content. *IEEE Transactions on Circuits and Systems for Video Technology* Vol. 7, No. 5, 771–785, 1997.

[7] Taniguchi, Y.; Akutsu, A.; Tonomura, Y. Panorama Excerpts: Extracting and packing panoramas for video browsing. In: Proceedings of the 5th ACM International Conference on Multimedia, 427–436, 1997.

[8] Hua, X.-S.; Li, S.; Zhang, H.-J. Video booklet. 2010. Available at http://dent.cecs.uci.edu/~papers/icme05/defevent/papers/cr1126.pdf.

[9] Goldman, D. B.; Curless, B.; Salesin, D.; Seitz, S. M. Schematic storyboarding for video visualization and editing. ACM Transactions on Graphics Vol. 25, No. 3, 862–871, 2006.

[10] Nguyen, C.; Niu, Y.; Liu, F. Video summagator: An interface for video summarization and navigation. In: Proceedings of the SIGCHI Conference on Human Factors in Computing Systems, 647–650, 2012.

[11] Shah, R.; Narayanan, P. J. Interactive video manipulation using object trajectories and scene backgrounds. IEEE Transactions on Circuits and Systems for Video Technology Vol. 23, No. 9, 1565–1576, 2013.

[12] Ma, C.-X.; Liu, Y.-J.; Wang, H.-A.; Teng, D.-X.; Dai, G.-Z. Sketch-based annotation and visualization in video authoring. IEEE Transactions on Multimedia Vol. 14, No. 4, 1153–1165, 2012.

[13] Truong, B. T.; Venkatesh, S. Video abstraction: A systematic review and classification. ACM Transactions on Multimedia Computing, Communications, and Applications Vol. 3, No. 1, Article No. 3, 2007.

[14] Viaud, M.-l.; Buisson, O.; Saulnier, A.; Guenais, C. Video exploration: From multimedia content analysis to interactive visualization. In: Proceedings of the 18th ACM International Conference on Multimedia, 1311–1314, 2010.

[15] Höferlin, M.; Höferlin, B.; Weiskopf, D. Video visual analytics of tracked moving objects. 2012. Available at http://www.vis.uni-stuttgart.de/uploads/tx_vispublications/Hoeferlin2009b.pdf.

[16] Meghdadi, A. H.; Irani, P. Interactive exploration of surveillance video through action shot summarization and trajectory visualization. IEEE Transactions on Visualization and Computer Graphics Vol. 19, No. 12, 2119–2128, 2013.

[17] Walton, S.; Berger, K.; Ebert, D.; Chen, M. Vehicle object retargeting from dynamic traffic videos for real-time visualisation. The Visual Computer Vol. 30, No. 5, 493–505, 2014.

[18] Höferlin, B.; Höferlin, M.; Heidemann, G.; Weiskopf, D. Scalable video visual analytics. Information Visualization Vol. 14, No. 1, 10–26, 2013.

[19] Caspi, Y.; Axelrod, A.; Matsushita, Y.; Gamliel, A. Dynamic stills and clip trailers. The Visual Computer Vol. 22, No. 9, 642–652, 2006.

[20] Correa, C. D.; Ma, K.-L. Dynamic video narratives. ACM Transactions on Graphics Vol. 29, No. 4, Article No. 88, 2010.

[21] Tang, A.; Greenberg, S.; Fels, S. Exploring video streams using slit-tear visualizations. In: Proceedings of Extended Abstracts on Human Factors in Computing Systems, 3509–3510, 2009.

[22] Tanahashi, Y.; Ma, K.-L. Design considerations for optimizing storyline visualizations. IEEE Transactions on Visualization and Computer Graphics Vol. 18, No. 12, 2679–2688, 2012.

[23] Li, F. C.; Gupta, A.; Sanocki, E.; He, L.-w.; Rui, Y. Browsing digital video. In: Proceedings of the SIGCHI Conference on Human Factors in Computing Systems, 169–176, 2000.

[24] Liu, Y.-J.; Ma, C.-X.; Fu, Q.; Fu, X.; Qin, S.-F.; Xie, L. A sketch-based approach for interactive organization of video clips. ACM Transactions on Multimedia Computing, Communications, and Applications Vol. 11, No. 1, Article No. 2, 2014.

[25] Jawaheer, G.; Weller, P.; Kostkova, P. Modeling user preferences in recommender systems: A classification framework for explicit and implicit user feedback. ACM Transactions on Interactive Intelligent Systems Vol. 4, No. 2, Article No. 8, 2014.

[26] Zhang, X.; Furnas, G. W. mCVEs: Using cross-scale collaboration to support user interaction with multiscale structures. Presence Vol. 14, No. 1, 31–46, 2005.

[27] McCarthy, J. F.; Meidel, E. S. ActiveMap: A visualization tool for location awareness to support informal interactions. In: Lecture Notes in Computer Science, Vol. 1707. Gellersen, H.-W. Ed. Springer Berlin Heidelberg, 158–170, 2000.

[28] Nesbitt, K. V. Getting to more abstract places using the metro map metaphor. In: Proceedings of the 8th International Conference on Information Visualisation, 488–493, 2004.

[29] Gansner, E. R.; Hu, Y.; Kobourov, S. GMap: Visualizing graphs and clusters as maps. In: Proceedings of IEEE Pacific Visualization Symposium, 201–208, 2010.

[30] Fu, X. L.; Cai, L. H.; Liu, Y.; Jia, J.; Chen, W. F.; Yi, Z.; Zhao, G. Z.; Liu, Y. J.; Wu, C. X. A computational cognition model of perception, memory, and judgment. Science China Information Sciences Vol. 57, No. 3, 1–15, 2014.

[31] Solway, A.; Botvinick, M. M. Goal-directed decision making as probabilistic inference: A computational framework and potential neural correlates. Psychological Review Vol. 119, No. 1, 120–154, 2012.

15

Single image super-resolution via blind blurring estimation and anchored space mapping

Xiaole Zhao[1] (✉), Yadong Wu[1], Jinsha Tian[1], and Hongying Zhang[2]

Abstract It has been widely acknowledged that learning-based super-resolution (SR) methods are effective to recover a high resolution (HR) image from a single low resolution (LR) input image. However, there exist two main challenges in learning-based SR methods currently: the quality of training samples and the demand for computation. We proposed a novel framework for single image SR tasks aiming at these issues, which consists of blind blurring kernel estimation (BKE) and SR recovery with anchored space mapping (ASM). BKE is realized via minimizing the cross-scale dissimilarity of the image iteratively, and SR recovery with ASM is performed based on iterative least square dictionary learning algorithm (ILS-DLA). BKE is capable of improving the compatibility of training samples and testing samples effectively and ASM can reduce consumed time during SR recovery radically. Moreover, a selective patch processing (SPP) strategy measured by average gradient amplitude |grad| of a patch is adopted to accelerate the BKE process. The experimental results show that our method outruns several typical blind and non-blind algorithms on equal conditions.

Keywords super-resolution (SR); blurring kernel estimation (BKE); anchored space mapping (ASM); dictionary learning; average gradient amplitude

---

1 School of Computer Science and Technology, Southwest University of Science and Technology, Mianyang 621010, China. E-mail: X. Zhao, zxlation@foxmail.com (✉); Y. Wu, wyd028@163.com.
2 School of Information Engineering, Southwest University of Science and Technology, Mianyang 621010, China. E-mail: zhy0838@163.com.

1 Introduction

Single image super-resolution has been becoming the hotspot of super-resolution area for digital images because it generally is not easy to obtain an adequate number of LR observations for SR recovery in many practical applications. In order to improve image SR performance and reduce time consumption so that it can be applied in practical applications more effectively, this kind of technology has attracted great attentions in recent years.

Single image super-resolution is essentially a severe ill-posed problem, which needs adequate priors to be solved. Existing super-resolution technologies can be roughly divided into three categories: traditional interpolation methods, reconstruction methods, and machine-learning (ML) based methods. Interpolation methods usually assume that image data is continuous and band-limited smooth signal. However, there are many discontinuous features in natural images such as edges and corners etc., which usually makes the recovered images by traditional interpolation methods suffer from low quality [1]. Reconstruction based methods apply a certain prior knowledge, such as total variation (TV) prior [2–4] and gradient profile (GP) prior [5] etc., to well pose the SR problem. The reconstructed image is required to be consistent with LR input via back-projection. But a certain prior is typically only propitious to specific images. Besides, these methods will produce worse results with larger magnification factor.

Relatively speaking, machine-learning based method is a promising technology and it has become the most popular topic in single image SR field. The first ML method was proposed by Freeman et al. [6], which is called example-based learning method. This method predicts HR patches from LR patches by solving markov random field (MRF) model by belief propagation algorithm. Then, Sun et al. [7] enhanced discontinuous features (such as edges and corners etc.) by primal sketch priors. These methods need an external database which consists of abundant HR/LR patch pairs, and time consumption hinders the application of this kind of methods. Chang et al. [8] proposed a nearest neighbor embedding (NNE) method motivated by the philosophy of locally linear embedding (LLE) [9]. They assumed LR patches and HR patches have similar space structure, and LR patch coefficients can be solved through least square problem for the fixed number of nearest neighbors (NNs). These coefficients are then used for HR patch NNs directly. However, the fixed number of NNs could cause over-fitting and/or under-fitting phenomena easily [10]. Yang et al. [11] proposed an effective sparse representation approach and addressed the fitting problems through selecting the number of NNs adaptively.

However, ML methods are still exposed to two main issues: the compatibility between training and testing samples (caused by light condition, defocus, noise etc.), and the mapping relation between LR and HR feature spaces (requiring numerous calculations). Glasner et al. [12] exploited image patch non-local self-similarity (i.e., patch recurrence) within image scale and cross-scale for single image SR tasks, which makes an effective solution for the compatibility problem. The mapping relation involves the learning process of LR/HR dictionaries. Actually, LR and HR feature spaces are tied by some mapping function, which could be unknown and not necessarily linear [13]. Therefore, the originally direct mapping mode [11] may not reflect this unknown non-linear relation correctly. Yang et al. [14] proposed another joint dictionary training approach to learn the duality relation between LR/HR patch spaces. The method essentially concatenates the two feature spaces and converts the problem to the standard sparse representation. Further, they explicitly learned the sparse coding problem across different feature spaces in Ref. [13], which is so-called coupled dictionary learning (CDL) algorithm. He et al. [15] proposed another

beta process joint dictionary learning (BPJDL) for CDL based on a Bayesian method through using a beta process prior. But, above-mentioned dictionary learning approaches did not take the feature of training samples into account for better performance. Actually, it is not an easy work to find the complicated relation between LR and HR feature spaces directly.

We present a novel single image super-resolution method considering both SR result and the acceleration of execution in the paper. The proposed approach firstly estimated the true blur kernel based on the philosophy of minimizing the dissimilarity between cross-scale patches [16]. LR/HR dictionaries then were trained via input image itself downsampled by the estimated blur kernel. The BKE processing was adopted for improving the quality of training samples. Then, L_2 norm regularization was used to substitute L_0/L_1 norm constraint so that latent HR patch can be mapped on LR patch directly through a mapping matrix computed by LR/HR dictionaries. This strategy is similar with ANR [17], but we employed a different dictionary learning approach, i.e., ILS-DLA, to train LR/HR dictionaries. In fact, ILS-DLA unified the principle of optimization of the whole SR process and produced better results with regard to K-SVD used by ANR.

The remainder of the paper is organized as follows: Section 2 briefly reviews the related work about this paper. The proposed approach is described in Section 3 detailedly. Section 4 presents the experimental results and comparison with other typical blind and non-blind SR methods. Section 5 concludes the paper.

2 Related work

2.1 Internal statistics in natural images

Glasner et al. [12] exploited an important internal statistical attributes of natural image patches named the patch recurrence, which is also known as image patch redundancy or non-local self-similarity (NLSS). NLSS has been employed in a lot of computer vision fields such as super resolution [12, 18–21], denoising [22], deblurring [23], and inpainting [24] etc. Further, Zontak and Irani [18] quantified this property by relating it to the spatial distance from the patch and the mean gradient magnitude |grad| of a patch. The three main conclusions can be perceived according to Ref. [18]: (i) smooth patches recur very frequently, whereas highly structured patches recur much less frequently; (ii) a small patch tends to recur densely in its vicinity and the frequency of recurrence decays rapidly as the distance from the patch increases; (iii) patches of different gradient content need to search for nearest neighbors at different distances. These conclusions consist of the theoretical basis of using the mean gradient magnitude |grad| as the metric of discriminatively choosing different patches when estimating the blurring kernels.

2.2   Cross-scale blur kernel estimation

For more detailed elaboration, we still need to briefly review the cross-scale BKE and introduce our previous work [16] on this issue despite a part of it is the same as previous one. We will illustrate the detailed differences in Section 3.1. Because of camera shake, defocus, and various kinds of noises, the blur kernel of different images may be entirely and totally different. Michaeli and Irani [25] utilized the non-local self-similarity property to estimate the optimal blur kernel by maximizing the cross-scale patch redundancy iteratively depending on the observation that HR images possess more patch recurrence than LR images. They assumed the initial kernel is a delta function used to down-sample the input image. A few NNs of each small patch were found in the down-sampled version of input image. Each NN corresponds to a large patch in the original scale image, and these patch pairs construct a set of linear equations which could be solved by using weighted least squares. The root mean squared error (RMSE) between cross-scale patches was employed as the iteration criterion. Figure 1 shows the main process of cross BKE of Ref. [25]. We follow the same idea with more careful observation: the effect of the convolution on smooth patches is obviously smaller than that on structured patches (refer to Fig. 2). This phenomenon can be explained easily according to the definition of convolution. Moreover, the mean gradient magnitude |grad| is more expressive than the variance of a patch on the basis of the conclusions in Ref. [18].

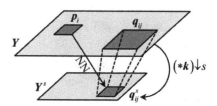

Fig. 1   Description of cross-scale patch redundancy. For each small patch p_i in Y, finding its NNs q_{ij}^s in Y^s which corresponds to a large patch q_{ij} in Y, q_{ij}^s and q_{ij} constitute a patch pair, and all patch pairs of NNs construct a set of linear equations which is solved using weighted least squares to obtain an updated kernel.

(a) Clean patches   (b) Blurred patches

Fig. 2   Blurring effect on non-smooth and smooth areas. Black boxes indicate structured areas, and red boxes indicate smooth areas. (a) Clean patches. It can be clearly seen that the structure of non-smooth patch is distinct. (b) Blurred patches corresponding to (a). The detail of non-smooth patch is obviously blurry.

2.3   ILS-DLA and ANR

ILS-DLA is a typical dictionary learning method. It adopts an overall optimization strategy based on least square (LS) to update the dictionary when the weight matrix is fixed so that ILS-DLA [26] is usually faster than K-SVD [17, 27]. Besides, ANR just adjusts the objective function slightly and the SR reconstruction process is theoretically based on least square method.

Supposing we have two coupled feature sets F_L and F_H with size $n_L \times L$ and $n_H \times L$, and the number of the atoms in LR dictionary D_L and HR dictionary D_H is K. The training process for D_L can be described as

$$\{\hat{D}_L, \hat{W}\} = \underset{D_L, W}{\arg\min} \sum_{i=1}^{L} \|w_i\|_p + \lambda \|F_L - D_L W\|_2^2,$$

$$s.t. \quad \|d_L^i\|_2^2 = 1 \quad (1)$$

where d_L^i is an atom in D_L, w_i is a column vector in W. $p \in \{0, 1\}$ is the constrain of the coefficient vector w_i, and λ is a tradeoff parameter. Equation (1) is usually resolved by optimizing one variable while keeping the other one fixed. In ILS-DLA case, least square method is used to update D_L while W is fixed. Once D_L and W were obtained then we could compute the D_{H} according to the same LS rule:

$$D_{\mathrm{H}} = F_{\mathrm{H}} W^{\mathrm{T}} (WW^{\mathrm{T}})^{-1} \qquad (2)$$

According to the philosophy of ANR, a mapping matrix can be calculated through the weight matrix and the both dictionaries. Then, it is used to project LR feature patches to HR feature patches directly. Thus, L_0/L_1 norm constrained optimization problem degenerates to an issue of matrix multiplication.

3 Proposed approach

3.1 Improved blur kernel estimation

Referring to Fig. 1, we use Y to represent the input LR image, and X to be latent HR image. Michaeli and Irani [25] estimated the blur kernel through maximizing the cross-scale NLSS directly, while we minimized the dissimilarity between cross-scale patches. Despite these two ideas look like the same with each other intuitively, they are slightly different and lead to severely different performance [16]. While Ref. [16] has introduced this part of content in detail, we need to present the key component of the improved blur kernel estimation for integrated elaboration. The following objective function has reflected the idea of minimizing the dissimilarity between cross-scale patches:

$$\underset{k}{\operatorname{argmin}} \sum_{i=1}^{N} \left\| p_i - \sum_{j=1}^{M_i} z_{ij} R_{ij} k \right\|_2^2 + \eta \| C k \|_2^2 \qquad (3)$$

where N is the number of query patches in Y. Matrix R_{ij} corresponds to the operation of convolving with q_{ij} and down-sampling by s. C is a matrix used as the penalty of non-smooth kernel. The second term of Eq. (3) is kernel prior and η is the balance parameter as the tradeoff between the error term and kernel prior. For the calculation of the weight z_{ij}, we can find M_i NNs in down-sampled version Y^s for each small patch p_i $(i = 1, 2, \cdots, N)$ in the input image Y. The "parent" patches q_{ij} right above q_{ij}^s are viewed as the candidate parent patches of p_i. Then the weight z_{ij} can be calculated as follow:

$$z_{ij} = \frac{\exp(-\| p_i - q_{ij}^s \|^2 / \sigma^2)}{\displaystyle\sum_{j=1}^{M_i} \exp(-\| p_i - q_{ij}^s \|^2 / \sigma^2)} \qquad (4)$$

where M_i is the number of NNs in Y^s of each small patch p_i in Y, and σ is the standard deviation of noise added on p_i. s is the scale factor (see Fig. 1). Note that we apply the same symbol to express column vector corresponding to the patch here. Setting the gradient of the objective function in Eq. (3) to zero can get the update formula of k:

$$\hat{k} = \left(\sum_{i=1}^{N} \sum_{j=1}^{M_i} z_{ij} R_{ij}^{\mathrm{T}} R_{ij} + \eta C^{\mathrm{T}} C \right)^{-1} \sum_{i=1}^{N} \sum_{j=1}^{M_i} z_{ij} R_{ij}^{\mathrm{T}} p_i \qquad (5)$$

Equation (5) is very similar to the result of Ref. [25], which can be interpreted as maximum a posteriori (MAP) estimation on k. However, there are at least three essential differentials with respect to Ref. [25]. Firstly, the motivation is different so that Ref. [25] tends to maximize the cross-scale similarity according to NLSS [12] while we minimize the dissimilarity directly according to Ref. [18]. This may not be easy to understand. However, the former leads Michaeli and Irani [25] to form their kernel update formula from physical analysis and interpretation of "optimal kernel". The latter leads us to obtain kernel update formula from quantitating cross-scale patch dissimilarity and directly minimizing it according to ridge regression [16]. Secondly, selective patch processing measured by the average gradient amplitude |grad| was adopted to improve the result of blind BKE. Finally, the number of NNs of each small patch p_i is not fixed which provides more flexibility during solving least square problem. Accordingly, the terminal criterion cannot be the totality of NNs. We use the average patch dissimilarity (APD) as terminal condition of iteration:

$$\mathrm{APD} = \sum_{i=1}^{N} \sum_{j=1}^{M_i} \| p_i - q_{ij}^s \|_2^2 \cdot \left(\sum_{i=1}^{N} M_i \right)^{-1} \qquad (6)$$

It is worth to note that selective patch processing is used to eliminate the effect on BKE caused by smooth patches; we selectively employ structured patches to calculate blur kernel. Specifically, if the average gradient magnitude |grad| of each query patch is smaller than a threshold, then we abandon it. Otherwise, we use it to estimate blur kernel according to Eq. (5). We typically perform search in the entire image according to Ref. [18] but this could not consume too much time because of a lot of smooth patches being filtered out.

3.2 Feature extraction strategy

There is a data preparation stage before dictionary learning when using sparse representation to do SR task, it is necessary to extract training features from the given input data because different feature extraction strategies will cause very different SR results. The mainstream feature extraction strategies include raw data of an image patch, the gradient of an image patch in x and y directions, and mean-removed patch etc. We adopt the back-projection residuals (BPR) model presented in Ref. [28] for feature extraction (see Fig. 3).

Firstly, we convolve Y with estimated kernel k, and down-sample it with s. From the view of minimizing the cross-scale patch dissimilarity, the estimated blur kernel gives us a more accurate down-sampling version of Y. In order to make the feature extraction more accurate, we consider the enhanced interpolation of Y', which forms the source of LR feature space F_{L}. The enhanced interpolation is the result of an iterative back-projection (IBP) operation [29, 30]:

$$\hat{Y}'_{t+1} = \hat{Y}'_t + [(Y^s - \hat{Y}^s_t) \uparrow s] * k' \qquad (7)$$

where $\hat{Y}^s_t = (\hat{Y}'_t * k) \downarrow s$, k' is a back-projection filter that spreads the differential error locally. It is usually replaced by a Gaussian function. The IBP starts with the bicubic interpolation, and down-sampling operation is performed by convolving with estimated blur kernel k. After a certain number of iterations, the error between Y^s and $\hat{Y}^s_t$ will be sufficiently small so that the enhanced version of Y' is adequately consistent with Y^s. The HR feature space F_{H} is obtained by extracting raw patches from residuals image $Y - Y'$. In fact, the back-projection residual image represents the high-pass filtered version of Y. It contains essential high frequencies

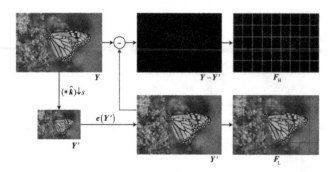

Fig. 3 Feature extraction strategy. $e(\cdot)$ represents the enhanced interpolation operation. The down-sampled version Y^s is obtained by convolving with estimated kernel $\hat{k}$ and down-sampling with s. LR feature set consists of normalized gradient feature patch extracted from Y', HR feature set is made up with the raw patches extracted from BPR image $Y - Y'$.

of Y, and this is substantially helpful for dictionary training. Besides, the directly down-sampled version Y^s with the estimated kernel usually is inconsistent with Y. The enhanced interpolation process gives an effective adjustment via reducing local projection error. When both LR and HR feature patches get prepared, we use ILS-DLA algorithm to train our coupled dictionaries presented in Ref. [26] for fast training and unified optimization rule, see Section 2.3.

3.3 SR recovery via ASM

Yang et al. [13] accelerated the SR process from two directions: reducing the number of patches and finding a fast solver for L$_1$ norm minimization problem. We adopt a similar manner for the first optimization direction, i.e., a selective patch process (SPP) strategy. However, in order to be consistent with BKE, the criterion of selecting patches is the gradient magnitude |grad| instead of the variance. The second direction Yang et al. headed to is learning a feed-forward neural network model to find an approximated solution for L$_1$ norm sparse encoding. We employ ASM to accelerate the algorithm similar with Ref. [17]. It requires us to reformulate the L$_1$ norm minimization problem as a least square regression regularized by L$_2$ norm of sparse representation coefficients, and adopt the ridge regression (RR) to relieve the computationally demanding problem of L$_1$ norm optimization. The problem then comes to be

$$\underset{w}{\operatorname{argmin}} \|y - D_{\mathrm{L}}w\|_2^2 + \mu\|w\|_2 \qquad (8)$$

where the parameter μ allows alleviating the ill-posed problem and stabilizes the solution. y corresponds to a testing patch extracted from enhanced interpolation version of input image. D_{L} is the LR dictionary trained by ILS-DLA. The algebraic solution of Eq. (8) is given by setting the gradient of objective function to zero, which gives:

$$w = (D_{\mathrm{L}}^{\mathrm{T}}D_{\mathrm{L}} + \mu I)^{-1}D_{\mathrm{L}}^{\mathrm{T}}y \qquad (9)$$

where I is a identity matrix. Then, the same coefficients are used on the HR feature space to compute the latent HR patches, i.e., $x = D_{\mathrm{H}}w$. Combined with Eq. (9):

$$x = D_{\mathrm{H}}(D_{\mathrm{L}}^{\mathrm{T}}D_{\mathrm{L}} + \mu I)^{-1}D_{\mathrm{L}}^{\mathrm{T}}y = P_{\mathrm{M}}y \qquad (10)$$

where mapping matrix P_{M} can be computed offline and D_{H} is computed by Eq. (2). Equation (10) means HR feature patch can be obtained by LR patch multiplying with a projection matrix directly, which reduces the time consumption tremendously in practice. Moreover, the feature patches needed to be mapped to HR features via $\boldsymbol{P}_{\mathrm{M}}$ will be further reduced due to SPP. Though the optimization problem constrained by L$_2$ norm usually leads to a more relaxative solution, it still yields very accurate SR results because of cross-scale BKE.

4 Experimental results

All the following experiments are performed on the same platform, i.e., a Philips 64 bit PC with 8.0 GB memory and running a single core of Intel Xeon 2.53 GHz CPU. The core differences between the proposed method and Ref. [16] are the feature extraction and SR recovery. The former is mainly aiming at reducing local projection error and improving the quality of the training samples further. The latter is primarily used to accelerate the reconstruction of the latent HR image.

4.1 Experiment settings

We quintessentially perform ×2 and ×3 SR in our experiments on blind BKE. The parameter settings in BKE stage are partially the same with Refs. [16] and [25], i.e., when scale factor $s = 2$, the size of small query patches $\boldsymbol{p}_i$ and candidate patches $\boldsymbol{q}_{ij}^s$ of NNs are typically set to 5 × 5, while the sizes of "parent" patches $\boldsymbol{q}_{ij}$ are set to 9 × 9 and 11 × 11; when performing ×3 SR, query patches and candidate patches do not change size but "parent" patches are set to be 13 × 13 patches. Noise standard deviation σ is assumed to be 5. Parameter η in Eq. (3) is set to be 0.25, and matrix $\boldsymbol{C}$ is chosen to be the derivative matrix corresponding to x and y direction of "parent" patches. The threshold of gradient magnitude |grad| for selecting query patches varies in 10–30 according to the different images. In the processing of feature extraction, the enhanced interpolation starts with the bicubic interpolation and down-sampling operation is performed by convolving with estimated blur kernel $\boldsymbol{k}$, and the back-projection filter $\boldsymbol{k}'$ is set to be a Gaussian kernel with the same size of $\boldsymbol{k}$. The tradeoff parameter μ in Eq. (8) is set to be 0.01 and the number of iteration for dictionary training is 20.

4.2 Analysis of the metric in blind BKE

Comparisons for blind BKE usually include the accuracy of the estimated kernels and the efficiency, and these two elaborations have been presented in our previous work [16] in detail. We intend to analyze the impact on blind BKE through discriminating the query patches instead of simply comparing the final results with some related works. The repeated conclusions will be ignored here. We collected patches from three natural image sets (Set2, Set5, and Set14) and found that the values of |grad| and variance mostly fall into the range of [0, 100]. So the entire statistical range is set to be [0, 100] and the statistical interval for |grad| and variance is typically set to be 10.

We sampled the 500 × 400 "baboon" image and got 236,096 query patches, and 235,928 patches from 540 × 300 "high-street" (dense sampling). It is distinctly observed that the statistical characteristics of |grad| and variance are very similar with each other in Fig. 4. The query patches with threshold ⩽ 30 account for the most proportion for both |grad| and variance, and we could get similar conclusion from other images. However, the relative relation between them reverses around 30 (value may be different from images but the reverse determinately exists). This is an intuitive presentation that why we adopt the |grad| instead of variance as the metric of selecting patches based on the philosophy of dropping the useless smooth patches as many as possible and keeping the structured patches as far as possible. More systemically theoretical explanations could be found in Ref. [18].

Moreover, the performance of blind BKE is obviously affected by the threshold on |grad|. The optimal kernel was pinned beside the threshold in Fig. 4. We can see that the estimated kernel by our method is not close to the ground-truth one infinitely as the threshold increasing because the useful structured patches reduce as well. Usually, the estimated kernel at the threshold of "turning point" is closest to the ground-truth. When the threshold is set to be 0, it actually degenerates to the algorithm of Ref. [25], which does not give the best result in most instances. In general case, the quality of recovery declines with the increase of |grad| like the second illustration in Fig. 4. But there indeed exist special cases like the first illustration in Fig. 4 for the PSNRs

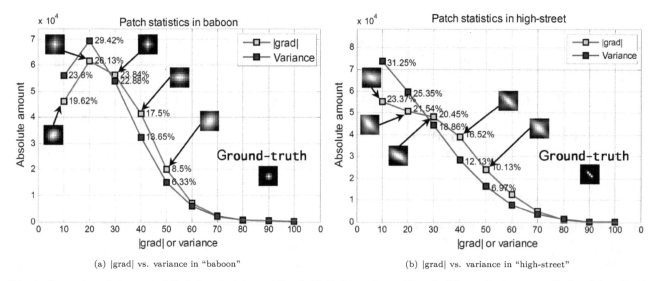

(a) |grad| vs. variance in "baboon"   (b) |grad| vs. variance in "high-street"

Fig. 4 Comparisons between statistical characteristics and threshold effect on estimated kernels. The testing images are "baboon" from Set14 and "high-street" from Set2, and the blur kernels are a Gaussian with $hsize = 5$ and $sigma = 1.0$ (9×9) and a motion kernel with $length = 5$, $theta = 135$ (11×11) respectively. We only display estimated kernels when threshold on $|grad| \leqslant 50$.

of recovered images rise firstly and then fell with the threshold increasing.

4.3 Comparisons for SR recovery

Compared with several currently proposed methods (such as A+ ANR [27] and SRCNN [31] etc.), the reconstruction efficiency of our method sometimes is slightly low but almost in the same magnitude. Due to the anchored space mapping, the proposed method was accelerated substantially with regard to some typical sparse representation algorithms like Refs. [11] and [32]. Table 1 and Table 2 present the quantitative comparisons using PSNRs and SR recovery time to compare objective index and SR efficiency. Four recent proposed methods including Ref. [32], A+ ANR (adjusted anchored neighborhood regression) [27], SRCNN (super-resolution convolutional neural network) [31], and JOR (jointly optimized regressors) [33] are picked out as the representative of non-blind methods (presented in Table 1), and three blind methods, NBS (nonparametric blind super-resolution) [25], SAR-NBS (simple, accurate, and robust nonparametric blind super-resolution) [34], and Ref. [16] are concurrently listed in Table 2 with the proposed method. It's worth noting that PSNR needs reference images as base line. Because the input images are blurred by different blurring kernels so that the observation data is seriously degenerated and non-blind methods usually give very bad results in this case, we referred the recovered

images to the blurred input images. The average PSNRs and running time are collected ($\times2$ and $\times3$) over four image sets (Set2, Set5, Set14, and B100). Besides, we set the threshold on $|grad|$ around to the "turning point" adaptively for the best BKE estimation instead of pinning it to a fixed number (e.g., 10 in Ref. [16]). The methods listed in Table 1 and Table 2 are identical to the methods presented in Figs. $5-8$.

As shown in Table 1 and Table 2, the proposed algorithm obtained higher objective evaluation than other blind or non-blind algorithms in both $s = 2$ and/or $s = 3$ case. For fairness, it excludes the time of preparing data and training dictionaries for all of these methods. Firstly, four non-blind methods in Table 1 fail to recover real images when the inputs are degraded seriously though some of them provided very high speed. And, both the accuracy and efficiency of estimating kernels via Michaeli et al. [25] are not high enough which has been illustrated in Ref. [16], and SR recovery performed by Ref. [11] is very time-consuming. While the same process of BKE with us was executed in Ref. [16] (fixed threshold on $|grad|$), the SR reconstruction with SPP is essentially still low-efficiency. The proposed method adopted adaptive $|grad|$ threshold to improve the quality of BKE and the enhanced interpolation on input images reduced the mapping errors brought by estimated kernels further. On the other hand, ASM increased the speed of the algorithm in essence. This is mainly

Table 1   Performance of several non-blind methods (without estimating blur kernel)

Image set	Scale	Zeyde et al. ([32])		A+ ANR ([27])		SRCNN ([31])		JOR ([33])	
		PSNR (dB)	Time (s)	PSNR (dB)	Time (s)	PSNR (dB)	Time (s)	PSNR (dB)	Time (s)
Set2	×2	30.4314	9.0178	30.6207	2.2749	30.5952	2.0517	30.6334	8.3200
Set5		30.4607	7.1648	31.1095	1.3894	31.1021	1.2044	31.1252	7.8399
Set14		30.8179	11.4795	31.1023	2.3714	31.0683	2.1742	31.1214	9.2874
B100		30.5784	8.4876	31.1007	1.5497	31.0271	1.4263	31.1098	8.1431
Set2	×3	28.0296	6.1883	28.2544	1.7831	28.2527	1.6397	28.2605	8.4166
Set5		28.1548	4.1546	28.3327	1.1173	28.3314	0.8564	28.3397	7.4879
Set14		28.4706	8.6470	28.6147	1.9406	28.6107	1.7867	28.6244	8.8371
B100		28.2381	6.0365	28.5836	1.5733	28.5694	1.5049	28.6042	8.2165

Table 2   Performance of several blind methods (adaptive threshold on |grad|)

Image set	Scale	NBS ([11] + [25])		SAR-NBS ([34])		Zhao et al. ([13] + [16])		Ours	
		PSNR (dB)	Time (s)	PSNR (dB)	Time (s)	PSNR (dB)	Time (s)	PSNR (dB)	Time (s)
Set2	×2	31.1417	126.7434	31.4371	—	31.8745	25.8316	32.1795	2.0476
Set5		31.4734	97.4641	31.7217	—	32.0146	19.7842	32.3914	1.2078
Set14		31.3043	108.7918	31.5841	—	31.9243	26.7849	31.9167	2.1607
B100		31.4971	102.4352	31.7638	—	31.9673	22.4876	32.2671	1.3844
Set2	×3	29.2549	98.4870	29.8749	—	30.3498	21.4876	30.6648	1.5743
Set5		29.3631	86.9237	29.8379	—	30.4716	15.9829	30.5176	1.0748
Set14		29.2461	95.4881	29.6477	—	29.9831	24.9573	30.2472	1.8476
B100		28.9771	91.4877	29.6942	—	30.2752	19.7481	30.3317	1.4977

due to the adjustment of the objective function and the constraint conversion from L_0/L_1 norm to L_2 norm. Actually, the improvement of our method is not only reflected in SR recovery stage, but also reflected in BKE (through SPP) and dictionary training (through ILS-DLA) which are not usually mainly concerned by most of researchers. But these preprocessing procedures are still very different when big data need to be processed.

Figures 5–8 show the visual comparisons between several typical SR algorithms and our method. For layout purpose, all images are diminished when inserted in the paper. Still note that the input images of all algorithms are obtained through reference images blurred with different blur kernel. Namely, input image data is set to be of low quality in our experiments for the sake of simulating many actual application scenarios. Though it is well known that non-blind SR algorithms presented in the illustrations are efficient for many SR tasks, they fail to offset the blurring effect in testing images without a more precise blurring kernel. There is also significant difference about the estimated kernels and reconstruction results among blind algorithms. The BKE process of Ref. [25] is actually close to our method when the threshold on |grad| is 0 and the criterion for iteration is

MSE. Shao et al. [34] solved the blur kernel and HR image simultaneously by minimizing a bi-L_0-L_2-norm regularized optimization problem with respect to both an intermediate super-resolved image and a blur kernel, which is extraordinarily time-demanding (so not shown in Table 1). More important is that the fitting problem caused by useless smooth patches still exists in these methods. Although the idea of our method is simple, it could avoid the fitting problem by dropping the smooth query patches reasonably according to the internal statistics of a single natural image.

Figures 9 and 10 present SR recovery results of other two real images ("fence" and "building"), which were captured by our cell-phone with slightly joggle and motion. It is easily noticed that all blind methods produce a better result than non-blind methods which even can not offset the motion deviation basically. Comparing Fig. 9(f)–Fig. 9(i) and Fig. 10(f)–Fig. 10(i), we can find the visible difference in estimated kernels and recovered results produced by different blind methods. Particularly, SAR-NBS tends to overly sharpen the high frequency region and gives obvious distortion in final images. The results of Zhao et al. [16] look more realistic but the reconstruction accuracy is not high enough compared with our approach.

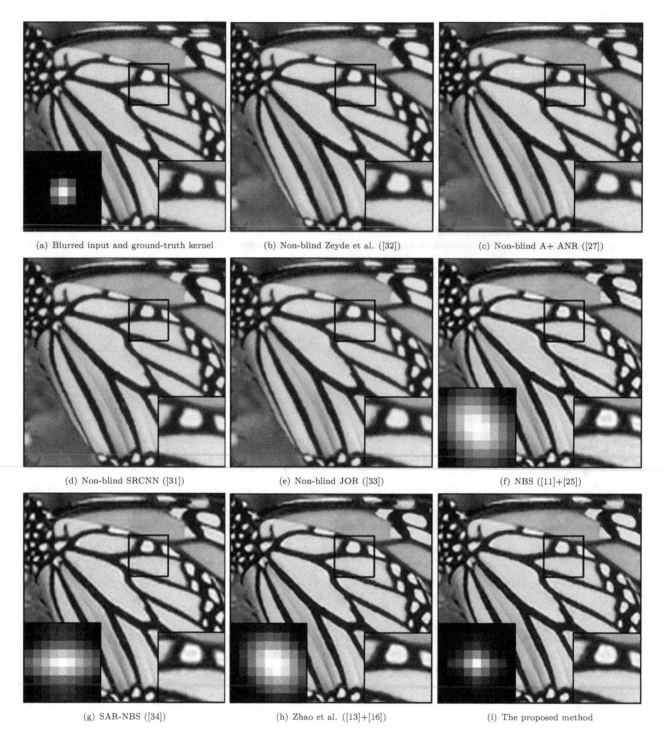

(a) Blurred input and ground-truth kernel   (b) Non-blind Zeyde et al. ([32])   (c) Non-blind A+ ANR ([27])

(d) Non-blind SRCNN ([31])   (e) Non-blind JOR ([33])   (f) NBS ([11]+[25])

(g) SAR-NBS ([34])   (h) Zhao et al. ([13]+[16])   (i) The proposed method

Fig. 5 Visual comparisons of SR recovery with low-quality "butterfly" image from Set5 (×2). The ground-truth kernel is a 9×9 Gaussian kernel with $hsize = 5$ and $sigma = 1.25$, and threshold on |grad| is 18.

5 Conclusions

We proposed a novel single image SR processing framework aiming at improving the SR effect and reducing SR time consumption in this paper. The proposed algorithm mainly consists of blind blur kernel estimation and SR recovery. The former is based on the idea of minimizing dissimilarity of cross-scale image patches, which leads us to obtain kernel update formula by quantitating cross-scale patch dissimilarity and directly minimizing it according to least square method. The reduction of SR time mainly relies on an ASM process

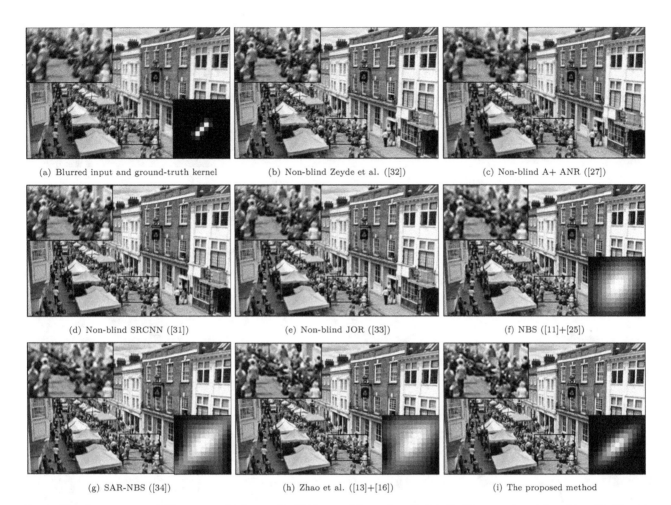

(a) Blurred input and ground-truth kernel   (b) Non-blind Zeyde et al. ([32])   (c) Non-blind A+ ANR ([27])

(d) Non-blind SRCNN ([31])   (e) Non-blind JOR ([33])   (f) NBS ([11]+[25])

(g) SAR-NBS ([34])   (h) Zhao et al. ([13]+[16])   (i) The proposed method

Fig. 6 Visual comparisons of SR recovery with low-quality "high-street" image from Set2 ($\times 3$). The ground-truth kernel is a 13×13 motion kernel with $len = 5$ and $theta = 45$, and threshold on $|grad|$ is 24.

with LR/HR dictionaries trained by ILS-DLA algorithms a selective patch processing strategy measured by $|grad|$. Therefore, the SR effect is mainly guaranteed by improving the quality of training samples and the efficiency of SR recovery is mainly guaranteed by anchored space mapping and selective patch processing. They ensure the improvement of time performance via reducing the number of query patches and translating L_1 norm constrained optimization problem into L_2 norm constrained anchor mapping process. Under the equal conditions, all above-mentioned processes make our SR algorithm achieve better results than several outstanding blind and non-blind SR approaches proposed previously with a much higher speed.

Acknowledgements

We would like to thank the authors of Ref. [34], Mr. Michael Elad and Mr. Wen-Ze Shao, for their kind help in running their blind SR method [34], which thus enables an effective comparison with their method. This work is partially supported by National Natural Science Foundation of China (Grant No. 61303127), Western Light Talent Culture Project of Chinese Academy of Sciences (Grant No. 13ZS0106), Project of Science and Technology Department of Sichuan Province (Grant Nos. 2014SZ0223 and 2015GZ0212), Key Program of Education Department of Sichuan Province (Grant Nos. 11ZA130 and 13ZA0169), and the innovation funds of Southwest University of Science and Technology (Grant No. 15ycx053).

References

[1] Freedman, G.; Fattal, R. Image and video upscaling from local self-examples. *ACM Transactions on Graphics* Vol. 30, No. 2, Article No. 12, 2011.

[2] Babacan, S. D.; Molina, R.; Katsaggelos, A. K. Parameter estimation in TV image restoration

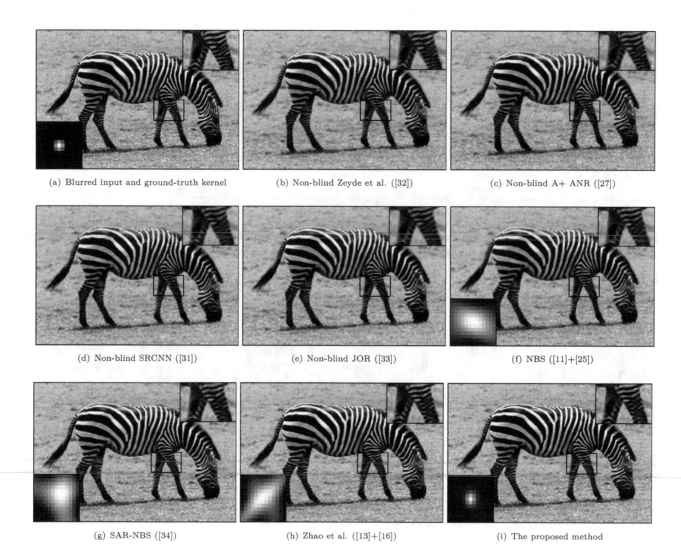

(a) Blurred input and ground-truth kernel   (b) Non-blind Zeyde et al. ([32])   (c) Non-blind A+ ANR ([27])

(d) Non-blind SRCNN ([31])   (e) Non-blind JOR ([33])   (f) NBS ([11]+[25])

(g) SAR-NBS ([34])   (h) Zhao et al. ([13]+[16])   (i) The proposed method

Fig. 7 Visual comparisons of SR recovery with low-quality "zebra" image from Set14 (×3). The ground-truth kernel is a 13×13 Gaussian kernel with $hsize = 5$ and $theta = 1.25$, and threshold on $|\text{grad}|$ is 16.

using variational distribution approximation. *IEEE Transactions on Image Processing* Vol. 17, No. 3, 326–339, 2008.

[3] Babacan, S. D.; Molina, R.; Katsaggelos, A. K. Total variation super resolution using a variational approach. In: Proceedings of the 15th IEEE International Conference on Image Processing, 641–644, 2008.

[4] Babacan, S. D.; Molina, R.; Katsaggelos, A. K. Variational Bayesian super resolution. *IEEE Transactions on Image Processing* Vol. 20, No. 4, 984–999, 2011.

[5] Sun, J.; Xu, Z.; Shum, H.-Y. Image super-resolution using gradient profile prior. In: Proceedings of IEEE Conference on Computer Vision Pattern Recognition, 1–8, 2008.

[6] Freeman, W. T.; Jones, T. R.; Pasztor, E. C. Example-based super-resolution. *IEEE Computer Graphics and Applications* Vol. 22, No. 2, 56–65, 2002.

[7] Sun, J.; Zheng, N.-N.; Tao, H.; Shum, H.-Y. Image hallucination with primal sketch priors. In:

Proceedings of IEEE Computer Society Conference on Computer Vision and Pattern Recognition, Vol. 2, 729–736, 2003.

[8] Chang, H.; Yeung, D. Y.; Xiong, Y. Super-resolution through neighbor embedding. In: Proceedings of IEEE Computer Society Conference on Computer Vision and Pattern Recognition, 275–282, 2004.

[9] Roweis, S. T.; Saul, L. K. Nonlinear dimensionality reduction by locally linear embedding. *Science* Vol. 290, No. 5, 2323–2326, 2000.

[10] Bevilacqua, M.; Roumy, A.; Guillemot, C.; Morel, M.-L. A. Low-complexity single-image super-resolution based on nonnegative neighbor embedding. In: Proceedings of the 23rd British Machine Vision Conference, 135.1–135.10, 2012.

[11] Yang, J.; Wright, J.; Huang, T.; Ma, Y. Image super-resolution as sparse representation of raw image patches. In: Proceedings of IEEE Conference on Computer Vision and Pattern Recognition, 1–8, 2008.

[12] Glasner, D.; Bagon, S.; Irani, M. Super-resolution from a single image. In: Proceedings of IEEE 12th

(a) Blurred input and ground-truth kernel   (b) Non-blind Zeyde et al. ([32])   (c) Non-blind A+ ANR ([27])

(d) Non-blind SRCNN ([31])   (e) Non-blind JOR ([33])   (f) NBS ([11]+[25])

(g) SAR-NBS ([34])   (h) Zhao et al. ([13]+[16])   (i) The proposed method

Fig. 8 Visual comparisons of SR recovery with low-quality "tower" image from B100 (×2). The ground-truth kernel is a 11×11 motion kernel with $len = 5$ and $tehta = 45$, and threshold on |grad| is 17.

International Conference on Computer Vision, 349–356, 2009.

[13] Yang, J.; Wang, Z.; Lin, Z.; Cohen, S.; Huang, T. Coupled dictionary training for image super-resolution. *IEEE Transactions on Image Processing* Vol. 21, No. 8, 3467–3478, 2012.

[14] Yang, J.; Wright, J.; Huang, T.; Ma, Y. Image super-resolution via sparse representation. *IEEE Transactions on Image Processing* Vol. 19, No. 11, 2861–2873, 2010.

[15] He, L.; Qi, H.; Zaretzki, R. Beta process joint dictionary learning for coupled feature spaces with application to single image super-resolution. In: Proceedings of IEEE Conference on Computer Vision and Pattern Recognition, 345–352, 2013.

[16] Zhao, X.; Wu, Y.; Tian, J.; Zhang, H. Single image super-resolution via blind blurring estimation and dictionary learning. In: *Communications in Computer and Information Science, Vol. 546*. Zha, H.; Chen, X.; Wang, L.; Miao, Q. Eds. Springer Berlin Heidelberg, 22–33, 2015.

[17] Timofte, R.; De, V.; Van Gool, L. Anchored neighborhood regression for fast example-based super-resolution. In: Proceedings of IEEE International Conference on Computer Vision, 1920–1927, 2013.

[18] Zontak, M.; Irani, M. Internal statistics of a single natural image. In: Proceedings of IEEE Conference on Computer Vision and Pattern Recognition, 977–984, 2011.

[19] Yang, C.-Y.; Huang, J.-B.; Yang, M.-H. Exploiting self-similarities for single frame super-resolution. In: *Lecture Notes in Computer Science, Vol. 6594*. Kimmel, R.; Klette, R.; Sugimoto, A. Eds. Springer Berlin Heidelberg, 497–510, 2010.

[20] Zoran, D.; Weiss, Y. From learning models of natural image patches to whole image restoration. In: Proceedings of IEEE International Conference on Computer Vision, 479–486, 2011.

[21] Hu, J.; Luo, Y. Single-image superresolution based on local regression and nonlocal self-similarity. *Journal of Electronic Imaging* Vol. 23, No. 3, 033014, 2014.

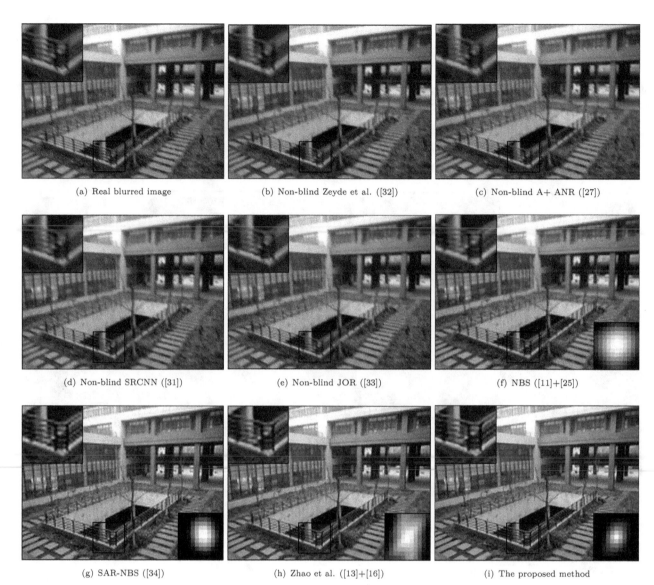

(a) Real blurred image   (b) Non-blind Zeyde et al. ([32])   (c) Non-blind A+ ANR ([27])

(d) Non-blind SRCNN ([31])   (e) Non-blind JOR ([33])   (f) NBS ([11]+[25])

(g) SAR-NBS ([34])   (h) Zhao et al. ([13]+[16])   (i) The proposed method

Fig. 9 Visual comparisons of SR recovery with real low-quality image "fence" captured with slight joggle (×2). Threshold on |grad| is 21.

[22] Zhang, Y.; Liu, J.; Yang, S.; Guo, Z. Joint image denoising using self-similarity based low-rank approximations. In: Proceedings of Visual Communications and Image Processing, 1–6, 2013.

[23] Michaeli, T.; Irani, M. Blind deblurring using internal patch recurrence. In: *Lecture Notes in Computer Science, Vol. 8691*. Fleet, D.; Pajdla, T.; Schiele, B.; Tuytelaars, T. Eds. Springer International Publishing, 783–798, 2014.

[24] Guillemot, C.; Le Meur, O. Image inpainting: Overview and recent advances. *IEEE Signal Processing Magazine* Vol. 31, No. 1, 127–144, 2014.

[25] Michaeli, T.; Irani, M. Nonparametric blind super-resolution. In: Proceedings of IEEE International Conference on Computer Vision, 945–952, 2013.

[26] Engan, K.; Skretting, K.; Husøy, J. H. Family of iterative LS-based dictionary learning algorithms, ILS-DLA, for sparse signal representation. *Digital Signal Processing* Vol. 17, No. 1, 32–49, 2007.

[27] Timofte, R.; De Smet, V.; Van Gool, L. A+: Adjusted anchored neighborhood regression for fast super-resolution. In: *Lecture Notes in Computer Science, Vol. 9006*. Cremers, D.; Reid, I.; Saito, H.; Yang, M.-H. Eds. Springer International Publishing, 111–126, 2014.

[28] Bevilacqua, M.; Roumy, A.; Guillemot, C.; Morel, M.-L. A. Super-resolution using neighbor embedding of back-projection residuals. In: Proceedings of the 18th International Conference on Digital Signal Processing, 1–8, 2013.

[29] Irani, M.; Peleg, S. Motion analysis for image enhancement: Resolution, occlusion, and transparency. *Journal of Visual Communication and Image Representation* Vol. 4, No. 4, 324–335, 1993.

[30] Irani, M.; Peleg, S. Improving resolution by image registration. *CVGIP: Graphical Models and Image Processing* Vol. 53, No. 3, 231–239, 1991.

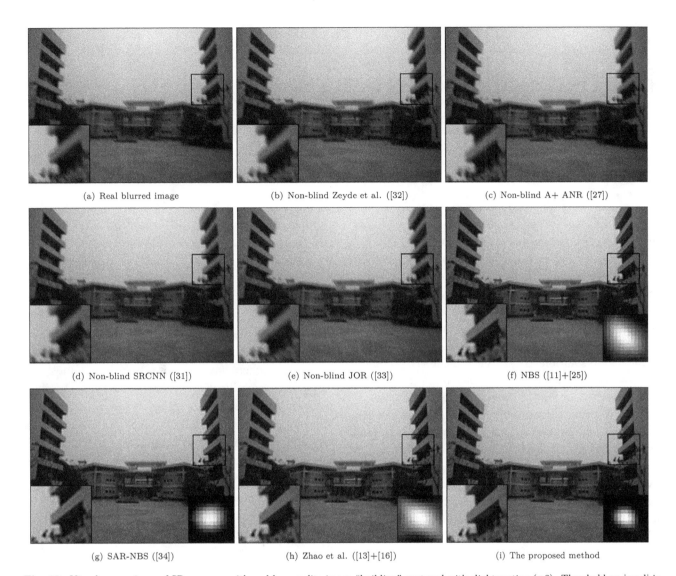

(a) Real blurred image   (b) Non-blind Zeyde et al. ([32])   (c) Non-blind A+ ANR ([27])

(d) Non-blind SRCNN ([31])   (e) Non-blind JOR ([33])   (f) NBS ([11]+[25])

(g) SAR-NBS ([34])   (h) Zhao et al. ([13]+[16])   (i) The proposed method

Fig. 10 Visual comparisons of SR recovery with real low-quality image "building" captured with slight motion (×2). Threshold on |grad| is 26.

[31] Dong, C.; Chen, C. L.; He, K.; Tang, X. Learning a deep convolutional network for image super-resolution. In: *Lecture Notes in Computer Science, Vol. 8692*. Fleet, D.; Pajdla, T.; Schiele, B.; Tuytelaars, T. Eds. Springer International Publishing, 184–199, 2014.

[32] Zeyde, R.; Elad, M.; Protter, M. On single image scale-up using sparse-representations. In: *Lecture Notes in Computer Science, Vol. 6920*. Boissonnat, J.-D.; Chenin, P.; Cohen, A. et al. Eds. Springer Berlin Heidelberg, 711–730, 2010.

[33] Dai, D.; Timofte, R.; Van Gool, L. Jointly optimized regressors for image super-resolution. *Computer Graphics Forum* Vol. 34, No. 2, 95–104, 2015.

[34] Shao, W.-Z.; Elad, M. Simple, accurate, and robust nonparametric blind super-resolution. In: *Lecture Notes in Computer Science, Vol. 9219*. Zhang, Y.-J. Ed. Springer International Publishing, 333–348, 2015.

16

High-resolution images based on directional fusion of gradient

Liqiong Wu[1], Yepeng Liu[1], Brekhna[1], Ning Liu[1], and Caiming Zhang[1](✉)

Abstract This paper proposes a novel method for image magnification by exploiting the property that the intensity of an image varies along the direction of the gradient very quickly. It aims to maintain sharp edges and clear details. The proposed method first calculates the gradient of the low-resolution image by fitting a surface with quadratic polynomial precision. Then, bicubic interpolation is used to obtain initial gradients of the high-resolution (HR) image. The initial gradients are readjusted to find the constrained gradients of the HR image, according to spatial correlations between gradients within a local window. To generate an HR image with high precision, a linear surface weighted by the projection length in the gradient direction is constructed. Each pixel in the HR image is determined by the linear surface. Experimental results demonstrate that our method visually improves the quality of the magnified image. It particularly avoids making jagged edges and bluring during magnification.

Keywords high-resolution (HR); image magnification; directional fusion; gradient direction

1 Introduction

The aim of image magnification is to estimate the unknown pixel values of a high-resolution (HR) version of an image from groups of pixels in a corresponding low-resolution (LR) image [1]. As a basic operation in image processing, image magnification has great significance for applications in many fields, such as computer vision, computer animation, and medical imaging [2]. With the rapid development of visualization and virtual reality, image magnification has been widely applied to diverse applications, such as high-definition television, digital media technology, and image processing software. However, image magnification methods face great challenges because of the increased demand for robust technology and application challenges. In recent years, although many researchers have proposed a variety of methods for image magnification, there is not yet a unified method suitable for all image types. Considering the characteristics of different types of images, it is still hard to achieve low computational time while maintaining edges and detailed texture during the process of magnification. Based on the analysis above, this paper focuses on generating an HR image maintaining the edge sharpness and structural details of a single LR image by means of the directional fusion of image gradients.

1.1 Traditional methods

Traditional methods, including nearest neighbor, bilinear [3], bicubic [4, 5], and Lanczos resampling [6], are widely applied in a variety of commercial software and business applications for image processing. The main advantages of such conventional methods are that they are easy to understand, simple to implement, and fast to calculate. However, there are limitations for these methods. Using a unified mathematical model causes loss of high frequency information at edges. Thus, conventional methods are likely to introduce jagged edges and blur details at significant transitions in an image, such as edges and texture details.

1.2 Advanced methods

Studies have shown that human eyes are more sensitive to the edges of an image that transmit most of the information of the image, so images with good

1 School of Computer Science and Technology, Shandong University, Jinan 250101, China. E-mail: L. Wu, wuliqiong.june@gmail.com; C. Zhang, czhang@sdu.edu.cn(✉).

quality edges can help to clearly describe boundaries and the outlines of objects. Edges that contain important information are of great significance in image magnification. Various edge-directed methods have been proposed in recent years, most of which take advantage of edge information to overcome the shortcomings of conventional methods, e.g., Refs. [7–13].

The edge-guided interpolation method put forward by Li and Orchard [10] is based on image covariance, and exploits local covariance coefficients estimated from the pixel values of the LR image to calculate the covariance coefficients of the HR image, utilizing the geometric duality between LR and HR images. These covariance coefficients are used to perform interpolation. Zhang and Wu [12] present a non-linear interpolation method, based on inserting a missing pixel in two mutually orthogonal directions, and use a minimum mean square error estimation technique to fuse them for realizing interpolation.

Zhang et al. [8] propose a method based on a combination of quadratic polynomials to construct a reverse fitting surface for a given image in which the edges of the image act as a constraint, which ensures the fitted surface has a better approximation accuracy. Fan et al. [14] present a robust and efficient high-resolution detail-preserving algorithm based on a least-squares formulation. A gradient-guided image interpolation method is presented in Ref. [9], assuming that the variation in pixel values is constant along the edge. The method can be implemented simply and has good edge retention, but it leads to a wide edge transition zone because of the diffusion of the HR image gradients, and so it is not suitable for magnification of images with complicated textures and detail.

Corresponding patches between low- and high-resolution images from a database can be used with machine learning-based techniques or sampling methods to achieve interpolation [15–20].

Traditional methods often introduce artifacts such as jagged edges and blurred details during magnification. Often, edge-based methods tend to generate artifacts in small scale edge structures and complicated texture details. Learning-based techniques are complex and time-consuming, with the outcome influenced by the training data. Because of these issues, this paper proposes a novel method to produce an HR image based on the directional fusion of gradients.

2 Related work

In this study, we use a degradation model that assumes the LR image can be directly down-sampled from the HR image, rather than by using Gaussion smoothing. Since the proposed method is partly based on CSF [8] and GGI [9], this section will briefly introduce both methods.

2.1 Quadratic surface fitting constrained (CSF) by edges

In CSF, image data is supposed to be sampled from an original scene that can be approximated by piecewise polynomials [8]. The fitted surface is constructed by a reversal process of image sampling using the edge information as constraints. That makes the surface a good approximation to the original scene, with quadratic polynomial precision. Assuming that $P_{i,j}$ is an image of size $N \times N$ generally sampled from the original scene $F(x,y)$ on a unit square, so

$$P_{i,j} = \int_{j-\frac{1}{2}}^{j+\frac{1}{2}} \int_{i-\frac{1}{2}}^{i+\frac{1}{2}} w(x,y)F(x,y)\mathrm{d}x\mathrm{d}y \qquad (1)$$

where $w(x,y)$ is a weight function set to be 1.

In the region $[i-1.5, i+1.5] \times [j-1.5, j+1.5]$, let $u = x - i, v = y - j$. See Fig. 1. The fitted surface $f_{i,j}(x,y)$ of $F(x,y)$ is defined as

$$f_{i,j}(x,y) = a_1 u^2 + a_2 uv + a_3 v^2 + a_4 u + a_5 v + a_6 \qquad (2)$$

where a_1, a_2, a_3, a_4, a_5, and a_6 are to be determined. Determination of the unknown coefficients is performed by a least-squares method constrained by edge information [8]. Since a good quality surface can help to produce high precision interpolation, we

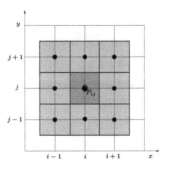

Fig. 1 Constructing surface.

will later make use of the constructed surface to interpolate gradients.

2.2 Gradient-guided interpolation (GGI)

In order to eliminate jagged edges, a gradient-guided interpolation method is proposed in Ref. [9], based on the idea that the variation in pixel values is constant along the edge direction. GGI uses a Sobel kernel to calculate gradients of the LR image, and adopts bicubic interpolation to determine the gradients of the HR image, then uses gradient diffusion. Finally, the unknown HR pixels $P_{i,j}$ to be interpolated are divided into three categories with different LR pixels $P_{x,y}$ in the neighborhood N_{ij}.

$$P_{i,j} = \sum_{P_{x,y} \in N_{ij}} w_{xy} P_{x,y} \qquad (3)$$

$P_{i,j}$ is estimated by summing the neighborhood pixels N_{ij} weighted by w_{xy}, where a shorter distance carries greater weight. Let d_{xy} denote the distance between $P_{x,y}$ and $P_{i,j}$ projected along the gradient direction of $P_{i,j}$. Then

$$w_{xy} = \frac{1}{S} e^{-\frac{d_{xy}}{a}} \qquad (4)$$

where $a = 0.2$ controls decrease of the exponential, and S is defined as

$$S = \sum_{P_{x,y} \in N_{ij}} e^{-\frac{d_{xy}}{a}} \qquad (5)$$

Although the method of Ref. [9] provides good quality interpolation at edges by significantly decreasing jagged edges, it can cause loss of detail in non-edge regions in some cases. In particular, it is unsuitable for image areas containing complex details and abundant texture.

3 High-resolution image based on directional fusion of gradient

In this section, a new magnification method is put forward based on fusion of gradient direction, which exploits the property that the pixel values change very quickly in the gradient direction. From the analysis above, maintaining is sharpness of edges and the clarity of detailed textures becomes the key mission in image magnification, since most information in the image is transmitted by edges and detail textures. Our method first finds approximate gradients of the LR image, then calculates those

of the HR image. We estimate the gray values of the unknown pixels in the HR image, using a linear approximation of the neighboring pixels. For simplicity of discussion, we mainly focus on enlargement by a factor of 2, to produce an HR image of size $2m \times 2n$ from an LR image of size $m \times n$. The general information flows in our proposed method are shown in Fig. 2.

3.1 Calculating the gradients of the HR image

In order to compute the LR gradients with high accuracy, our method adopts Eq. (2) to compute the LR gradient for each $P_{i,j}$. The gradient vector of the LR image is defined as $\vec{g} = (g_x, g_y)$, where g_x and g_y are defined as

$$\left. \begin{array}{l} g_x = 2a_1 u + a_2 v + a_4 \\ g_y = a_2 u + 2a_2 v + a_5 \end{array} \right\} \qquad (6)$$

Thus, for each $P_{i,j}$ we can get the LR gradients as $g_x = a_4, g_y = a_5$. The LR gradients are used to calculate HR gradients, denoted by $\vec{IG} = (G_X, G_Y)$, by bicubically interpolating the LR gradients.

3.2 Diffusing the gradients of the HR image

The GGI method [9] utilizes the gradient information in order to maintain the sharpness of edges. However, the spatial distribution of gradients is not considered effectively during diffusion: the norm of the gradient takes a local maximum in the gradient direction [21]. It may cause the gradient direction to change in an inapprorpiate way in detail-rich portions by directly replacing the gradient at a central pixel by the mean of some region, which may

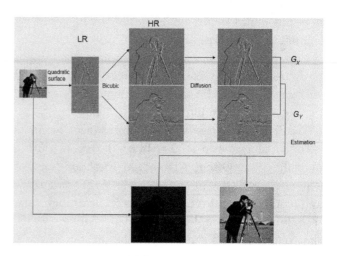

Fig. 2 Flowchart of the method.

result in distortion of details.

Therefore, we take account of the spatial correlation between the gradient directions to improve the diffusion of gradients $\overrightarrow{IG}$. Diffusion deals with gradient values in the vertical G_X and horizontal G_Y directions. A local window of size 5×5, with $P_{i,j}$ as the central pixel, see Fig. 3, is used to adjust the gradient direction. Our method adjusts the gradient vector of the center pixel using the average value of gradients whose direction falls within a certain rage relative to that of the central pixel.

By considering the spatial correlations between gradient directions, our method can approximate HR gradients that not only maintain the sharpness of edges, but also better retain the structure of textures and details. Let k denote the number of pixels satisfying the condition $\beta_{xy} < \alpha$, and $\alpha = 45°$.

$$\left. \begin{aligned} G'_{X_{ij}} &= \frac{\sum\limits_{\beta_{xy}<45°} G_{X_{xy}}}{k} \\ G'_{Y_{ij}} &= \frac{\sum\limits_{\beta_{xy}<45°} G_{Y_{xy}}}{k} \end{aligned} \right\} \quad (7)$$

After conducting the diffusion of $\overrightarrow{IG} = (G_X, G_Y)$, we obtain the adjusted HR gradients $\overrightarrow{CG} = (G'_X, G'_Y)$, which are used to calculate the gray values of HR pixels.

3.3 Estimation of HR image

In this section, we give the strategy for calculating the unknown pixels of the HR image. In Section 2.2 we noted that the GGI method [9] yields a precise constant. In comparison with GGI, our method provides higher precision of polynomial interpolation by constructing a linear surface to approximate the intensity of the HR image. It performs well in maintaining the details of the image. Depending on the known pixels in the neighborhood window with the unknown pixel as the center (see Fig. 4(b)), the unknown pixels of the HR image may be divided into three categories:

(1) Black $I(2n-1, 2m-1)_H$;

(2) Blue $I(2n, 2m)_H$;

(3) Pink $I(2n-1, 2m)_H$ and $I(2n, 2m-1)_H$, where $n = 1, \cdots, N$, $m = 1, \cdots, M$. Therefore, the estimation of the unknown pixels in the HR image is achieved in three steps.

Step 1:

In this step, we assign the values of LR pixels to the corresponding HR pixels. For an LR image I_L of size $n \times m$ enlarged to give an HR image of size $2n \times 2m$, we have $I(2n-1, 2m-1)_H = I(n, m)_L$, where $n = 1, \cdots, N$ and $m = 1, \cdots, M$. $I(n, m)_L$ and $I(2n-1, 2m-1)_H$ are the solid black dots shown in Fig. 4(a) and Fig. 4(b), respectively.

Step 2:

In this step, we use four neighboring black pixels to calculate the central pixels $P_{i,j}$ (the blue dots in Fig. 5(a)) satisfying $P_{i,j} \in I(2n, 2m)_H$. In order to precisely obtain $P_{i,j}$, we construct a linear surface to approximate the image data via directional fusion of gradients. Within the neighborhood window N_{ij} centered on $P_{i,j}$, our method constructs a linear surface $f^H_{i,j}$ using a linear polynomial as follows:

$$f^H_{i,j}(x, y) = a * x + b * y + c \quad (8)$$

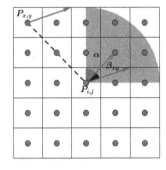

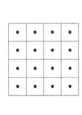

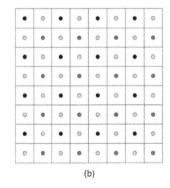

(a)　　　　　　　　(b)

Fig. 3 Diffusion of gradient. The blue dots $P_{x,y}$ stand for neighboring HR pixels of $P_{i,j}$, and the blue arrow represents the gradient direction at $P_{x,y}$, while the red arrow indicates the gradient direction at $P_{i,j}$. β_{xy} is the angle between the gradient directions $P_{i,j}$ and $P_{x,y}$. The dashed area defines the range of angles for which the gradient direction of $P_{x,y}$ is positively correlated with that of $P_{i,j}$.

Fig. 4 Degradation mode. (a) Pixels of LR image. (b) Pixels of HR image. The solid black dots in (a) represent pixels of the LR image. The dots in (b) are pixels of the HR image, where the black dots are the known pixels of HR image $I(2n-1, 2m-1)_H$ that are directly determined by the corresponding LR image pixels, blue dots stand for the case where $I(2n, 2m)_H$, while the pink points represent the cases where $I(2n-1, 2m)_H$ or $I(2n, 2m-1)_H$.

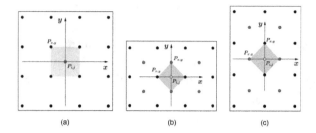

Fig. 5 Three cases for constructing the linear surface $f_{i,j}^{\mathrm{H}}$. (a) represents the linear surface constructed in *Step* 2. (b) and (c) represent the linear surface constructed in *Step* 3. In the figure, black dots give known pixels of the HR image from the corresponding LR pixels, and the blue dots stand for unknown HR pixels calculated in *Step* 2.

where a, b, and c are unknown coefficients to be found.

We determine the unknown coefficients (i.e., a, b, c) in Eq. (8) by a least-squares method, weighted by the gradients and the values of pixels in the neighborhood window.

$$G(a,b,c) = \sum_{P_{x,y} \in N_{ij}} w_{xy} * (a * x + b * y + c - P_{x,y})^2$$

$$(9)$$

where N_{ij} represents the neighboring pixels $P_{x,y}$ of the central pixel $P_{i,j}$, satisfying $(x,y) \in \{(-1,1),(1,1),(-1,-1),(1,-1)\}$. The procedure to calculate w_{xy} is given in Eq. (4) (see Fig. 6(a)).

Minimizing Eq. (9) requires

$$\frac{\partial G}{\partial a} = 0 \qquad (10)$$

$$\frac{\partial G}{\partial b} = 0 \qquad (11)$$

$$\frac{\partial G}{\partial c} = 0 \qquad (12)$$

Substituting the variables (a,b,c) into Eq. (8) gives the approximate pixel value, i.e., $P_{i,j} = c$.

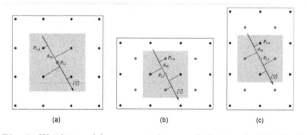

Fig. 6 Weighting. (a) represents the case of what is solved in *Step* 2. (b) and (c) are the two situations to be determined in *Step* 3 using the results of *Step* 2. The black dots are known pixels of the HR image, and the blue dots are the unknown HR pixels. $P_{x,y}$ stands for the neighboring pixels of $P_{i,j}$. $\overrightarrow{CG}$ is the gradient direction at the center pixel $P_{i,j}$.

Step 3:

In this step, we use the results of *Step* 1 and *Step* 2 to estimate the remaining unknown HR pixels (the pink dots in Fig. 4(b), i.e., $P_{i,j} \in \{I(2n-1,2m)_{\mathrm{H}}, I(2n,2m-1)_{\mathrm{H}}\}$). The gray value of the central pixel $P_{i,j}$ is calculated using the same procedure as in *Step* 2. We use Eq. (8) to construct a linear surface (see Figs. 5(b) and 5(c)). The surface is constrained by Eq. (9) in order to get an approximate surface, where $(x,y) \in \{(-1,0),(0,1),(1,0),(0,-1)\}$. The weight w_{xy} is calculated from Eq. (4) (see Figs. 6(b) and 6(c)).

Finally, the pixels located on the image boundary are calculated by averaging the existing neighboring pixels, instead of by constructing a surface.

4 Results and discussion

In order to verify the effectiveness of the proposed method, we have carried out many experiments with different kinds of images, including natural images, medical images, and synthetic images. The results of our experiments demonstrate that the proposed method can obtain better quality image magnification, especially at edges and in detail-rich areas. To demonstrate the advantages of our proposed method, we compare magnification results with several methods, including bicubic interpolation (*Bicubic*) [4], cubic surface fitting with edges as constraints (*CSF*) [8], the new edge-directed interpolation method (*NEDI*) [10], and gradient-guided interpolation (*GGI*) [9]. We now analyze the experimental results in detail.

In the experiment, we carried out tests with different types of images by magnifying LR images of size 256×256 to get HR images of size 512×512. Figures 7 and 8 show the magnified images with labeling of local windows containing edges and details extracted from the HR image. Comparing the corresponding regions of the boat image in Fig. 7, we can see that our method is more capable of dealing with edge portions of an image, while other methods introduce jagged edges or blurring artifacts near edges. It is also clear from Fig. 8 that Bicubic [4] and CSF [8] methods tend to introduce bluring artifacts: see the moustache of the baboon. NEDI [10] produces zigzags that are particularly

Fig. 7 Results of magnifying the boat image: (a) ground truth; (b) Bicubic; (c) CSF; (d) NEDI; (e) GGI; (f) ours.

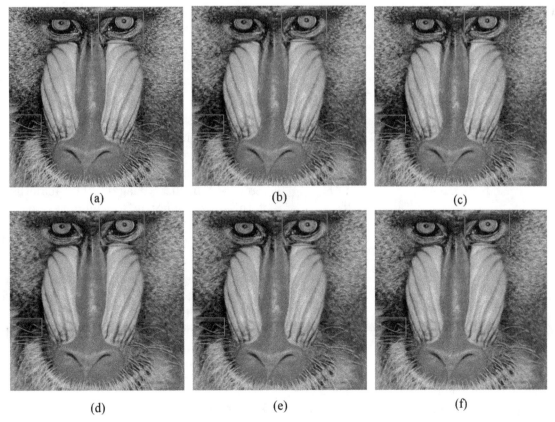

Fig. 8 Results of magnifying the baboon image: (a) ground truth; (b) Bicubic; (c) CSF; (d) NEDI; (e) GGI; (f) ours.

evident, while GGI [9] causes loss of detail in the area of the moustache. Our method leads to better visual quality than other methods.

We also conducted experiments with MRI images of a brain which were segmented into four classes by the MICO (multiplicative intrinsic component optimization) segmentation algorithm [22]. Although the results of MICO algorithm provide high accuracy segmentation, there are still rough edges due to limitations of the segmentation method. Figures 9(a)–9(f) show Bicubic, CSF, NEDI, GGI, and our results from top to bottom. The results of magnification shown in Fig. 9 illustrate that our method can deal well with a segmented image with severe zigzags, effectively retaining sharp edges while avoiding jagged artifacts during magnification.

For synthetic images, Fig. 10, Fig. 11, and Fig. 12 show the map of gray values at edge portions after applying several methods mentioned above. It is clear that our method is able to maintain the sharpest edges with less blur: other methods produce fuzzy data around the edges which results in blurring artifacts.

In order to evaluate the quality of the magnification results, we use the three objective methods based on comparisons with explicit numerical criteria [23] , including peak signal to noise ratio (PSNR), structural similarity (SSIM), and percentage edge error (PEE). PSNR measures the disparity between the magnified image and the ground truth image, and is defined as

$$\text{PSNR} = 10 \times \log_{10} \frac{255^2}{\text{MSE}} \quad (13)$$

where the mean square error (MSE) between two images is

$$\text{MSE} = \frac{1}{mn} \sum_{i=0}^{m-1} \sum_{j=0}^{n-1} \|I_{(i,j)} - S_{(i,j)}\| \quad (14)$$

SSIM measures the similarity of the structural information between the magnified image and the ground truth image [24]. It is related to quality perceived by the human visual system (HVS), and is given by

$$\text{SSIM}_{\text{S,I}} = \frac{(2\mu_{\text{S}}\mu_{\text{I}} + C_1)(2\sigma_{\text{S}}\sigma_{\text{I}} + C_2)(\sigma_{\text{SI}} + C_3)}{(\mu_{\text{S}}^2 + \mu_{\text{I}}^2 + C_1)(\sigma_{\text{S}}^2 + \sigma_{\text{I}}^2 + C_2)(\sigma_{\text{S}}\sigma_{\text{I}} + C_3)} \quad (15)$$

where μ_{S} and μ_{I} denote the mean value of the ground truth image and the magnified image respectively, σ_{S} and σ_{I} represent variances of the corresponding images, and σ_{SI} denotes the covariance of the two images.

For the images shown in Fig. 13, values of PSNR and SSIM are listed in Table 1 and Table 2, respectively. It is clear that our proposed method performs well in most cases, giving the highest values for PSNR and SSIM.

In addition, the percentage edge error (PEE) [25] was also used to measure perceptual errors. PEE is very suitable for measuring dissatisfaction of image magnification, where the major artifact is blurring. PEE measures the closeness of details in the interpolated image to the ground truth image. Generally in image interpolation, a positive value of PEE means that the magnified image is over smoothed, with likely loss of details. Thus, a method with smaller PEE performs better at avoiding blurring artifacts. PEE is defined by

$$\text{PEE} = \frac{\text{ES}_{\text{S}} - \text{ES}_{\text{I}}}{\text{ES}_{\text{S}}} \quad (16)$$

where ES_{S} denotes the edge strength of the ground truth image and ES_{I} is that of the magnified image. ES is defined as

$$\text{ES} = \sum_{i=1}^{M} \sum_{j=1}^{N} \text{EI}_{(i,j)} \quad (17)$$

where $\text{EI}_{(i,j)}$ denotes the edge intensity value of the image.

The PEE values for each interpolation method are shown in Table 3. It is clear that the PEE value for the proposed method is very low compared with the values for other techniques, so structural edges are better preserved and less blurring is produced in our method.

The analysis of the experimental results above shows that the proposed method achieves a good balance between edge-preservation and blurring, performing especially well on synthetic images and segmented medical images. The major drawback of this method lies in the limitation of using the gradients only in horizontal and vertical directions, making it hard to get accurate gradient values for images with very low contrast. Our future work will consider how to calculate gradients in more directions, and use a surface of high accuracy to approximate the image data. We hope to develop a method for magnification that can maintain edges and detailed texture perfectly with low computational time.

5 Conclusions

This paper presents a novel method of producing an

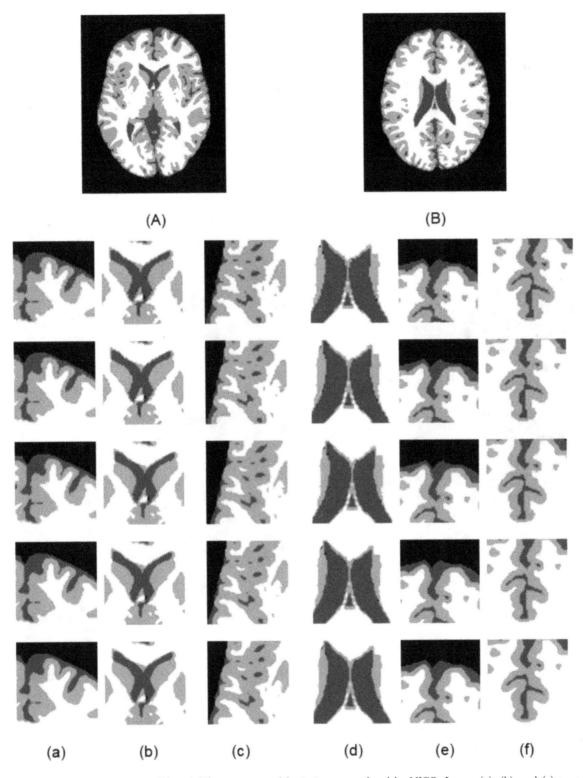

Fig. 9 Enlarged image of a brain. (A) and (B) are segmented brain images produced by MICO. Images (a), (b), and (c) are results of enlarging a specified area of (A). Images (d), (e), and (f) are the results of enlarging a specified area of (B).

HR image by making use of gradient information. It maintains sharpness of edges and clear details in an image. Our proposed method first obtains LR image gradient values by fitting a surface with quadratic polynomial precision, then the method adopts a bicubic method to get initial values of the HR image gradients. It then adjusts the gradients according to the spatial correlation in the gradient direction

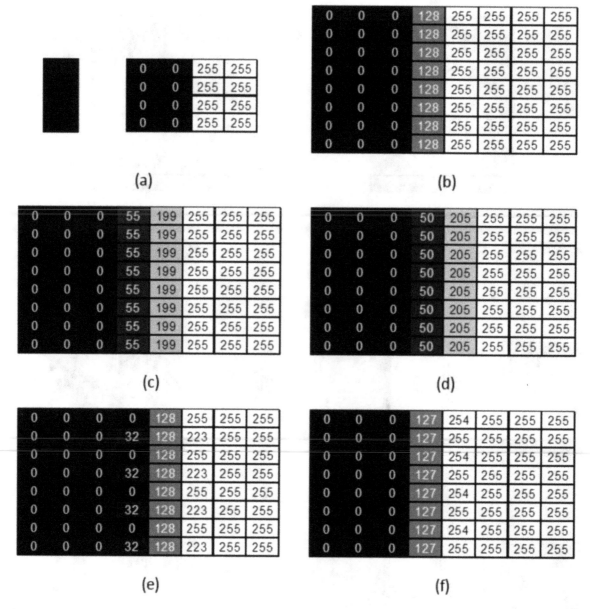

Fig. 10 Magnification of vertical edges: (a) original image and gray value; (b) ours; (c) Bicubic; (d) CSF; (e) NEDI; (f) GGI.

to constrain the gradients of the HR image. Finally it estimates the missing pixels using a linear surface weighted by neighboring LR pixels. Experimental results demonstrate that our proposed method can achieve good quality image enlargement, avoiding jagged artifacts that arise by direct interpolation; it preserves sharp edges by gradient fusion.

Acknowledgements

The authors would like to thank the anonymous reviewers for their valuable suggestions that greatly improved the paper. This project was supported by the National Natural Science Foundation of China (Nos. 61332015, 61373078, 61572292, and 61272430), and National Research Foundation for the Doctoral Program of Higher Education of China (No. 20110131130004).

References

[1] Siu, W.-C.; Hung, K.-W. Review of image interpolation and super-resolution. In: Proceedings of Asia-Pacific Signal & Information Processing Association Annual Summit and Conference, 1–10, 2012.

[2] Gonzalez, R. C.; Woods, R. E. *Digital Image Processing*, 3rd edn. Upper Saddle River, NJ, USA: Prentice-Hall, Inc., 2006.

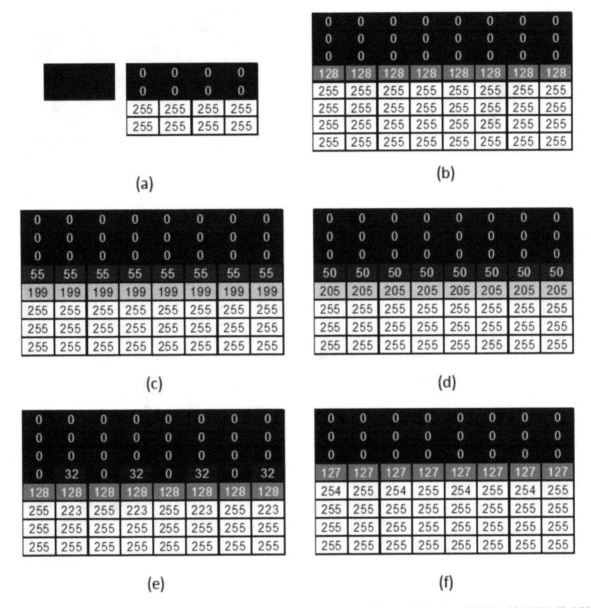

Fig. 11 Magnification of horizontal edges: (a) original image and gray value; (b) ours; (c) Bicubic; (d) CSF; (e) NEDI; (f) GGI.

[3] Franke, R. Scattered data interpolation: Tests of some methods. *Mathematics of Computation* Vol. 38, No. 157, 181–200, 1982.

[4] Keys, R. G. Cubic convolution interpolation for digital image processing. *IEEE Transactions on Acoustics, Speech and Signal Processing* Vol. 29, No. 6, 1153–1160, 1981.

[5] Park, S. K.; Schowengerdt, R. A. Image reconstruction by parametric cubic convolution. *Computer Vision, Graphics, and Image Processing* Vol. 23, No. 3, 258–272, 1983.

[6] Duchon, C. E. Lanczos filtering in one and two dimensions. *Journal of Applied Meteorology* Vol. 18, No. 8, 1016–1022, 1979.

[7] Allebach, J.; Wong, P. W. Edge-directed interpolation. In: Proceedings of International Conference on Image Processing, Vol. 3, 707–710, 1996.

[8] Zhang, C.; Zhang, X.; Li, X.; Cheng, F. Cubic surface fitting to image with edges as constraints. In: Proceedings of the 20th IEEE International Conference on Image Processing, 1046–1050, 2013.

[9] Jing, G.; Choi, Y.-K.; Wang, J.; Wang, W. Gradient guided image interpolation. In: Proceedings of IEEE International Conference on Image Processing, 1822–1826, 2014.

[10] Li, X.; Orchard, M. T. New edge-directed interpolation. *IEEE Transactions on Image Processing* Vol. 10, No. 10, 1521–1527, 2001.

[11] Tam, W.-S.; Kok, C.-W.; Siu, W.-C. Modified edge-directed interpolation for images. *Journal of Electronic Imaging* Vol. 19, No. 1, 013011, 2010.

[12] Zhang, D.; Wu, X. An edge-guided image interpolation algorithm via directional filtering and data fusion.

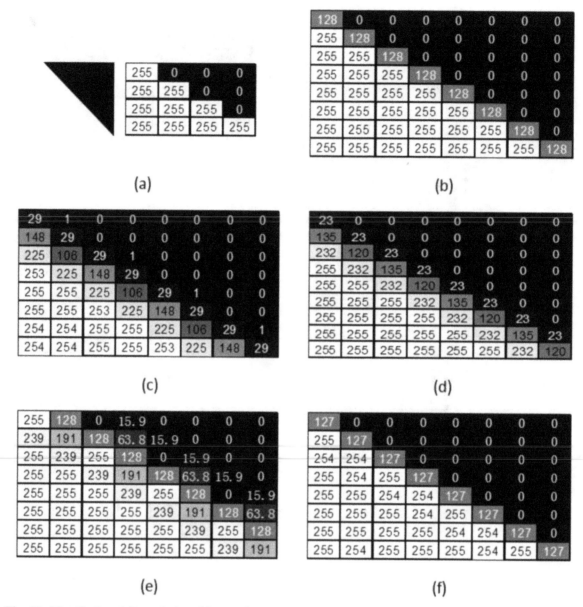

Fig. 12 Magnification of diagonal edges: (a) original image and gray value; (b) ours; (c) Bicubic; (d) CSF; (e) NEDI; (f) GGI.

Fig. 13 Test images. Top row, left to right: cameraman, baboon, boat, goldhill, lake. Bottom row: peppers, couple, Lena, crowd, medical.

IEEE Transactions on Image Processing Vol. 15, No. 8, 2226–2238, 2006.

[13] Zhang, L.; Zhang, C.; Zhou, Y.; Li, X. Surface interpolation to image with edge preserving. In: Proceedings of the 22nd International Conference on Pattern Recognition, 1055–1060, 2014.

[14] Fan, H.; Peng, Q.; Yu, Y. A robust high-resolution details preserving denoising algorithm for meshes. *Science China Information Sciences* Vol. 56, No. 9, 1–12, 2013.

[15] Chang, H.; Yeung, D.-Y.; Xiong, Y. Super-resolution through neighbor embedding. In: Proceedings of IEEE Computer Society Conference on Computer Vision and Pattern Recognition, Vol. 1, I, 2004.

[16] Dong, W.; Zhang, L.; Lukac, R.; Shi, G. Sparse representation based image interpolation with nonlocal autoregressive modeling. *IEEE Transactions on Image Processing* Vol. 22, No. 4, 1382–1394, 2013.

[17] Freeman, W. T.; Jones, T. R.; Pasztor, E. C. Example-based super-resolution. *IEEE Computer Graphics and Applications* Vol. 22, No. 2, 56–65, 2002.

Table 1   Values of PSNR

Image	Bicubic	CSF	NEDI	GGI	Ours
Cameraman	30.37	30.09	33.94	34.27	**35.45**
Baboon	20.91	20.88	**22.79**	22.31	22.62
Boat	25.61	25.53	28.79	28.54	**28.84**
Goldhill	25.96	25.89	28.33	28.13	**28.42**
Lake	24.18	24.10	27.41	26.77	**27.72**
Peppers	27.35	27.27	30.44	30.49	**30.66**
Couple	23.99	23.91	26.82	26.65	**26.89**
Lena	26.90	26.80	29.37	30.11	**30.38**
Crowd	24.89	24.83	27.86	27.75	**28.25**
Medical	24.51	24.72	26.05	25.99	**26.39**

Table 2   Values of SSIM

Image	Bicubic	CSF	NEDI	GGI	Ours
Cameraman	0.943	0.941	0.891	0.944	**0.965**
Baboon	0.511	0.515	**0.662**	0.627	0.649
Boat	0.769	0.770	0.853	0.847	**0.854**
Goldhill	0.654	0.655	0.773	0.775	**0.782**
Lake	0.708	0.708	0.800	0.803	**0.808**
Peppers	0.754	0.754	0.819	0.809	**0.821**
Couple	0.664	0.666	0.785	0.775	**0.786**
Lena	0.780	0.782	0.834	0.841	**0.849**
Crowd	0.786	0.787	0.874	0.868	**0.882**
Medical	0.732	0.776	0.858	0.847	**0.865**

Table 3   Values of PEE as percentages

Image	Bicubic	CSF	NEDI	GGI	Ours
Cameraman	25.79	19.89	23.41	15.26	**10.73**
Baboon	13.62	9.44	11.37	−3.40	**−6.82**
Boat	23.67	16.12	18.52	12.33	**8.14**
Goldhill	19.24	17.95	16.92	13.08	**11.32**
Lake	21.74	14.75	19.02	10.23	**7.93**
Peppers	30.57	25.31	28.94	17.78	**14.43**
Couple	23.67	16.03	17.95	9.86	**6.39**
Lena	18.83	16.45	17.65	9.25	**7.82**
Crowd	15.76	10.85	14.16	6.79	**4.28**
Medical	27.51	25.02	20.43	14.77	**9.61**

[18] Sun, J.; Sun, J.; Xu, Z.; Shum, H.-Y. Image super-resolution using gradient profile prior. In: Proceedings of IEEE Conference on Computer Vision and Pattern Recognition, 1–8, 2008.

[19] Wu, W.; Liu, Z.; He, X. Learning-based super resolution using kernel partial least squares. *Image and Vision Computing* Vol. 29, No. 6, 394–406, 2011.

[20] Yang, J.; Wright, J.; Huang, T. S.; Ma, Y. Image super-resolution via sparse representation. *IEEE Transactions on Image Processing* Vol. 19 No. 11,

2861–2873, 2010.

[21] Ohtake, Y.; Suzuki, H. Edge detection based multi-material interface extraction on industrial CT volumes. *Science China Information Sciences* Vol. 56, No. 9, 1–9, 2013.

[22] Li, C.; Gore, J. C.; Davatzikos, C. Multiplicative intrinsic component optimization (MICO) for MRI bias field estimation and tissue segmentation. *Magnetic Resonance Imaging* Vol. 32, No. 7, 913–923, 2014.

[23] Hore, A.; Ziou, D. Image quality metrics: PSNR vs. SSIM. In: Proceedings of the 20th International Conference on Pattern Recognition, 2366–2369, 2010.

[24] Wang, Z.; Bovik, A. C.; Sheikh, H. R.; Simoncelli, E. P. Image quality assessment: From error visibility to structural similarity. *IEEE Transactions on Image Processing* Vol. 3, No. 4, 600–612, 2004.

[25] Al-Fohoum, A. S.; Reza. A. M. Combined edge crispiness and statistical differencing for deblocking JPEG compressed images. *IEEE Transactions on Image Processing* Vol. 10, No. 9, 1288–1298, 2001.

Semi-supervised dictionary learning with label propagation for image classification

Lin Chen[1], Meng Yang[1,2,3] (✉)

Abstract Sparse coding and supervised dictionary learning have rapidly developed in recent years, and achieved impressive performance in image classification. However, there is usually a limited number of labeled training samples and a huge amount of unlabeled data in practical image classification, which degrades the discrimination of the learned dictionary. How to effectively utilize unlabeled training data and explore the information hidden in unlabeled data has drawn much attention of researchers. In this paper, we propose a novel discriminative semi-supervised dictionary learning method using label propagation (SSD-LP). Specifically, we utilize a label propagation algorithm based on class-specific reconstruction errors to accurately estimate the identities of unlabeled training samples, and develop an algorithm for optimizing the discriminative dictionary and discriminative coding vectors simultaneously. Extensive experiments on face recognition, digit recognition, and texture classification demonstrate the effectiveness of the proposed method.

Keywords　　semi-supervised learning; dictionary learning; label propagation; image classification

1 Introduction

In recent years, sparse representation has gained much interest in the computer vision field [1, 2] and has been widely applied to image restoration [3, 4], image compression [5, 6], and image classification [7–11]. The success of sparse representation is partially because natural images can be generally and sparsely coded by structural primitives (e.g., edges and line segments) and the images or signals can be represented sparsely by dictionary atoms from the same class.

In the task of image classification based on sparse representation, signals need to be encoded over a dictionary (i.e., a set of representation bases) with some sparsity constraint. The dictionary, which encodes the testing sample, can directly consist of the training samples themselves. For example, Wright et al. [12] firstly constructed a dictionary by using the training samples of all classes, then coded the test sample with this dictionary, and finally classified the test sample into the class with the minimal class-specific representation residual. So-called sparse representation based classification (SRC) [12] has achieved impressive performance in face recognition. However, the number of dictionary atoms used in SRC can be quite high, resulting in a large computational burden in calculating the coding vector. What is more, the discriminative information hidden in training samples cannot be exploited fully. To overcome the above problems, the problem of how to learn an effective dictionary from training data has been widely studied.

Dictionary learning methods can be divided into three main categories: unsupervised [13], supervised [14–17], and semi-supervised [11, 18–23]. K-SVD [13] is a representative unsupervised dictionary learning model, which is widely applied to image restoration tasks. Since no label information is exploited in the phase of dictionary learning,

1 College of Computer Science and Software Engineering, Shenzhen University, Shenzhen, China. E-mail: L. Chen, chen.lin@email.szu.edu.cn; M. Yang, yang.meng@szu.edu.cn (✉).

2 School of Data and Computer Science, Sun Yat-sen University, Guangzhou, China.

3 Key Laboratory of Machine Intelligence and Advanced Computing (Sun Yat-sen University), Ministry of Education, China.

unsupervised dictionary learning methods are useful for data reconstruction, but not advantageous for classification tasks.

Based on the relationship between dictionary atoms and class labels, prevailing supervised dictionary learning methods can be divided into three categories: shared, class-specific, and hybrid. In the first case, discrimination provided by shared dictionary learning is typically explored by jointly learning a dictionary and a classifier over the coding coefficients [9, 10]. Using the learned shared dictionary, the generated coding coefficients, which are expected to be discriminative, are used for classification. In class-specific dictionary learning, each dictionary atom is predefined to correspond to a unique class label so that the class-specific reconstruction error can be used for classification [14, 24]. However, the learned dictionary can be very large when there are many classes. In order to take advantage of the powerful class-specific representation ability, and to reduce the coherence between different sub-dictionaries, the hybrid dictionary learning [15, 25, 26] combines shared dictionary atoms and class-specific dictionary atoms.

Sufficient labeled training data and high quality training images are necessary for good performance in supervised dictionary learning algorithms. However, it is expensive and difficult to obtain the labeled training data due to the vast human effort involved. On the other hand, there are abundant unlabeled images that can be collected easily from public image datasets. Therefore, semi-supervised dictionary learning, which effectively utilizes these unlabeled samples to enhance dictionary learning, has attracted extensive research.

In recent years, semi-supervised learning methods have been widely studied [27–31]. One classical semi-supervised learning method is co-training [29] which utilizes multi-view features to retrain the classifiers to obtain better performance. In co-training, the multi-view features need to be conditionally independent so that one classifier can confidently select unlabeled samples for the other classifier. Another important semi-supervised learning method is the graph-based method [27]. In classification, graph-based semi-supervised learning methods can readily explore the class information in

unlabeled training data via a small amount of labeled data. A representative method based on graphs is label propagation (LP), which has been widely used in image classification and ranking. Label propagation algorithms [27, 28, 33–35] perform class estimation of unlabeled samples by propagating label information from labeled data to unlabeled data. This is done by constructing a weight matrix (or affinity matrix) based on the distance between any two samples. The basic assumption of LP algorithms is that if the weight linking two samples is high, they are likely to belong to the same class.

Semi-supervised dictionary learning [11, 18, 19, 21–23, 36] has gained considerable interest in the past several years. In semi-supervised dictionary learning, the issue of whether the unlabeled samples can be accurately estimated for use as labeled samples for training is very important. For instance, a shared dictionary and a classifier may be jointly learned by estimating the class confidence of unlabeled samples [18]. In Ref. [23], the unlabeled samples are utilized to learn a discriminative dictionary by preserving the geometrical structure of both the labeled and unlabeled data. However, the class-specific reconstruction error which carries strong discriminative ability cannot be utilized to estimate the identities of unlabeled samples in the shared dictionary. A semi-supervised class-specific dictionary has also been learned in Ref. [19]. However, its model is a little complex due to many regularizations.

By combining the label information of the labeled samples and reconstruction error of unlabeled samples over all classes, the identities of the unlabeled training samples can be estimated more accurately. In this paper, we propose a novel semi-supervised dictionary model with label propagation. In our proposed model, we design an improved label propagation algorithm to evaluate the probabilities of unlabeled data belonging to a specific class. Specifically, the proposed label propagation algorithm is based on the powerful class-specific representation provided by the reconstruction error of unlabeled samples for each sub-dictionary. Simultaneously, the label information of labeled data can be utilized better by this graph-based method via label propagation. We also well exploit the discrimination provided by the labeled training data in dictionary learning by minimizing the within-class variance. We have conducted several experiments on face recognition, digit recognition, and texture classification, which show the advantage of our proposed SSD-LP approach.

Our main contributions are summarized as follows:

1. We propose a novel discriminative semi-supervised dictionary learning method which can effectively utilize the discriminative information hidden in both unlabeled and labeled training data.

2. By using label propagation, we estimate a more accurate relationship between unlabeled training data and classes, and enhance exploration of the discrimination provided by the unlabeled training data.

3. The discrimination provided by the labeled training data by minimizing within-class variance is explored during semi-supervised dictionary learning.

4. Experimental results show that our method has a significantly better discrimination ability using unlabeled training data in dictionary learning.

The rest of this paper is organized as follows. In Section 2, we briefly introduce related work on semi-supervised dictionary learning. Our model is presented in Section 3, and Section 4 describes the optimization procedure. Section 5 presents experimental results and Section 6 concludes the paper with a brief summary and discussion.

2   Related work

Based on the predefined relationship between dictionary atoms and class labels, semi-supervised dictionary learning approaches can be divided into two main categories: discriminative class-specific dictionary learning and discriminative shared dictionary learning.

Motivated by Ref. [24], Shrivastava et al. [19] learnt a class-specific dictionary by using Fisher discriminant analysis on the coding vectors of the labeled data. However, its model is complex: the training data is represented by a combination of all class-specific dictionaries, and the coding coefficients are regularized by both intra-class and inter-class constraints.

Another approach to semi-supervised dictionary learning is to learn a shared dictionary. Pham and

Venktesh [11] took into account the representation errors of both labeled data and unlabeled data. In addition, the classification errors of labeled data were incorporated into a joint objective function. One major drawback of the above approach is that it may fall into a local minimum due to the dictionary construction and classifier design. Wang et al. [18] utilized an artificially designed penalty function to assign weights to the unlabeled data, greatly suppressing the unlabeled data having low confidence. Zhang et al. [22] proposed an online semi-supervised dictionary learning framework which integrated the reconstruction error of both labeled and unlabeled data, label consistency, and the classification error into an objective function. Babagholami-Mohamadabadi et al. [23] integrated dictionary learning and classifier training into an objective function, and preserved the geometrical structure of both labeled and unlabeled data. Recently, Wang et al. [21] utilized the structural sparse relationships between both the labeled and unlabeled samples to learn a discriminative dictionary in which the unlabeled samples are automatically grouped into different labeled samples. Although a shared dictionary usually has a compact size, the discrimination provided by class-specific reconstruction residuals cannot be used.

3   Semi-supervised dictionary learning with label propagation (SSD-LP)

Although several semi-supervised dictionary learning approaches have been proposed, there are still some issues to be solved, such as how to build a discriminative dictionary by using unlabeled data, how to utilize the representation ability of a class-specific dictionary, and how to estimate the class probabilities of the unlabeled data. In this section, we propose a discriminative semi-supervised dictionary learning method using label propagation (SSD-LP) to address the issues mentioned above.

3.1   SSD-LP model

Let $\boldsymbol{A} = [\boldsymbol{A}_1, \ldots, \boldsymbol{A}_i, \ldots, \boldsymbol{A}_C]$ be the labeled training data, where $\boldsymbol{A}_i$ is the ith-class training data and each column of $\boldsymbol{A}_i$ is a training sample, and $\boldsymbol{B} = [\boldsymbol{b}_1, \ldots, \boldsymbol{b}_j, \ldots, \boldsymbol{b}_N]$ is the unlabeled training data with unknown labels from 1 to C, where N is the number of unlabeled training samples. Here, as in prevailing semi-supervised dictionary methods [11, 18, 19, 21–23, 36], we assume that the unlabeled training data belongs to some class of the training set.

In our proposed model, the dictionary to be learnt is $\boldsymbol{D} = [\boldsymbol{D}_1, \ldots, \boldsymbol{D}_i, \ldots, \boldsymbol{D}_C]$, where $\boldsymbol{D}_i$ is the class-specific sub-dictionary associated with class i; it is required to well represent the ith-class data but to have a poor representation ability for all other classes. In general, we make each column of $\boldsymbol{D}_i$ a unit vector. We can write $\boldsymbol{D}_i$, the representation coefficient matrix of $\boldsymbol{A}_i$ over $\boldsymbol{D}$ as $\boldsymbol{X}_i = [\boldsymbol{X}_i^1; \ldots; \boldsymbol{X}_i^j; \ldots \boldsymbol{X}_i^C]$, where $\boldsymbol{X}_i^j$ is the coding coefficient matrix of $\boldsymbol{A}_i$ on the sub-dictionary $\boldsymbol{D}_j$. Further, $\boldsymbol{y}_j^i$ is the coding coefficient vector of the unlabeled sample $\boldsymbol{b}_j$ on the class-specific dictionary $\boldsymbol{D}_i$.

Apart from requiring the coding coefficients to be sparse, for the labeled training data we also minimize the within-class scatter of coding coefficients, $||\boldsymbol{X}_i^i - \boldsymbol{M}_i||$, to make the training samples from the same class have similar coding coefficients, where $\boldsymbol{M}_i$ is the mean coefficient matrix with the same size as $\boldsymbol{X}_i^i$ and takes the mean column vector of $\boldsymbol{X}_i^i$ as its column vectors.

We define a latent variable, $P_{i,j}$, which represents the probability that the jth unlabeled training sample belongs to the ith class. $P_{i,j}$ satisfies $0 \leqslant P_{i,j} \leqslant 1$ and $\sum_{i=1}^C P_{i,j} = 1$. If the labeled training sample k belongs to class j, then $P_{j,k} = 1$ and $P_{i,k} = 0$ for $i \neq j$.

Our proposed SSD-LP method can now be formulated as

$$\min_{\boldsymbol{D},\boldsymbol{X},\boldsymbol{P},\boldsymbol{y}} \sum_{i=1}^C (||\boldsymbol{A}_i - \boldsymbol{D}_i \boldsymbol{X}_i^i||_F^2 + \gamma||\boldsymbol{X}_i^i||_1 - \lambda||\boldsymbol{X}_i^i - \boldsymbol{M}_i||_F^2)$$
$$+ \sum_{j=1}^N \left\{ \sum_{i=1}^C P_{i,j}||\boldsymbol{b}_j - \boldsymbol{D}_i \boldsymbol{y}_j^i||_F^2 + \gamma||\boldsymbol{y}_j^i||_1 \right\} \quad (1)$$

where γ and λ are parameters, and $\boldsymbol{P}$ is learned via our proposed improved label propagation (ILP) algorithm.

For the labeled training data, a discriminative representation term, i.e., $||\boldsymbol{A}_i - \boldsymbol{D}_i \boldsymbol{X}_i^i||_F^2$, and a discriminative coefficient term, i.e., $||\boldsymbol{X}_i^i - \boldsymbol{M}_i||_2^2$, are introduced. Since $\boldsymbol{D}_i$ is associated with the ith-class, it is expected that $\boldsymbol{A}_i$ should be well represented by $\boldsymbol{D}_i$ but not by $\boldsymbol{D}_j$, $j \neq i$. This implies that $\boldsymbol{X}_i^i$ should have some significant coefficients such

that $||\boldsymbol{A}_i - \boldsymbol{D}_i \boldsymbol{X}_i^i||_F^2$ is small, while $\boldsymbol{X}_i^j$ should have nearly zero coefficients. Thus the term $||\boldsymbol{D}_i \boldsymbol{X}_i^j||_F^2$ is eliminated as shown in Eq. (1).

For the unlabeled training data, the probability that the sample belongs to each class is required. For instance, $P_{i,j} = 1$ indicates that the jth unlabeled training sample comes from the ith-class, and the class-specific dictionary $\boldsymbol{D}_i$ should well represent the jth unlabeled training sample in that $||\boldsymbol{b}_j - \boldsymbol{D}_i \boldsymbol{y}_j^i||_F^2$ is small.

Due to the good performance of graph-based label propagation on semi-supervised classification tasks, we utilize it to select the unlabeled sample with high confidence and assign the unlabeled sample a high weight, as explained in detail in Section 4.1.

3.2 Classification scheme

Once the dictionary $\boldsymbol{D} = [\boldsymbol{D}_1, \ldots, \boldsymbol{D}_i, \ldots, \boldsymbol{D}_C]$ has been learned, a testing sample can be classified by coding it over the learned dictionary. Although the learned dictionary is class-specific, the testing sample is not always coded on each sub-dictionary corresponding to each class. As the discussion in Ref. [24], there are two methods of coding the testing sample.

When the number of training samples in each class is relatively small, the sample sub-space of class i cannot be supported by the learned sub-dictionary $\boldsymbol{D}_i$. Thus the testing samples $\boldsymbol{b}^t$ are represented on the collaborative combination of all class-specific dictionaries. In this case, the sparse coding vector of the testing sample should be found by solving:

$$\hat{\boldsymbol{y}} = \arg\min_{\boldsymbol{y}} \{||\boldsymbol{b}^t - \boldsymbol{D}\boldsymbol{y}||_2^2 + \gamma||\boldsymbol{y}||_1\} \quad (2)$$

where γ is a constant for the sparsity constraint. Then the class of the testing sample $\boldsymbol{b}^t$ is predicted by

$$\text{label} = \arg\min_i ||\boldsymbol{b}^t - \boldsymbol{D}_i \boldsymbol{y}_i||_2^2 \quad (3)$$

where $\hat{\boldsymbol{y}} = [\boldsymbol{y}_1; \ldots; \boldsymbol{y}_i; \ldots; \boldsymbol{y}_C]$ and $\boldsymbol{y}_i$ is the coefficient vector associated with class i.

When the number of training samples in each class is relatively large, the sub-dictionary $\boldsymbol{D}_i$, which has enough discrimination, can support the sample sub-space of class i. Thus, we can directly code testing sample $\boldsymbol{b}^t$ on each sub-dictionary:

$$\hat{\boldsymbol{y}} = \arg\min_{\boldsymbol{y}} \{||\boldsymbol{b}^t - \boldsymbol{D}_i \boldsymbol{y}||_2^2 + \gamma||\boldsymbol{y}||_1\} \quad (4)$$

The class of testing sample $\boldsymbol{b}^t$ is then predicted by

$$\text{label} = \arg\min_i \{e_i\} \quad (5)$$

where $e_i = ||\boldsymbol{b}^{\mathrm{t}} - \boldsymbol{D}_i \hat{\boldsymbol{y}}||_2^2$.

4 Optimization of SSD-LP

The SSD-LP objective function is not convex in the joint variables of $\{\boldsymbol{D}, \boldsymbol{X}, \boldsymbol{P}, \boldsymbol{y}\}$, but it is convex in each variable when the others are fixed. Optimization of Eq. (1) can be divided into three sub-problems: updating $\boldsymbol{P}$ by fixing $\boldsymbol{D}$, $\boldsymbol{X}$, $\boldsymbol{y}$; updating $\boldsymbol{X}$, $\boldsymbol{y}$ by fixing $\boldsymbol{P}$, $\boldsymbol{D}$; and updating $\boldsymbol{D}$ by fixing $\boldsymbol{P}$, $\boldsymbol{X}$.

4.1 Updating $\boldsymbol{P}$ by improved label propagation

Unlike the approach used in Ref. [28] to construct the weight matrix, our weight matrix is constructed from the reconstruction errors of the unlabeled samples over all classes rather than the distances between any two samples. Intuitively, since sub-dictionary $\boldsymbol{D}_i$ is good at representng the ith-class but is poor at representing other classes, any pair of samples is likely to belong to the same class if they achieve minimum reconstruction error in the same class.

Specifically, to compute the weight value w_{ij} (if w_{ij} is large, then sample $\boldsymbol{b}_i$ and sample $\boldsymbol{b}_j$ are likely to have the same class), we first compute the reconstruction errors of both training samples $\boldsymbol{b}_i$ and $\boldsymbol{b}_j$ over all classes. This gives $\boldsymbol{e}_i = [e_{i1}; \ldots; e_{ik}; \ldots e_{ic}]$ and $\boldsymbol{e}_j = [e_{j1}; \ldots; e_{jk}; \ldots e_{jc}]$ where $e_{ik} = ||\boldsymbol{b}_i - \boldsymbol{D}_k \boldsymbol{y}_i^k||_2^2$ is the reconstruction error value of sample $\boldsymbol{b}_i$ on the class k and $\boldsymbol{y}_i^k$ is the coefficient vector for class k.

After obtaining $\boldsymbol{e}_i$ and $\boldsymbol{e}_j$, we compute the distance d_{ij}^2 between them:

$$d_{ij}^2 = ||\boldsymbol{e}_i - \boldsymbol{e}_j||_2^2 \qquad (6)$$

Finally, the weight linking samples $\boldsymbol{b}_i$ and $\boldsymbol{b}_j$ is

$$w_{ij} = \exp(-d_{ij}^2/\sigma^2) \qquad (7)$$

where σ is a constant. After finding all weight values for every pair of samples, we can get the transition matrix $\boldsymbol{T}$, which can be defined by normalizing the weight matrix using:

$$T(i,j) = \frac{w_{ij}}{\sum_{k=1}^{C} w_{ik}} \qquad (8)$$

so that $\sum_{j=1}^{C} T(i,j) = 1$ and $\boldsymbol{T}$ is asymmetric after normalization.

Let $n = n_{\mathrm{l}} + n_{\mathrm{u}}$ where n_{l}, n_{u} are the total numbers of labeled and unlabeled training samples respectively. For the multi-class problem, the probability matrix is $\boldsymbol{P} = [\boldsymbol{P}^{\mathrm{l}}; \boldsymbol{P}^{\mathrm{u}}] \in \Re^{n \times C}$, where C is the number of classes, $\boldsymbol{P}^{\mathrm{l}}$ is the probability matrix for labeled samples, and $\boldsymbol{P}^{\mathrm{u}}$ is the probability matrix for unlabeled samples. We set $\boldsymbol{P}^{\mathrm{l}}(i,k) = 1$ if sample $\boldsymbol{b}_i$ is a labeled sample with class k, and 0 otherwise. We initialize the probability matrix as $\boldsymbol{P}_0 = [\boldsymbol{P}_0^{\mathrm{l}}; \boldsymbol{0}]$, i.e., the probability for the unlabeled training samples is set to zero. The improved label propagation algorithm for updating $\boldsymbol{P}$ is presented in Algorithm 1. Its convergence can be seen by refering to Ref. [27]. $\boldsymbol{P}_{t+1}$ denotes the next iteration of $\boldsymbol{P}_t$. Please note that the step 3.b is crucial as it ensures the label information of the labeled samples is preserved.

Compared with using a weight matrix based on the distances of any two original samples, there are two main advantages in our method. On one hand, the original method of constructing the weight matrix is a kind of single-track feedback mechanism in which the update of the probability matrix $\boldsymbol{P}$ can affect the dictionary update, but the update of the latter cannot affect the former because the distances between the original samples do not change. On the other hand, a weight matrix based on reconstruction errors over all classes more realistically reflects the similarity between two samples, which is helpful in estimating the class labels of unlabeled data.

4.2 Updating $\boldsymbol{X}$ and $\boldsymbol{y}$

By fixing the estimated class probabilities of the unlabeled training data (i.e., $\boldsymbol{P}$), the discriminative dictionary (i.e., $\boldsymbol{D}$) and coding coefficients (i.e., $\boldsymbol{X}$ and $\boldsymbol{y}$) can now be updated.

When the dictionary $\boldsymbol{D}$ is fixed, the coding coefficients of the labeled training data can be easily updated. The objective function in Eq. (1) now reduces to

$$\min_{\boldsymbol{X}} \sum_{i=1}^{C} (||\boldsymbol{A}_i - \boldsymbol{D}_i \boldsymbol{X}_i^i||_F^2 + \gamma ||\boldsymbol{X}_i^i||_1 + \lambda ||\boldsymbol{X}_i^i - \boldsymbol{M}_i||_F^2) \qquad (9)$$

Algorithm 1: Improved label propagation based on reconstruction error

---

1: Construct a transition matrix $\boldsymbol{T}$ by Eq. (8);
2: Initialize the probability matrix $\boldsymbol{P}_0 = [\boldsymbol{P}_0^{\mathrm{l}}; \boldsymbol{0}]$;
3: Repeating the following steps until $\boldsymbol{P}$ converges:
    3.a $\boldsymbol{P}_{t+1} = \boldsymbol{T} * \boldsymbol{P}_t$;
    3.b $\boldsymbol{P}_{t+1}^{\mathrm{l}} = \boldsymbol{P}_0^{\mathrm{l}}$;
4: Output the probability matrix $\boldsymbol{P}$.

In our approach, we update $\boldsymbol{X}_i^i$ for the ith-class of data by using the coding method in Ref. [24].

As discussed in Section 3.2, when the number of training samples in each class is relatively small, updating the coding coefficients of the unlabeled training data using a collaborative representation can achieve better classification performance. Conversely, we choose a local representation when there are sufficient training samples of each class. For the unlabeled training data, two coding strategies, i.e., collaborative representation and local representation, are used. In the collaborative representation, the coding coefficient is solved via

$$\min_{\boldsymbol{y}_j} ||\boldsymbol{b}_j - \boldsymbol{D}\boldsymbol{y}_j||_F^2 + \gamma ||\boldsymbol{y}_j||_1 \qquad (10)$$

where $\boldsymbol{D} = [\boldsymbol{D}_1, \dots, \boldsymbol{D}_i, \dots, \boldsymbol{D}_C]$ and $\boldsymbol{y}_j = [\boldsymbol{y}_j^1; \dots; \boldsymbol{y}_j^i; \dots; \boldsymbol{y}_j^C]$; $\boldsymbol{y}_j^i$ is the coding vector of the unlabeled sample $\boldsymbol{b}_j$ for the sub-dictionary $\boldsymbol{D}_i$. Here the different class-specific dictionaries $\boldsymbol{D}_i$ will compete with each other to represent $\boldsymbol{b}_j$. In order to ensure fair competition between different class-specific dictionaries, the encoding phase of collaborative representation ignores $\boldsymbol{P}$.

In the local representation, the SSD-LP model associated with $\boldsymbol{y}_i$ changes to

$$\min_{\boldsymbol{y}_j^i} \sum_{i=1}^{C} P_{i,j}(||\boldsymbol{b}_j - \boldsymbol{D}_i\boldsymbol{y}_j^i||_F^2) + \gamma ||\boldsymbol{y}_j^i||_1 \qquad (11)$$

which is a standard sparse coding problem.

4.3 Updating D

After updating $\boldsymbol{P}$, further unlabeled training samples are selected to train our model. If we fix the size of the learnt dictionary, the discrimination of our dictionary cannot improve. Thus, after updating the probability matrix $\boldsymbol{P}$, we should increase the size of each sub-dictionary to explore the discriminative information hidden in the unlabeled samples (i.e., an additional dictionary atom $\boldsymbol{E}_i$ must be initialized and added to sub-dictionary $\boldsymbol{D}_i$).

Since the unlabeled samples provide more discrimination, $\boldsymbol{E}_i$ is initialized by using unlabeled data:

$$\min_{\boldsymbol{E}} \sum_{j=1}^{N} \sum_{i=1}^{C} P_{i,j}||\boldsymbol{b}_j - \boldsymbol{E}_i\tilde{\boldsymbol{y}}_j^i||_F^2 \qquad (12)$$

where $\tilde{\boldsymbol{y}}_j^i$ is the unknown coding coefficient. We update $\boldsymbol{E}_i$ class by class:

$$\min_{\boldsymbol{E}_i} \sum_{j=1}^{N} P_{i,j}||\boldsymbol{b}_j - \boldsymbol{E}_i\tilde{\boldsymbol{y}}_j^i||_F^2 \qquad (13)$$

Then we combine all terms in Eq. (13):

$$\min_{\boldsymbol{E}_i} ||[\sqrt{P_{i,1}}\boldsymbol{b}_1, \dots, \sqrt{P_{i,j}}\boldsymbol{b}_j, \dots, \sqrt{P_{i,N}}\boldsymbol{b}_N] - \boldsymbol{E}_i[\sqrt{P_{i,1}}\tilde{\boldsymbol{y}}_1, \dots, \sqrt{P_{i,j}}\tilde{\boldsymbol{y}}_j, \dots, \sqrt{P_{i,N}}\tilde{\boldsymbol{y}}_N]||_F^2 \qquad (14)$$

Since we require the coding coefficients to be sparse, we compute the extended dictionary by singular-value decomposition (SVD):

$$[\boldsymbol{U}, \boldsymbol{S}, \boldsymbol{V}] = \text{svd}((\sqrt{P_{i,1}}\boldsymbol{b}_1 \dots (\sqrt{P_{i,j}}\boldsymbol{b}_j) \dots \sqrt{P_{i,N}}\boldsymbol{b}_N)) \qquad (15)$$

The extended dictionary is defined such that:

$$\boldsymbol{E}_i = \boldsymbol{U}(:, n) \qquad (16)$$

where n is the number of atoms in the extended dictionary. In all experiments shown in this paper, we set $n = 1$, i.e., each sub-dictionary adds a single dictionary atom after the update of probability matrix $\boldsymbol{P}$.

The new sub-dictionary for class i is initialized using $\hat{\boldsymbol{D}}_i = [\boldsymbol{D}_i, \boldsymbol{E}_i]$. By fixing the coding coefficient $\boldsymbol{X}$ and probability matrix $\boldsymbol{P}$, the problem in Eq. (1) is reduced to

$$\min_{\boldsymbol{D}} \sum_{i=1}^{C}(||\boldsymbol{A}_i - \hat{\boldsymbol{D}}_i\boldsymbol{X}_i^i||_F^2) + \sum_{j=1}^{N}(\sum_{i=1}^{C} P_{i,j}||\boldsymbol{b}_j - \hat{\boldsymbol{D}}_i\boldsymbol{y}_j^i||_F^2) \qquad (17)$$

Dictionary updating can be easily performed atom by atom by using Metaface [8]. After updating the extended dictionary $\boldsymbol{E}$, we need several iterations to update the dictionary and coefficients to guarantee the convergence of the discriminative dictionary. In our experiment, the number of additional iterations is set to 5.

The whole algorithm of the proposed semi-supervised dictionary learning is summarized in Algorithm 2. The algorithm converges since the total objective function value in Eq. (1) decreases in each iteration. Figure 1 shows the total objective function value for the AR dataset [37]. In all the experiments mentioned in this paper, our algorithm converges in less than 10 iterations.

5 Experiment results

We have performed experiments and corresponding analysis to verify the performance of our method for image classification. We evaluate our approach on two face databases: the Extended YaleB

Algorithm 2:   Semi-supervised dictionary learning with label propagation (SSD-LP)

1. Initialization
The class probabilities of the unlabeled training samples are all initialized to zero; the sub-dictionary D_i is initialized using the classes of the ith-class labeled training samples A_i; and each column of D_i is given unit l_2-norm.
2. Class estimation of the unlabeled training data
Update each $P_{i,j}$ for every unlabeled training sample using Algorithm 1.
3. Discriminative dictionary learning
  3.1 Compute the extended dictionary E_i for each class by solving Eq. (16).
  3.2 Update the coding coefficients X and y, and the dictionary D over several iterations:
    3.2.1 Update the coding coefficients by solving Eqs. (9)–(11);
    3.2.2 Update the dictionary atom by atom by solving Eq. (17).
4. Return to step 2 unless the values of the objective function in Eq. (1) in adjacent iterations are close enough or the maximum number of iterations is reached.
5. Output D.

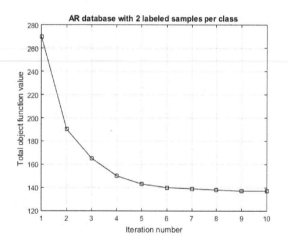

Fig. 1 Total objective function value on the AR database [37] versus number of iterations.

database [38] and the AR face database [37], two handwritten digit datasets: MNIST [39] and USPS [40], and an object category dataset: Texture-25 [41]. We compare our method with SRC [12], M-SVM [17], FDDL [24], DKSVD [10], LCKSVD [16], SVGDL [42], S2D2 [19], JDL [11], OSSDL [22], SSR-D [36], and the recently proposed USSDL [18] and SSP-DL [21] algorithms. The last six methods (S2D2, JDL, OSSDL, SSR-D, USSDL, and SSP-DL) are semi-supervised dictionary learning models; the others are supervised dictionary learning methods.

We repeated each experiment 10 times with different random splits of the datasets and report the average classification accuracy together with standard deviation; the best classification results are in boldface. For all approaches, we report their best results obtained after tuning their parameters.

5.1 Parameter selection and comparison with original label propagation

In our all experiments, the parameters of SSD-LP are fixed to $\gamma = 0.001$ and $\lambda = 0.01$. The number of additional iterations is set to 5 in step 3.2 of Algorithm 2. In our experiment, since the sub-dictionary D_i is initialized using the ith-class of labeled samples, the number of atoms D_i is equal to the number of labeled samples for the ith-class (e.g., in the AR database, these are 2, 3, 5 as there are 2, 3, 5 labeled samples respectively). After each update of the probability matrix P, each sub-dictionary adds an additional dictionary atom (the number of atoms of each sub-dictionary does not increase if the number of iterations exceeds the number of unlabeled training examples).

In order to show the effectiveness of our algorithm, a test was conducted on the Extended YaleB dataset. As shown in Fig. 2, we can see that for face recognition, recognition significantly improves with iteration number.

We also compare our proposed improved label propagation method with the original label propagation method (LP). As Fig. 3 shows, SSD-LP has at least 10% improvement over the performance when the images are classified directly

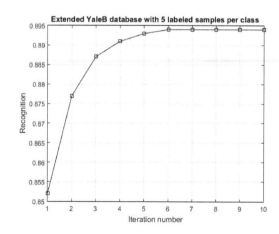

Fig. 2 Recognition rate versus iteration number for the Extended YaleB database with five labeled training samples per class.

by the original label propagation method. With an increasing number of iterations, the recognition rate of our method grows, while the performance of the original label propagation algorithm is essentially unchanged. This is because the original label propagation is dependent on the distribution structure of the input data which does not change as the dictionary is updated. This is a kind of single-track feedback mechanism between the original label propagation and dictionary learning as explained in Section 4.1.

We also compare the running time of our improved LP and the original LP using MATLAB 2015a on an Intel i7-3770 3.40 GHz machine with 16.0 GB RAM. The running time for the improved LP and original LP is 11.21 s and 7.54 s, respectively for two training examples per person (see Fig. 3 up), and 11.73 s and 7.75 s, respectively for five training examples per person (see Fig. 3 bottom). We can see that the running time of the improved LP and original LP is comparable.

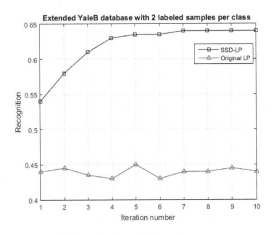

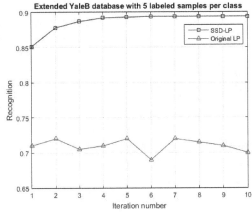

Fig. 3 Recognition rate versus iteration number for the Extended YaleB database with two labeled training samples per person (up) and five training samples per person (bottom).

5.2 Face recognition

In this section, we evaluate our method in a face recognition problem, for both AR and Extended YaleB databases, using the same experimental setting as Ref. [18]. In both face recognition experiments, the image samples are reduced to 300 dimensions by PCA.

The AR database consists of over 4000 images of 126 individuals. In the experiment we chose a subset of 50 male and 50 female subjects. Focusing on illumination and expression changes, for each subject we chose 7 images from Session 1 for training, and 7 images from Session 2 for testing. We randomly selected {2, 3, 5} samples from each class in the training set as the labeled samples, and the remaining as the unlabeled samples. Five independent evaluations were conducted for the experiment with different numbers of labeled training samples.

As shown in Table 1, when the number of labeled samples was small (2 or 3), our algorithm performed better than all other methods, especially supervised dictionary learning models. This is because supervised dictionary methods cannot utilize the discriminative information hidden in the unlabeled training samples. The semi-supervised dictionary learning methods usually perform better than supervised dictionary learning methods: for instance, USSDL performs the second best. From Table 1, we can see that USSDL has very close results to SSD-LP, but we should note that USSDL needs more information in the dictionary learning task, including classifier learning of the coding vectors. In addition, the optimization procedure of USSDL is more complex than that of SSD-LP.

We also evaluated our approach on the Extended

Table 1 Recognition rate for various methods, for different number of labeled training samples, for the AR database   (Unit: %)

Method	2	3	5
SRC	72.2±1.0	79.1±0.9	88.2±0.5
M-SVM	60.1±2.2	74.3±1.2	84.9±2.0
FDDL	83.6±1.8	89.7±2.1	93.6±0.9
LC-KSVD	67.4±4.2	89.2±3.6	91.5±2.1
SVGDL	82.1±1.8	90.3±2.0	93.8±1.5
S2D2	85.3±3.1	89.2±1.9	92.1±1.1
JDL	87.2±2.0	88.2±1.8	90.7±1.2
USSDL	89.1±2.3	91.3±1.4	**94.1±1.3**
SSD-LP	**90.9±0.9**	**91.6±0.6**	93.7±0.5

YaleB database. The database consists of 2414 frontal face images of 38 individuals. Each individual has 64 images; we randomly selected 20 images as the training set and used the rest as the testing set. We randomly selected {2, 5, 10} samples from each class in the training set as the labeled samples, and used the remainder as the unlabeled samples. The classification results are shown in Table 2.

It is clear that our proposed method provides better classification performance than other dictionary learning methods. Especially when a small number of label samples is involved, the SSD-LP performs singificantly better than supervised dictionary learning methods which are dependent on the number of the labeled samples. It also can be seen that SSD-LP improves by at least 1.5% over the other semi-supervised dictionary learning methods. When the number of labeled samples is small, the improvement is more obvious. That is mainly because our method has strong capability to utilize the unlabeled samples by accurately determining their labels and using them as labeled samples to train our discriminative dictionary.

5.3 Digit classification

Next, we evaluated the performance of our method on both the MNIST and USPS datasets, with the same experimental setting as Ref. [21]. The MNIST dataset has 10 classes. The training set has 60,000 handwritten digital images and the test set has about 10,000 images. The dimension of each digital image is 784. We randomly selected 200 samples from each class, using 20 images as the labeled samples, 80 as the unlabeled samples, and the rest for testing.

The USPS dataset has 9298 digital images in 10 classes. We randomly selected 110 images from each class, using 20 as the labeled samples, 40 as the unlabeled samples, and 50 as the testing samples. We used the whole image as the feature vector, and normalized the vector to have unit l_2-norm.

The results for the ten independent tests are combined in Table 3. It can be seen that our proposed SSD-LP method can effectively utilize information from the unlabeled samples, achieving a classification accuracy clearly higher than for the other dictionary methods. Using the additional unlabeled training samples, the size of the dictionary is enlarged adaptively to better utilize the discrimination provided by the unlabeled samples, which is why we can achieve better performance than other semi-supervised dictionary methods mentioned in Table 3.

5.4 Object classification

In this experiment we used the Texture-25 dataset which contains 25 texture categories, with 40 samples of each. We used low-level features [43, 44], including PHOG [32], GIST [45], and LBP [46]. Using the experimental setting in Ref. [18], PHOG was computed with a 2-layer pyramid in 8 directions, and GIST was computed on rescaled images of 256×256 pixels, in 4, 8, and 8 orientations at 3 scales from coarse to fine. Uniform LBP were used. All the features are concatenated into a single 119-dimensional vector. In this experiment, 13 images were randomly selected for testing and we randomly select {2, 5, 10, 15} samples from each class in the training set as labeled samples. The average accuracies together with the standard deviation in five independent tests are presented in Table 4.

It can be seen that SSD-LP improves by at least 3% over supervised dictionary learning when the number of labeled samples is 2 or 5. As the number

Table 2 Recognition rate for various methods, for different number of labeled training samples, for the Extended YaleB database

(Unit: %)

Method	2	3	5
SRC	47.8±2.9	79.1±1.9	90.5±0.5
M-SVM	38.0±2.6	66.6±1.1	83.8±0.8
FDDL	52.4±2.5	82.3±0.7	92.1±0.3
LC-KSVD	48.5±2.8	69.6±3.6	84.6±3.8
SVGDL	53.4±2.2	81.1±1.0	91.7±5.8
S2D2	53.4±2.1	76.1±1.3	83.2±1.9
JDL	55.2±1.8	77.4±2.8	85.3±1.6
USSDL	60.5±2.1	86.5±2.1	93.6±0.8
SSD-LP	**67.0±2.9**	**89.8±0.9**	**95.2±0.2**

Table 3 Recognition rate for various methods, for digit databases USPS and MNIST

(Unit: %)

Method	USPS	MNIST
SRC	68.6±2.7	72.9±2.3
DKSVD	67.5±1.8	71.4±1.7
FDDL	85.2±1.2	82.5±1.3
LC-KSVD	76.9±1.3	73.0±1.3
OSSDL	80.8±2.8	73.2±1.8
S2D2	86.6±1.6	77.6±0.8
SSR-D	87.2±0.5	83.8±1.2
SSP-DL	87.8±1.1	85.8±1.2
SSD-LP	**90.3±1.3**	**87.8±1.6**

Table 4 Recognition rate for various methods, for different number of labeled training samples, for the Texture-25 database (Unit: %)

Method	2	5	10	15
M-SVM	24.9±3.4	41.6±1.7	52.9±2.7	55.3±1.2
FDDL	31.4±4.0	48.9±1.7	52.6±3.1	56.7±1.4
LC-KSVD	28.0±4.1	38.2±1.3	48.6±2.9	54.1±2.9
SVGDL	29.8±3.9	37.9±1.3	40.3±2.3	56.8±1.3
S2D2	31.7±2.3	43.8±1.4	47.9±2.4	50.9±1.7
JDL	27.6±2.1	39.2±1.9	43.3±0.8	50.3±0.8
USSDL	34.2±3.7	51.1±2.2	54.6±1.6	57.7±1.6
SSD-LP	**38.2±1.3**	**54.2±2.0**	**64.1±1.3**	**73.7±2.5**

of labeled samples increases, the effect is clearly enhanced, by about 10%. Table 4 shows that our method also gives better results than the other three semi-supervised dictionary methods. That is because as more samples are used for training, the estimates of the labels of the unlabeled training data become more accurate. The result fully demonstrates the classification effectiveness of label propagation based on reconstruction error. In addition, adaptively adding dictionary atoms makes our learnt dictionary more discriminative. JDL, which only uses the reconstruction error of both labeled and unlabeled data, does not work well.

6 Conclusions

This paper has proposed a discriminative semi-supervised dictionary learning model. By integrating label propagation with that class-specific reconstruction error of each unlabeled training sample, we can more accurately estimate the class of unlabeled samples to train our model. The discriminative property of labeled training data is also well explored by using a discriminative representation term and minimizing within-class scatter of the coding coefficients. Several experiments, including applications to face recognition, digit recognition, and texture classification have shown the advantage of our method over supervised and other semi-supervised dictionary learning approaches. In the future, we will explore more classification questions, e.g., the case in which the training samples may not belong to any known class.

Acknowledgements

This work was partially supported by the National Natural Science Foundation for Young Scientists of China (No. 61402289), and the National Science Foundation of Guangdong Province (No. 2014A030313558).

References

[1] Elad, M.; Figueiredo, M. A. T.; Ma, Y. On the role of sparse and redundant representations in image processing. *Proceedings of the IEEE* Vol. 98, No. 6, 972–982, 2010.

[2] Wright, J.; Ma, Y.; Mairal, J.; Sapiro, G.; Huang, T. S.; Yan, S. Sparse representation for computer vision and pattern recognition. *Proceedings of the IEEE* Vol. 98, No. 6, 1031–1044, 2010.

[3] Chen, Y.-C.; Patel, V. M.; Phillips, P. J.; Chellappa, R. Dictionary-based face recognition from video. In: *Computer Vision–ECCV 2012*. Fitzgibbon, A.; Lazebnik, S.; Perona, P.; Sato, Y.; Schmid, C. Eds. Springer Berlin Heidelberg, 766–779, 2012.

[4] Mairal, J.; Elad, M.; Sapiro, G. Sparse representation for color image restoration. *IEEE Transactions on Image Processing* Vol. 17, No. 1, 53–69, 2008.

[5] Bryt, O.; Elad, M. Compression of facial images using the K-SVD algorithm. *Journal of Visual Communication and Image Representation* Vol. 19, No. 4, 270–282, 2008.

[6] Bryt, O.; Elad, M. Improving the k-svd facial image compression using a linear deblocking method. In: Proceedings of the IEEE 25th Convention of Electrical and Electronics Engineers in Israel, 533–537, 2008.

[7] Yang, J.; Yu, K.; Huang, T. Supervised translation-invariant sparse coding. In: Proceedings of the IEEE Computer Society Conference on Computer Vision and Pattern Recognition, 3517–3524, 2010.

[8] Yang, M.; Zhang, L.; Yang, J.; Zhang, D. Metaface learning for sparse representation based face recognition. In: Proceedings of the IEEE International Conference on Image Processing, 1601–1604, 2010.

[9] Mairal, J.; Ponce, J.; Sapiro, G.; Zisserman, A.; Bach, F. R. Supervised dictionary learning. In: Proceedings of the Advances in Neural Information Processing Systems, 1033–1040, 2009.

[10] Zhang, Q.; Li, B. Discriminative K-SVD for dictionary learning in face recognition. In: Proceedings of the IEEE Computer Society Conference on Computer Vision and Pattern Recognition, 2691–2698, 2010.

[11] Pham, D.-S.; Venkatesh, S. Joint learning and dictionary construction for pattern recognition. In: Proceedings of the IEEE Conference on Computer Vision and Pattern Recognition, 1–8, 2008.

[12] Wright, J.; Yang, A. Y.; Ganesh, A.; Sastry, S. S.; Ma, Y. Robust face recognition via sparse representation. *IEEE Transactions on Pattern Analysis and Machine Intelligence* Vol. 31, No. 2, 210–227, 2009.

[13] Aharon, M.; Elad, M.; Bruckstein, A. K-SVD: An algorithm for designing overcomplete dictionaries for sparse representation. *IEEE Transactions on Signal Processing* Vol. 54, No. 11, 4311–4322, 2006.

[14] Mairal, J.; Bach, F.; Ponce, J.; Sapiro, G.; Zisserman, A. Discriminative learned dictionaries for local image analysis. In: Proceedings of the IEEE Conference on Computer Vision and Pattern Recognition, 1–8, 2008.

[15] Yang, M.; Dai, D.; Shen, L.; Van Gool, L. Latent dictionary learning for sparse representation based classification. In: Proceedings of the IEEE Conference on Computer Vision and Pattern Recognition, 4138–4145, 2014.

[16] Jiang, Z.; Lin, Z.; Davis, L. S. Learning a discriminative dictionary for sparse coding via label consistent K-SVD. In: Proceedings of the IEEE Conference on Computer Vision and Pattern Recognition, 1697–1704, 2011.

[17] Yang, J.; Yu, K.; Gong, Y.; Huang, T. Linear spatial pyramid matching using sparse coding for image classification. In: Proceedings of the IEEE Conference on Computer Vision and Pattern Recognition, 1794–1801, 2009.

[18] Wang, X.; Guo, X.; Li, S. Z. Adaptively unified semi-supervised dictionary learning with active points. In: Proceedings of the IEEE International Conference on Computer Vision, 1787–1795, 2015.

[19] Shrivastava, A.; Pillai, J. K.; Patel, V. M.; Chellappa, R. Learning discriminative dictionaries with partially labeled data. In: Proceedings of the 19th IEEE International Conference on Image Processing, 3113–3116, 2012.

[20] Jian, M.; Jung, C. Semi-supervised bi-dictionary learning for image classification with smooth representation-based label propagation. *IEEE Transactions on Multimedia* Vol. 18, No. 3, 458–473, 2016.

[21] Wang, D.; Zhang, X.; Fan, M.; Ye, X. Semi-supervised dictionary learning via structural sparse preserving. In: Proceedings of the 30th AAAI Conference on Artificial Intelligence, 2137–2144, 2016.

[22] Zhang, G.; Jiang, Z.; Davis, L. S. Online semi-supervised discriminative dictionary learning for sparse representation. In: *Computer Vision–ACCV 2012*. Lee, K. M.; Mu, K.; Matsushita, Y.; Rehg, J. M.; Hu, Z. Eds. Springer Berlin Heidelberg, 259–273, 2012.

[23] Babagholami-Mohamadabadi, B.; Zarghami, A.; Zolfaghari, M.; Baghshah, M. S. PSSDL: Probabilistic semi-supervised dictionary learning. In: *Machine Learning and Knowledge Discovery in Databases*. Blockeel, H.; Kersting, K.; Nijssen, S.; Železný, F. Eds. Springer Berlin Heidelberg, 192–207, 2013.

[24] Yang, M.; Zhang, L.; Feng, X.; Zhang, D. Fisher discrimination dictionary learning for sparse representation. In: Proceedings of the IEEE International Conference on Computer Vision, 543–550, 2011.

[25] Zhou, N.; Shen, Y.; Peng, J.; Fan, J. Learning inter-related visual dictionary for object recognition. In: Proceedings of the IEEE Conference on Computer Vision and Pattern Recognition, 3490–3497, 2012.

[26] Deng, W.; Hu, J.; Guo, J. Extended SRC: Undersampled face recognition via intraclass variant dictionary. *IEEE Transactions on Pattern Analysis and Machine Intelligence* Vol. 34, No. 9, 1864–1870, 2012.

[27] Zhu, X.; Lafferty, J.; Rosenfeld, R. Semi-supervised learning with graphs. Carnegie Mellon University, Language Technologies Institute, School of Computer Science, 2005.

[28] Wang, B.; Tu, Z.; Tsotsos, J. K. Dynamic label propagation for semi-supervised multi-class multi-label classification. In: Proceedings of the IEEE International Conference on Computer Vision, 425–432, 2013.

[29] Blum, A.; Mitchell, T. Combining labeled and unlabeled data with co-training. In: Proceedings of the 11th Annual Conference on Computational Learning Theory, 92–100, 1998.

[30] Mallapragada, P. K.; Jin, R.; Jain, A. K.; Liu, Y. SemiBoost: Boosting for semi-supervised learning. *IEEE Transactions on Pattern Analysis and Machine Intelligence* Vol. 31, No. 11, 2000–2014, 2009.

[31] Gong, C.; Tao, D.; Maybank, S. J.; Liu, W.; Kang, G.; Yang, J. Multi-modal curriculum learning for semi-supervised image classification. *IEEE Transactions on Image Processing* Vol. 25, No. 7, 3249–3260, 2016.

[32] Bosch, A.; Zisserman, A.; Munoz, X. Image classification using random forests and ferns. In: Proceedings of the IEEE 11th International Conference on Computer Vision, 1–8, 2007.

[33] Xiong, C.; Kim, T.-K. Set-based label propagation of face images. In: Proceedings of the 19th IEEE International Conference on Image Processing, 1433–1436, 2012.

[34] Cheng, H.; Liu, Z.; Yang, J. Sparsity induced similarity measure for label propagation. In: Proceedings of the IEEE 12th International Conference on Computer Vision, 317–324, 2009.

[35] Kang, F.; Jin, R.; Sukthankar, R. Correlated label propagation with application to multi-label learning. In: Proceedings of the IEEE Computer Society Conference on Computer Vision and Pattern Recognition, 1719–1726, 2006.

[36] Wang, H.; Nie, F.; Cai, W.; Huang, H. Semi-supervised robust dictionary learning via efficient l-norms minimization. In: Proceedings of the IEEE International Conference on Computer Vision, 1145–1152, 2013.

[37] Martinez, A. M. The AR face database. CVC Technical Report 24, 1998.

[38] Lee, K.-C.; Ho, J.; Kriegman, D. J. Acquiring linear subspaces for face recognition under variable lighting. *IEEE Transactions on Pattern Analysis and Machine Intelligence* Vol. 27, No. 5, 684–698, 2005.

[39] LeCun, Y.; Bottou, L.; Bengio, Y.; Haffner, P. Gradient-based learning applied to document recognition. *Proceedings of the IEEE* Vol. 86, No. 11, 2278–2324, 1998.

[40] Hull, J. J. A database for handwritten text recognition research. *IEEE Transactions on Pattern Analysis and Machine Intelligence* Vol. 16, No. 5, 550–554, 1994.

[41] Lazebnik, S.; Schmid, C.; Ponce, J. A sparse texture representation using local affine regions. *IEEE Transactions on Pattern Analysis and Machine Intelligence* Vol. 27, No. 8, 1265–1278, 2005.

[42] Cai, S.; Zuo, W.; Zhang, L.; Feng, X.; Wang, P. Support vector guided dictionary learning. In: *Computer Vision–ECCV 2014*. Fleet, D.; Pajdla, T.; Schiele, B.; Tuytelaars, T. Eds. Springer International Publishing, 624–639, 2014.

[43] Boix, X.; Roig, G.; Van Gool, L. Comment on "Ensemble projection for semi-supervised image classification". *arXiv preprint* arXiv:1408.6963, 2014.

[44] Dai, D.; Van Gool, L. Ensemble projection for semi-supervised image classification. In: Proceedings of the IEEE International Conference on Computer Vision, 2072–2079, 2013.

[45] Oliva, A.; Torralba, A. Modeling the shape of the scene: A holistic representation of the spatial envelope. *International Journal of Computer Vision* Vol. 42, No. 3, 145–175, 2001.

[46] Ojala, T.; Pietikainen, M.; Maenpaa, T. Multiresolution gray-scale and rotation invariant texture classification with local binary patterns. *IEEE Transactions on Pattern Analysis and Machine Intelligence* Vol. 24, No. 7, 971–987, 2002.

Permissions

List of Contributors

Yuliang Rong, Tianjia Shao and Kun Zhou
State Key Lab of CAD and CG, Zhejiang University, Hangzhou 310058, China

Youyi Zheng
ShanghaiTech University, Shanghai 200031, China

Yin Yang
The University of New Mexico, Albuquerque, NM 87131, USA

Haozhi Huang, Xiaonan Fang, Yufei Ye and Songhai Zhang
Department of Computer Science, Tsinghua University, Beijing, 100084, China

Paul L. Rosin
School of Computer Science and Informatics, Cardiff University, Cardiff, CF24 3AA, UK

Chao Wang and Xiaohu Guo
University of Texas at Dallas, Richardson, Texas, USA

Chunping Zhang, Zhe Ji and Qing Wang
School of Computer Science, Northwestern Polytechnical University, Xi'an 710072, China

Yang Song, Qing Li, Dagan Feng and Weidong Cai
School of Information Technologies, the University of Sydney, NSW 2006, Australia

Ju Jia Zou
School of Computing, Engineering and Mathematics, Western Sydney University, Penrith, NSW 2751, Australia

Changmin Choi, YoonSeok Lee and Sung-Eui Yoon
Korea Advanced Institute of Science and Technology(KAIST), 291 Daehak-ro, Yuseong-gu, Daejeon, Republic of Korea

Shaoning Zeng and Yang Xiong
Huizhou University, Guangdong 516007, China

Jun Song, Siliang Tang, Jun Xiao and Fei Wu
College of Computer Science and Technology, Zhejiang University, Hangzhou 310027, China

Zhongfei (Mark) Zhang
Department of Computer Science, Watson School of Engineering and Applied Sciences, Binghamton University, Binghamton, NY, USA

Yoshikatsu Nakajima and Hideo Saito
Department of Science and Technology, Keio University, Japan

Yuxin Ma, Wei Chen, Xiaohong Ma, Jiayi Xu and Xinxin Huang
State Key Lab of CAD and CG, Zhejiang University, Hangzhou, 310058, China

Ross Maciejewski
Arizona State University, USA

Anthony K. H. Tung
National University of Singapore, Singapore

Shuang Liu, Xiaosong Yang and Jian J. Zhang
Bournemouth University, Poole, BH12 5BB, UK

Yongqiang Zhang and Daming Shi
Harbin Institute of Technology, Harbin, 150001, China

Sheng Yang and Kang Chen
Tsinghua University, Beijing, China

Jie Xu
Massachusetts Institute of Technology, Cambridge, USA

Hongbo Fu
City University of Hong Kong, Hong Kong, China

Craig Henderson and Ebroul Izquierdo
Multimedia and Vision Research Group, School of Electronic Engineering and Computer Science, QueenMary University of London, London, E1 4NS, UK

Cui-Xia Ma and Hong-An Wang
State Key Lab of Computer Science, Institute of Software, Chinese Academy of Sciences, Beijing 100190, China
Beijing Key Lab of Human–Computer Interaction, Institute of Software, Chinese Academy of Sciences, Beijing 100080, China

Yang Guo
School of Computer and Control Engineering, University of Chinese Academy of Sciences, Beijing 100080, China

Xiaole Zhao, Yadong Wu and Jinsha Tian
School of Computer Science and Technology, Southwest University of Science and Technology, Mianyang 621010, China

Hongying Zhang
School of Information Engineering, Southwest University of Science and Technology, Mianyang 621010, China

Liqiong Wu, Yepeng Liu, Brekhna, Ning Liu and Caiming Zhang
School of Computer Science and Technology, Shandong University, Jinan 250101, China

Lin Chen
College of Computer Science and Software Engineering, Shenzhen University, Shenzhen, China

Meng Yang
College of Computer Science and Software Engineering, Shenzhen University, Shenzhen, China
School of Data and Computer Science, Sun Yat-sen University, Guangzhou, China
Key Laboratory of Machine Intelligence and Advanced Computing (Sun Yat-sen University), Ministry of Education, China

Index

CPSIA information can be obtained
at www.ICGtesting.com
Printed in the USA
LVHW061855300820
664469LV00033B/29